INVENTING PARADISE

THE **POWER BROKERS** WHO CREATED THE **DREAM** OF **LOS ANGELES**

PAUL HADDAD

SANTA
MONICA
PRESS

Published by: Santa Monica Press LLC
P.O. Box 850
Solana Beach, CA 92075
1-800-784-9553
www.santamonicapress.com
books@santamonicapress.com

SANTA
MONICA
PRESS

Printed in China

Santa Monica Press books are available at special quantity discounts when
purchased in bulk by corporations, organizations, or groups. Please call our
Special Sales department at 1-800-784-9553.

ISBN-13 978-1-59580-127-2 (Print)
ISBN 978-1-59580-758-8 (Ebook)

Publisher's Cataloging-in-Publication data

Names: Haddad, Paul, author.
Title: Inventing paradise : the power brokers who created the dream of Los
Angeles / by Paul Haddad.
Description: Includes bibliographical references and index. | Solana Beach, CA:
Santa Monica Press, 2024.
Identifiers: ISBN: 978-1-59580-127-2 (paperback) | 978-1-59580-758-8 (ebook)
Subjects: LCSH Los Angeles (Calif.)--History. | Los Angeles Metropolitan Area
(Calif.)--History. | Los Angeles (Calif.)--History--Biography. | Los Angeles
Metropolitan Area (Calif.)--Biography. | City planning--California--Los
Angeles. | BISAC HISTORY / United States / State & Local / West (AK, CA, CO,
HI, ID, MT, NV, UT, WY) | HISTORY / United States / General | BIOGRAPHY
& AUTOBIOGRAPHY / Historical | POLITICAL SCIENCE / Public Policy /
City Planning & Urban Development | TECHNOLOGY & ENGINEERING /
Civil / General | ARCHITECTURE / Urban & Land Use Planning | BUSINESS
& ECONOMICS / Entrepreneurship
Classification: LCC F869.L857 H33 2024 | DDC 979.4/94--dc23

Front cover map courtesy of Los Angeles Public Library Map Collection
Cover and interior design and production by Future Studio

"It is no more possible to stop Los Angeles than to push back the rising sun."

—HARRY CHANDLER
President, *Los Angeles Times*, 1932

CONTENTS

PART III: PARADISE FRAYED

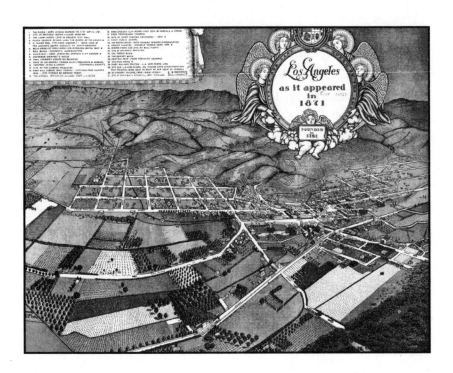

A map showing Los Angeles in 1871, ninety years after its founding. The Los Angeles River cuts across the lower right corner. The pueblo had not advanced much beyond "four square leagues," or twenty-eight square miles, as originally mandated by Spanish Governor Felipe de Neve. (Map commissioned by the Women's University Club of L.A. in 1929.)

INTRODUCTION

LOS ANGELES IS A city that should not exist. The city boasts no natural features that could sustain its current population of about four million people, let alone twelve million in its metropolitan region. For centuries, Indigenous peoples lived comfortably within their means in L.A.'s semi-arid coastal basin. In 1781, Spanish settlers established El Pueblo de Nuestra Senora la Reina de Los Angeles (shortened to Los Angeles) at its main water source, today's Los Angeles River. But the Spaniards and, later, Mexicans who governed Alta California took a pragmatic view of this agrarian hub. The river was fickle; it could support one hundred thousand people, maybe two. The city was hemmed in by mountain ranges, which made overland routes challenging. It also had no suitable seaport. The closest natural harbor, twenty-one miles to the south, was cursed with shallow water, which limited larger vessels needed for maritime trade. In short, the pueblo was just that—a simple village with nice climate but no aspirations for big city status due to constraints of geography.

But natural limitations don't explain how Los Angeles did come to exist—indeed, was *predestined* to exist. For that, one must turn to the human factor. After the United States acquired California during the Mexican-American War in 1848, not much changed on the local landscape until the run-up to the American Civil War. A looming Gilded Age ushered in a period of rapid economic growth and can-do optimism in which nature's limitations were mere trifles to be overcome. Los Angeles's frontier town status made it particularly ripe for well-heeled industrialists to shape the city's future. Reflective of the times, power coalesced around a patriarchal hierarchy, led by General Phineas

Banning, Gen. Harrison Gray Otis, Harry Chandler, Gen. Moses Sherman, Henry Huntington, and William Mulholland. Starting in 1859, when L.A. expanded its borders for the first time since its founding, these six successive titans of industry spearheaded the city's meteoric rise over several decades, culminating with its greatest moment—the Olympic Games—in 1932. That year also marked the end of what can be termed the Annexation Era (1896–1932), a stunningly prolific, thirty-six-year span in which ninety percent of L.A.'s present total area was secured. This book retraces the city's improbable growth through the prism of these six men, whose omnipotence, influence, and drive transformed Los Angeles from an agricultural hamlet to a global megalopolis.

Nonetheless, to borrow an old aphorism, it takes a village to raise a city, and Los Angeles had no shortage of architects. Financier Isaias W. Hellman, oil tycoon Edward Doheny, realtor Billy Garland, and Chamber of Commerce trailblazer Frank Wiggins were among the city's prime movers. All make appearances in this book and are the subject of others. But Hellman and Doheny spent considerable time residing outside of Southern California; even on their own, each excelled in one specific sector, lacking the breadth of ambition necessary to unilaterally affect the trajectory of Los Angeles. A similar argument could be made about Garland, Wiggins, and dozens of other figures in this book. In the annals of history, they remain strong supporting characters, relegated below the line of our marquee players in the story of how modern Los Angeles was willed into being.

On that note, the first dramatis personae to take the stage is Gen. Phineas Banning. His presence in these pages is relatively short-lived but vital. It is through Banning's efforts that landlocked L.A.'s southern tentacles eventually touched the Pacific Ocean, earning him the nickname "The Father of Los Angeles Harbor." In addition to obtaining a commitment from the federal government to deepen San Pedro Bay, Banning built the first railroad between the harbor and the City of Angels. Both actions brought global commerce to L.A.'s shores, and the Port of Los

Angeles is now the largest shipping gateway in the United States.

By the time of Banning's premature death in 1885, Gen. Harrison Gray Otis was on his way to building the *Los Angeles Times* into the town's foremost newspaper. In an age when virtually everybody got their information from daily periodicals, Otis broadcast his personal agenda in the guise of news, intent on selling L.A. as the most business-friendly city in America. Heavily spun articles laid bare the city's Wild West roots, promoting the merits of free labor, open markets, deregulation, and, most importantly, expansionism. It was a successful formula, and anyone who disagreed with these points was an "enemy of the city," ruthlessly pilloried in print. In the words of one historian, the general "quickly developed the fixed idea that he owned Los Angeles, and that he alone was destined to lead it to greatness."

As Los Angeles transitioned into the twentieth century, an aging Otis gradually yielded control of the *Times* to his son-in-law Harry Chandler. Discarding the general's combative tactics, Chandler continued to use the newspaper as a tool to uplift Los Angeles. Famously secretive, he was a consummate consensus-builder and dealmaker, a puppet master who pulled strings behind the scenes and enriched those in his orbit. He also became L.A.'s largest landowner. "Land lust tempted me," he later admitted. Los Angeles was his golden goose, and both his and the city's fortunes were inextricably tied. Thanks to his diverse holdings, access to capital, and cozy relationships with politicos and power brokers, no one was more instrumental in the growth of Los Angeles than Chandler.

Chandler's well-off wingman in many of his dealings was Gen. Moses Sherman. When the duo weren't forming syndicates that led to L.A.'s expansion into the Hollywood Hills and San Fernando Valley, Sherman held prominent positions on city committees, where he could do Chandler's bidding by shaping policy. But Moses wasn't solely defined by his relationship with his best friend. He and a partner, Eli Clark, opened up the westside of Los Angeles through an extensive railway system in the 1890s

and early 1900s. Ingeniously, these streetcars whisked Angelenos
to lots for sale, which were owned by Sherman, or by speculators
who paid him "subscriptions" to have trains pass by their properties. Long operating in Chandler's long shadow, Sherman's legacy
has dimmed over time but is properly restored here.

Because he took over several Sherman and Clark trolley franchises, Henry Huntington played a part in the whitewashing of
Sherman from Los Angeles lore. A beloved philanthropist whose
estate remains a popular cultural oasis, Huntington reigned over
the world's largest streetcar empire, dominating routes across Los
Angeles County. Old photos of his Pacific Electric Red Cars and
Los Angeles Railway Yellow Cars elicit instant nostalgia among
generations of Angelenos who weren't even born when they operated. But as with Sherman, Huntington's railways were a means
to an end, providing easy access to housing developments in
which he had a stake. "Keep your money rolling," was his philosophy. "Reinvest." For Huntington, that meant building a utility
network that could provide gas and electricity to his communities, tightening a monopoly that directly influenced L.A.'s boundaries and population trends.

But it was water—the most precious of all utilities—that
formed the lifeblood for all development in Los Angeles. Without
a sufficient supply of it, there would be no oligarchy, no metropolis, no basis for this book's raison d'être. Perhaps that explains
why William Mulholland, our sixth protagonist, achieved something close to sainthood among Angelenos. For forty-two years,
the tetchy engineer headed up L.A.'s water department. He was
serenaded with not one, not two, but three day-long dedications
in his honor between 1913 and 1925. His greatest achievement
was the construction of the 233-mile Los Angeles Aqueduct, a
controversial project that fleeced Owens Valley residents of their
water while enabling L.A. to accommodate another two million
people. Besides prompting the annexation of the San Fernando
Valley, the opening of the aqueduct led to a tripling of L.A.'s area
within three years as neighboring towns, their wells running

dry, voted themselves into the big city to access its artificial river. Nonetheless, "Old Bill" also waged a decades-long tug-of-war with L.A.'s ruling elite, who pressured him to keep the water—and money—flowing. This would have tragic consequences. As Angel City's resident miracle worker, Mulholland had carte blanche over future infrastructure projects to meet the demands of a thirsty city. Facing lax oversight, he finally flew too close to the sun.

The reckoning that awaited Mulholland speaks to an essential component of this book. Despite their successes, the founding fathers of modern Los Angeles had flaws like any other human. While it is true each hungered for power, distilling their accomplishments to pure greed is a reductive view that ignores their inner lives, for it is there where their demons and desires lay. At a time when the written word was the primary means of communication, their preserved letters, memos, and telegrams—often in correspondence with each other—offer keen insight into what made them tick, or at least the motives behind their actions. Like the proverbial butterfly whose flapping of wings can be felt on the other side of the world, seemingly unremarkable whims often bore disproportionate weight on the future of Los Angeles.

As the two kingpins with firsthand experience of the Civil War, Banning and Otis took pride in their "General" titles (spurious as they were), storming toward an eternal quest for personal glory that was always just out of reach. Conquering Los Angeles helped fulfill their missions, particularly in Otis's case. His Los Angeles was a surrogate for the battlefield, the *L.A. Times* its best defense. When outside agitators tried to infiltrate the city—be it labor organizers or railroad conglomerates intent on owning the harbor—the former Union Army captain was never more alive, "liberating" the city from disruptive forces that might otherwise thwart its destiny.

Succeeding his father-in-law at the *Times*, Chandler traded public glory for immortality. His legacy is permanently etched in an array of institutions and industries that make up Los Angeles.

More literally, he also developed a strange fixation—and regimen—similar to contemporary billionaires who seemingly aspire to live forever. It was as if he wanted to survive long enough to witness the flowering of all the investments he had seeded.

In contrast to Chandler, Huntington had the soul of a poet. He yearned for high culture, perhaps seeing it as a sort of salvation. As a child, Henry kept a journal in which he jotted self-improvement maxims and endlessly perfected his signature, often adding a wishful "Esq." at the end of it. After decades building up and profiting from L.A., the multi-millionaire finally had the means to deliver on his childhood promise by retiring to his Xanadu, cloistering himself in nature and inspiring works of art. "I am just beginning to live," he wrote his sister in 1913, revealing his true calling. He would go on the rest of his years chasing beauty, luring visitors to his estate so he could share his treasures with the world.

Mulholland didn't have the time—nor the resources—for such lofty pursuits. He defined himself by his work ethic; so much so, newspapers kept running tabs on the last time he took a vacation. By devoting himself so much to "my water," as he provincially referred to the city's waterworks, Mulholland unwittingly fed into his untouchable status. He developed a savior complex, which created an insatiable need for recognition that could never be filled, while also inuring him to critics who could never comprehend his engineering genius.

Though he was roughly the same age as Mulholland, Sherman lacked the water chief's vigor, his life beset by health problems. Like a gambler chasing a high, his cure was to throw himself into high-risk, high-reward ventures. In letters to Chandler, he talked about the thrill of the chase as if it were a tonic that imbued him with superpowers. The times he was recuperating, away from the office, were his darkest moments. "I am not going to die. I am going to live," he once wrote his family, as if trying to reassure himself as much as them. "I am going to stay here, in the beautiful country, where the grass is green and the birds sing, as long as I can."

If there was one thing this gang of six had in common, it was their mutual belief that they were living in "paradise." Consequently, each earnestly bought what they were selling. Like other transplants, they had fallen in love with the Los Angeles region and, in some cases, even credited it with saving their lives. "We have the advantage of 'climate,'" Sherman wrote a relative in 1908, referencing the "astonishing" number of people who flocked to L.A. to improve their well-being. Around that time, Huntington observed, "There's nothing like this Southern California anywhere else in the world." To *not* build a metropolis in such an ideal environment, with so much room to grow, was almost a crime against the tenets of sound investing. Huntington predicted "it will be the one center for all that is beautiful and worthwhile," while Chandler cheered the possibilities for the "man-made end of California." The fact that Los Angeles was engineered by human hands was another shared point of pride, a way to claim superiority over naturally blessed San Francisco. Every milestone was carefully measured against its Bay Area counterpart, and L.A.'s visionaries wouldn't rest until their city had surpassed its smug rival in every way.

To justify their enterprises, these purveyors of paradise eagerly welcomed new arrivals, just so long as the right people punched a ticket to get in. During the 1920s, 1.2 million Americans migrated to Southern California, diluting L.A.'s Waspy makeup. As the Southland's dominant landowners, Chandler, Sherman, and Huntington backed new developments that excluded people of color from owning property. Such policies were standard among realtors, who pitched neighborhoods as economic "white spots" that were code for "whites only." Chandler was particularly guilty of perpetuating discrimination by aligning himself with eugenics and, through the *Times*, diminishing the needs of L.A.'s increasingly diverse populace. The stigmatization of Latino and African American residents created long-lasting racial tensions that would boil over in the form of the Zoot Suit Riots of 1943, the

Watts and Rodney King uprisings of 1965 and 1992, and other flashpoints that have become part of the city's firmament.

But history also shows that, once Los Angeles became synonymous with paradise—real or imaginary—the idea became a self-fulfilling prophecy. More industries led to more jobs and more people, and adjacent districts often felt they had no choice but to wed themselves to the megacity. From 1859 to 1932, Los Angeles absorbed ten cities and seventy-three communities—eighty-three districts in all. The results can be traced in L.A.'s famously jagged borders, which include several "island" municipalities floating within its 468 square miles. This book aims to bring order to the chaos, explaining how some towns succumbed to Angel City while others, like Santa Monica, Beverly Hills, and San Fernando, retained their autonomy. Naturally, not every historical undertaking was directly tied to Banning, Otis, Chandler, Sherman, Huntington, or Mulholland. But as true forces of nature, their supremacy lorded over the landscape, creating and contributing to the conditions that led to the manufacturing of the city of Los Angeles.

PART I

A COALESCING OLIGARCHY

CHAPTER 1

The Father of the Harbor

ONE MEAGER SQUARE MILE.

For seventy-eight years, Los Angeles had remained stubbornly fixed at the twenty-eight square miles established by Spanish Governor Felipe de Neve in 1781. It was bounded, roughly, by Hoover Street on the west, present-day Silver Lake on the north, and the Los Angeles River on the east. Then, in 1859, the pueblo recorded one additional mile (1.2 to be exact), nudging parts of its southern border beyond Exposition Boulevard. In a town of barely 4,000 residents, this registered as a non-event, unworthy of reportage by the local press. Not so for city charter members. Mired in years of litigation in their quest to boost Los Angeles's profile, the anemic addition represented, per L.A. scholar James M. Guinn, "pitiful compensation for the blasted hopes of municipal expansion."

It also served as a stark reminder that the fast-and-loose rules of the former frontier town would no longer play in a larger union. Unlike established Eastern cities, Los Angeles claimed amorphous borders for much of the nineteenth century. Starting in the 1860s, charter members enlisted lawyer and surveyor Henry Hancock—whose heirs would establish Hancock Park—to subdivide dozens of square miles. By including Spanish and Mexican land grants, or ranchos, L.A.'s unofficial borders bulged ten miles across and ten miles longitudinally, which would've qualified it as the largest city by area in America. But the United States Claims Commission threw cold water on the new 100-square-mile figure, refuting the legality of several grants. L.A.'s city limits shriveled back to the boundaries of the original

pueblo, with only the southern border remaining fluid. After negotiations with the commission, twenty-nine square miles were
locked into place on June 1, 1869.

That same year, an overachiever from Delaware laid the
foundation for Los Angeles's first big—and most important—expansion. His name was Phineas Banning. These days the desert
town of Banning is a convenient rest stop on the way to Palm
Springs, the name commemorating a stagecoach line operated by
Banning through San Gorgonio Pass. But it was his development
of San Pedro, and its link to landlocked Los Angeles, that altered
the course of history and cemented his legacy as The Father of
Los Angeles Harbor.

Banning arrived in Los Angeles in 1851, shortly after California became the nation's thirty-first state. Like L.A.'s other heavy-
weights, he inhabited an outsize presence—six-feet tall, strong
and stocky, with a self-possession common to young men chasing dreams out West. Eschewing the hirsute stylings of the time,
Phineas wore his face clean, which accentuated his soul-piercing
eyes. In photographs, he could pass as a distant relative of Tom
Cruise, inhabiting the actor's intensity of gaze and certitude. Not
long before his death, the industrialist dictated an unpublished
memoir to writer Edward Newkirk. Banning's account of his life
reads like an adventure story sprung from the pen of Herman
Melville, with vainglorious references to himself in the third person, as in "our hero." After stepping off a ship in San Pedro—a
vestige of New Spain's Rancho San Pedro—the twenty-one-year-
old bachelor rendered himself "a man both in mind and estate,"
seized by "an uncontrollable desire . . . to seek his fortune, in the
then far away land of California." What he found was a settlement caught between eras. "Some native tribes still lived in tra-
ditional ways," recounted one historian, "increasingly precarious
in the face of changes the Spanish missions and soldiers, Mexican
dons, and American gold rushers introduced to control them."

Mid-nineteenth century San Pedro was a humble fishing
hamlet with a serviceable port, believed to be the same one that

Iberian explorer Juan Rodriguez Cabrillo called the "Bay of the Smoke" in 1542. It was a reference to the Tongva peoples' cooking fires, whose fumes were trapped by the Southland's distinctive marine layer (technically, an early form of smog). While not of the deep-water variety like San Francisco Bay, the harbor remained the best option between San Diego and Santa Barbara throughout Spanish, Mexican, and American rule.

Another feature L.A. lacked compared to San Francisco was reliable infrastructure. Though only twenty-one miles separated San Pedro from Los Angeles, it could take up to one week to transport goods along a rickety road. As a stagecoach driver along that route, Banning sought to exploit this underserved market. "Banning was always thinking about transportation," says Michael Sanborn, who oversees the Banning Residence Museum in Wilmington. "He was very entrepreneurial, always focused on how fast he could get luggage and mail from the port to downtown [L.A.]." Partnering with investors, Banning spent the next two years acquiring fifteen wagons and seventy-five mules to haul passengers and freight between the two cities. He also built warehouses for storage.

Having improved land transport, Banning now had a new problem: San Pedro Harbor. As ships grew larger and heavier, they were unable to anchor at his wharf—dubbed Banning's Landing—lest they get stuck in the bay's shallow waters. As a stopgap, Banning invested in steam tugs and barges to shuttle cargo to the dock, where holds were loaded onto wagons. Banning sank his profits into further port improvements, including a telegraph line to Los Angeles. By the late 1850s, surges in maritime traffic convinced Banning to expand the harbor by purchasing several hundred acres of land abutting San Pedro. He eventually called this new town Wilmington after his Delaware birthplace. It was the perfect spot to build his estate and settle in with his new bride, Rebecca Sanford, who would bear him eight children.

When the American Civil War broke out in 1861, Banning was well-positioned to capitalize on it. A staunch Unionist in a region where most residents were Confederate sympathizers, he leveraged his relationship with Union General Winfield Scott Hancock by selling the government sixty acres of land in Wilmington in return for several commissions. One assignment was to run supplies to Fort Yuma on the Arizona border. But the biggest was a contract to build Camp Drum. Not only did it serve as the Union's Southwestern command post for California and the territory of Arizona, but it resulted in Wilmington having a greater population than Los Angeles during the Civil War. An army officer marveled at Banning's prolific nature, finding him "forever in a hurry and doing the business of a half dozen of men." Besides their patriotic service, soldiers at the Wilmington post became local heroes. On April 27, 1863, a San Francisco-bound steamer owned by Banning blew up in San Pedro Bay due to a faulty boiler. Twenty-six people were killed, a toll that would have been higher if not for military personnel courageously aiding passengers in need of medical attention. Banning was absolved of liability, though he was seen as getting preferential treatment due to his importance to the region.

After the war ended in 1865, Camp Drum was decommissioned, its historic barracks now part of a Civil War museum. Gen. Hancock and the U.S. government promoted Banning to Brigadier General of the First Brigade of a new state militia. Banning named a son after Hancock, and insisted on being called General Banning for the rest of his life—a predilection shared by two subsequent L.A. magnates (Generals Otis and Sherman). Though Banning's title was purely honorary, he claimed to "always hold himself in readiness to lead his army to the field" should the occasion ever arise.

Now that he had elevated the profile of San Pedro-Wilmington, Banning parlayed his relationship with the government to even bigger dreams—deepening the harbor and converting his wagon line to rail. But getting chummy with army commanders wasn't enough. "In order to accomplish this desired object," Phineas pronounced in his unpublished memoir, "it became necessary for our hero to enter the political arena."

And that's just what our hero did, serving as a California state senator from 1865 to 1868. It was here where Banning's "fertile genius" truly began to blossom. "His magnetic influence was a power," the general recalled, "and he so successfully wielded it." Huddling with Senator Cornelius Cole, Banning and his constituents secured pledges to dredge the harbor and install a breakwater, two monumental projects that would take years to be realized. A more achievable short-term goal was the establishment of a twenty-one-mile railway, for which Banning received state funds. "The Bill introduced by him appropriating money for the purpose of building a Railroad from tide water to Los Angeles was successfully passed and became a law," he said.

Though public sentiment was clearly on his side—Banning framed everything he did as "for the ultimate benefit of the People"—not everyone was enthused. One newspaper wrote of a "crazy old coot" caught up in a longtime vendetta against Banning, who tried to oust the old-timer from his home along the shores of San Pedro. Captain J. F. Janes was a colorful ex-sailor who, like a human hermit crab, had built his house out of the hulks of wrecked ships, with rooms crafted out of bulkheads, bulwarks, and rusty lockers. But it was a memento of his own making that he was most proud of: twenty-eight legal documents pinned to his wall in the shape of a giant starfish. Each notice was issued by a judge or sheriff ordering him to vacate for Banning's railroad. "Those papers are my lawsuits," the captain explained to a reporter. "I keep them on exhibition like an Indian does his scalps. . . . I have defied them all." In a sweet irony, Janes maintained that the suits provided him with the means to survive: "Each one represents money."

For his part, Banning found a work-around, brushing aside the old salt as just another of his "bitter opponents, who threw every obstacle their petty spite could invent in the way." On November 1, 1869—exactly five months after L.A. solidified the addition of its southern boundary—Banning presided over the opening of the Los Angeles & San Pedro Railroad. It was the first railroad in Southern California. But it was a bittersweet feat, as his wife Rebecca was not on his arm for the celebratory grand ball. She had died during childbirth one year earlier. Their infant, Vincent, succumbed as well.

Meanwhile, 1869 marked another prominent railway christening—certainly the most symbolic in American history. The Golden Spike Ceremony launched the First Transcontinental Railroad near Promontory, Utah. Once again, Banning's keen foresight would serve him well. America's rail industry grew at a 151 percent clip in the West throughout the 1870s, two to four times higher than other regions in the United States. As political stability settled across the land, Americans of leisure took excursions on luxury Pullmans and seafaring steamships. Congress eagerly spent on energy, transportation and infrastructure projects to precipitate more growth. Not coincidentally, the decade also marked the rise of the Gilded Age, when titans of industry would amass obscene wealth under a corrupt and unchecked socio-economic system.

Banning was not in the same league as multi-millionaires like Cornelius Vanderbilt or John D. Rockefeller, but he did see his own investments ripen throughout the 1870s. With his Short Line railroad up and running, he secured initial federal funding for his desired dredging of the harbor. The gargantuan task was clearly in the government's best interests. "To accomplish this purpose," Banning related about himself, "he, at his own costs, and expenses, made the journey to Washington, in the year 1871 . . . to obtain an appropriation of some $200,000 for the purpose of improving the approach toward the protection of Wilmington Harbor." The work was "so thoroughly and promptly done, was beneficial to the harbor, that again and again, was he successful in obtaining [more] appropriations from the Government . . . to the enormous sum of half a million dollars." Banning also enjoyed good fortune in his personal life. Two years after Rebecca's death, he married Mary Hollister, whose family founded

Hollister, California. The heiress bore him three more children while further increasing the value of his estate.

"About this time, the Southern Pacific Railroad Co. began feeling its way toward the Southern end of the states," Banning recorded. The company, established in 1865, was looking to establish a foothold in the West. It announced a route from San Francisco through Arizona and points east, bypassing Los Angeles altogether. This was alarming news. In 1870, San Francisco's population stood at 149,473. Los Angeles claimed only 5,728. How could this upstart pueblo ever achieve its desired "municipal expansion" if it wasn't served by major rail systems?

Not to worry, said Southern Pacific. The conglomerate offered to swing the line through Los Angeles to the tune of $600,000 in so-called aid, an amount that represented five percent of L.A.'s assessed valuation. Elected officials were outraged, but business leaders didn't see where the city had much choice. They worried that another municipality—perhaps San Bernardino—would emerge as Southern California's defining metropolis if L.A. didn't step up. The issue was put to voters in 1872. By a three-to-one margin, Angelenos approved the subsidy.

Once again, Banning stood to prosper. Southern Pacific was interested in acquiring his Los Angeles & San Pedro Railroad and its right-of-way to the harbor. The company also sought the general's counsel in securing unrestricted access through Arizona, valuing his experience with the Yuma wagon route. Banning drove a hard bargain: "After some negotiation, wherein Mr. Banning displayed much diplomatic talent, the short line . . . was turned over to them, and became the southern terminus of their line." The last spike connecting Los Angeles with San Francisco was staked on September 6, 1876. Eight months later, the Southern Pacific reached Texas, where it fused with eastern terminals. No longer isolated, Southern California's interconnectivity with the rest of the nation was a tectonic milestone. Banning, flush with cash, took the time to wistfully reflect on his humble beginnings. Back in 1851, "three or four hundred tons of freight" were transported via horsepower along his wagon route, often with Banning at the reins. Now, as part of a sleek interstate railway connected to his beloved harbor, freight tonnage "increased to as many as thousands per day . . . and an army of employees to handle it."

No doubt about it, Los Angeles was having a moment. The city's improved accessibility came just in time for its Centennial in September 1881. Newspaper accounts called it "the grandest affair that the city has ever witnessed." A parade featured some 3,000 marching civilians and public servants—more than one quarter of L.A.'s entire population. Establishing a tradition that Los Angeles would revisit time and again for subsequent milestones, the ceremony included ritual romanticizing of past conquered cultures. Native peoples danced in "rich costumes of the last century," and an oxen-led carriage carried "two Mexican women" whose birthdays predated that of the City of Angels itself—Laura, age 102, and Benjamina, age 117 (highly unlikely, but who would dare challenge a sweet old lady?).

From its northern perspective, the *Sacramento Record-Union* dished out awkward compliments. Los Angeles was, by virtue of rail interconnectivity, at last a Yankee city in a Yankee nation, building upon the "spirit of his race" while the "ancient and lazy efforts of the early California pioneers" were in the past, where they belonged. Also gone were Northern California's jibes of its nascent counterpart as the Hell-Hole of the West. "Where the Indian worshipped his absolute god Chinigchinich," the *Record-Union* opined, "there [now] stand temples of trade, shrines of commerce and the indestructible walls of a better civilization." How fitting that Indians and Mexicans were part of the pageantry, allowing them to bear witness to the "progress which, in 100 years, has transformed a simple settlement of a non-progressive people into a typical American city."

Playing to its mostly white readership, the California press also denigrated Chinese immigrants, claiming that the community had only itself to blame for the massacre of nineteen Chinese people in an 1871 race riot in Los Angeles. Ten years later, in the Centennial year of 1881, the *Los Angeles Daily Times*—in only its fourth issue since launching on December 4—sent an intrepid reporter into L.A.'s Chinatown to observe how its exotic residents lived. "A Chinaman never dreams of observing even the simplest sanitary rules," he remarked. "He knows nothing of them and does not care to learn." The scribe warned of heathens who "can't eat like a Christian," favoring squatting positions in their "grimy apartment" with its "mysterious odors." Underlying these attacks was a grudging acknowledgment that Chinese households were resourceful and family-oriented, which posed a threat to hard-working Caucasians: "These strange men band themselves together with families of three or four or even a dozen, and live. The strictest domestic economy is practiced, and herein lies the secret of their ability to under-bid white labor and thrive on a pittance."

Los Angeles was merely a microcosm of rising national resentment toward Chinese migrants, scapegoated for lowering American values and stealing jobs. After a series of measures in California made it harder for Chinese inhabitants to own businesses, Congress, responding to pressure from Western states, passed the Chinese Exclusion Act in 1882. The law suspended immigration from China for ten years and prohibited those of Chinese descent from becoming citizens. It was the most restrictive immigration policy in American history.

Not that these were concerns for Gen. Banning. Having entered his fifties in the early 1880s, the intransigent opportunist had softened with age, his 240 pounds reined in by red suspenders. He and Mary loved hosting soirees at their Wilmington residence, a Greek Revival-Victorian mansion with thirty rooms and enough quarters for servants, company employees and extended family. He doted on his three adult sons from Rebecca—the only of their eight children to survive to adulthood—who were making their way in the world while maintaining ties to the family business. In letters to them, the general addressed each by affectionate nicknames: "Captain William," "Uncle Hancock," and

"Judge Joseph," the latter of whom had just entered law school. "Do not forget it is hard to be a good lawyer without being a hypocrite," he advised the "judge," "and you must pretend to be a follower of the 'meek and lowly' if you want to succeed." Meanwhile, his youngest brought out Phineas's goofier side, with the father appealing to his son's "fine appreciation of the fine arts." While on a business trip, he wrote:

> My dear Uncle Hancock Banning:
>
> I would have written you sooner but it was my desire to give you a full account of our trip over the plains from Los Angeles here which I could not do unless having some <u>fine</u> steel engravings prepared, which you know takes time.

The inserted "steel engravings" were, in fact, nothing more than doodles scribbled by Banning of colorful characters he met on his trip, each given a snarky caption.

But perhaps nothing gave Phineas greater satisfaction than the solitary pursuit of parking his generous frame on the upper balcony of his palace. Under a fourth-floor cupola, he would have glimpsed the cargo ships and steamers plying his beloved bay. His view would have included a rudimentary breakwater awaiting upgrades, and one could imagine his eager anticipation of the channel's further widening. In the distance lay the contours of Catalina Island, which, acting on their father's wishes, his sons would acquire after his death and turn into a popular resort. (The Banning family sold Catalina to chewing gum magnate William Wrigley Jr. in 1919.) It had been thirty years since Phineas had fallen for "this golden shore." Thanks to his prescience, San Pedro Harbor was poised to become the busiest commercial port on the West Coast, with property assessments in Wilmington equally primed to explode. Several newspapers were starting to refer to the bay as "Los Angeles Harbor." Even though it was not part of

L.A., the underlying message was that it was just a matter of time before it would be. As for the celebrated Banning, he had already served as an L.A. City Council member and a state senator. With his money, popularity, and civic connections, it was not out of the realm that he could run for mayor of Los Angeles in the next election and easily win.

But the general would never get to bask in the glory that he had earned. On a trip to San Francisco in the summer of 1884, Phineas stepped off a cable car and got struck by a passing horse-driven wagon. The carriage ran over him, leaving him with severe injuries to internal organs. Just as Los Angeles was shedding its adolescence, Banning was cut down in middle age, counting down the days to a premature death.

CHAPTER 2

Men of Brains, Brawns, and Guts

ONE YEAR AFTER ITS Centennial, Los Angeles saw the arrival of two outsiders who didn't know each other, but whose fates would converge to leave a lasting impact on the city. Harry Chandler's L.A. story was set into motion in the winter of 1882, when the burly nineteen-year-old Dartmouth student pulled a bone-headed stunt that only could have occurred in the nineteenth century. Trying to make good on a dare, Chandler dove head-first into a vat of ice-covered starch. He immediately came down with severe pneumonia. Doctors advised his parents that their violently coughing son with hemorrhaged lungs would die unless he convalesced in a warm environment. Chandler's family put him on a Pullman bound for sunny Los Angeles in May of 1882.

When he stepped off the train at Plaza de Los Angeles, the six-foot-two, blond Ivy Leaguer would have stood out from the crowd in the twenty-nine-square-mile pueblo. Water was still pumped out of crude irrigation ditches called zanjas, delivered to adobes through wooden pipes. Pedestrians and wagons competed with grubby dogs and chickens on dusty, odoriferous streets. Roaming past saloons and bordellos, Chandler had just enough money to rent a room at a boardinghouse. But his coughing jags concerned other guests, who feared he had tuberculosis. He was promptly evicted. Even in this pit of pestilence, Chandler was deemed too hazardous to people's lives.

Homeless and destitute, the sickly Chandler had an epiphany—not the first for this deeply fervent Congregationalist. While passing by a storefront, he noticed a stereographic slide in the window. It showed a young lad with a mop of curly hair, whispering into the ear of a towheaded girl. Chandler stopped dead in his tracks. The image was of *him*, captured just after the Civil War by a photographer who thought young Harry embodied the quintessential American boy. "I felt that if my picture was something people wanted to display, maybe there was some reason for me to be alive after all," Chandler recalled. "I took new courage. It was a turning point in my life."

Following a familiar script written by many a white man in an era of rugged individualism, Chandler pulled himself up by his bootstraps and marched toward greatness. He pitched a tent in Cahuenga Pass and found work breaking horses, clearing trees, and hauling water, his naked torso browning in the sun. The healthy regimen of clean air and manual labor restored his stamina. A doctor who owned an orchard in the pass took a liking to Harry and hired him to maintain his orange and grapefruit trees for market. Looking to make a few extra bucks, Chandler peddled surplus fruit to Mexican farmhands in the San Fernando Valley. One day, a man on horseback cried out, "Get out of here, you son of a bitch!" The proprietor was Isaac Van Nuys, owner of 60,000 acres of Valley wheatland. He thought Harry was a moonshiner trying to get his workers drunk. Once he realized his mistake, Van Nuys allowed Chandler to hawk his fruit, admiring his industriousness. By the end of the harvest season, Chandler had socked away $3,000, a staggering sum in 1883. Still, though he liked Southern California, he missed his college chums and returned to Dartmouth to resume his studies. But after two days, he started coughing up blood again. It was a sign. Destiny was not done with him. Chandler returned to Los Angeles and made it his permanent home.

In July 1882, two months after Chandler first set foot in the Plaza, the City of Angels received another man who would prove to be an agent of growth. Six-foot-one with a barrel chest and Van Dyke goatee, Harrison Gray Otis strode into the offices of a struggling newspaper then known as the *Los Angeles Daily Times* and proclaimed his intention to invest in it. Like Phineas

Banning, Otis was a loyal Unionist during the Civil War. Unlike Banning, Otis had seen action, fighting in the 23rd Ohio Infantry. Twice injured for "gallant and meritorious conduct," Otis was promoted seven times, eventually earning the rank of captain. With a background as a printer for Midwestern newspapers, Otis was enamored by the endless possibilities of Southern California. "It is the fattest land I ever was in," he later said. After running the *Santa Barbara Press* in the 1870s, Otis borrowed $5,000 to purchase a quarter share of the *L.A. Daily Times*. The city was not much more advanced than Santa Barbara. It had only one non-horse-powered railway, and telephones and electrified lighting were but flickering blips on the scene. Within a few short years, Otis owned the paper outright, ascending to president and general manager, and dropping the word "Daily" from the masthead.

If Harrison Gray Otis didn't exist, he'd be invented. Using the *Times* as a mouthpiece for his extreme pro-business, anti-socialism stances, Otis became so enmeshed with his publication, they became almost one and the same. If anything, he set the baseline for newspaper blowhards decades before Orson Welles created Charles Foster Kane in 1941's *Citizen Kane*, itself drawn from William Randolph Hearst and his newspaper empire. L.A.'s own poet laureate, Joan Didion, perfectly captured Harrison Gray Otis's grandiose vision for his adopted city in a 1990 essay:

> "Los Angeles wants no dudes, loafers and paupers; people who have no means and trust to luck," the new citizen announced in an early [*Times*] editorial. . . . Los Angeles as he saw it was all capital formation, no service. It needed no "cheap politicians, failures, bummers, scrubs, impecunious clerks, bookkeepers, lawyers, doctors," he said. "The market is overstocked already. We need workers! Hustlers! Men of brains, brawn and guts! Men who have a little capital and a good deal of energy —first-class men!"

Considering the context of the times, Otis's bluster was un-derstandable. Much as the United States of America manifested democracy from the ground up, Los Angeles represented a lim-itless horizon, a chance to create the next American metropolis *the right way*—free of blight, free of non-European immigrants, free of those meddling unions that had infiltrated the East Coast and San Francisco. With the arrival of the railroads, scores of Americans were purchasing tickets to Angel City, with the Santa Fe Railroad launching the first direct route from the East. De-spite Otis's call for men of brawn and energy, many of those who stepped off the train were, well, invalids. One study determined that one quarter of the hundreds of thousands of Americans who migrated westward from 1865 to 1900 had done so for reasons of recuperation. The sunny Southland had become a prescription for whatever ailed you, be it arthritis, exhaustion, senility, or just a general sense of the blahs. Viewing health-seekers as good busi-ness, Otis began to promote L.A. as a "mecca for sick pilgrims" in his newspaper. A recent hire fit this mold. In 1884, Cincinnati journalist Charles Fletcher Lummis had recently contracted ma-laria when he secured a job with the *Times*. Forgoing train travel, Lummis set out for Los Angeles on foot, chronicling his 3,500-mile adventure in widely read dispatches. By the time he arrived in L.A., he was semi-famous, and Otis promoted him to city ed-itor. Meanwhile, the largest category of enfeebled Americans to blaze a trail to California were "lungers": people suffering from asthma, bronchitis, pneumonia, tuberculosis, or other respiratory ills. People with the courage to uproot their lives and risk it all in spite of their ailments.

People like Harry Chandler.

After returning from his second aborted stint at Dartmouth, Chandler quickly recovered in L.A.'s restorative sunshine. But rather than resume back-breaking work in the fields, the now-twenty-one-year-old hired on as a clerk in the circulation depart-ment of the *L.A. Times*. The event served as a kind of Big Bang for Chandler's supernova career. "I joined the staff December

5th, 1885, when the paper was just four years and one day old," he reminisced decades later. Over the next two years, Chandler worked his way up to circulation manager. To make money on the side—and without telling his boss—he bought the rights to the morning delivery routes of the *Los Angeles Express, Los Angeles Herald*, and *Los Angeles Tribune*. It was during this side hustle that the legend of Chandler's ruthlessness took hold. Through various schemes, he had figured out a way to line his own pockets—up to $1,000 a month—while also driving down the subscription volumes of the *Times'* biggest competitors. He escalated delivery charges for the other papers but kept the *Times'* rates the same. He invited *Herald* carriers to Big Bear so that they were not in L.A. to deliver their rounds. He took *Tribune* carriers on a picnic, where young charges got so drunk, they failed to deliver papers for days. Bit by bit, readers tired of the unreliable deliveries of the other dailies and switched to the *Times*. The avowed Bible-thumper had successfully sabotaged the competition while worshipping at the altar of deceit.

When Otis got wind of Chandler's stunts, he was outraged. Not because it was unscrupulous, but because Chandler had been skimming eighteen bucks a day off delivery of the *Tribune* without sharing it with the *Times*. Chandler told him not to worry; he had cut the *Times'* main rival off at the knees. Sure enough, the *Tribune* quickly went under—well worth the money Chandler had hoarded for himself. Intrigued, Otis seized on the idea of purchasing the distressed *Tribune's* typesetting equipment at a bargain-basement price. But when he talked to the *Tribune's* liquidator, the confused agent said, "Why, Harry bought the type yesterday." Of *course* he did!

Otis's volcanic temper erupted again. But like Isaac Van Nuys before him, once he settled down, he had to admire Chandler's moxie. He promoted him to business manager.

BOTH IN manner and appearance, Chandler was not a man who was easily ruffled. Though he towered over his peers, he came across like a cerebral college professor in his wire-rim glasses and ill-fitting pinstripe suits. But his unassuming demeanor was an impenetrable shield that hid the shark within. During the latter 1880s, Los Angeles teemed with opportunities for Chandler to make money for the *Times*, and, more importantly, enrich himself through his association with the paper—a recurring pattern throughout his life. As late as 1930, an L.A. high school teacher told her history class it was common knowledge that "Harry Chandler of the *Los Angeles Times* never does anything unless first he sees an opportunity to benefit his own interests." It was a charge Chandler denied throughout this career, even though his track record showed otherwise.

In 1886, Los Angeles underwent a land boom that was spurred by the arrival of interstate railroads. The Southern Pacific and Santa Fe companies danced the limbo, each seeing how low it could go to attract passengers. At one point, the fare between Chicago and the West Coast dropped to a single dollar. For those who had missed out on the Northern California Gold Rush, Southern California offered up its own reward: real estate. It was cheap and it was plentiful, and, unlike elusive gold, it was a tangible asset there for the taking. But local companies were ill-prepared for the crush of visitors—120,000 in 1887 alone. To meet demand, Escrow and Recorder offices kept their doors open twenty-four hours a day while prospectors stood in all-night lines to purchase lots in any of the seventy new townsites laid out on plat maps. Investors were known to flip the same property upward of six times a day. Speculators bought on credit, sight unseen. As buyers overwhelmed sellers, a bubble formed. Acres that went for $100 a year prior sold for $1,500 in 1887. The movement came to be known as the Mad Eighties. And the *L.A. Times* helped fuel the madness.

Starting in 1886, the *Times* put out a yearly Midwinter Edition for upscale East Coast and Midwest markets. Thousands of free copies were printed and delivered every New Year's Day, often through blistering ice storms. The issues promised a veritable Eden stretching from the mountains to the sea, where one could pluck oranges and avocados in clean, balmy air and build one's castle. Though it was Otis's brainchild, the Midwinter Edition quickly became Harry's baby. The *Times'* business manager beamed with pride at the number of paid advertisements that populated the special edition, making it the "fattest newspaper in the country." Eventually, it turned into a 200-page magazine, with a typical glossy color cover depicting happy people frolicking on the beach under impossibly blue skies. The Midwinter Edition was such a money-maker for the paper—and so effective at selling Los Angeles—that it continued through three generations of Otis-Chandler ownership into the early 1960s.

Local daily editions of the *Times* also cashed in. In 1886, the average front page of the newspaper consisted of nine columns of news and features, with a smattering of property ads. In 1887, under Chandler's aegis, the ratio flipped. The front page was a carnival of classifieds, bursting with superlatives and exclamation points. For the next two years, real estate postings promised the "Very Finest Speculation of the Day" and "Large Profits and Quick Returns," though sometimes an ad's copy would be more teasy: "Magnolia—Keep your eye on this town." Or simply: "Ramirez!" Chandler's priorities were telegraphed at the top of column one, just below the masthead, where "*Times* Advertising Rates" were clearly laid out ("payable at the counter" at Times-Mirror headquarters at Temple and New High streets).

By early 1888, the party was over. In the hangover that followed, people who were sold land by vulturine agents discovered that their lots were often fifty miles away from Los Angeles, on a mountaintop, in the desert, or even under the ocean. Dozens of towns disappeared from maps—Sunset, Clearwater, Chicago Park, Waterloo. Those told to keep an eye on Magnolia saw it too vanish. Plummeting real estate prices rippled through L.A., wiping out $14 million in assessed value. Looking back at "the height of the infection," businessman Harris Newmark remarked that "two-thirds of our population were, in a sense, more insane than sane." Aside from a desperate few who committed suicide, broke buyers licked their wounds and returned home or found some other line of work.

Not surprisingly, Chandler held all aces after everyone else went bust. Left with hundreds of outstanding advertising accounts to worthless lots, he collected on the unpaid debts by acquiring the properties' deeds. These investments helped both his and the *Times'* bottom lines, instilling in Chandler a hunger to get in on the ground floor of land development. Sure, the market had succumbed to irrational exuberance, but Los Angeles had too much going for it to fail. He was convinced it would rebound and become "the most important city in this country, if not the world."

Chandler's faith was based on the progress L.A. had made during the Mad Eighties, a decade in which it finally started to shed its backwater pueblo image. Among its civic improvements were dozens of interurban cable routes, eighty-seven miles of paved streets, and seventy-eight miles of cement sidewalks, many now lined with novel electrical lampposts. Intercontinental railroads allowed L.A.'s prized citrus to reach every part of the union. Two institutions of higher learning were founded—the University of Southern California and Occidental College. And several boom towns *did* manage to survive the bust, absorbed by Los Angeles in subsequent decades.

But in order to graduate to megacity status, the city still needed access to a world-class, deep-water port. This would be especially important given the news out of Central America. Though the United States would eventually take over the project, France was excavating a shipping canal through the Isthmus of Panama (Nicaragua had also been surveyed). The channel would obviate the need for long and dangerous passages around Cape Horn, an expected boon for Los Angeles upon its completion. Otis's *Times* regularly pushed the government to continue dredging San Pedro Harbor and improve its existing breakwater. In other words, to complete the work that Gen. Phineas Banning never had a chance to finish.

Banning, meanwhile, was never the same after his freak accident in 1884. The following March, he died at age fifty-four with his family by his bedside. Tributes poured in. His funeral was one of the best-attended in the history of the Southland—a showing that would've no doubt thrilled him. The *Times* published a front-page obit, calling him "a pioneer" and "one of the most enterprising and energetic citizens Los Angeles County has ever had." The *Los Angeles Herald* eulogized his complicated glory: "He saw in the distance the coming greatness of Southern California. And worked wisely to hasten the day of its coronation. . . . Like the rest of us he had his faults. He was apt at times to be peremptory and domineering, but his heart was always in the right place." All agreed that Los Angeles was "indebted" to the "wheel-horse of Wilmington." In recognition of his eventual moniker as The Father of Los Angeles Harbor, perhaps it's only fitting to grant the proud general the last word, pulled from the final pages of his unpublished memoir in the twilight of his career. "Various as have been the projects in which he has ventured," he reflected, "none have been failures."

BY THE end of the 1880s, even counting those who abandoned the city after going broke, Los Angeles's population had soared to 50,395—almost five times what it was in 1880. While City Hall did its best to meet demands, a new problem arose: More people now resided *outside* L.A.'s twenty-nine square miles than lived within them. Townships that survived the bust had their own challenges, often wanting in water, utility, and transportation needs. This wasn't L.A.'s problem per se. However, many Angelenos did business in adjacent districts or relocated to homes outside city limits, creating a dilemma. Los Angeles couldn't afford to pay for improvements in places like Garvanza, Colegrove, and Palms, yet it was in the city's best interests to see them prosper.

Annexation was an obvious solution; the additional tax base could offset expanded municipal services while also building toward its vanguard's prophecy of a thriving metropolis.

But any talk of annexation was premature in 1890. Before Los Angeles could seriously entertain the idea of gobbling up its neighbors, it needed to upgrade its own infrastructure. Water was, and would remain, the primary concern. Through the 1860s, the city was still relying on the Zanja Madre, or "Mother Ditch," an antiquated system inherited from Spanish settlers in which water was scooped out of the Los Angeles River by a creaky wheel, funneled into a conduit, and often hauled to houses on horse-drawn carts. On July 22, 1868, the Los Angeles City Water Company—a private enterprise comanaged by Prudent Beaudry—signed a thirty-year lease to provide reliable water for domestic services for up to 100,000 inhabitants. An overhaul couldn't come soon enough. Potable water from zanjas intermixed with open sewer ditches, creating a toxic cauldron that led to breakouts of dysentery, cholera, and typhoid. Houses on fire often burned to the ground because of low water pressure, or no water at all. Those fortunate enough to have working spigots periodically found something else deposited into their sinks: small wriggling fish that survived the journey from the L.A. River. Even a delay in a homeowner's morning newspaper delivery could be traced to this fishy system. The printing press for the *L.A. Times* was operated by water from a zanja. Occasionally, fish would flop into the machine and clog it up, literally stopping the presses until their gutsy remains could be cleared out.

Piscine issues aside, placing the city's water supply in the hands of a private company proved problematic. Whereas a municipally run utility would be held to account, the City Water Co. provided little transparency. Beaudry ran it like the business it was, seemingly putting his own interests before the city's. In May 1879, the company announced that it would charge extra for houses with bathtubs. This drew protests from L.A.'s health officer, who argued that "bathing should be encouraged in the city." Additionally, council members accused the utility of failing to fulfill an agreement to supply free water to hospitals, public schools, and jails. One issue was so contentious, it ended up in a prolonged legal battle. The water firm insisted that it was not responsible for providing the 300,000 daily gallons needed to spray down L.A.'s dusty streets. But even by its own narrow standards, the company fell short of its obligations. Throughout the 1880s, houses still burned down from a lack of fire hydrants, and people still found fish shimmying in their pipes.

Los Angeles also had a hard time keeping up with transportation needs. (The first "motor carriage," or automobile, wouldn't arrive in L.A. until 1897.) As trains continued making inroads across America, Los Angeles was pockmarked with private railways that did not necessarily go where one wanted to go . . . unless it was to a new housing development that subsidized its operations. One exception was L.A.'s first streetcar line, the Spring and Sixth Street Railroad, established on July 1, 1874. But like others that came online over the next ten years, it was horse-drawn. It wasn't until 1885 that the city saw its inaugural cable car line—twelve years after San Francisco opened the world's first. And yet L.A.'s cable-driven lines proved less reliable than plodding horses. The huge steam engines that ran the cable wheels were prone to breaking down, and tracks regularly flooded out from rainstorms. Other than the occasional funicular, the technology proved short-lived. In 1886, the first electric trolley finally appeared when the Los Angeles Electric Railway Company launched the first route on the Pacific Coast, its cars powered by a "trolley" that rolled along overhead wires. Within two years, however, operations shut down after a boiler exploded. Other trolley lines opened—a dizzying twenty-seven by the end of the 1880s—but, again, their routes often followed an exurb-driven agenda. "It would never do for an electric line to wait until the demand for it came," streetcar sultan Henry Huntington would later say, unapologetically. "It must anticipate the growth of communities and be there when the home builders arrive."

Not exactly practical for a homemaker who simply wanted to run errands around town.

As the calendar flipped to 1890, two new figures—one in the field of water, the other in transportation—were about to rise in prominence. The change they would bring to these infrastructure networks would make them household names by the close of the decade, and lead Los Angeles on a path of unprecedented expansion.

CHAPTER 3

The Teacher and the Autodidact

ON PAPER, MOSES HAZELTINE Sherman seemed an unlikely future tycoon. Born in Vermont in 1853, he matriculated at the Oswego Normal School and followed his father into teaching. Like fellow New Englander Harry Chandler—who would become a lifelong friend—Sherman came down with a lung illness in college that doctors diagnosed as tuberculosis. Their prescription was predictable: Move to a warmer climate. Sherman settled in Prescott, Arizona (population: 2,000) for a modest life as an instructor in a single-room schoolhouse.

He certainly looked the part. Six feet tall with thinning hair and calculating, deep-set eyes, Sherman exuded quiet aplomb, prone to folding his arms across his chest in posed photographs. He also exhibited a quality that would serve him well throughout his life—an ability to forge relationships with people of influence by mastering the art of ingratiation. After convincing voters to support a bond issue to build a larger school, Sherman deftly arranged for the complex to include offices for the territorial government. In 1883, Governor Frederick Augustus Tritle appointed Sherman the Adjutant General of Arizona, overseeing the territory's militia. Like Phineas Banning before him, the assignment came with the title "General." Henceforth, he too adopted the honorific. Any similarities to the more famous General Sherman were entirely intentional.

His teaching days behind him, Sherman moved to Phoenix with his family, which included wife Harriet (who went by Hattie), daughters Lucy and Hazeltine, and Hattie's son Robert from her first marriage. The city would serve as a fertile proving ground for Sherman, who threw himself into various business ventures—cofounding a bank, purchasing shares of Phoenix Water Works, investing in the Arizona Canal, and, crucially, building and operating a street railway. He also acquired real estate. Sherman was credited with persuading the territorial government to relocate the capital from Prescott to Phoenix by generously donating a ten-acre plot. The capitol building still stands on Sherman's former land. By 1890, he claimed to pay more in taxes than any other individual in Arizona, which tallied about 25,000 voting-eligible males in its population. Now thirty-six-years old, it was as if the sparsely populated desert colony could no longer contain the general's grand ambitions. Fortunately, there was a place that could.

In the summer of 1890, Sherman and his family decamped to Los Angeles. He exhibited kid-in-a-candy-store glee at the myriad opportunities the town presented. As in Phoenix, he diversified. "Looking for some cheap ostriches for $25 to $40 a piece for some land in Los Angeles," he wrote a Colonel Marble, hoping to capitalize on the craze for ostrich-feathered women's hats. But he was chagrined to find only "old more expensive ones." One area where he did find success was L.A.'s budding but chaotic streetcar system. As he snatched up troubled electric railways, newspapers tracked his dealings, and he and Hattie started showing up in society pages, hobnobbing with the city's movers and shakers.

In 1891, Hattie's brother Eli P. Clark entered the picture. Eli and Moses had become close during their teaching days in Prescott—so close, Eli married Moses's sister Lucy. Sherman enlisted his brother-in-law to form the Los Angeles Consolidated Electric Railway Company (LACE), with Sherman as president and Clark as vice president and general manager. It was the first of many business partnerships, and their personal relationship would well outlast Sherman's own marriage. Over the next two years, LACE constructed a fairly reliable rail system with astonishing speed. The partners also bought up bankrupt companies like Pacific Railway, which they renamed the Los Angeles-Pacific

Railroad (LAP)—hinting at their eventual plan to link L.A. with the Pacific Ocean. By the end of 1893, they were operating thirty-five miles of electric lines in the heart of Los Angeles, with another thirty-five miles of horse- or cable-drawn lines that would soon convert to electrical power. All told, the routes shuttled 32,000 passengers a day.

With their emphasis on city transit, Sherman's franchises were financed by hundreds of owners who benefitted from his coaches rumbling past their properties or businesses, thus increasing their valuations. It was a hard proposition to pass up. "We might build five, or six, or even seven miles of road, and we might build less, according to the amount of money [the landowners] raise," Sherman explained. "But the understanding is that the Railway Company does not put in anything." At first blush, this practice carried an uneasy whiff of extortion. And yet viewed through a modern lens, Sherman's policy was essentially the private equivalent of present-day rules that require new builders to pay various development fees for civic improvements. In some ways, the general was simply following the same playbook as water boss Prudent Beaudry. Los Angeles was in a race against time to provide infrastructure for its exploding populace; however, its base wasn't big enough yet to raise the necessary funds in an expedient manner. This opened the door for the private sector to fill the gap in public services, each party taking advantage of the other.

Besides, Sherman needed the revenue streams as a hedge against the Panic of 1893, which triggered a four-year recession that historians often cite as the end of the Gilded Age. Even Sherman's San Francisco banker friends stopped offering loans. But Sherman kept plugging away on projects, adding to his significant debt load. In 1895, he and Clark rolled out the popular Pasadena & Los Angeles Electric Railway, making both cities easily accessible for the first time. Pasadena, however, was already well-established, settled in 1874 by wealthy Midwesterners. Sherman knew that the *real* money would come from extending his rail empire into undeveloped areas. There he could invest in sellable land, then run his trains out to subdivisions under his control. He set his sights on the westside of Los Angeles, in the sixteen miles between downtown and the coast.

MEANWHILE, THE year 1890—the same year that Moses arrived in Los Angeles—proved equally eventful for a ruggedly handsome, thirty-five-year-old Irish immigrant with a walrus mustache and flinty blue eyes that betrayed a signature twinkle. William Mulholland had been working in the L.A. vicinity for thirteen years, the last four as the superintendent of the Los Angeles City Water Company. On the home front, 1890 saw Bill finally marry his young sweetheart, Lillie Ferguson. On the job, he received a gold watch from company president William Hayes Perry. The gift was a token of appreciation for going beyond the call of duty last Christmas Eve to personally unclog a conduit along the L.A. River that had threatened to leave the city bone-dry. As the *Los Angeles Times* put it, Mulholland "jumped out of bed when the alarm was given . . . and he didn't get a chance to undress and go to bed like a Christian for four days." Mulholland later confirmed, "I never had my shoes off from Tuesday until Friday night." Slaving away for four straight days and nights in torrential rain, he managed to fix the culvert and avert a shutdown—a huge relief for Perry, who envisioned a nightmarish scenario in which "the city would have to go back to water carts for its supply." Mulholland was the maven who had saved Christmas. Plenty more miracles were to come, each elevating this holy water man to new heights among the Angel City faithful. It was a dangerous place to be for the self-professed autocrat to live.

The truth was, there was no place Bill would rather be than slogging through the muddy banks of the Los Angeles River. He first laid eyes on the waterway in 1877, when he stepped off a ship in San Pedro Bay with five bucks to his name and vague notions of outdoor employment. The river stirred something within him, evoking feelings of his native Belfast, which he left at fifteen years old. "It was a beautiful, limpid little stream, with willows on its banks," he recalled. "It was so attractive to me that it at once became something about which my whole scheme of life was woven, I loved it so much." Working his way up to Los Angeles, he was drawn to the splendor of its countryside, the simple charms of its Spanish and Mexican heritage. "It was the most attractive town I had ever seen," he said. "The world was my oyster and I was just opening it."

From the start, Mulholland viewed Los Angeles as his own iambic pentameter, a lyrical dreamland requiring structure. Lacking a high school education, he devoured books, cultivating an appreciation for classic literature and poetry. This tendency to romanticize his journey as a Homeric Odyssey perhaps imbued him with a sense of greater purpose while also insulating him from self-doubt. Mary Foy, the city's first female librarian, remembered him being extremely "studious" as she watched the young man haunt the nonfiction aisles for real-world knowledge. Yet it is a testament to his complex nature that, even at the height of his powers, Bill still possessed the beating heart of an impressionable young bloke from the Emerald Isle. A man's destiny, he determined, was ultimately guided by blessings and curses: "I went to school in Ireland when I was a boy, learned the three R's and the Ten Commandments—or most of them—made a pilgrimage to the Blarney Stone, received my father's blessing, and here I am."

After one year in L.A., Mulholland landed a job digging wells for the Los Angeles City Water Co. It was adventurous, rewarding work, reminding him of his seaman days with the British Merchant Navy. "When we were down six hundred feet, we struck a tree," he said of one well excavation. "A little further, we got some fossil remains, and these fired my curiosity. I wanted to know how they got there." Back to the library he went, checking out volumes on geology, hydrology, and engineering. It was settled. He would become a hydraulic engineer in his beloved adopted hometown. Oyster fully opened, Bill had found his pearl.

In those early days, well before gifting Mulholland a gold watch in 1890, William Perry had no reason to give Mulholland a second thought. To the president of City Water, the anonymous staffer was just another lowly zanja digger. Likewise, Mulholland never had occasion to meet Perry. One day in 1880, Perry happened upon Bill clearing out a ditch in Elysian Park. Perry asked the grizzled man who he was. Mulholland, whose legendary temper was probably inflamed by the backbreaking work, growled, "None of your goddamn business." Perry rode off on his horse, after which Bill's fellow zanjeros informed him that he had just told off their boss. Accounts vary on what happened next, but Mulholland's own version has him making his way downtown to pick up his last paycheck, since he would clearly be fired. When he got to the office, Perry's clerk asked, "You're the one from the ditch out by the river?" Mulholland nodded gravely. The clerk came around the desk and shook his hand. "Mr. Perry says you're the foreman of the ditch gang out there from now on." Mulholland would often recount this incident when describing his career, for better or worse. He said what he felt and felt what he said. Who needs to collaborate when your instincts are their own reward?

Mulholland's approach to his job may have been unorthodox, but it was well-suited in a city that indulged risk-takers. With all his years repairing and laying down pipes, Bill never bothered to keep records; the inventory was all in his head. Even after he was promoted to superintendent in 1886, he happily spent more time in the field than he did at his desk. His photographic memory was put to the test during an arbitration meeting at the City Council in the 1890s. Initially, some councilmen were put off by the fact that Mulholland showed up without maps in hand. Mulholland quickly wowed them. In great detail, according to one newspaper, the super recited "the size and character of the various pipes of the system, the dates on which they were laid and the character of the soil in which they were placed." Mulholland knew the exact locations of 300 miles of pipes, 500 fire hydrants, and every pumping station. After the meeting, the arbitration board ran a spot check, sending crews out to verify pipes in 200 subterranean spots. All matched up with Mulholland's mental map. Knowledge was power, and Bill's total recall of L.A.'s water-works contributed to his eventual promotion as the city's water chief. But it also led to an overreliance on one man's judgment to marshal an emerging metropolis into the next century.

The Nephew

IN 1894, SOUTHERN PACIFIC Railroad opened the Long Wharf some twenty miles west of Los Angeles's borders. It instantly earned the distinction as the longest pier in the world, with dual railroad tracks gliding almost one mile over Santa Monica Bay. The length was necessitated to reach sufficient ocean depths to handle ship traffic. More than anything, the Long Wharf represented a hostile act—a flipping of the bird by Southern Pacific (SP) to the influencers of Angel City. By bypassing San Pedro, the company had planted its own Southern California beachhead with the intent of monopolizing global commerce, effectively stunting L.A.'s growth. In fact, the president of SP boasted that he would "make the grass grow in [Los Angeles's] streets."

This would not do for Harrison Gray Otis. Since the days of Gen. Phineas Banning, the city of Los Angeles—to say nothing of California and the District of Columbia—had invested time, energy, and money in San Pedro Harbor. During more cooperative times, Southern Pacific had acquired Banning's Short Line in 1872, a signal that it too was on board with San Pedro. Now, SP was building "Port Los Angeles" thirty miles up the coast. The new port wasn't even *in* Los Angeles; it was in Santa Monica, a recently incorporated town that, like Pasadena, had steadfastly resisted any notions of affixing itself to Los Angeles. The implications were clear. If the West's most dominant railway made Santa Monica the dominant harbor, Los Angeles would lose its dominance. Any talk of annexations would be rendered insignificant.

Southern Pacific's truculent tactics were sparked by its president, Collis Potter Huntington, the same man who promised

to turn L.A. into a grassy ghost town. In 1890, Collis got wind
of a St. Louis outfit buying up land in San Pedro to build the
Los Angeles Terminal Railway. Worried that Southern Pacific's
presence in San Pedro was getting diluted, he turned his attention to Santa Monica, scooping up waterfront property without
telling his SP partners. Huntington may have also been tipped
off that Congress was planning to allocate four million dollars
toward improving San Pedro's breakwater, which created even
more urgency. Well-connected with lobbyists, he had an ally in
Nevada Senator John P. Jones, who just happened to be one of
the founders of Santa Monica. The two had gotten to know each
other years earlier, after SP purchased Jones's failed railroad from
Los Angeles to Santa Monica.

Evoking imagery from his Civil War days, Otis fired off com-
mentaries in his *Los Angeles Times*. He framed the dispute as
a battle for freedom—calling it the Great Free Harbor Fight—
with Huntington as an enemy who had crossed state lines. "The
Southern Pacific of Kentucky, a foreign corporation controlled
by a resident of New York city, proposes to thwart the will of this
people," one screed started off. Then, in a plea to readers:

> Are the citizens of Los Angeles slaves and curs that they
> should permit themselves to be whipped into line by
> Collis P. Huntington? Is this a community of free and in-
> dependent American citizens, or are we the vassals of a
> bandit, creatures open to bribery, slaves to a plutocratic
> master, who has neither bowels of compassion, common
> decency, nor an organ in his putrid carcass so great as
> his gall?

Throughout the battle, Otis's *Times* beat the drum of a "free
harbor" and Los Angeles as a "free community of free American citizens." No dog whistles here. Labor movements and railroad worker strikes were on the rise in America, and Otis was
intent on keeping these "socialist freaks," "born mob leaders,"

and "leeches upon honest work" out of Southern California. So powerful was Otis's influence, organized labor leaders referred to Los Angeles as the "Otistown of the Open Shop." Indeed, by keeping guilds at the gates, L.A.'s labor costs were thirty percent lower than San Francisco's. Southern Pacific threatened to up-end all that, leading to higher wages and inspiring more unions. Of course, such results would benefit workers, which was exactly what business leaders didn't want, and what Otis's readership didn't need to hear.

In the end, Collis Huntington's vision for a seaport in Santa Monica never amounted to much. Though it operated for a period of time, it was dealt a death blow in 1897 when the Senate put its full weight behind San Pedro. As Pedro's harbor got its improvements, the Long Wharf gradually deteriorated until it was finally torn down in 1921. Collis's port war also exposed a rift not just within his company, but his own family. In 1897, Collis was seventy-six years old and ceding more responsibilities to Henry E. Huntington, his forty-seven-year-old nephew. In letters between them, Henry's loyalty to his uncle came in conflict with his personal belief that San Pedro was the superior location. As early as April 7, 1893, Henry prosaically advised Collis that "if the Government do not build a breakwater at Santa Monica and should build one at San Pedro, we should be benefited by the building of San Pedro on account of our real estate holdings there. . . . Of course, if the Government built at San Pedro, it would be a great setback for our wharf at Santa Monica as there is no doubt the underwriters would insure for a much less rate for a wharf protected by a breakwater than is not." Truth be told, Henry was not interested in ports or interstate railroads. His passion was real estate and streetcars, domains that would put him on a collision course with Gen. Moses Sherman. But Henry loved his Uncle Collis like a father. After all, he would never even be in a position to shape the future of Los Angeles were it not for the old man.

Born in 1850 in Oneonta, New York, Henry was the fourth of

seven children raised by Solon and Harriet Huntington. The family was solidly middle class, with no aspirations to leave their pleasant burg. The same could not be said for Collis. Solon's younger brother had an entrepreneurial streak and wasn't encumbered by a wife and kids. Seduced by the Gold Rush of 1849, he left New York to seek his fortune in California, one year before Henry was born.

As Collis set up shop in Sacramento, he kept tabs on his brother's family, updating them on his new ventures out West. These letters must have seemed exciting and exotic to young Henry, who toiled away at his father's modest hardware store throughout his teen years. Coincidentally, as part of his growing portfolio, Collis co-owned a hardware manufacturing facility in New York City called Sargent & Company. Bored with Oneonta, Henry moved to the big city when he was twenty and hired on as a porter. He explained his sudden move in a letter to his parents: "I wanted to get into someplace soon as it was getting lonesome here doing nothing, and I proposed to Uncle that I should go there till I could do better."

At Sargent & Co., Collis found his nephew uncommonly disciplined, an eager sponge absorbing the ways of business. But Henry was frustrated by his $3 weekly salary and having to rely on his uncle's charity for room and board. "I do not think that [Uncle Collis] would like it if I were to leave here; he seems so willing to help me all the time," he wrote in another letter. "Yet I am getting to the age that I do not like to feel dependent on anyone." Collis convinced him to stick it out; he had big plans for his nephew beyond the hardware store. Henry was heartened by his uncle's faith in him: "He said he was thinking what he should do for me and told me not to be in any hurry. I think Uncle will do what is right with me."

The following year, Collis brought his nephew along on an inspection of his expanding eastern railroad network. In May 1871, Henry's apprenticeship under his uncle yielded its first test: overseeing the manufacturing of railroad ties in Coalsmouth,

West Virginia. The job had a high potential of going sideways. The mill employed thirty hardscrabble workers who were now being bossed by the twenty-one-year-old nephew of his blue-blood uncle. But Henry passed with flying colors. Lean and broad-shouldered, with pensive blue eyes that told of unwavering focus, he commanded the respect of his workforce. He not only increased the output of railroad ties, but also lowered the cost of production. Returning to New York in 1872, Henry met Mary Alice Prentice, the sister of Collis's adopted daughter. They were married the following year. Already bound to Collis professionally, Henry was now also in bed with the family.

Using the knowledge and experience he gleaned from his uncle, Henry began to invest on his own, often with loans from Collis. He had some early successes. "I am glad to hear that your prospects for business are so good," Collis conveyed, "but I did not expect anything else." However, Henry stumbled as well, usually with enterprises in which he had entered into a partnership. Unlike his outgoing uncle, Henry was introverted and reserved, qualities better served for a man who prized his independence. This modus operandi would define his career. Though he would join the occasional syndicate, especially if it was endorsed by friends like Sherman and Harry Chandler, the quiet dreamer in him flourished under the freedom that came from not having to answer to others.

Looming over all of this, Collis was preparing his nephew to potentially take over Southern Pacific, installing him on an executive ladder that led to the position of First Vice President. "I received an encouraging letter from Uncle Collis about my work here," Henry wrote his mother in 1882. "I cannot tell you how gratified I am to know that he appreciates [me], and I feel fully repaid for my labor." By the early 1890s, Henry's family, which now included his children Clara, Elizabeth, Marian, and Howard, was firmly ensconced in San Francisco near SP's headquarters. Though he called New York his permanent home, Collis was a constant presence. A photographer caught Henry and Collis walking along a San Francisco street during this period. Clad in overcoats on a typically gray day, the pair posed in front of a skyscraper. In the photo, it is striking how much they look like actual father and son. Sporting a salt-and-pepper mustache, Henry oozes self-confidence, his body language erect but relaxed, a rolled-up newspaper pinned under his right arm. Next to him, Collis leans on a cane but otherwise looks hearty and hale, his other hand fisting his jutted hip as if to say, "Look at us!" The elder Huntington radiates pride, with mirthful eyes and a smile pushing out his shiny, plump cheeks and snow-white whiskers.

But the happy times would not outlive this snapshot. Collis would soon be embroiled in the Long Wharf drama and Henry would wrestle with controversy after acquiring several San Francisco streetcar lines on behalf of SP. The biggest problem child was the Market Street Railway Company, whose 170 miles of tracks ran through dense neighborhoods from the bay to the Mission District. One evening in the spring of 1895, a grand jury was convened to get to the bottom of a spate of fatal accidents involving young children getting run over. As the Market Street line's president, Henry was forced to explain why he had not affixed safety guards—similar to cowcatchers, but for pedestrians—on the front of the electrified cars, which traveled faster than cable cars. A reporter outside the room could hear Henry vehemently argue that his railway was not culpable in the latest death, a three-year-old named James Madigan. "[Huntington] is possessed of good after-dinner lungs, and his voice could be heard through the two thicknesses of doors," the reporter wryly observed. Within months, the San Francisco Board of Supervisors drafted Fender Ordinance 2866, making it unlawful for any person or corporation to operate a streetcar without a regulated fender, "so constructed as to prevent any person from getting under or being run over by the wheels of said car."

Despite the ordinance, the Market Street Railway continued to operate "fenderless" cars. Tragedies continued. In early 1898, William Randolph Hearst's incendiary *San Francisco Examiner* published a shrill headline—"WHEN WILL HUNTINGTON ACT?"—in relation to its running tally of "Street-Car Murders." Since Madigan's death in 1895, twenty-nine more people had been killed, the majority on routes owned by Henry Huntington. The paper sensationalized their deaths with a gory cartoon that portrayed Henry as the grim reaper. Perched at the front of a trolley car, he lowered a giant scythe that read "Huntington's Fender." Its blade mangled eight little girls—some already dead, others bug-eyed in fear—leaving them disemboweled along the track like discarded doll parts. By any era's standards, the sketch was in shockingly poor taste.

The latest victim was a two-and-a-half-year-old girl, Hulda Johnson, who toddled in front of a fenderless Huntington car. In grisly prose, the *Examiner* reported that the coach that struck Hulda "ground the little tot into the paving stone, crushed her baby head, and passed her along to the wheels, which cut off her tiny limbs and mangled her until the people turned from the sight in horror." Without proof, the newspaper cited faulty brakes. Meanwhile, an accompanying article spoke of an Oakland man who fell in front of a trolley owned by a competing company. *That* car had a fender, which scooped the man off the tracks and saved him from certain death—proof that Huntington's dereliction was costing lives. "The law in the case has been disregarded for two and a half years," the newspaper stated. "The trouble is H. E. Huntington [sets himself] above the law."

The following morning, the *Examiner* injected itself into the story, which now occupied all of page one. "'The Examiner' is Compelled to Take the Initiative and to Cause the Arrest of H. E. Huntington" read one heading. Dominating the upper-right corner was an illustration of an officious mustachioed man at his desk, signing his name to a document. The caption read: "Yesterday, on complaint of the managing editor of 'The Examiner,' Police Judge Conlan issued a warrant for the arrest of H. E. Huntington." The *Examiner* included a statement from San Francisco Mayor James D. Phelan, who decried the profits of rapid transit barons paid in the blood of children.

Of course, there was always more than meets the eye with Hearst. Though he was still decades away from peak powers, the young publisher was already skilled at channeling populist causes. Huntington was the perfect adversary. "Hearst had an infallible instinct for the adolescent maturity level of the American people," noted California historian Gray Brechin. "He was a perennial adolescent himself, so he really keyed in to the American need for fairy tales and sex and violence, and he'd give it to them." The *Examiner's* attacks on the Huntington clan also reflected Hearst's wariness of a Southern Pacific monopoly—a sentiment shared by many of his readers, who had come to resent the fact that SP, like an octopus, had its tentacles wrapped around so many rail lines and industries. After a while, the words "Southern Pacific" and "octopus" became so synonymous, the *Examiner* resorted to simply invoking Octopus as a substitute; readers understood the shorthand.

Several months after calling for Henry's head on a pike, the *Examiner* buried an article in its July 17, 1898, issue conceding that he was never arrested. The paper's target this time was the Board of Supervisors, which had amended Fender Ordinance 2866 to allow railroad owners more time to comply with the new safety standards. The Huntingtons' relationship with business-friendly pols undoubtedly helped their predicament. As if to save face, the *Examiner* trotted out the same judge who issued the arrest: "Judge Conlan's Decision Shows How Corrupt Supervisors Saved the Magnate," read its headline. "Applauds 'The Examiner.'"

Though the bad press weighed on Huntington, he was not always around to read it. Lately, he was spending more time in Los Angeles at his uncle's behest. Santa Fe had eclipsed Southern Pacific in railroad traffic in Southern California, and a perturbed Collis tasked Henry to look for new opportunities while keeping tabs on their rival. Henry had first visited Los Angeles in 1892. It was love at first sight. "I feel as if I could remain here all my

life and never leave," he wrote his family. He mingled with power players, established relationships, and joined fraternal organizations like the California Club. Huntington was there when
prospector Edward Doheny struck oil near downtown, leading
to the latter's fortune from "black gold." "There is no limit to the
possibilities," Henry observed about L.A. (Doheny would later convince Huntington to convert a fleet of locomotives from
coal-powered to oil-powered.) Another person Huntington met
was Moses Sherman. In 1895, the two partnered up to build the
Pasadena and Altadena Railroad, which served as a connector
to the Mt. Lowe Railway in the San Gabriel Mountains. It was
during this period that Henry grew familiar with Shorb Ranch in
Pasadena—the area that would become San Marino—where he
would build his wondrous estate later in life.

But it was Southern California's agreeable weather that ultimately won him over. "People will inevitably seek the best cli-
mates," he wrote in one letter. "This is the finest country in the
world out here. You can't say too much in its favor." Henry himself benefitted from the city's agreeable virtues. Years of stressful
living in San Francisco had taken a toll on his health, alarming
those close to him. After he left for an East Coast trip in 1896,
his private secretary took the liberty of urging Collis to pare back
her boss's workload. "He has not been looking well for sometime
back," she wrote, "and he has been working very hard ever since
I have been with him." Collis also registered concern, frequent-
ly imploring his nephew to get steady exercise: "He who walks
much is paced by health, while he who sits much has disease for
a caller."

As if L.A.'s balmy weather wasn't enough of an incentive, local
newspapers began to lay on the flattery, tracking Huntington's every move in the Southland as if he were visiting royalty. Even the
L.A. Times dropped its grudge against the family. With the Santa Monica port fiasco now in the past—which was always driven
more by Collis anyway—Harry Chandler smartly bonded with
the younger Huntington, their business relationship evolving to

genuine friendship. In late 1897, one local paper opined, "Whatever may be said about the Huntington influence, it cannot be denied that it has transformed the Southern Pacific [into] one the equal of the best managed Eastern lines, and this has largely been done by H. E. Huntington, the nephew."

On August 13, 1900, Collis Huntington died suddenly from a heart attack. The news shook Henry to his core. "The shock of his death was the severest blow I have ever received," he said, "for I loved him as a boy loves his own father and received from him the kindest treatment that any son could possibly get." A special train hurried Henry to New York City for the funeral. His uncle's passing was the final impetus for Henry to relocate to Los Angeles. In a slap in the face, Southern Pacific's board passed him over to succeed Collis as company president. Instead, they gave it to E. H. Harriman, a Union Pacific Railroad veteran who was looking to merge the railway giants. Regardless, Huntington was tired of fighting battles—with bad health, hostile unions, warring SP board members, and a vituperative San Francisco press (although he couldn't escape Hearst forever; the *Examiner* tycoon would establish a *Los Angeles Examiner* in 1903). After resigning as vice president of Southern Pacific, Huntington cashed out his company stock and sold his interest in the cursed Market Street railway, pocketing a cool $20 million. He was now fifty years old. He was no longer the "nephew," no longer required to carry someone else's water. The Huntington name was now his alone. In addition to his payout from SP, he inherited $15 million from Collis's estate. Here was a chance to build his own empire. Los Angeles would be his new playground.

But first, he'd have to kick Moses Sherman out of the sandbox.

CHAPTER 5

Sherman's March Westward

THE FRESHLY SCRUBBED SANTA Monica firehouse gleamed in anticipation. Locals speckled its grounds with calla lilies and draped its palm trees in garlands. Schools shut down at noon. By three o'clock, 1,500 people had congregated in front of the engine house amidst the trilling of a brass band and percussive blasts from a ceremonial gun. As three electric streetcars pulled up to the station, the guest of honor was spotted. A bevy of beauties streaked toward him, "bearing wreaths and decorated palms" as they "turned loose their floral weapons on him." Gen. Moses Sherman playfully surrendered. "It was a battle of flowers," reported the *Los Angeles Times*, "but it was all one-sided, and he had to capitulate, but not till he was enveloped in a mass of the decorations."

It was April 1, 1896, and Santa Monica was saluting the arrival of the first electric railway connecting Los Angeles to the beach city. After a bedecked Sherman unfolded his large frame and exited the car to a loud ovation, the celebration moved to the Town Hall for a spread of sandwiches and lemonade. Dignitaries took turns praising Sherman, president of Los Angeles-Pacific Railroad. He had delivered on his promise to bring public transportation to the Pacific Ocean. The route represented, in the words of L.A. Mayor Frank Rader, "Sherman's march to the sea"—a quip that newspaper copy editors found irresistible.

After the festivities, the three cars switched directions to head back to Los Angeles. In addition to connecting two cities, the sixteen-mile line featured many highlights. It included a stop at the Soldiers' Home (today's Veterans Affairs campus in West

L.A.), where Civil War vets serenaded the train with "Marching Through Georgia," another play off Union Army Gen. William Sherman's reaching the Atlantic coast. At the halfway point, the track traversed a tent city—appropriately called Sherman—which included a Sherman-owned train yard and a massive generator that powered his streetcars. The railway also went through the Colegrove district (today's southern Hollywood) along Colegrove Boulevard (eventual Santa Monica Boulevard), with an eastern terminus at Bellevue Avenue.

Behind all the genuflection for the former schoolteacher was a dirty little secret. The primary purpose of the LAP Railroad, of course, wasn't rapid transit. It was to sell lots, either those belonging to Moses (and partner Eli Clark) or other parties, who helped underwrite the enterprise. Sherman was just one of many speculators nationwide who understood the connection between streetcar accessibility and increased property values in outlying areas. As far back as 1856, a horse-drawn line enticed residential development outside Boston. "From the late 1800s through the first decade of the nineteenth century, that was the model," says writer Josh Stephens, an expert in urban planning and development. "If you had a piece of land, you'd be willing to pay for infrastructure to get people out there." But the self-serving relationship between real estate holders and railways was drawing increased scrutiny. The same month that Sherman opened the L.A.-Pacific, Henry Huntington was subdividing Shorb Ranch through a similar ploy. *The San Francisco Examiner*—never one to ignore Henry's exploits, even from afar—shredded the mogul for unfairly rewarding himself by wearing different hats:

> It must be borne in mind that there are several H. E. Huntingtons, all of whom have intimate dealings with each other. There is H. E. Huntington, the assistant to the President of the Southern Pacific Company, and H. E. Huntington, President of the Pacific Improvement Company, and H. E. Huntington, the land speculator. . . . How

perfectly the various H. E. Huntingtons work together. The one sells the land to the other, and the third makes it an important railroad point.

The *Examiner* claimed that Huntington sold the Shorb Ranch to himself at one-tenth its assessed value. Eventually, he changed the 500-acre plot's name to San Marino Ranch, with the resultant San Marino community accessible by his Pacific Electric trolley.

As a contrast, Los Angeles-based newspapermen and policymakers were far more forgiving—even accommodating—regarding the business practices of transportation titans. A 1905 article in the *Los Angeles Herald* was typical of the editorial flattery that often passed for news. It commended Sherman and Clark as "pioneers of interurban transportation [who] are endowed with an enterprise and sagacity that would command fortune anywhere." Los Angeles harbored a long-running inferiority complex vis-à-vis San Francisco, like a little sister who could never measure up to her older sibling. Anyone who could help the city get a leg up on its bête noire was an asset, even if they disproportionately benefited. After all, a rising tide lifted all boats.

As important as Sherman's route was to opening up the Westside, Moses didn't rest on his laurels. He was thinking bigger—always bigger. His goal was to expand the Los Angeles-Pacific railway to even more beach communities. The LAP had already proved the power of PR. What if he could attract passengers with sightseeing trips that lasted all day? Along the way, silky salesmen could shill Sherman-owned property at each tourist stop. But real life delayed his dream, as Sherman was financially overextended in the middle of a recession. It also didn't help that Henry Huntington—his partner on the Pasadena and Altadena Railroad—was muscling in on his transportation stronghold. Regardless, the general had earned himself a well-deserved vacation after launching the Santa Monica line. He and Clark departed with family members to the Hotel del Coronado in San Diego.

If the coronation of Sherman's railway pointed toward the

creeping western advancement of Los Angeles, the following
day confirmed it. On April 2, 1896, registered voters approved
the annexation of 3,250 acres known as the Western Addition. A
common misconception about Western Avenue is that the north-
south arterial got its name because it once marked the western
border of L.A.'s original territory. The street, however, had opened
for traffic in 1885, and Los Angeles did not absorb it until this
1896 annexation; even then, the new city limits extended several
blocks beyond Western Avenue to Arlington Avenue (now Wilton
Place, farther north). Nevertheless, the Western Addition included the affluent enclaves of Rosedale and Pico Heights. That same
day, Los Angeles voted in the Southern Addition, an area bounded by Hoover Street on the west, Alameda Street on the east, and
Slauson Avenue on the south. Together the Western and Southern
additions comprised ten square miles. The city now totaled forty
square miles, a thirty-three percent increase.

The admittance of these areas culminated eighteen-month
campaigns by neighborhood groups like the Southwest Improvement Association and the Pico Heights Association, who eyed
L.A.'s superior municipal services. Though the pro-annex faction
was initially outflanked by dissenters, they garnered key support
from the *L.A. Times* and the City Council. In trying to keep up
with the Joneses, influential L.A. voices argued that larger, more
established cities across the U.S. were actively consolidating adjacent towns. This was especially true after the Panic of 1893, when
bankruptcy concerns prompted many municipalities to merge.
Subscribing to the economy of scale, larger cities became their
own economic engine, too big to fail.

Thanks to miles of unincorporated land in every direction,
Los Angeles had multiple pathways to annexation. One way to
look at L.A. on the brink of its long expansion phase is to imagine
it through the laws of physics, as if it were a celestial body exerting
a gravitational pull. Typically, the greater the planet, the greater
its number of natural satellites. For the first seventy-eight years
of its existence, Los Angeles was like Mercury—its critical mass

too small to draw another moon into its orbit. The city absorbed its first satellite in 1859 with the one-mile Southern Extension. As it kept growing, L.A. reached and surpassed the gravitational equivalents of Neptune (fourteen moons), Uranus (twenty-seven moons), and finally, the gas giants Saturn and Jupiter, each with some eighty moons. Los Angeles would eventually absorb over 200 satellite districts, though there were also plenty of holdouts. Beverly Hills, Culver City, Glendale, Pasadena, and Santa Monica are among the eighty-eight dwarf planets free-floating within L.A.'s sphere.

Around the time of the Western and Southern Addition election, another vote revealed the push-pull dynamics behind the issue of annexation. Both Vernon and present-day University Park were on the same ballot that day. Both districts had enough "no" votes to remain autonomous. Four years later, the University section joined L.A. after all, while Vernon remained unhitched. (Vernon incorporated in 1905 and has remained a bizarre, often troubled fiefdom ever since.) Meanwhile, a balkanized Highland Park couldn't agree on anything. Six months after the Western and Southern annexation, a 1.4-square-mile portion was voted into Los Angeles. Another part of Highland Park chose to remain independent . . . only to change its mind years later.

So what advantages did Highland Park, Pico Heights, and Rosedale enjoy from joining their larger neighbor? Access to the Los Angeles Public Library, beefed-up fire and police services, reliable garbage removal, electric streetlights, and improved water and sewers. Also, children now had the privilege of a free education at Los Angeles High School, whereas localities outside the city limits paid a tuition. On the flip side, communities that married into the City of Angels risked losing their identities or getting wiped off the map altogether. (RIP Pico Heights, which later became part of Pico-Union.) Taxes could get contentious. Johnny-come-lately residents often felt passed over when paying into a municipal pool that prioritized the needs of older communities. In Pico Heights, weekend boozers dreaded capricious L.A.

rules that intermittently shut down saloons on Sundays. Then there was Rosedale. Residents there looked forward to the inevitable higher land values that would come from being part of Los Angeles. It was assumed that its main asset—twelve-year-old Rosedale Cemetery, the first in L.A. to accept all races and religions—would be sold off and subdivided to create residential housing and a nice park. Neither happened, and the graveyard (now called Angelus-Rosedale Cemetery) is still there, having survived into a third century.

However, there was one upshot that no one from Pico Heights, Rosedale, or Los Angeles could really argue with: improved streets. Prior to 1896, travel between Pico Heights/Rosedale and L.A. was erratic. Dirt roads abruptly petered out near Hoover Street, the dividing line between the Western Addition and Los Angeles. Now that all roadways were brought under L.A. control, users could count on regularly sprinkled streets (to minimize dust) and more streamlined traffic—to an extent, at least. Even to this day, several routes emanating from Hoover make for a disorienting driving experience. Major streets on the original Los Angeles side—Occidental, Rampart, Alvarado—still abruptly end at Hoover at thirty-degree angles due to L.A.'s slanted street grid. Ordinal numbered streets like 11th, 12th, and 25th maddeningly stop at Hoover, only to pick up again a block north or south—that is, if they don't end at Hoover entirely. In another reminder of the past, boulevards like Pico, Venice, and Washington, after passing through Hoover, curve southeast upon entering L.A.'s original borders. Street maps of this area are akin to seismology maps of the San Andreas Fault, the "shift" between the former Western Addition and Los Angeles resembling the sedimentary scars of an old earthquake. Lacking a cohesive urban plan, Los Angeles still had not developed a central vision. Harry Chandler would help bring it into focus.

CHAPTER 6

Gen. Otis, Freedom Fighter

HARRISON GRAY OTIS LIVED for the fight. The churlish Civil War vet continued to press for the unfettered growth of Los Angeles. Relying on his usual palette of colorful epithets, anyone who stood in the way was a "corpse defacer," "moral leper," or even pro-bestiality. By the mid-1890s, two battles played out with regularity on the pages of his *Los Angeles Times*. One was the need to maintain a "free harbor" in San Pedro by staving off Southern Pacific Railroad and pressuring Washington to upgrade the port. The other hit closer to home. The *Times*, like so many other industries, was dealing with rumblings of strikes and unionization among its workers. This was clearly socialism at work, and it would lead to the decline of a "free Los Angeles" if left unchecked.

In 1898, a third conflict of far bigger proportions flared up. On April 20, President William McKinley signed a joint Congressional resolution declaring war on Spain. McKinley just happened to be an old army cohort of Otis's. Eager to defend Old Glory against Spanish aggression—and perhaps trying to recapture the glory of his youth—the rotund, sixty-one-year-old newspaper magnate appealed to the president to join the campaign. Within weeks, Otis was appointed Brigadier General and assigned to Manila to oversee American volunteers in the Spanish-American War. Just like that, the *Times* was minus its president and general manager.

But the paper was in more than capable hands with now-Vice President Harry Chandler. Just before setting sail, Otis anointed him "interim General Manager." The situation echoed that timeworn cliché of Dad entrusting his son to manage household affairs in his absence. That's because Chandler now held another important role: son-in-law.

Harry had first married in 1888, when he was twenty-four years old. His wife was Magdalena Schlador, the friend of a clerk at the *Times*. Their first child, Frances, was born in 1890. But after the delivery of a second daughter, May, in 1892, Magdalena died from complications during childbirth. A year and a half after her death, Chandler married into the *Times* family by wedding Marian Otis, his boss's daughter. (Redolent of Henry's finding his wife through Collis Huntington.) By 1898, Marian and Harry had two daughters of their own. Four more children would round out the Chandler brood over the next ten years.

During Otis's leave, Chandler maintained the *Times'* bullish messaging regarding Los Angeles. However, consistent with his M.O., Harry's interest was driven more by principal than principle. He continued to see the *Times* as a fulcrum from which to form business relationships. "Chandler saw that speculation could be even more profitable, and performed on a much larger scale, if links were made not only with streetcar builders but also with financiers, politicians, the press, and other key players," noted historian William Fulton. Chandler had also learned the lessons from the economic bust of 1887, leaning on the most stable pillars in the community for future growth. Once all these leaders agreed on a mutual interest—for example, a new real estate subdivision—a syndicate would be formed. Chandler would then set about promoting the new property in the *Times*, donating so much ad space that the "fattest newspaper in the country" soon crushed all other U.S. papers in advertising volume. Simultaneously, a budding relationship with Gen. Moses Sherman morphed into a kind of brotherhood—what might be termed today a bromance—that would enrich them both. "Every good citizen with money who is brought to Southern California to live, through the Midwinter *Times*, helps you and helps me," Moses wrote Harry with regard to his friend's pet project that beckoned Americans westward.

Chandler also worked hand in glove with the Los Angeles Chamber of Commerce. Cofounded by Otis in 1888, Chandler helped build it into a peerless juggernaut. He had a kindred spirit on the committee in Frank Wiggins. Like Chandler, the Indiana native had been a lunger, desperate to cure his ailing body. By the time he arrived in L.A. in 1885—shortly after Chandler joined the *Times*—doctors gave him only a few weeks to live. He miraculously survived, solidifying his loyalty to his adopted city. After joining the Chamber of Commerce in 1890, Wiggins soon took over, cranking out colorful leaflets extolling the virtues of Southern California. It was "the garden spot of the world" and the "sanatorium of the universe." He dreamed up a "California on Wheels" train, which tooted across the country with displays of agriculture and bushels of Sunkist oranges ("Oranges for Health, California for Wealth"). He also created eye-popping exhibits for traveling expos. At the Chicago World's Fair in 1893, he unveiled a larger-than-life, 850-pound elephant made out of California walnuts. Closer to home, Wiggins was a powerful proponent of the *Times*' efforts behind the Port of Los Angeles and, later, the Los Angeles Aqueduct.

Meanwhile, the Spanish-American War ended on August 12, 1898, with the U.S. acquiring the Philippines from Spain. General Brigadier Harrison Gray Otis and his squad stayed behind in the Philippines to quell an uprising against the American occupation. Otis's letters back to the States carried the stench of the white man's burden. "The Filipinos are without doubt incapable of governing themselves satisfactorily," he wrote California Senator Stephen White. "The necessity of Uncle Sam holding on is obvious to me." By February of 1899, Filipino nationalists took over the city of Malolos; some of Otis's soldiers got caught up in the chaos and died. Otis blasted the "ignorant, misguided and bumptious natives" who had "wantonly assailed" his authority. Though guerrilla warfare would continue another three years, the rebels were finally driven out of Malolos. As far as Otis was concerned, it was Mission Accomplished. He put in his resignation, received an honorable discharge, and was hailed a conquering hero in his newspaper.

Otis's return to Los Angeles in April 1899 was conveniently timed. The Army Corps of Engineers had begun dredging San Pedro Bay and Congress had just approved $2.9 million for a two-mile breakwater. The Great Free Harbor was ready for its official groundbreaking. For Otis, it marked his second great triumph within a month's time, and there was no way he was going to miss it. The two-day Free Harbor Jubilee kicked off on April 26, 1899, cosponsored by San Pedro and Los Angeles interests. Color posters for the event displayed a distinct ecclesiastical glow. Naked cherubs flitted around the rays of the sun, which formed an aureole behind a bejeweled goddess blowing Gabriel's horn while clutching the stars and stripes. Behind these figures was a bird's-eye view of the envisioned harbor, teeming with boats, their safe passage protected by a breakwater. A locomotive steamed toward San Pedro from Los Angeles, visible on the raised horizon like a mythical City upon a Hill.

At eleven o'clock that first morning, Otis's former comrade, President William McKinley, pushed a button in the White House that flashed a signal 2,700 miles away in Pedro. Upon receiving the executive order, soldiers on a bluff overlooking the harbor fired a volley of shots: Commence breakwater!

Bobbing in boats, photographers fixed their lenses on the first load of boulders—600 tons' worth quarried from Catalina Island that would be dumped into the ocean by day's end. As a gate slid open, the barge began to list. Everyone waited for the first batch of rocks to breach the swells with a rumbling *splash*. But there was no splash. The rocks were stuck. The barge tilted some more. Still no splash. Finally, after some more tilting and nudging, the boulders gave way. As they tumbled into the water, spectators onshore whooped and whistled, waving their hats. Though it would take twelve years for the Army Corps of Engineers to complete the jetty, today was about the promise of prosperity. Both the breakwater and the deepening of the harbor heralded that Southern California was finally on the cusp of global greatness heading into the twentieth century.

A procession of notables took to the dais. San Francisco was a reliable punchline, its best days behind it. More than one speaker pointed to the port's southerly location as more convenient for northbound vessels after passing through the anticipated canal in Central America. Like those ships, freighters from the Far East would find, upon arrival, more favorable transcontinental conditions. "Two through-lines, the Southern Pacific and the Santa Fe systems, cross the continent from Los Angeles at much lower elevations than the northern lines," observed now ex-Senator Stephen White, "and also connect the Pacific with the Gulf of Mexico, and their operation is never obstructed by snow or ice." California Governor Henry T. Gage alluded to the USA's victory in the Spanish-American War—and its recent absorption of Hawaii—with imperialistic overtones that surely made Otis puff with pride:

> On account of . . . the lately-annexed [Hawaiian] Islands, almost in a direct ocean line westward from San Pedro; the Philippine possessions ceded by Spain, and over which now floats, and over which forever ought to float, the victorious American flag, and the prospect of an early opening of the interoceanic canal at Nicaragua, affording an eastern outlet to our trade incident to our newly-acquired territory in the Far West, we may well be assured of a great commercial future for Southern California.

The only thing people seemed to disagree on was whether the capital of commerce would be centered in San Pedro or Los Angeles. "Los Angeles is now practically united as to this harbor," said White, foreshadowing a future in which San Pedro was subsumed by its larger cousin. Governor Gage's future saw room for both: "Our little city of San Pedro will, with the progress of trade, blossom into an industrial metropolis."

If so, no one told San Pedroans. The scrappy fishing village wasn't quite ready to shed its buccaneer image. The two-day extravaganza represented easy money, a chance to plug into a captive audience of 20,000 visitors from all over Southern California. Almost every street corner featured games of chance—poker, craps, faro, roulette—along with a suspiciously high number of "blind" musicians seeking donations. Saloons did record business. So did storefronts that reinvented themselves as saloons. Forty police officers came down from L.A. to patrol the debauchery, but they weren't needed. It was a surprisingly congenial and diverse affair—whites, Blacks, Hispanics, and Chinese all carousing in harmony.

The bonanza culminated with a free barbecue serving up 15,000 pounds of roast beef, 5,000 pounds of clams, and enough baked beans to fuel the harbor boats. The distance from the waterfront to the eating area was a mile-and-a-half uphill—daunting for women, children, and the aged—but enterprising locals offered every conceivable mode of transportation for a nominal fee. Carriages were powered by horses, mules, donkeys, humans, and on one occasion, a dog that was whipped into action by his pint-sized master. Of course, there is no such thing as a free lunch. When exhausted visitors finally arrived at the feast, they discovered it was hosted by John T. Gaffey, on whose land they were now sitting. The developer was on hand to hawk his lots.

Otis's *Times* framed the federal consecration of the harbor as preordained, instigated by the "first jubilee" 357 years of yore when explorer Juan Rodriguez Cabrillo "found it a very good port." Declaring April 27, 1899, "San Pedro Day," the paper illustrated Lady Liberty flying the banner of "Progress" while a rising sun spelled out "Commercial Supremacy." Who could blame Otis for feeling vindicated? After presiding over the acquisition of the Philippines for a pugilistic, expansionist-minded nation, he was now firing the final salvo against Collis Huntington's monopolistic railway. "The great fight for a Free Harbor," the *Times* declared, was over. Freedom had won. Nonetheless, Otis, now a veteran of two U.S. wars, retrenched as if gearing up for a third one. Like Banning and Sherman before him, he now insisted on being addressed as General Otis. He named his homes in Westlake and Hollywood, respectively, The Bivouac and The Outpost. He affixed a large eagle atop The Fortress—his term for the formidable *Times* building—and referred to members of his staff as the Phalanx, all with access to his cache of fifty rifles and loaded shotguns. As the years crept on and his mind softened, the general was known to conduct military drills, strutting around his office in a faded army uniform jangling with medals and epaulets.

Paranoid or just patriotic? Whatever the case, Gen. Otis was still fighting one more war—the one between himself and union-bent workers, a slow-burning fuse with explosive ramifications that neither party saw coming.

TWO MONTHS after the festival that telegraphed Los Angeles's future destiny as a seaport, the city officially annexed two more districts. After not making the cut in 1895, University Park and its 1.77 square miles were granted entrée into Los Angeles on June 12, 1899. The area included Exposition Park—then called Agricultural Park—a wild patch southwest of the city core where kids hunted jackrabbits and adults once attended bullfights. The other area was Garvanza, which was eager to tap L.A.'s water supply. One of the few townships to survive the bust of 1887, Garvanza added less than one square mile to Los Angeles but was just as densely populated as its larger, already-annexed neighbor, Highland Park. This concerned water superintendent William Mulholland. After L.A.'s thirty-year lease with the problematic City Water Co. expired, Mayor Fred Eaton charged Mulholland with overseeing the formation of a municipal water department. (The transition was marred by lawsuits and countersuits involving how to compensate City Water for the infrastructure it had already laid.) Unfortunately, the Los Angeles River—still the city's primary water source—was under stress to meet the demands of L.A.'s now 100,000 people. The water chief groused to fellow commissioners that Garvanza residents were swilling far more water per capita than the rest of Los Angeles. Not only that, these ingrates had the gall to complain about the quality of the water. There was also the issue of the young employee who, presumably hungover, was regularly snoozing well past his 5 A.M. call time to activate Garvanza's water pump. No fan of malingerers himself, Mulholland was about to offer a solution when a department member piped up, "I know a good old man. . . ."

"I'm not here to investigate the merits or demerits of old men!" Bill snapped back. "I'll get someone that can run that pump."

Garvanzans weren't the only ones consuming more than their fair share of water. To curb other Angelenos from abusing the precious resource, Mulholland emulated cities like Cleveland, Detroit, and St. Louis, which equipped random homes with meters to extrapolate overall water usage. One of his targets was Howard E. Wright, a corrupt former Assemblyman who had resigned in disgrace but was now living comfortably in Boyle Heights. "For more than two years I have gone by Mr. Wright's place many times, and I never went by, either day or night, that sprinklers were not running," Mulholland fulminated. "If everybody used water like he does, only three thousand consumers in the entire city would get water." At a hearing, Wright did not take well to the public shaming. He didn't deny his indulgence for water; what he resented was Bill's men digging up his property "without so much as saying 'good morning, sir.'" If the crew tried to install a meter, Wright promised to "kick the whole outfit into the street." The fallen politician ended up getting a restraining order against Mulholland and his water posse.

Unfortunately, the *Times* didn't do Mulholland any favors either. While he was busy preaching conservation, Otis drowned him out with a constant stream of articles promoting unlimited growth: "Let the arid wastes be provided with an abundance of water," implored one editorial. "Plant new orchards and vineyards. Build new railroads." If calls for L.A.'s rapid expansion weren't enough to give Mulholland an ulcer, now he had a new concern: vertical growth. Due to advances in steel and engineering, skyscrapers were sprouting up across America. Even earthquake-prone San Francisco could proudly point to its 218-foot Chronicle building, erected in 1890. As building envy swept through Angel City, Mulholland told a journalist, "I don't know what we'll do if they keep on climbing skyward. It will not be possible to put on enough [water] pressure to supply them, even if we were inclined to try it." Some cities had imposed laws requiring buildings over five stories to provide their own pumping apparatuses, but that was not a practical long-term solution. No doubt the Chief gulped when he saw the blueprints for architect John Parkinson's twelve-story, 173-foot Beaux Arts citadel that would come to be known as the Continental Tower. But he need not have worried. After it opened in 1903, no other L.A. structure eclipsed its height for twenty-five years until City Hall was built. That's because Parkinson himself helped craft a civic ordinance that capped buildings at 150 feet high. The restriction was not so much about earthquake worries as it was about aesthetics. Adhering to the City Beautiful movement, a city design committee called for "broad and harmonious lines of beauty and symmetry," which created more space and light while avoiding the "dark walled-in streets" of older cities found in the Midwest and East. "A building 150 feet high is plenty tall enough for any city," said Stanley L. McMichael, a visiting Cleveland realtor, who found in Los Angeles "an evenness of growth that is pleasing."

As L.A.'s preeminent engineer, Mulholland could see that the city's water capacity did not compute with its projected growth. To compound the problem, the final three years of the nineteenth century were marked by such paltry rainfall amounts, they wouldn't look out of place in the drought-laden 2000s: 7.06 inches (1897–1898), 5.59 inches (1898–1899), and 7.91 inches (1899–1900)—well below the average of fifteen inches. Privately, Bill felt the weight of an entire city on his shoulders. Publicly, he soft-pedaled his concerns, not wanting to come across as a Cassandra. Part of him still relished playing the role of a miracle worker who could fix any problems thrown at him. As Mulholland tried to square his conflicting impulses, Otis, Chandler, Sherman, and Henry Huntington were busy plotting out L.A.'s onrushing metropolis, whether he liked it or not.

CHAPTER 7

Tracking the Future

GEN. MOSES SHERMAN'S TRIUMPHANT march to Santa Monica was a mirage. Belying the success of his Los Angeles-Pacific railway was the fact that he and Eli Clark were cash poor, owing to their frenetic five-year stretch of streetcar construction and assumption of debt of acquired lines. In 1895, after missing several bond payments, bondholders of their Los Angeles Consolidated Electric Railway Company (LACE) rebelled. Though Sherman stayed on as a director, investors wrested control and renamed the line the Los Angeles Railway (LARy). In 1898, LARy was sold to Henry Huntington. Under his watch, its city coaches would come to be known colloquially as Yellow Cars. Sherman and Clark's Pasadena & Los Angeles Electric Railway also fell into Huntington's hands. It would form the basis of Huntington's interurban Pacific Electric Railway Company (PE), with Sherman's green-colored cars giving way to Huntington's Red Cars. For a while, Sherman and Clark even lost control of their prized Los Angeles-Pacific Railroad. But the brothers-in-law regained ownership of the franchise when the bondholders themselves went broke. The dizzying tangle of new names and corporations was a byproduct of Sherman and Clark's constant financial restructuring as lines fell in and out of receivership. For now, at least, Huntington's intrusion into L.A.'s rail market—mostly in eastern and southern regions—was little more than sand kicked in their faces. The partners still owned the key route connecting Los Angeles to Santa Monica, with Sherman's dream of expanding and capitalizing on his westerly empire still very much alive.

On February 1, 1901, the first of many newspaper ads touted

Sherman's "BALLOON ROUTE – LOS ANGELES-PACIFIC R.R."
No, the capitalist wasn't promoting a party train with festive in-
flatables; the descriptor referenced the fact that the loop's overhead map looked like an elongated balloon. Not to be outdone,
Santa Fe Railway advertised its own geometrically inspired route:
The "Kite-Shaped Track," which toured the Inland Empire within
a quadrilateral area resembling a kite. There were in fact many
creatively named rail tours in the Southland in the days before
tour buses. But the Balloon Route was *the* premium route for prospective property owners to scope out beach-adjacent land, much
of it owned by Sherman and far cheaper than lots within L.A.'s
core district. The initial Balloon Route mimicked the original Los
Angeles-Pacific Railroad circuit to Santa Monica, but with added
stops in Ocean Park and Palms via the newly created Venice Short
Line, which traversed the median of Venice Boulevard. Eventually, the Balloon Route added so many stops in so many interesting places, it became better known as a sightseeing must-do.
Drawn by the gimmick of "101 miles for $1.00," 10,000 people
per month bought tickets. "JUST THINK!" read the route's brochure, "That within an hour's ride of Los Angeles reached only by
the Los Angeles-Pacific Railroad (BALLOON ROUTE) are found
the most delightful Valley, Mountain and Beach Resorts on the
Pacific Coast."

Every morning, the all-day adventure departed Hill and 4th
Streets at 9:30 with an exhilarating blast through the Hill Street
tunnels. First stop: the Hollywood estate of still life artist Paul de
Longpré, where riders disembarked to fawn over his picture-post-
card flower garden. From there the trolley visited Cahuenga
Valley (the "Valley" in the brochure), Sherman (residential lots
offered at $150), and the Soldiers' Home, where the conductor
kept a wary eye for wayward veterans passed out on the tracks
with liquor bottles. (The original train station still stands on VA
property.) Passengers posed in front of the Soldiers' Home dining hall for an official photo. Once the Balloon Route reached the
Santa Monica coastline, the real fun began. Remember Southern

Pacific's ill-fated Long Wharf? It had become a salty relic by the early 1900s, fading into irrelevance. The railroad company leased the nearly mile-long pier to Sherman, who rebranded it as a tourist attraction. Chugging over its tracks, guides informed passengers that they were experiencing "the only ocean voyage in the world on wheels."

One Santa Monica landmark that withstood the test of time was Camera Obscura. Commissioned by Santa Monica's mayor in 1898, passengers took turns staring into its mysterious optics to spy on unsuspecting beachgoers. (The novelty now resides at Palisades Park.) Continuing southbound, the trolley connected the dots of "10 beaches" from Ocean Park to South Bay. Highlights included a fish fry at the Sherman-operated Playa del Rey Pavilion, scavenging for moonstones in Redondo Beach, and, from 1905 onward, strolling along the canals of Venice Beach. The Venice Short Line hurtled passengers back to L.A. by five o'clock, but not before the photographer from the Soldiers' Home reboarded the train. During the intervening hours, he had developed his film. Now he passed out framed prints as keepsakes to the delight of all.

Like so many Sherman and Clark rail operations, the Balloon Route passed on to other parties. In 1906, Southern Pacific assumed control under its president, E. H. Harriman. Five years later, Pacific Electric (under SP's auspices) took over and kept the line running until 1923. Nonetheless, Sherman had achieved his goal. Like moths to a flame, he had lured thousands of potential homeowners to the bright, wide-open plats abutting his lines. While locales like Santa Monica, Manhattan Beach, and Sherman (West Hollywood) would remain independent, others, such as Playa del Rey, Palms, Venice, and Mar Vista, would eventually merge with Los Angeles. With the smashing success of the Balloon Route in opening the portals of the Westside, Moses had truly charted an exodus to what became—and remains—L.A.'s most exclusive real estate.

Closer to the city's center, a region that would draw even

more hype also bore Sherman's imprint. Hollywood has been called "the best-known proper noun" in the world, a tribute to its association as the capital of mythmaking in addition to being a geographical place. But in one of the great paradoxes of L.A., Hollywood's reputation as a den of depravity belies its wholesome origins. In 1886, Harvey and Daeida Wilcox—a wealthy Christian couple from the Midwest—purchased 120 acres in Cahuenga Valley. The following year, Harvey subdivided the land and Daeida came up with the name. According to one version, Mrs. Wilcox heard a woman on a cross-country train trip chatting about her country estate in Illinois called "Hollywood" and admired the name. In another telling, it was her husband—or was it a family friend?—who came up with "Hollywood," inspired by the wild toyon bushes in the hills that produce red California hollies. Either way, the couple soon endured a rough patch. Harvey had to recall several deeds after the bubble-burst of 1887. Then the couple's only child died at 18 months, followed by Harvey's own passing in 1891. Daeida threw herself into the Lord's work, tirelessly promoting Hollywood as a utopian community with high moral standards. She gave away land to churches, schools, and banks, hit up entrepreneurs to get a railway up and running, and remarried a wealthy property owner named Philo Beveridge. By 1900, Hollywood was an alcohol-free Christian community of five hundred people, many of whom lived in Victorian and Craftsman homes with beautiful grounds. Indeed, it was Daeida's "dream of beauty" that beckoned French painter Paul de Longpré, who acquired his home and gardens in exchange for three paintings.

Despite earning the moniker the "Mother of Hollywood," Mrs. Wilcox Beveridge was against incorporating her community for fear that it would raise taxes and create a burdensome bureaucracy. Nonetheless, on November 14, 1903, the issue was put to eligible Hollywood voters. Cityhood won out by an 88–77 margin. Its boundaries were fixed at Normandie Avenue on the east, Fairfax Avenue on the west, the foothills on the north, and

Sunset Boulevard on the south. (The section south of Sunset was still known as Colegrove.) Daeida had no say in the election; as a woman, she was unable to vote in those pre-Nineteenth Amendment days. But she still held sway, making sure that Hollywood remained a temperate zone that prohibited alcohol, bowling alleys, and pool halls. Even before it attained cityhood, however, Daeida's pious paradise was already being tested by the high priests of capitalism, creating two diametrically opposed visions vying for the soul of Hollywood.

At first, Moses Sherman was a welcome presence in Daeida's life. In the late 1890s, he and Clark laid electric train tracks up Vermont Avenue to Prospect Avenue (now Hollywood Boulevard). Running west along Prospect, the line became part of their Balloon Route, creating great buzz for Hollywood. Wary of the risks of speculation, the partners funded their endeavor with other people's money. Thus, they essentially held the community hostage by refusing to complete the lines until property owners forked over either land or cash. Daeida and Colonel Griffith J. Griffith (of Griffith Park fame) made substantial contributions. Sherman possessed an uncanny ability to "hypnotize" investors into opening their wallets, according to financier Isaias W. Hellman of Wells Fargo Nevada National Bank. Hellman himself admitted to falling under his spell. Perhaps he was influenced by the general's pronounced brow, or his air of amicable persuasiveness.

As the Wilcox-Beveridges subdivided the eastern half of Hollywood, including the several-block radius emanating from the Cahuenga Corridor, Sherman bought land close to Sherman, his titular district to the west. On April 25, 1903, a few months before the incorporation of Hollywood, his Balloon Route scheduled a special trip for potential property owners to the 300-acre Hollywood Ocean View Tract, billed as "the finest suburb of Los Angeles." Located in the foothills currently occupied by Outpost Estates and Hollywood Heights, it was bankrolled by the Los Angeles Pacific Boulevard and Development Company, whose principal investors included Sherman, Clark, Harry Chandler, and

Gen. Harrison Otis. Passengers boarded two coaches, festooned in flowers and bunting, at the Hill Street terminal. As an orchestra saw them off, the express whisked the home-seekers to the new Hollywood Hotel on the corner of Highland and Prospect Avenues. The palatial Mission Revival resort, built on property owned by Otis, was a welcome contrast to dowdy eastern Hollywood. Disembarking passengers were greeted by a scrum of real estate agents talking up the Hollywood Ocean View Tract. (And while it's true that movies made Hollywood world-famous, these realtors were sloganeering "The Tract That Made Hollywood Famous" at least a decade before the studios started rolling in.)

Next, a quick jaunt over to Outpost Drive brought the VIPs to an old adobe built in 1853. This was The Outpost, Otis's famed retreat in the hills. The general boasted that the structure held militaristic import as the setting where Mexico ceded California to the United States with the signing of the Treaty of Cahuenga. This made for a good story, but it wasn't true. (The *Los Angeles Times* waited until Otis was nearly dead before finally admitting that his claim was not "strictly accurate historically.") All the same, The Outpost was the oldest building in Hollywood and made a great first impression as a model for other country villas in the hills above it. To create urgency, the syndicate members populated empty tracts with fake "SOLD" signs and building materials, as if construction were about to begin. Otis materialized at one lot with a wonderful view, waving an American flag, backlit by the sun against the distant ocean.

The special day also saw the flag-raising of Whitley Heights, a swank enclave in the foothills just east of Ocean View. Named after developer Hobart Whitley, Whitley Heights would later gain fame as Hollywood's first celebrity colony during the Silent Movie Era. Though he also served as president of the Ocean View consortium, Whitley's self-named Mediterranean-style subdivision was his pride and joy. According to Arnold Haskell, a friend of Sherman's who got to know his colleagues, Whitley petitioned to change the name of Hollywood to Whitley to reflect his sizable financial footprint. The other members rejected his request, figuring Whitley Heights was plenty enough. In fact, Haskell asserted, it was *Chandler* who named the region Hollywood after seeing a boy emerge from the hills on a burro loaded down with toyon berries, or California holly. "Let's call it Hollywood," Chandler is to have said. "All the canyons are full of holly." However, Haskell's version of events does not line up with the fact that Harry's own newspaper, the *L.A. Times*, started referring to the region as "Hollywood" as far back as 1887, shortly after Harvey and Daeida Wilcox named the land. That same year, Chandler was a low-level circulation manager, still years away from marrying his boss's daughter. However, the etymology behind Hollywood can't seem to shake its holly berry inspiration. It's possible Haskell somehow grafted Harry into the holly origin story attributed to the Wilcoxes.

In the late afternoon, the Hollywood excursion party cruised back to the Hollywood Hotel for a barbecue and "light refreshments." There was Otis again, greeting guests alongside Sherman, Clark, Whitley, even de Longpré. Hands were shaken, cigars were lit, and toasts were made (it's a safe bet that even in dry Hollywood, they weren't drinking Martinelli's sparkling apple juice). "Behold what God hath wrought!" crowed Sherman, sizing up all the potential sales. The pageantry spilled outside with automobile races down Prospect Avenue. Leon Schellter bested his competition in the "half-mile dash" by revving up to thirty-four miles an hour, crossing the finish line in front of the hotel in fifty-three seconds. The speedster also won a "hill-climbing contest," ascending "250 yards over a twenty-two percent grade" in about seventy-five seconds. As passengers gamboled back to the trolley for the return trip, a local observed, "The guests departed for their respective homes, like Sheba, to tell the wonders they had seen."

Given Hollywood's bipolar state, the town had entered a kind of bloodless "civic war." West of Highland Avenue was controlled by the Sherman-Chandler-Otis-Clark-Whitley bloc, looking to drag Hollywood into the twentieth century; east of Highland (and south of Whitley Heights) were Daeida's interests, wanting to keep it in the nineteenth. But the pastoral party was losing the feud. The Balloon Route brought a wave of well-to-do home-owners to the Ocean View and Whitley tracts whose tastes were more sophisticated. Hollywood's population leapt from 1,000 in 1903 to 3,400 in 1907, much of it cloistered around the bustling new business district along Highland and Prospect. As land values climbed in this section, the Wilcox-Beveridges were forced to buy into Hollywood's new catchline (created by Sherman and company) as the "City of Homes" lest they lose out. Sherman's group also engaged Daeida in a zoning war, each trying to out-maneuver the other in the development of Prospect Avenue. The outcome was a main drag with two distinct commercial corridors, separated by a half-mile residential stretch, whose blocks would later be converted to a business zone. Highland and Cahuenga would be in the news again a few years later, as the rivals behind each street competed to secure a north-south railway. For a while, it appeared that a generous donation from Daeida had convinced Henry Huntington to run a Red Car along Cahuenga. But the deal fell apart, and Highland eventually claimed the coveted interurban line.

Ultimately, the bucolic township that Daeida Wilcox Beveridge carefully nurtured succumbed to progress. The future movieland locale would follow a framework that played out in countless neighboring towns: People move in, utilities get stretched thin, towns consider joining L.A. In the coming years, the coalitions controlled by Chandler, Sherman, Otis, Clark, and Whitley would be justly rewarded. Hollywood emerged as the premier address to work, stay, and play for film industry glitterati. Whitley banked $26 million from his Whitley Heights subdivision, and Ocean View made a tidy sixty percent profit. The men weren't done with Hollywood, either. In 1905, Sherman and Clark acquired 640 acres for a future subdivision that would become far more "famous" than the Ocean View Tract. Chandler ensured that it would be, quite literally, the most visible residential neighborhood in the world.

More significantly, the group's umbrella company, Los Angeles Pacific Boulevard and Development, functioned as a blueprint for another syndicate that would divvy up the San Fernando Valley in a few short years. It would lead to Los Angeles's biggest annexation yet.

CHAPTER 8

A Right to Water

IT'S A WELL-KNOWN ADAGE that oil and water don't mix. In Los Angeles, their commingling represented yet another threat to the city's supply of fresh water. In the years since Edward Doheny struck oil in 1892, Los Angeles had become a petroleum boom town, where any wildcatter could strike it rich. "I had found gold and I had found silver and I had found lead," Doheny later observed, "but this ugly-looking substance was the key to something more valuable than any or all of these metals." Over the next couple decades, thousands of derricks fueled an "oildorado." Housing developments popped up in oil districts, promising overnight windfalls. "Beautiful Homesites—All Oil Rights Included," read ads for Petroleum Gardens in Artesia. Each additional pool of goo fueled more jobs and growth. Flush with Big Oil capital, city officials did little to regulate safety standards. By the late 1920s, one quarter of the world's petroleum output originated in Los Angeles. Even today, as drilling phases out, it's estimated that 1.6 billion gallons of recoverable crude still sloshes beneath the city's terra firma.

Environmental destruction caused by oil production was already an issue for William Mulholland in the early 1900s. The water superintendent warned city officials that refinery plants were a "menace" to water tables. He pushed for reinforced concrete holding tanks to contain the toxic runoff. By this point in his career, Bill was like the Dutch boy with his finger in the dike, except the dike kept cracking and he was out of fingers. In 1903, Los Angeles was in its eighth year of a nine-year stretch in which rainfall levels failed to reach their yearly average of fifteen inches.

The Los Angeles River was temperamental; the zanja system was useless (Mulholland was dismantling it); and water tables, when they weren't compromised by contaminants, were overpumped.

Nor could one discount the menace of L.A.'s neighbors. Hollywood claimed that it could make do with its own water system—provided by the Union Hollywood Water Company—for up to 10,000 inhabitants. But what would happen once Hollywood's population surpassed 10,000? What about towns like San Pedro and Wilmington, and settlements like Colegrove and Hermon? As their wells inevitably ran dry, they will be lining up with empty buckets, pleading for water from Los Angeles—or asking to merge. In its best years, the L.A. River could support a quarter-million people. The city was well on its way to reaching that figure by 1910, if not sooner. These scenarios reinforced the central problem: Los Angeles was running out of water.

Mulholland responded to the crisis by calling for a pause on further annexations and instituting austerity programs, like limiting irrigation and allowing park lawns to go brown. These unpopular measures were no match against boosterism. New homes bragged of plush landscaping and showers and bathtubs, raising L.A.'s daily per capita water usage to an all-time high—230 gallons per household. "If cleanliness is next to godliness," the Chief snarked, "then the City of the Angels must occupy a high place in the scale of municipal virtue." But this was precisely the problem. The oligarchy behind Angel City had sold it as an Eden. It was incumbent upon Mulholland to find a way to keep it blooming.

Enter Fred Eaton, the former mayor who had known Bill for twenty-five years. After leaving office, Eaton remained a fixture among business circles, once even investing in a railway with Gen. Moses Sherman. From his perspective, L.A. needed to think not just outside the box, but outside the city itself. Born twelve days after Mulholland in 1856, Eaton was a native Angeleno whose father Benjamin helped found Pasadena. (Newspapers liked to refer to Fred as the "sixth white child born in Los Angeles.") Like Mulholland, Eaton was a self-taught engineer, advancing to superintendent of the Los Angeles City Water Co. when he was only nineteen. In 1878, he hired Mulholland as a ditchdigger. The two became good friends, sharing an affinity for whiskey and a call of duty to the city they loved. In 1898, Eaton was elected to a two-year term as L.A.'s twenty-fourth mayor. By 1900, he was the rare individual who was well-versed in both water engineering and local politics, with the added advantage of having seen first-hand how the city had changed since the Civil War. And what he saw concerned him as much as it did Mulholland.

For the last nine months of 1903, less than half-an-inch of rain fell on most of Los Angeles County. Fires raged through Malibu, cattle starved in Antelope Valley, and pine trees wilted in Elysian Park. For the first time, L.A.'s most prized export—bountiful produce—couldn't meet the demands of U.S. markets. How could the *Los Angeles Times* Midwinter Edition and Frank Wiggins's Chamber of Commerce promote a paradise on Earth when fruit was no longer fruitful and sprinklers weren't allowed to sprinkle? With gallows humor, Mulholland suggested that the only way to snuff out newcomers and save the city from it-self would be by "killing Wiggins . . . for the present rush to this country will cease until he is dead."

By early 1904, desperation had set in. On January 10, the city's religious leaders called upon people to pray for rain on the com-ing Sabbath. Then, a vision arrived in the form of a dapper man with aquamarine eyes and waxy skin. His name was Charles M. Hatfield. His business card read "Rainmaker." A former sewing machine salesman, Hatfield had already made a name for himself throughout the Golden State, leaving behind a wake of ranchers who had paid him thousands of dollars to induce precipitation with mixed results. Hatfield's methods involved standing on a wooden tower and blasting the atmosphere with a proprietary twenty-three-chemical solution. One observer equated its odor to "a Limburger cheese factory broken loose." Cunningly, the wa-ter wizard pooh-poohed any magical powers. His practices were rooted in science. "I do not make rain. That would be an absurd claim," he sniffed. "I simply attract clouds, and they do the rest." Later in 1904, a group of Los Angeles businessmen hired Hatfield to seed the clouds for $1,000. The clouds delivered. L.A. experienced its wettest winter since 1895. Hatfield was feted, then took his talents to San Diego, Ventura, and other California towns. But his track record remained spotty. Even when he was successful, meteorologists have since pointed out that Hatfield typically timed his visits to water-starved communities only after years of drought, which increased the odds of an overdue rainy season. However, he remained in the picture long enough to inspire *The Rainmaker*, a 1956 movie starring Burt Lancaster, whose character was loosely based on Hatfield. At 81 years old, Hatfield was invited to the premiere. He died about a year later, buried on a sunny winter's day in Glendale.

But before the soggy winter of 1904–1905, the parched summer of 1904 brought Los Angeles to the brink of an all-out water war. In the last week of July, the city's rising water consumption exceeded its allocation by sixteen million gallons. As Mulholland's water police installed residential meters to catch water-wasters, officials were often met at gunpoint. One haughty railway executive insisted that his extravagant bill was due to a faulty meter, to which the Chief pointed out that if the meter was broken, it wouldn't register at all. The City Attorney slapped injunction suits on 163 San Fernando Valley ranch owners, depriving them of water from the L.A. River. The ranchers countersued, arguing that L.A.'s riparian rights were clouded by years of piecemeal deals with private companies (which was true). The dispute even made its way up to the United States Supreme Court. "If they can take any part of our water, they can take all of it," Mulholland cried in exasperation, "and our great conduit would be a dusty runway for squirrels and coyotes." Realizing that their superintendent was at a boiling point, the water commission encouraged Mulholland to take a two-week summer vacation. But he refused, opting to stay in L.A. to fight water scofflaws and manage the crisis.

By mid-September, newspapers reported that Mulholland finally relented to a country sabbatical in the Sierra Nevada Mountains. But his respite masked the real purpose of his trip: to scout
a possible new water source for Los Angeles. It was his traveling
companion's idea. Fred Eaton had first visited Owens Valley in
1880, during a trip with his father. Struck by its alpine beauty,
Eaton returned on family camping trips in the 1890s, fantasizing
about retiring near the base of Mt. Whitney. It was during one of
these jaunts to Inyo County that he noticed abundant mountain
snowmelt draining into the Owens River. Eaton had previously
mentioned the region to Mulholland and other water commissioners. Now, the time had come for the Chief to lay eyes on this
watery wonderland himself.

On September 14, 1904, he and Eaton rode a team of mules
200 miles to Owens Valley. It was an invigorating adventure for
the old pals. Freshly divorced from a wife who blamed their breakup on whiskey, Fred could freely indulge his habit with someone
who appreciated a nip now and then, whereas Bill could recali-
brate in the great outdoors, where he always felt more at home.

Trekking into the valley, Mulholland immediately saw its potential. By his estimates, there was enough water to support two
million Angelenos. The trick, of course, would be securing rights
to the water and building an aqueduct to Southern California.
The first part was not Mulholland's domain. Eaton was already
one step ahead of him anyway, posing as a cattle rancher for the
last few months, buying up land options with the intent of being reimbursed by the city of Los Angeles. But the second part
tapped right into Mulholland's savior complex. If the money was
there, he felt he could pull off this conquest of engineering. "It
is big, but it is simply big," Mulholland shrugged. Back home,
the men relayed their scheme to water commissioners and L.A.'s
power nucleus, including the *Times*' Gen. Harrison Gray Otis
and Harry Chandler and other newspaper bigwigs. All agreed it
was an idea worth exploring. But discretion would be essential.
If word leaked out too soon, it could trigger protests, especially

in the northern part of the state. "The city could not disclose its purpose of going to the Owens Valley for water and we had to be secret about our movements," Mulholland later attested. Better to allow time to run the numbers, build consensus, and frame the messaging before taking it to the public. And so, armed with the knowledge that they were about to potentially change the entire face of Los Angeles, everyone took a vow of confidentiality.

The secret leaked out almost immediately among L.A.'s business leaders. As recon teams headed to Owens Valley, Mulholland shared his findings with members of the Sunset Club, an exclusive fraternal order whose accumulated wealth came with the power to shape city politics. During one lecture, the Chief set up a slide presentation of the planned enterprise on a 3-D stereopticon projector. But he couldn't get the blasted thing to work, so he simply showed the men relief maps and blown-up photos of white-capped mountains draining their slushy cargo into Owens Lake. "The supply that will be obtained from this source will be 260 million gallons a day," he explained, a marked increase from L.A.'s current sixty million gallons a day. Scanning the roomful of suits under a haze of cigar smoke, Mulholland delivered a crash course on local geology, which was hindering Los Angeles from further growth—read, fulfilling its full business potential. Pointing to the San Gabriel Mountains, the craggy range in northeastern L.A. County, he said, "You will note the rugged character of these mountains. There is no possibility for any great run-off of storage in the mountains themselves as they exist. They are so steep in character, the gradients are so high in the canyons, that there are no good reservoir sites in the mountains." As a result, "We cannot depend on the run-off from the natural watersheds . . . if we expect to add very much to the population of our towns." He ended with an ominous note: "The public must be prepared for somewhat of a shock at the enormous expenditure that will be required to bring a remote but reliable supply of water to this country."

On the morning of July 29, 1905, Mulholland and officials

got their first read of the general public's reaction to this out-
landish scheme when the *L.A. Times* blew the secret open on its
front page: "TITANIC PROJECT TO GIVE CITY A RIVER."
Under that headline was a declaration that turned out to be wild-
ly untrue: "Los Angeles' water supply has been solved for the next
hundred years." The paper disclosed that preliminary negotiations were underway to secure "30,000 inches of water, or about
ten times our present total supply, enough for 2,000,000 people."
If voters agreed to fund a 233-mile aqueduct through the issuance
of bonds—estimated by Mulholland to be about $21 million—it
will be "the most important movement for the development of
Los Angeles in all the city's history." The magnitude of this news
prompted scripture-inspired imagery that seemed to bear Chandler's ink-stained fingerprints:

> Water, living water; the oblation of the hills poured upon
> the plains; the snows of far Sierras melting upon the bo-
> som of the South. Water—gift of God! Thanks be to God
> and blessed be His name!

> Then will Los Angeles county indeed become the Prom-
> ised Land. More precious than milk and honey will be
> the flow of the pure mountain water—aye, more precious
> than gold and diamonds.

Indeed, mountain water from upstate wasn't just ordained
by Providence; it rightfully belonged to Angelenos in the first
place. In some brazen revisionist history—and more biblical
overtones—the *Times* submitted that the Owens River used to
connect to the Los Angeles River as recently as a thousand years
ago. No geologists were quoted. However, unnamed engineers
deduced that the tributary was blocked when "a mighty earthquake threw mountain ranges across the river bed," and thus was
necessary this "feasible plan for tunneling these mountains and
bringing the water again into the San Fernando Valley." Another

unsourced expert said, "Back to the headwaters of the Los Angeles River will be turned the flow of a thousand mountain streams that ages ago were tributaries of the current that swept past the site of the ancient pueblo of Los Angeles to the ocean." These comments contradicted what Mulholland, the city's top engineer, told the members of the Sunset Club only a few months earlier. Of the San Fernando Valley, he had said, "It has not been cut out by the water. It has been created by the uplift of the mountains surrounding, leaving a depression in the center." Ever the team player, though, Mulholland now stated in the *Times* that the rivers used to be connected, probably "a few thousand years ago." In short, the newspaper's spin was that the Chief's gravity-powered aqueduct would simply be correcting nature's mistake. Once that happened, so long to guilt! San Fernando Valley ranchers could "devote the entire flow of the river to agriculture," parks and lawns could get drunk on Adam's ale, and manufacturing could grow unabated thanks to hydroelectric plants. "The Owens River will be to Los Angeles what Niagara is to Buffalo," the *Times* prophesied.

As a contrast, picking up a newspaper in Inyo County meant reading the region's obituary. "Los Angeles Plots Destruction," read one headline. "Would Take Owens River, Lay Lands Waste, Ruin People, Homes and Communities." Yet the *Times* continued to trot out insensitive passages that only seemed to invite a date with schadenfreude: "There is something romantic . . . about impounding the melted snows of the highest mountain in the United States that seems entirely in keeping with the dauntless history of Southern California."

Beneath these layers of entitlement, however, were troubling fault lines. The *Times* reported that Fred Eaton bought "50,000 acres of water-bearing land" three months prior. "It was thought that Eaton was going into the stock-raising business," the paper said, "but it has since been learned he was securing options for Los Angeles city." In fact, Eaton had started buying up lots in Owens Valley for at least a year and a half, and Chandler and Otis were privy to his cattle charade far earlier than three months ago.

Eaton's acquisitions were not necessarily illegal, but they were
certainly disingenuous. Clearly, had Owens Valley landowners
known that they were signing away their properties so Los Angeles could take their water, Eaton would've been run out of town.
Yet the *Times* took unbridled joy in portraying the residents there
as gullible rubes. Eaton was seen as a "locoed millionaire" from
the big city. "In the eyes of the ranchers he was land mad. When
they advanced the price of their holdings a few hundred dollars
and found that he stood the raise, the cup of their joy fairly overflowed." The paper's conclusion that "everyone is happy" in newly
enriched Owens Valley was its biggest whopper.

Even Mulholland had to admire his companion's temerity. "I
do not believe that there is another man in the country that could
have conducted those negotiations to a successful conclusion like
Fred did without getting found out." Only on their last visit together did a "canny old Scotch woman" unravel the scheme. Mulholland himself participated in the con, relating a story about an
old acquaintance in Mojave who wondered why Mulholland was
making so many trips to Owens Lake. "I said that I had taken
a flyer in the stock-raising business," Mulholland recalled. "He
chuckled gleefully as he told me that the week before he had sold
his Owens River ranch to Fred Eaton. He called Fred an easy
mark." The Mojave man got three times what his property was
worth, telling Mulholland, "I never saw a fellow so daffy about
stock land."

The *Times*' coverage included a photograph of the Los Angeles Water Board members who had signed off on the project. Sitting front and center was Moses Sherman. By this point in L.A.'s
legacy-building, Sherman was like Zelig—always in the thick of
things, although if one followed the money, the trail usually led
to him. Sherman had joined the Water Board in lieu of Eaton,
who wanted to create distance while retaining a proxy vote. As
non-elected officials, committee members had lifetime tenure.
One noticeably absent figure from the aqueduct coverage was
the *Times*' eminence grise, Harry Chandler. But his shadowy

presence would soon be cast into stark relief. Both he and Sherman—nicknamed "the spy" by conspiracists—would face blistering critiques for their roles in the scheme. Otis also drew heat,
criticized for betraying the handshake deal made between newspaper owners. They had all agreed to hold onto the "secret" until
all the land options were completed, at which point they would
publish the news on the same day. Nonetheless, after hearing
about the final property recording from Mulholland, Otis broke
the story without telling the others. Even Eaton was caught off
guard by the *Times'* exclusive. Still in Owens Valley, he noticed
a hostile crowd gathering around his wagon and quickly shed
his red sweater—a visible target for potential assassins. He then
hightailed it to San Francisco. "When I go back for my cattle, they
will drown me in the river," he told a Bay Area reporter.

Interestingly, the wrangling of Sierra Nevada runoff never
would have happened if not for an assist from Uncle Sam. Just
three years earlier, Congress had passed the Reclamation Act,
designed to promote water storage and conservation in the arid
West. Mulholland and Eaton had befriended a slippery reclamation agent named Joseph B. Lippincott, who worked out a sweet
consultant deal with Los Angeles. Sharing deeds and plat maps
with city representatives while working for the government was
clearly a conflict of interest. But in the end, the U.S. relinquished
its hold on the Owens River when President Theodore Roo-
sevelt declared, "[The water] is a hundred- or a thousand-fold
more important to the state and more valuable to the people as
a whole if used by the city than if used by the people of Owens
Valley." Normally disdainful of Progressive Era politics, here the
L.A. Times applauded Teddy's stance. "The law is intended to afford the greatest good to the greatest number," the paper cheered.
The government's insinuation of placing a higher value on Los
Angeles over Owens Valley provided further grist that the city's
motives were moral and just, even considering the duplicitous
methods used to achieve them; after all, didn't the end justify the
means? For his part, Lippincott may have padded his pockets,

but it came at a cost. Inyo's newspaper called him "Judas B. Lip-pincott" for ruining "the very lands [the federal government] was supposed to reclaim." He received death threats for double-cross-ing townsfolk, with some aiming to hunt him down.

Meanwhile, this was the second time in eight years that Washington, D.C., had paved the way for Angel City's future growth. In 1897, it declared San Pedro Bay the official port for Greater Los Angeles, throwing open the southern flank for de-velopment. Now, in 1905, it set up rapid expansion to the north, into the untapped frontier that was the San Fernando Valley. The city's land-hungry lords couldn't wait to carve it up.

PART II

THE TAKE

CHAPTER 9

She Has But Just Begun to Grow

"BEFORE YOU GIRLS DIE, this valley will be filled with people working in the city, and living in the country." The middle-aged man made a sweeping motion with his hands. "We're going to put a town here, we're going to put a road there. . . ."

The girls giggled. Their father had driven them out to the bleak, barren landscape of the San Fernando Valley. Their destination was a 2,300-acre parcel for which he paid $200,000, a rather oversized spot for their family picnic. The girls huddled behind the car, out of earshot. "Papa's *really* crazy this time!" whispered one sister to the others. Papa was Harry Chandler, and he was crazy alright . . . crazy for land. Now, two decades after scrounging up his first few bucks selling produce to Isaac Van Nuys's laborers at the rancher's Valley fields, Chandler had made his first solo Valley purchase. Farther north, he also acquired a minority share in the San Fernando Mission Land Company, a syndicate formed by his father-in-law, Gen. Harrison Gray Otis, in 1903. Its objective was firmly fixed on the future: to push the northern boundary of Los Angeles beyond the range of the Santa Monica Mountains.

The syndicate obtained a $575,750 option on 16,450 acres of ranchland from developer George K. Porter. Located sixteen miles from L.A., the tract was principally owned by Otis, Edwin T. Earl (publisher of the rival *Los Angeles Express*), Leslie C. Brand (who would develop much of Glendale), and banker Joseph F. Sartori. Minority investors counted Chandler, Gen. Moses Sherman, and Henry Huntington, who was looking to expand his Pacific Electric Railway (PE) to the Valley. All saw water on the horizon. According to William Mulholland, Fred Eaton had been talking up Owens Valley to water employees since at least 1892—thirteen years before plans for an aqueduct were made public. At a deposition later in his career, the Chief reiterated that it was commonly known among L.A.'s gentry that a conduit originating from up north would, at some point, funnel water into the San Fernando Valley. One reason policymakers were looped in was to evaluate whether an aqueduct was worth it. If it wasn't, no one would be the wiser. "It was necessary in order to get money to buy the water rights in the Owens Valley that some knowledge should be had of the possible cost of the work," Mulholland said.

Considering his high ranking as a member of the water commission, and his close relationship with Chandler, Sherman would have been hip to the scheme. Many historians have speculated that this intel is what led the San Fernando Mission Land Co. to option land near the eventual terminus of the aqueduct. Sherman's advance knowledge could also explain why he maintained a low profile; his and Chandler's minority interests in the syndicate ensured that their names would not be published alongside the principal members. (Sherman's defenders argued that the promise of a Huntington railway to the Valley was the main impetus for his involvement.) However, one thing is certain: When news of the aqueduct broke in 1905, Sherman, still on the Water Board, invested in yet another syndicate—this time, as a principal partner—that bought up most of the remaining San Fernando Valley, sparking a bitter vendetta against him before the close of the decade.

But that was still a few years off. In 1903, one could understand why Chandler's picnicking children thought their father mad. The San Fernando Valley was still a hostile hellscape, fairly unchanged since the founding of San Fernando Mission in 1797. And though the Southern Pacific Railroad rolled through the Valley in 1874, the steamer's presence didn't lead to the same kind of development seen in the coastal basin. Only the most hardened hands could scrape by a living in the Valley, even if it meant fighting to the death to hold onto water. "The ranchers say they will shoot to kill rather than abandon their wells," Mulholland remarked. The superintendent was public enemy number one. As the man who sicced a court injunction on them to stop taking L.A. River water, the ranchers threatened his life and continued to sink new wells as others went dry, siphoning groundwater near the river.

The Valley may have continued indefinitely as a desert-like outpost if not for the San Fernando Mission Land Co. Though George K. Porter's old property included robust orange, lemon, and olive orchards, the syndicate didn't acquire it for farming. "The purchase was made with the view of ultimate subdivision," the *Los Angeles Times* said bluntly. Then, in passive language that messaged the coming of water without getting *too* into details, the paper added, "Further development of water will be made, and when these preliminaries to subdivision are completed the property will undoubtedly become desirable for suburban homes." The article concluded that "the purchase marks an important step in the development of the country adjacent to Los Angeles." In short, Otis's syndicate openly envisioned a future in which the former Porter ranchland would form L.A.'s first suburb· in the northwestern Valley. (George K. Porter's brother Benjamin held onto another 4,148 acres of ranchland. Paradoxically, the actual suburb called Porter Ranch, carved out of this final acreage in 1962, would be the last community in the San Fernando Valley to join Los Angeles.)

The *Times'* tease about impending water was published ten months before Mulholland made his first scouting trip to Owens Valley with Fred Eaton in September 1904, when there were vague notions of a man-made waterway among L.A.'s inner sanctum. In November 1904, after Mulholland gave the Owens Valley project his blessing, the Water Board approved the aqueduct. One day later, Otis and his partners exercised their three-year option early, officially securing the Porter acreage. There are no records that expressly implicate syndicate members in any shady dealings, but the rush to close the deal hints at inside knowledge of a coming aqueduct. Either way, the purchase raised ethical questions for Otis. After his own newspaper broadcast the aqueduct project in July 1905, it was clear that his San Fernando Mission Land Co. would reap the benefits. But contrition wasn't in the general's nature. Taking risks—and dealing with the consequences later—was.

The *Los Angeles Examiner* was the first to jump on Otis's hubris and the whole aqueduct ordeal. After William Randolph Hearst opened an L.A. shingle of his incendiary *Examiner* in 1903, the daily wasted no time in fighting for labor and trade unions at the expense of L.A.'s power hierarchy. Among those investigated by *Examiner* general manager Henry Lowenthal's corps were Sherman and old whipping boy Huntington. But it was Otis—from whom Hearst was looking to peel away subscribers—who made an easy target now. Why was the general suddenly so gung-ho on the San Fernando Valley?

In the weeks leading up to the election calling for the aqueduct's first bonds, Lowenthal divulged that he had sent two reporters to Owens Valley. They found residents apoplectic about being misled into selling their water rights to Los Angeles. Lowenthal also avowed that Otis pressured Mulholland into manufacturing the water crisis in order to create a favorable outcome for the upcoming bond election. The *Examiner* accused Mulholland of dumping water from the city's reservoirs into the ocean after midnight—"flushing the system," the Chief allegedly called it. There is no proof that he wantonly drained reservoirs. There *is* proof that L.A.'s creaky waterworks, unequipped to handle an exploding population, had been springing leaks for years, often preventing reservoirs from filling to full capacity (and requiring temporary drainage for maintenance). Mulholland estimated that six million gallons of water seeped out of pipes every night. Nonetheless, the accusation that he created an artificial drought made for juicy copy; the myth even inspired a key plot twist in the 1974 movie *Chinatown*, Robert Towne's compelling drama about L.A.'s water wars that some have mistaken for the truth.

Otis responded to the *Examiner's* accusations of collusion as if swatting away a mosquito. "Fudge for Cry-Baby Lowenthal!" the *Times* mocked. Never mind that Otis reneged on the gentlemen's agreement that all the papers would simultaneously break news about the aqueduct. Lowenthal, the paper argued, was simply humiliated for being scooped:

> Everybody is laughing at the baby antics of the impossible Lowenthal, presiding howler of the *Examiner*, who takes pains to exploit the fact that the *Examiner* did not hear of the most important piece of local news that has come up in Los Angeles in a generation, till almost every other daily newspaper in the city had printed it. . . . The simple, straightforward fact is that The Times got the anxiously-awaited news of the consummation of the deal before anybody else, and printed it . . . but the sleepy Lowenthal did not hear of it till it had been published to the four corners of the earth.

The *Times* dismissed Hearst as an interloper who had no roots in Southern California and thus wasn't devoted to its development. Still, with the water bond vote looming, Otis was not taking any chances. Resorting to familiar jingoistic rhetoric, his newspaper huffed that anyone voting against the aqueduct would be "placing himself in the attitude of an enemy of the city." During the dog days of summer, scare quotes attributed to Mulholland appeared more ominous with each passing day. Reservoir levels were dropping at the rate of three million gallons a day. If the bond issue was defeated, it would lead to a "mass exodus" out of Los Angeles. Claiming there was "barely enough" water to last a few more weeks, the Chief predicted that half of L.A.'s population would bolt if the bond didn't pass. "If you don't get the water now, you'll never need it," he intoned. "The dead never get thirsty." Privately, though, Bill expressed less alarm. The previous winter (1904–05), L.A. had experienced its wettest rainy season since 1892–93, which helped buy some time during a sustained drought. (The next two winters would also yield above-average rainfall. Combined with the impending Owens Valley water, the revised outlook prompted Mulholland to assure city officials that the city had "an ample supply for several years.")

The *Times* supplemented the doom-and-gloom with promises of prosperity. Other towns would surely catch annexation fever, which would allow Los Angeles to fulfill its imperial destiny: "Adjacent towns will soon be knocking at our doors for admission in order to secure the benefits to be derived from our never-failing supply of life-giving water, and Greater Los Angeles will become a magnificent reality." This had an element of truth. Pasadena was already inquiring about purchasing surplus water from the aqueduct. But L.A. Mayor Owen McAleer and City Attorney W. B. Mathews made it clear that any reserves would first be offered to San Fernando Valley ranchers. If the likes of Pasadena, Long Beach, or Santa Monica wanted to tap the aqueduct, they would have to pony up for some construction costs. Short of that, they could simply annex with the City of Angels down the line. The officials' stance was rooted in the city charter, which stipulated that municipalities seeking L.A.-owned water could only access it through amalgamation.

Then, just five days before the September 1905 election—a twist! The *L.A. Examiner* now endorsed the water bonds. As polls showed the referendum heading for a landslide win, Hearst likely did not want to appear out of touch with his readership. The mogul reportedly flew down from San Francisco, told Lowenthal to cool his jets, and even met with good-cop Harry Chandler, who may have reminded Hearst how much they all had to gain from a larger population base. The *Los Angeles Herald* also urged readers to vote affirmatively, drawing a parallel to events in northern Europe at that time: "The vote on the water bond proposition should be relatively as emphatic as the vote of the Norwegians on the question of severing connection with Sweden. That vote was

95,935 affirmative to 37 negative."

On September 7, 1905, forty percent of eligible voters went to the polls to decide Ordinance No. 11,418, which called for taking on a debt of $1.5 million. The money would be used to gain Owens Valley water rights, secure rights of way, and greenlight initial construction of the aqueduct, essentially a down payment that would allow the project to move forward. (The estimated $21 million in completion funds would come up for another vote in a year or two.) Needing a two-thirds majority for ratification, the 1905 water-bond vote passed by a 14 to 1 margin—10,693 yeas, 754 nays. "Let me tell you how I feel," Mulholland exclaimed, mere days before his fiftieth birthday. "I'm intoxicated, drunk with delight. I want to whoop and yell like a kid!" Calling it the "proudest" day in L.A. history, councilman G. A. Smith saw it as nothing less than the city's conception: "This is our birthday and we are no longer a minor among the cities of the United States."

"Viva Los Angeles!" brayed Otis's *L.A. Times* the following morning. "Los Angeles joyously announces to all the world that she has but just begun to grow; that she has hitched her wagon to a star, and nothing can stop her progress. . . . To suppose that Los Angeles would hesitate to secure the opportunity presented to her in the Owens River project would be to assume that she entertained designs of suicide." As for the 6.5 percent who deigned to vote "no"? "Timorous, ignorant, penurious . . . every opponent of the Owens River project went to the polls and did his pitiful, futile worst to ruin Los Angeles." The paper's gloating coverage included an editorial cartoon with good ole Lady Liberty—a sash of "Progress" flowing off her neck—steering a horse-drawn chariot labeled "Los Angeles" toward snow-covered mountains. Lowenthal's prostrate body lay in the tracks of the wagon, severed at the waist from the wagon wheels, an "Examiner" club harmlessly by his side. As was the general's wont, he enlisted a *Times* poet to encapsulate the victory in an epinicion:

Mulholland was a gentleman
Of credit and renown,
A water expert eke was he
Of famous Angel Town.

He measured Owens River and
He told us 'twould cost;
We've bought the snowy water—but
For the knockers what a frost!

Fred Eaton was an engineer
Who knew a stream or two;
And Lippincott could figure out
The proper thing to do;

"No, no," said Papa Lowenthal,
"They're criminals and guys!"
The votes have now been counted and
The city has gone wise.

So let us say, oh, long live [Commissioner John] Fay,
And Sherman, long live he!
To all our faithful Water Board,
Great praise and glory be!

Decades later, commemorating the historic Owens Valley vote, the *Times* credited its battle-tested leader for shepherding through one of the most monumental days in the city's history: "The brunt of the [water] campaign fell upon The Times. Gen. Otis fought for the necessary water supply with the same vigor that won the free harbor fight."

Indeed, the campaign for a "free harbor" in San Pedro remained an ongoing concern in 1905. Otis and the *Times* were still advocating for that town's annexation, along with Wilmington and its outer harbor. Now there was a palpable sense of urgency. The city of Long Beach was looking to lock up both San Pedro and Wilmington, and was already exercising legal motions to annex East San Pedro and Terminal Island through a piecemeal approach of special elections. If Long Beach seized control of the entire industrial waterfront, it would undo all the efforts Otis and company had exerted—a disaster for Los Angeles. Complicating matters was the fact that L.A. had no legal pathway to absorb San Pedro and Wilmington. State laws required that any new territory must be contiguous to the city that was annexing it, creating a flow analogous to water through pipes. The harbor towns were roughly twenty miles away from L.A.'s southern limits. Worse, they sat next door to Long Beach, which could much more easily ingest them. Otis had once led the charge to designate San Pedro the main port of Southern California, but now the city's brightest minds would have to devise a strategy to outflank Long Beach and summon the destiny that was rightfully Los Angeles's.

It was the legacy of Gen. Phineas Banning that pointed toward a solution. In 1869, his Los Angeles & San Pedro Railroad established a rail link between those two cities. Eventually, he deeded the right-of-way to Southern Pacific. Since then, the U.S. Supreme Court increasingly recognized the efficacy of eminent domain—essentially, land grabs backed by the federal government to serve the greater good. (Condemnation laws would later be used—and abused—to construct much of L.A.'s freeway system.) Realtor Gabor Hegyi was credited with the idea of using eminent domain to secure a narrow ribbon between Los Angeles and the harbor. The proposed strip would ostensibly parallel the railroad route, bolstering L.A.'s claim to a major trade corridor. City Attorney W. B. Mathews determined that the expropriation plan had legal merit, and convinced the L.A. City Council to call a special election.

City planners mapped out a swath of land that started as a blocky section south of the University Addition, then narrowed to a half-mile width. The western border of this "Shoestring Strip"—so-called because of its graphical resemblance to a shoestring—shadowed Vermont Avenue and, just past Gardena, Western Avenue. Farther south, it skirted western Wilmington and plugged into the northwestern tip of San Pedro like an umbilical cord. Council members wisely decided not to include the annexation of San Pedro and Wilmington on the ballot. San Pedroans were viciously prideful, and its leaders were already seeking concessions from Los Angeles—for example, the allowance of self-governing powers akin to a borough—before considering a merger. The harbor annexation question was shelved until the following year.

Unlike the aqueduct vote, which garnered huge numbers for a special election, the Shoestring Strip drew low turnout. Part of that was because polls were closed in certain precincts. But it also reflected the sparse population of the unincorporated parcel, which participated in the election. As the results trickled in on November 13, 1906, Shoestring inhabitants accounted for only 410 votes, with a razor-thin margin of 208 yeas and 202 nays. One area that was adamantly anti-annexation lay just over L.A.'s southern border, where the Ascot Park horse racing track welcomed gamblers who couldn't get their kicks in Angel City. It sat on land owned by Henry Huntington, who ran a trolley to and from the popular attraction. On the other side of the ledger, Angelenos carried annexation by a large margin (6,741 to 925).

The vote was ratified by the Secretary of State the day after Christmas. The new territory added 18.5 square miles to Los Angeles, whose citizens could now, as the *Times* enthused, "toss pebbles into the sea," a reference to the fact that the city brushed up against Wilmington's inner-harbor. L.A. now measured just over sixty square miles. Overnight, it became the sixth largest city in America by area; outside the U.S., only London was deemed larger. As expected, wet blanket council members prohibited betting on horses at Ascot Park. The state would soon follow, and racetrack betting wouldn't be legalized again until 1933.

With the Shoestring Strip officially part of Los Angeles, the city was now bearing down on San Pedro and Wilmington. In the meantime, there was the inglorious aspect of governing the new territory. The community of Gardena was a case study, proving to be a migraine-sized headache for both L.A. officials and residents of Gardena. The district was cleaved in half by the strip, causing, as one local put it, "her schoolhouse on one side and the school district on the other, and the harpoon of Los Angeles thrust through her heart." True, Gardena voters endorsed the annexation by a 50 to 21 spread. But many were motivated out of fear that if they didn't say "yes" to Los Angeles, they would be taken over by Long Beach.

Decades later, the left-behind part of Gardena incorporated, only to find itself dealing with confusing repercussions from the 1906 strip vote. "I tell people that the First United Methodist Church of Gardena is not in Gardena, and people just kind of stare in disbelief," Reverend Dick Haddon told the *L.A. Times* in 1989. The church's post office address indicated Gardena, but its physical location was in Los Angeles. Homeowners in the section of Gardena absorbed by L.A. felt that the city neglected their neighborhood, resulting in gangs and higher crime, while those in incorporated Gardena took pride in its boundaries. "We're like in limbo," said a resident of Harbor Gateway, the name L.A. gave to the corridor alongside Gardena. "We're only here because Los Angeles needs this little piece of land to attach to the harbor. Nobody cares about us. . . . We're like the forgotten people." For years, Los Angeles never bothered to put fire or ambulance stations in the strip, relying on mutual aid from adjoining regions. This practice led to a tragic incident in 1984. After a nurse named Linda Jefferis suffered a heart seizure while driving along the Harbor Freeway's "Gateway" corridor, no ambulances assisted her even though five paramedic units were within a ten minutes' drive. By the time help arrived, it was too late to save the forty-year-old's life. Jefferis had fallen through administrative cracks, victimized by vague jurisdictions among Los Angeles, Los Angeles County, and local municipalities. Sadly, this was not the first time that cardiologist Dr. Michael Criley from the Harbor-UCLA Medical Center had seen an avoidable death. He called the Shoestring Strip the "valley of death." Residents in the

Gateway strip still complain of being forgotten by first-respond-
ers, though some prefer the term "medical desert."

It is understandable why citizens in the shoestring neighborhoods might feel "forgotten." From the outset, they were pawns
trapped in a higher purpose. Policymakers at the time viewed the
strip as nothing more than an economic runway to the eventual
harbor, paving over the petty concerns of those residing within
it. "Now that the plan for the annexation of the 'shoestring' district has been indorsed, there has been a rush for the Greater Los
Angeles band wagon," reported the *L.A. Herald*. "And when the
harbor cities enter the charmed circle, the dream of a Greater Los
Angeles, reaching from the mountains to the sea, will become a
grand reality."

As 1907 kicked off, Los Angeles was now home to some
quarter-million people spread over sixty-two square miles. On
January 25, members of the Realty Board gathered for their annual banquet at the Angelus Hotel. Real estate visionary Billy
Garland—later known for helping bring the Tenth Olympiad
to Los Angeles—served as the toastmaster. His companion this
evening was Mayor Arthur C. Harper. One hundred twenty-five
men made merry to the strains of a live orchestra, drunk on the
promise of a new year. Legislation was being drafted to consolidate San Pedro and Wilmington, which would give Los Angeles
an international seaport. And the expected passage of the second
aqueduct bond would divert the Owens River to the city's door-
step, serving up enough water for two million people. It was all
enough to make the roomful of wheeler-dealers rise in a melodic
call-and-response. "Water! Water! Water! Roads! Roads! Roads!"
whooped one side, while others cheered, "And sunshine! Sand
lots! Subdivisions! And population!"

CHAPTER 10

Huntington Goes All In

JUST AS LOS ANGELES was enjoying its moment in the sun, three of its top power players had entered a period of darkness. After the death of his wife Eliza in late 1904, Gen. Harrison Gray Otis's forty-one-year-old daughter Beulah Lillian Otis succumbed to tuberculosis in March of 1906. That same year, Otis's own health took a turn for the worse, resulting in a month-long hospital stay for an undisclosed disease. Harry Chandler assumed a more active role running the *Los Angeles Times* in his absence. His influence began to permeate the paper, and it was just a matter of time before he would take over it completely.

Up north, the Great San Francisco Earthquake pummeled the Bay Area on the morning of April 18, 1906, killing 3,000 people. Eighty percent of San Francisco was destroyed, leaving half its population homeless. Collis Huntington's former residence was among the 25,000 buildings burned to the ground; as a memento, Henry Huntington had a Canary Island date palm tree from Collis's estate transported to his San Marino Ranch. (The charred tree still clings to life at Huntington Botanical Gardens.) More alarmingly, Gen. Moses Sherman's family was living in San Francisco at the time of the temblor. He chartered a private train to make sure they were okay and stayed the summer. Chandler arranged to have the *L.A. Times* delivered to him so he could keep up on affairs in Southern California, for which Moses was extremely grateful. "The people of San Francisco are very brave," Sherman wrote his friend, "and I really believe they will build a more wonderful city than ever."

The trauma had a serendipitous effect on Los Angeles. The

earthquake and subsequent fires impelled more people and industries to relocate to the city, which, since its founding, had not
recorded anything close to the convulsions that shook San Francisco. L.A. newspapers were quick to remind edgy readers of that.
"EVERYBODY KEEP COOL" read an April 20, 1906, headline
in the *Los Angeles Herald*, two days after the quake. The paper
claimed, falsely, that Los Angeles is "completely outside the natural pathway of earthquakes." It beseeched readers to stop worrying about the Big One, and instead "appreciate again the delicious
sunshine, the green trees, and the rose-embowered cottages of
beautiful Los Angeles," while embracing all the Northern Cali-
fornians now flocking to this "city of refuge." Even as hundreds
of city blocks still smoldered in San Francisco, the *Herald* took an
almost perverse joy in forecasting its demise: "This is the longest
state in the United States, and one end might be wiped off the map
without the other feeling a jar."

Settling back in Los Angeles in August 1906, Sherman had
issues of his own. His marriage to Hattie was in tatters—she
had been living up north with their kids for years—which both
blamed on his workaholic ways. "I know well that you do not
want us all in Los Angeles," she wrote him, "and I fancy that you
do not want me there either." Around this time, an insomniac
Moses penned a morose late-night letter to Hattie to settle the
affairs of his estate, establishing his wife and adult daughters Hazeltine and Lucy as directors of a newly created Sherman Investment Company. Moses grew darker as the letter went on, saying,
"The journey is soon over and I will soon be out of it," before
signing off with "I guess I'll try and see if I cannot sleep a little
before day light."

Sherman's fatalism wasn't just a pity party about the state
of his marriage. Now in his early fifties, he could no longer rely
on youthful ardor to carry him through his hard-charging days
and nights. He suffered from poor circulation, and had taken to
wearing wool frocks, even in the heat, to compensate. This get-
up often led to autograph seekers confusing him for a thespian

along Broadway's theatre district. In a letter to his sister-in-law, Sarah Carr, Moses all but confessed to a nervous breakdown. "I need a long vacation more than any man on the Coast," he wrote. "God knows, I am willing to do anything to get health. I have been in such bad condition physically, that my nerves have all gone back on me, and I cannot control myself. I laugh when I do not want to laugh, and I cry when I do not want to cry, and I go all to pieces, which is no one's fault, excepting that I am exhausted and used up."

But Sherman was a man conflicted. In a life defined by its accomplishments, he could not conceive of giving up the powerful succor that his hectic work schedule provided. Even Hattie had to admit, "You are growing constantly and maturing more & more instead of degenerating after forty as some men do." It's no coincidence that his two best friends, Eli Clark and Harry Chandler, were also his two most active business partners. The general had only grown closer to Chandler, joining him for dominos on Sunday evenings while becoming an uncle figure to Harry's children. Chandler instilled in Sherman a spirit of generosity. Even if his ultimate goal was to feather his nest, Chandler was known for his gift-giving and encouraged charity in others. Perhaps not wanting to upend their lucrative business relationship, Sherman donated to his crony's causes. "I know how you are helping others all the time, and I love and admire you for it," Moses wrote Harry in September of 1906 after one contribution. "Life is short . . . it makes me feel better. When we die, what little we have is left behind."

The Shermans' twenty-two-year marriage ended in 1907. They remained on good terms, and Moses maintained close relationships with his daughters and adopted son Robert. Recognizing that he was married to his work, he never came close to an altar again. Hattie was in Europe when word of the divorce was finalized. In a wistful letter from her Paris hotel room, she included several lines from the Ella Wheeler Wilcox poem "Resolve," stressing its message of moving on with no regrets:

Moist no tears
Upon the blotted record of lost years,
But turn the leaf, and smile, oh, smile, to see
The fair white pages that remain for thee.

Sherman at least had company. At the same time his marriage was in a death spiral, Mary Huntington stepped into a New
York courtroom to seek a divorce from Henry. She told the judge
that her husband "had not maintained conjugal relations for the
past six years," and that she had never "given her husband any
excuse for deserting her." It took just seven minutes for the court
to dissolve their thirty-three-year union. After securing a $2 mil-
lion trust fund (Henry's estate was pegged at $40 million), Mary
boarded a passenger ship for Japan later that day with family
members. Like Hattie Sherman, her marital freedom would be
spent halfway around the world.

In other parallels to the Shermans, the Huntingtons' six-year
estrangement had begun after Henry made Los Angeles his home
in 1900. Mary remained in San Francisco with Elizabeth, Marian, Clara, and Howard. It was a stressful time for all. His daughters wrote letters expressing how much they missed their father
during the holidays, and Mary spent a month in Germany seeking
treatment for "intense nervousness." Occasionally, his children
came down to visit when Henry wasn't in New York on business.
At first, they could find him at the Van Nuys Hotel. In 1905, he
moved into a suite in the Jonathan Club at his newly built Pacific
Electric Building. (Howard took a job with PE and moved into
quarters down the hall from Dad.) Though they worshipped their
father, Henry's daughters couldn't help feeling like afterthoughts
to his Los Angeles empire. "For my own part, I see how the few
have to be sacrificed for the benefit of the greater number, mean-
ing that we rarely saw Father," recollected Clara, his eldest daughter, "and his ambitions, his dreams, [and] his plans that would
have been interesting to hear about, we just didn't."

Family issues aside, leaving San Francisco for his new

"mistress"—the City of Angels—*had* greatly improved Henry's mental and physical well-being. He resolved to give back to the land that had blessed him, multifold. "I am a foresighted man. . . . I believe Los Angeles is destined to become the most important city in this country, if not the world," he said. Howard noticed the change in his father. "[Dad] is certainly buying a great deal of real estate and ranches and seems to have the greatest faith in the future development of Southern California," he wrote his grandmother. Indeed, the senior Huntington seemed a man on a mission, his influence on the city unmatched during the first decade of the twentieth century. Some even felt his mind and body worked in such close harmony, he was biologically programmed to succeed.

These days, if someone tells you to get your head examined, it's a good-natured barb that you're crazy. But in the early 1900s, phrenology—the pseudoscience of examining one's skull to determine mental traits—was serious business, often employed to measure mental superiority (or inferiority, as was conveniently found in non-Caucasian subjects). When Collis Huntington died in 1900, Henry came under intense scrutiny. Did he have what it took to manage his uncle's Southern Pacific holdings? In order to alleviate all doubt as to Henry's capacity for leadership, J. A. Fowler, Vice President of the American Institute of Phrenology, was commissioned to analyze Huntington's character. His conclusions—and a sketch of Henry's head—were published in newspapers:

> His forehead showed intuitiveness, perseverance, and energy; the base of his brain revealed executive force; his eyebrows indicated perception and memory; his eyes, acuteness; his nose, analytical powers; his jaw, endurance; and his chin, deliberateness.

In one article, Fowler emphasized the importance of ears in determining one's longevity and vital attributes. Photos of "twenty different kinds" of ears were spread across a centerfold. Huntington's head possessed No. 13 Ears, with thin but nicely curved upper rims—a clear sign of intelligence, independence, and self-regard. Fowler's findings excited the business community. "Can Triple Huntington Millions," raved a headline about the study. "Well Fitted to Succeed His Uncle and Continue Many Projects. Healthy Organization." Southern Pacific shareholders may have agreed Henry had a head for business, but, as previously covered, they had misgivings about his ability to run the company. In retrospect, Huntington's snubbing was a blessing for him. Credit his intuitive skull contours or perceptive eyebrows (or neither), but he quickly learned how to manage a fragile relationship with his late uncle's successor, E. H. Harriman. After the new SP president boldly declared his intentions to encroach on Huntington's Southern California transportation dominion, it motivated Henry to diversify and forge more partnerships, even with Harriman.

Like Los Angeles County, San Diego County experienced remarkable growth in the early twentieth century. Its population, which sat at 35,100 in 1900, would increase seventy-five percent by the end of the decade. For a foresighted man like Huntington, this presented an opportune moment to extend an interurban line to San Diego from his southernmost depots in Santa Ana and Newport Beach. Now it was Harriman's turn to feel threatened. In contrast to SP's lumbering steamers, Pacific Electric was nimble and efficient, able to make more stops and more runs. Harriman pressured Huntington to abandon his project, claiming it would unfairly compete with SP's plans to reach San Diego. Harriman also convinced Huntington to give up any notions of running a PE line to San Francisco. Even with his millions, Huntington knew he would lose a protracted fight with the better-funded Octopus. He abandoned the San Diego and San Francisco routes, scaling back the outer reaches of his empire to Orange and San Bernardino Counties while continuing to expand his intra- and interurban lines in metro L.A., now chiefly Pacific Electric and the Los Angeles Railway (LARy).

Harriman wasn't the only obstacle to Huntington's expansion plans. In 1894, William Spencer Hook, a Chicago banker, visited Los Angeles on a summer vacation. Like so many before him, he loved it so much, he never left. Within years, he and his brother Edwin built their own trolley system—the California Pacific, which connected to San Pedro. By the end of 1902, they owned fifteen percent of the local market, making them an attractive party for Huntington to buy out. In 1903, Huntington and the Hook brothers held discussions to consolidate lines. Huntington was extremely paranoid of Harriman getting wind of his plans. In a June 18, 1903, telegram to his trusted financier Isaias W. Hellman in San Francisco, he included this passage: "Fabulous is leniency the patriot launch to soapstone." Only Hellman knew how to decipher the cryptic message, which alluded to their strategy regarding Southern Pacific's anticipated moves. Later in the telegram, Huntington wrote, "But if Samian looks after unlucky Hollywood easily crooken also all easily demon hook's dorsal." Translation: "But if Harriman looks after Santa Monica and Hollywood matters, he should also look after all matters in connection with Hook's lines." In the end, covert telegrams didn't help Huntington land the Hooks' most prized franchises. The brothers had been holding their own backdoor meetings with Harriman, who outbid Huntington to the tune of $1.8 million. (Henry was so distraught, he offered the Hooks a higher price even after the transaction was complete.) "Huntington Came Within an Ace of Capturing the Line" read a headline in the *L.A. Times*.

Frantic to stay ahead of the Octopus, Huntington went on a shopping spree. He raised $10 million to start a second city line known as the Los Angeles Inter-Urban Electric Railway (LAIU). Neither red nor yellow, LAIU's cars were painted green. The *Los Angeles Evening News* published a cartoon that commented on his expanding reach. Under the banner "Henry E. Huntington: The Modern Colossus of Roads," a monster-sized Henry bestrode the entire Los Angeles region—one foot planted in San

Pedro, the other in Huntington Beach—his giant hands yanking on strings tied to communities he helped build as if they were his own personal puppets. As Los Angeles celebrated the Fourth of July in 1905, it was estimated that 100,000 out of 150,000 passengers that day rode a trolley that Huntington either owned or co-owned. A reporter from the *Los Angeles Record* asked the mogul to comment on a "well-grounded report" that he was looking to expand his rail empire as far north as Oxnard. Hip to the *Record's* anti-monopoly agenda, Henry scoffed, "Would you believe it if . . . I was about to build a railroad to the moon and open up mines of green cheese there?"

When the general manager of the LARy division suddenly died in 1904, Huntington replaced him with his son Howard. It was a lot to lay on the twenty-eight-year-old, who had only minimal railway experience. "Much to my surprise, I was selected GM of LARY Co.," wrote Howard in another letter to his grandmother. "I hope to be able to take more of the load off father's shoulders as time goes on." Unfortunately, it was Henry who ended up helping Howard more than the other way around. Juggling the infinite responsibilities of the Yellow Car system proved too much for the younger Huntington, who punted to his dad for complex decisions, or simply yielded to his iron will. When Hellman warned Howard that his father was overleveraged by borrowing too much against the railroads, Henry snapped back to the banker, "There can be but one head in the management of the property. . . . I think I understand the needs of the property and what is essential better than anyone else." Eventually, Howard suffered a "mental breakdown" and was replaced by his assistant general manager, his own title downgraded to vice president. Any hopes Henry had that his and Howard's relationship might emulate the mentor-protégé one he had enjoyed with Collis were dashed.

Still, under the junior Huntington, LARy added eighty miles of track from 1904 to 1908, most of it operating within eight miles of L.A.'s city center. The firm also eked out a modest profit, with dividends reinvested in the company. However, the interurban lines—PE and LAIU, which comprised over 500 miles of track—were not money-making ventures. In LAIU's "best" year, 1906, the trolley lost $93,032. One reason for the interurbans' unprofitability was the fact that Huntington often connected them to sparsely populated areas to secure the suburban market. Although these railways lost money on paper, they were invaluable in their ability to promote Henry's new subdivisions. A partial list of San Gabriel Valley communities that benefited from PE and LAIU routes and became their own cities includes Alhambra, Azusa, Monrovia, Pomona, Sierra Madre, Glendora, Covina, and San Gabriel. Even aside from his namesake Library, Museum, and Botanical Gardens, the Huntington name remains a fixture in the region, gracing a middle school, a hospital, and a resort hotel.

Meanwhile, a December 1906 letter from home builder Allen P. Nichols illustrated just how much speculators looked to cash in on the Huntington imprimatur, which had become synonymous with prosperity. After Nichols asked if Huntington would be willing to lend his name to new development, Huntington replied, "I would not like to have my name put at the head of anything which is not or is not likely to be a success; but the character of yourself and friends seems to me to be a pretty good guaranty that what you are doing will prove a decided success." Nichols thanked Huntington for his "willingness to permit the use of your name in connection with a subdivision," which was called the Huntington Boulevard Tract. In a classic quid pro quo, Nichols offered Huntington the middle forty feet of a 120-foot-wide boulevard—today's Huntington Drive—as a right-of-way for his Pacific Electric trolley. To guard against undesirables tainting the Huntington brand, Nichols added that his eighty-acre suburb will include "building restrictions which will insure a higher class of residences than can be found in other subdivisions." Nichols and Huntington had the law on their side. In 1892, federal courts granted individual property owners in California the right to discriminate whom they sold to, leading to the widespread practice of restrictive deed covenants in white communities.

Huntington's other major developments spoked off his Southern Division Lines, helping lead to the incorporation of places like Whittier, Redondo Beach, and of course Huntington Beach and Huntington Park ("Buy Where Huntington Buys!" read one post. "Is Good Advice to Follow.") By one account, all seventeen cities incorporated in Los Angeles County during the aughts were located along his streetcar lines. Though not part of Los Angeles, these "destination cities" were instrumental in sowing communities that are now familiar names within L.A. city limits—South Los Angeles, West Adams Heights, Watts, Central Alameda, Crenshaw, and Baldwin Hills, all of which were served by Huntington trolleys. Other localities also benefitted from his interurban network, including Willowbrook, Walnut Park, Florence-Graham, and Rancho Dominguez, unincorporated pockets that lie in the vast Gateway Cities Region of L.A. County. As with Pasadena-adjacent communities, many southeast districts permitted deeds that restricted Black or "alien" races from purchasing homes. Nat Laws, a longtime Angeleno who grew up in Huntington Park shortly after its 1906 incorporation, remembered that the city brandished signs informing Blacks and Asians that they were not welcome. "Huntington Park?" Laws said. "Man, a Negro couldn't walk the streets in Huntington Park." As recently as 1960, Huntington's eponymous community was still almost 100 percent white. Within a few years, the courts legally closed the loopholes on housing restrictions. Huntington Park is now over ninety-seven percent Latino, and the Gateway Cities Region is one of the most densely populated melting pots in the United States, home to some two million people.

When he wasn't running trolleys to communities built by his Huntington Land and Improvement Company, Huntington was supplying electricity through his Pacific Light and Power Company (PL&P). The utility primarily powered his streetcars, but by the end of the 1910s it was providing almost twenty percent of the electrical needs for Los Angeles. The firm drew its power from two massive Huntington-financed hydroelectric plants in Central California. Big Creek powerhouse, on the San Joaquin River, sat 280 miles from Los Angeles City Hall—an even farther distance than the water paradise of Owens Valley. Upstream from the power plant, three dams formed a reservoir that was christened Huntington Lake. High-voltage transmission wires traveled to a substation in Eagle Rock, where distribution lines fanned out across L.A. (Both the power plant and substation are still in use, now owned by Southern California Edison.) Huntington also formed what later became the Southern California Gas Company, which serviced one-fifth of the region's natural gas consumption. "Wherever the Huntington railways extend their lines," the *Times* declared, "the Huntington electric and gas companies are preparing to furnish fuel and light." At one point, the entrepreneur controlled twenty-three utility firms that provided water, electricity, and gas across Southern California. So pervasive was his presence, a resident of, say, Alhambra could take a Huntington-built trolley along Huntington Drive to his Huntington-built house, flick on lights powered by Huntington's PL&P, fill a tea kettle with water from Huntington's Alhambra Water Company, and boil the water on a gas stove fueled by Huntington's SoCal Gas. Since Huntington had interests in many other industries—and was one of L.A.'s largest employers—our imaginary Alhambra homeowner could well have been a company man himself.

Meanwhile, after Harriman purchased the Hook lines in 1903, Huntington worked out a deal with his rival that called for both men to assume a majority interest in Henry's troubled PE and LAIU railways; in return, Huntington acquired several SP-owned lines in Los Angeles and San Gabriel. Still, the power dynamic between the two remained unchanged. Whenever Huntington wanted to construct a new route in Southern California, he had to get Harriman's blessing, lest he run afoul of the Octopus or get hit with a lawsuit. Such was the case when Huntington sought approval to string a trolley to Covina, which would mirror an SP route. "All right, Huntington," Harriman sighed, "if you want to build it, go ahead." Harriman had determined that PE's focus on passengers would not steal away business from SP's freight traffic. By this point, it was clear to Huntington that his freight sector was never going to grow as long as he helmed PE and Harriman controlled SP. Though Henry may have chafed privately, he didn't begrudge his antagonist; Harriman was simply looking to maximize profits for shareholders. "So far as Mr. Harriman and I are concerned," Henry wrote friend Harry Chandler, "I can say with exact truth that I shall be fair and square with him as long as he shall be so with me." But in March 1906, Huntington felt a dagger in his back from another man he considered his friend—Moses Sherman.

Sherman and Huntington's business relationship dated back to 1895, when the pair partnered up on the Pasadena and Altadena Railroad. Since then, the transit kings had become tentatively friendly competitors, with Henry bailing out Moses's distressed routes when bondholders revolted. The cohorts also encountered each other at private clubs. When Sherman was prescribed bed rest after a malady in 1900, Huntington wrote him encouraging letters while smiling on his peer's business fortunes: "Things seem to be coming your way right along now." Weeks later, after the general's condition required a visit to a Northern California sanitarium, Huntington regularly checked in on his well-being. After Henry's uncle Collis died in August 1900, a still-institutionalized Sherman found the time to send his colleague a heartfelt note of sympathy and, later, a bouquet of flowers.

Though Sherman and Eli Clark had largely gotten out of the railway business by early 1906, they still owned the Los Angeles-Pacific Railroad—the backbone of their popular Balloon Route that linked L.A., Hollywood, the Westside, and South Bay. (As a refresher, the partners briefly lost control of the line in the 1890s before getting it back.) In March 1906, they were actively looking to unload it. The 180-mile-long LAP railway was the most coveted missing piece of Huntington's own streetcar empire. He wanted it—badly. But once again, he found himself checkmated. Sherman and Clark sold LAP to Southern Pacific for $6 million (over $200 million today). With Harriman now in charge, the brothers-in-law were retained as minority stockholders and executive officers. *The Daily Outlook* reported that Huntington found out about the deal while he was in New York. He promptly queried Sherman to ask if it was true. "The reply [by Sherman] is said to have been discourteous in the extreme, embodying a refusal to impart the information," the paper said. "This reply was construed to mean that the transfer had taken place as the relations between the Los Angeles-Pacific and the Pacific Electric had been such as to make diplomacy a necessity in the past." The secretive transaction also reignited animus between Huntington and Harriman. "A lively war is booked for Los Angeles," the *Outlook* foretold, gleefully.

Adding insult to injury, Sherman allegedly spread rumors after the sale that Huntington was getting out of the railway business, which was news to Huntington. When Chandler telegrammed Henry to ask if this was true, the normally measured baron unloaded on Moses in a letter back to Harry, his words dripping with venom:

My dear Mr. Chandler:

I really and deeply appreciate the very kind expression of your hope that I shall not dispose of my railway interests. . . . I'm afraid that fellow Sherman has for purposes of his own been trying to lead you astray. That he is no friend of mine—and through no fault of mine—goes without saying. I have no doubt whatever of his anxious desire now to vex and injure me as far as lies in his power; for I have always recognized the truth of what my late Uncle [Collis] used to say . . . that when a man betrays you he is bound thereafter to do his best to show that you deserved the betrayal. It is, in fact, the only justification for his own baseness.

I know him well. He has done some very dirty work; but I think his character is so well known by the better class of people in Los Angeles that he will never be able to make much headway with them and it doesn't matter how he stands with anybody else.

I have sometimes thought that I would publish his letters to me just to show him up in his true light; but perhaps it would be better not to do so quite yet. When one hunts a fox he must first get between him and his hole. . . . He had better keep out of my chicken-yard if he wants any mercy.

What made the letter even more astounding was that Huntington felt so comfortable openly demonizing Sherman. "I don't think Sherman is fooling you very much, if you are the judge of men I have always taken you to be," Henry told Harry. Yet by 1906, it was well known in business circles that Chandler and Sherman were tight. In fact, at the same time Huntington was venting his spleen, Chandler was granting Sherman direct access to *Times* managing editor Harry Andrews to help give Sherman's enterprises a more positive light. "My dear Andrews," Sherman wrote during the railroad imbroglio, "I thought that what you put in the paper this morning was splendid and I thank you for it." Sherman's letter goes on to make clear that Chandler—Andrews's boss—had Sherman's back regarding future business: "There is no one living that knows just what our plans are except ourselves. . . . I have had many talks with Mr. Chandler on this subject . . . please wait until Gen. Otis and Mr. Chandler return until we can get all the data and everything else ready for you." Chandler's policy of allowing a non-employee like Sherman to help shape reportage is a classic example of unethical journalism. But it also demonstrates his aptitude to manipulate the news to achieve a desired business outcome, and his skill at playing both sides—here, Sherman and Huntington—while playing the role of a placid mediator.

Reading behind the lines, Huntington could have simply been trying to get Chandler to rethink his relationship with Sherman. "I should certainly feel very great regret if I had the slightest belief [as to your friendship]," Huntington added, mendaciously. It's a fair bet that Sherman and Huntington would not be exchanging Christmas cards from 1906 onward. But as voracious capitalists, both placed profits over friendships. And in a few short years, they would reunite as partners as part of a historic syndicate that would double the size of Los Angeles and boost their considerable net worths. The man who would bring them to the table was their mutual ally—Harry Chandler.

CHAPTER 11

Here, There, Chandler

AFTER THE BREAKUP OF his marriage, Gen. Moses Sherman was free to log long hours on his entrepreneurial pursuits minus his customary guilt. Even ex-wife Hattie noticed his new zing. "I must admit to myself the fact that life for you seems to be better without me than with me," she commented. Sherman was also buoyed by new ventures with his partner-in-crime, Harry Chandler. It wasn't uncommon for the men to exchange multiple letters or telegrams a day. "I do enjoy working with you so much," Moses wrote. "You know, all we get out of it is the 'fun' of the 'game.'" Unlike Henry Huntington, whose growing appreciation of the arts defined the second half of his life, Sherman and Chandler had no consuming passions. Their bag was supercharging Los Angeles's growth. Any accumulated wealth, at least in Sherman's view, was a mere byproduct. "Harry, it is <u>not</u> the money we make, at all," he emphasized, "but it is the <u>fun</u> of success (that beats money all to pieces)." As with Huntington, sometimes the "game" required complete secrecy. In a June 1906 letter disclosing a new business opportunity, Sherman asked of Chandler, "Please be sure and tear this up as soon as you have read the same for it is bad to have these things lying around." He signed the letter "Thomas"—Moses's code name for himself. Around the same time, Huntington contacted Chandler about a business proposition, then added, "I must confess that the progress and prosperity of Los Angeles and its environs is quite a hobby of mine." Despite personal differences among Huntington, Sherman, Chandler, and Gen. Harrison Gray Otis, Huntington spoke for them all when he expressed his joy at seeing "anything published that makes Los Angeles look bigger and bigger in the public eye, for she deserves it." The power quartet would soon get their wish. The next year, the fate of Los Angeles would again be put to the public trust, with the *Los Angeles Times* playing its usual persuasive role.

"WHY BE AFRAID OF $3.20 A YEAR?" asked a headline in the June 9, 1907, issue. It had been one year and nine months since the initial water-bond election, when Angelenos overwhelmingly approved $1.5 million to initiate proceedings on the Los Angeles Aqueduct. Now, with another election three days away, the *Times* was imploring its readers to vote "yes" on the second bond issuance of $23 million, which would guarantee the construction and completion of the project. With a population of 250,000, each household would owe only $3.20 per year in water taxes. As always, Otis's tyrannical voice rang through. Anyone who opposed the plan was "deficient in intelligence . . . perversely disposed . . . or so false in civic duty." Similar to the San Pedro "free harbor" in 1897 and the first water bond in 1905, nothing less than the city's survival was at stake. As the campaign inched closer to election day, city officials asked William Mulholland to stump for votes. But the water supervisor stuck by his longstanding credo that "politics and water don't mix" when he inveighed, "Why, I'd sooner skin a dead dog than make a speech!"

Turns out, he wasn't needed. By a ten-to-one margin, 24,051 registered voters approved the bond issuance. The following morning, on June 13, 1907, the *Times'* editorial section was a study in contrasts by its two leaders—President and General Manager Otis, and VP and Assistant GM Chandler. Otis used the occasion to trash William Randolph Hearst's *Los Angeles Examiner* for being out of touch with the will of the people. The *Examiner's* revived takedown of the aqueduct included claims that Owens River water was teeming with typhoid. To which the *Times* quoted a city chemist: "One of the streams might become infected by those germs if some person suffering from the disease camped on its banks and the excrements were thrown on the snow. . . . It would be just as reasonable to say that the waters were infected with live monkeys. Monkeys are not natives of that territory; no more are typhoid fever germs."

Elsewhere on the *Times'* editorial page, however, Chandler's deliberate and aspirational tones could be heard behind the headline "MILLION POPULATION CLUB." Water was just the first step. The article stressed that social clubs will be equally instrumental to L.A.'s future, modeling Chandler's use of fraternal organizations to incubate some of the city's best ideas. Voted the "Most Valuable Citizen in Los Angeles" by the Chamber of Commerce, Chandler seemed everywhere at once. He was a charter member of the Automobile Club of Southern California, which helped drive the oil, automotive, road-building, and real estate industries that he also had a hand in. He founded the All-Year Club, cajoling businessmen to pool their money to promote Los Angeles as a tourist destination during "off-months." And he was arguably the most prominent member of the California Club, where he did his most serious fundraising by strong-arming wealthy peers into investing thousands of dollars into causes that would benefit L.A. With Owens Valley water now a fait accompli, the last impediment had been lifted. The *Times* called on an entire city to think big:

> We have it in sight now. It will come in good time. There will be no check to our growth. We can provide in all ways for the comfort of a million souls inside the city and for another million outside. . . . It is time today to organize the Million Population Club.

Shortly after the bond election's positive outcome, Chandler absconded to the alpine hamlet of Idyllwild in the San Jacinto Mountains to recharge. Long days had taken their toll. The *Times'* chieftain rarely went to bed before 2 A.M., opting to stay at the office to "put the [morning's] paper to bed" after already spending a full day managing countless non-newspaper enterprises. He was also picking up the slack for his father-in-law, whose deteriorating condition led to an operation at Johns Hopkins Hospital in Baltimore. "I hope you will not return until you feel perfectly well and strong," Sherman wrote Chandler. "The trouble with us is that we overwork. You will find that you cannot keep up the everlasting toil night and day the way you have for many years past." Sherman recommended sanitariums and hot springs that *he* frequented whenever he felt "tired and worn out." Not that Sherman followed his own advice. He admitted to his ex-sister-in-law Sarah Carr that he worked "from morning until night," although he had at least gotten someone to help him with his poor circulation. "I have a man come here to give me gymnastics," he wrote. Sherman would need all the strength he could muster, because he was about to be put through the wringer.

In a letter to Sarah in 1908, Moses boasted that he served on the Los Angeles Water Board, which gave him influence in pushing through the aqueduct project and general "development of this locality"—essentially, confiding his desire to subdivide the San Fernando Valley to take advantage of the incoming water source. Sherman and Chandler were already plotting their move to develop the northern half of the Valley, close to the aqueduct's eventual southern terminus. It had been twenty-six years since Isaac Van Nuys barked, "Get out of here, you son of a bitch!" to Chandler for trespassing on his ranch. By 1908, the two were still in touch. Now in his early seventies, Van Nuys was in declining health and looking to unload his remaining property. Chandler had been salivating over the domain for decades. Totaling about 47,500 acres, it extended east to the borders of Burbank and Lankershim (North Hollywood), west to present-day Canoga Park and Tarzana, and south to the Santa Monica Mountains (Encino and other pockets were excluded). The northern demarcation was marked by a sixteen-mile-long plow furrow that would become Roscoe Boulevard. The territory was mostly wheat and barley fields, scattered barns, and an old cattle range in the shadows of the crumbling San Fernando Mission. If

Chandler could put together another group to complement the 16,450 acres purchased by the San Fernando Mission Land Co. in 1903, the combined syndicates would control *one hundred square miles* of Valley real estate.

With Sherman and Otis already on board ("We will have a whole lot of fun out of this, with the biggest men in the country," Sherman effused), Chandler set about finding investors for what would be called the Los Angeles Suburban Homes Company. "He was a great catalyst," noted businessman Arnold Haskell of Chandler. "He was a man who had the ability to pull the abilities of many other people together and form something concrete . . . he would get others enthusiastic about the project and he had the ability to inspire them." The deal came together in 1909, when Chandler's syndicate offered Van Nuys $2.5 million. Rival industrialists submitted higher bids, including one for $3 million. But the prickly doyen maintained a soft spot for Harry, and instructed his family, "Sell the ranch to Harry Chandler."

As the transaction went public, it raised red flags with the local Democratic League, which had already been scrutinizing the affairs of Sherman, Huntington, and the gatekeepers at the *L.A. Times*—all staunch Republicans. Pro-labor newspapers *Los Angeles Examiner* and *Los Angeles Record* provided sympathetic outlets for the organization to air its grievances. As a member of the city's Water Board, Sherman drew the most fire for perceived self-dealing. Mayor Arthur C. Harper promised the Democratic League that he would look into the situation . . . only to find himself recalled in a special election in March of 1909.

Chandler—behind the scenes, as usual—orchestrated a rebuttal to the Democratic League's charges. He instructed Sherman to send him a letter of defense that he could excerpt in the *Times*. The general mailed back a reply on behalf of himself and fellow water commissioners. The memo included arguments made by a top lawyer apparently recommended by Chandler. "It seems to me now is the time to 'nail' the 'enemy,'" Sherman added confidentially, his disgust evident. "They must have fired their last 'gun' by this time, although they may have more 'rot' up their sleeves."

But the opposition was just getting started. Starting in April 1909, the *Record* eviscerated Sherman with a barrage of near-daily attacks targeting his financial interest in the syndicate, including one under the headline "GEN. SHERMAN MUST RESIGN FROM THE WATER BOARD."

> A member of the water board is shown to be the business associate of members of a land speculating syndicate, which will measure its profits according to the disposition of the water from the San Fernando reservoirs. . . . No additional reasons need to be advanced to establish the entire impropriety of General Sherman retaining his position on the water board.

The *Record* also published open letters to new mayor George Alexander, urging him to demand Sherman's immediate resignation. As Mayor Alexander dickered, the *Record* turned up the heat, savaging both men (and other potentates) in its June 2 edition with an editorial cartoon titled "Moses in L.A. Bullrushes." There was "Baby Moses"—the baby had Sherman's adult face—floating down a river in a basket, reaching out to Mayor Alexander on the riverbank. "Will This 'Moses' Be Rescued?" asked the caption. Alexander, dressed like a high priest, pretended not to see Moses through the thick bullrushes, whose cattails were made up of the heads (and name tags) of the syndicate's most well-known investors, including Otis and Huntington. "My, but those rushes are thick," cartoon Alexander remarked.

Eventually, the mayor got the message. On July 20, he came out in favor of removing Sherman from the board but failed to muster enough votes from the Los Angeles City Council. Meanwhile, the more the *Record* tried to humiliate Sherman, the more he dug in his heels. He refused to "resign under fire," threatening to take his case to the highest court.

Privately, Sherman expressed thanks to Otis and Chandler for defending him in the *Times* but allowed that the attacks were taking a toll. "I was very foolish to ever accept this office," he said. "It takes a great deal of my time, and it takes a great deal of patience to perform the duties that come to my associates and myself." The tension only intensified. Normally friendly periodicals now openly questioned the wisdom of having someone with a large stake in arid Valley lands also being in charge of water distribution. After rejecting more requests to step down, Sherman was finally sacked by the City Council on January 20, 1910. His position on the commission was vacated, then replaced.

Of course, Chandler's hands were just as dirty. "He had inside information from Moses," says historian Abraham Hoffman. "Chandler's land syndicate bought property close to where the aqueduct would come in, in the [San Fernando] Valley." But like a scene out of a Vaudeville pie-throwing sketch, the targets never smeared Chandler's face—always someone else's. "Father was the one who had the ideas to start [the syndicate], but he never had his name on anything, because he didn't want to be connected," recalled his daughter May Goodan. "He wasn't a man who wanted to take the lead," Haskell concurred, echoing statements from Chandler that he dodged the limelight to avoid accusations of impropriety due to his role at the *Times*.

Sure enough, even though Chandler was the chairman of the Los Angeles Suburban Homes Co., his name was not associated with it, either in the *Record's* cartoon flaying Sherman or in other newspapers announcing the deal. When the *Times* finally got around to writing about the group, it name-dropped thirteen bankers and industrialists as "a partial list of the members of the syndicate." There was no mention of the five controlling members—Chandler, Otis, Sherman, Hobart Whitley, and Otto Brant, president of a title company. There was also no mention of well-known investors Huntington and Eli Clark. Only after outrage subsided were all the partners revealed.

Overall, the Los Angeles Suburban Homes Co. was

comprised of thirty shareholders, each contributing a $25,000 down payment toward a $2.5 million pot. It was the largest land transaction ever recorded in Los Angeles County. Typically, a spokesperson would be made available to discuss a high-profile sale of this nature. But that would expose Chandler to criticism. Thus, all quotations in the *Times* about the Suburban Homes Co. were attributed to anonymous parties or couched in the passive voice. "It was stated yesterday by one of the members of the purchasing syndicate that it has two purposes in mind," the *Times* printed. "One, of course, is to make money; the other is to afford an opportunity for home-makers to secure desirable land close to Los Angeles at a reasonable price." This suburbia blurb parroted the announcement of the San Fernando Mission Land Co.'s purchase of the Porter tract in 1903. "The syndicate will build highways and establish towns, to be sold in parcels to suit buyers."

Back behind his *Times* desk, Chandler tallied up the newspaper's ad sales figures, always a good barometer of L.A.'s success. He noticed a ten percent uptick in the number of advertising columns bought through July 31, 1909—after the Suburban Homes Co. announcement—compared with the first seven months of 1908. In the paper's business section, the *Times* ascribed these "significant business gains" to three bullish developments in Los Angeles: the continuing influx of investors and tourists; the coming municipal aqueduct; and, if early polls were accurate, the imminent annexations of San Pedro and Wilmington, which would finally provide Los Angeles with a world-class seaport.

CHAPTER 12

Ready Suitors

ON MAY 26, 1906—six months before the election in which Los Angeles annexed the Shoestring Strip—delegates of the newly convened Los Angeles Consolidation Committee met with the San Pedro Chamber of Commerce. Even though San Pedro and Wilmington were not on the ballot for that November's election, it was clear to all that if the strip vote went through, L.A. would be gunning for the port cities next. That was, after all, the whole point of the umbilicus. The consolidation commission asked its San Pedro counterpart to draft talking points with its citizens on the advantages of uniting with the City of Angels. Chief among them, Los Angeles would continue to improve the harbor in ways that dinky San Pedro could not in the form of citywide bond issuances. With the Panama Canal estimated to be completed in less than a decade, an international port would bring more trade, more jobs, and a more prosperous future to all of Southern California.

Concurrently, members of L.A.'s most prominent bodies—including its own Chamber of Commerce, Board of Supervisors, City Council, and merchant groups with whom Harry Chandler counseled—joined forces with the Consolidation Committee to meet with Governor George Pardee. Their goal was to request special legislation that would amend the California constitution to allow for the consolidation of two or more contiguous municipalities. (Technically, a union of Los Angeles, San Pedro, and Wilmington would be a "consolidation," since all three were cities. "Annexation" referred to unincorporated land. Both terms came to be used interchangeably.) A voter-approved consolidation law would also open the door for other Southland cities looking to join Los Angeles.

The delegation achieved its mission. The consolidation proposition was put to Los Angeles voters. Though it didn't pass the first time around in 1907, it eventually garnered enough support. The stage was set for a citywide consolidation vote of San Pedro and Wilmington in the summer of 1909, the same period in which the Los Angeles Suburban Homes Co. bought up most of the southern half of the San Fernando Valley.

Alarmingly for L.A.'s ruling class, however, the consolidation movement among San Pedroans—also empowered to vote—was trending in the wrong direction. Four months before the August 12 election, straw polls indicated more "antis" than "pros." Ultimately, it was expected that the sheer volume of favorable Angeleno voters would more than compensate for the thousand or so registered voters in Pedro. But what if the negative feelings of that city's voting bloc bled into L.A.'s? Also, from a public relations standpoint, it was important to send a clear message to future communities—and frankly, all of Greater Los Angeles—that San Pedro was equally excited about the union, rather than being portrayed as a defenseless seaside colony conquered by a bullying big sister.

Many San Pedro residents remained concerned that, once subsumed by Angel City, the town would be scrubbed clean of its hard edges. The Consolidation Committee had already vowed to clean up the "deplorable conditions brought about by saloons." Taverns dominated downtown, many of them open at all hours. Respectable couples were known to avoid the main part of Pedro to get to church, lest they stumble over drunks in the streets. But saloons also had an affiliation with labor unions, whose control extended to docks, workplaces, and school boards. Cognizant of the pubs' power, the committee held several negotiations with saloon owners. Only after proprietors were reassured that their liquor licenses would not be revoked did they come around to supporting admission to Los Angeles, though they did make a show of condemning consolidation to appease barflies and bartenders.

In the weeks before the election, the tide began to turn. Newspapers and community leaders from San Pedro and Los Angeles ran education campaigns. Even neighboring Long Beach, which had a historically litigious relationship with San Pedro over waterfront rights, supported consolidation, a stance reaffirmed by a respected reverend, F. M. Rogers. "I believe traffic will grow so that everybody will realize the absolute need for our harbor," he said. "With the completion of the Panama Canal, San Pedro harbor will not be near big enough. . . . Long Beach, San Pedro and Wilmington harbors will be like the old lady's hair, 'You can't tell which from switch.' The harbors will become one." When L.A. Mayor George Alexander showed up to a South Bay rally on the eve of the election, he received a minutes-long ovation. Annexation supporters heaved a sigh of relief. San Pedro had finally caught the fever as vehicles flew consolidation pennants and soused citizens buzzed through town with consolidation pins. The town even dropped its request for borough-like self-governance.

San Pedro's final tally stood at 726 for and 227 against. In little-populated Wilmington, the outcome was 107 to 61 in favor. Angelenos carried the vote in a landslide. Papers were filed with the Secretary of State for ratification on August 28, 1909. Between Wilmington's 9.93 square miles and San Pedro's 4.61 square miles, Los Angeles ballooned to seventy-five square miles. San Pedro Harbor was redesignated Los Angeles Harbor, and a newly created Board of Harbor Commissioners would tap $30 million from voter-approved measures to improve the port between 1910 and 1924. At last, Los Angeles could now be included in the pantheon of global seaport cities—New York; Buenos Aires; Bombay; Shanghai; London; Antwerp; New Orleans; and, of course, San Francisco. Leave it to Chandler to somehow spin the beautifully natural bay of L.A.'s upstate rival into a negative asset. When a visiting engineer checked out California's two main anchorages, Harry was delighted by the man's preference for Los Angeles's. "A man-made harbor is as you want it," said the engineer, "whereas a natural harbor is makeshift. It's the difference between a built house and a cave." *The Saturday Evening Post* characterized Angelenos' view of their city as "the man-made end of California," with the Bay Area "the God-made end." Chandler could be forgiven if he saw this comparison as a point of pride. That a city lacking in abundant natural resources had come this far in such a short time was a masterstroke largely made possible by Gilded Age-bred torchbearers like Harry.

The additions of San Pedro and Wilmington, combined with the guarantee of Owens Valley water, set up a row of suitors jostling to marry into Los Angeles. Colegrove was first in line. The district just south of Hollywood never did incorporate like its northern neighbor; it had been angling to join L.A. ever since Sherman's Los Angeles-Pacific line pierced its border. The area's jagged 8.72 miles looked like the state of Idaho flipped upside down. Its upper section stretched from, alternately, then-Prospect and Fountain Avenues down to Wilshire Boulevard. A panhandle ran south of Wilshire along Arlington Avenue, ending at Jefferson Boulevard—much of today's Arlington Heights. Its western border was fixed at Seward Street; to the east, it hugged the northwest corner of L.A.'s original territory. Though it was founded by former California Senator Cornelius Cole, Colegrove was actually named after his wife, Olive Colegrove. In 1909, it was an increasingly popular place to live, home to 10,000 residents. It also maintained a thriving lemon industry, inspiring Lemon Grove Avenue, whose name has survived to the present. (More famously, so has Vine Street, named after Cole's vineyard.)

Within days of the consolidation of the harbor towns, Cole met with the Board of Trade to map out a strategy for merging with Los Angeles. Improved streets, schools, and water services were the main benefits cited. There was not a dissenting voice in the room. The ex-senator, also a lawyer for the Hancock family (of Hancock Park fame), carried enough clout to petition L.A.'s governing body to call for an annexation election on October 19, 1909—an extremely fast turnaround. Only 6,683 votes were cast in Los Angeles. This was a far cry from the 65,000 Angelenos who participated two months earlier for the more important San Pedro-Wilmington referendum, though, as subsequent years would bear out, special-election apathy seemed to be setting in. Nonetheless, the result was satisfactorily lopsided. Angelenos voted affirmatively by an 18 to 1 margin (Colegrove's precinct was 5 to 1). On the downside, Colegrove suffered the fate of many districts that were now guided by L.A.'s city council: a loss of identity. While Cole Street still lives on, Colegrove Avenue was dropped for Santa Monica Boulevard. By the 1920s, the neighborhood of Colegrove disappeared altogether as realtors, seeking to capitalize on the popularity of Hollywood, began to call the Hollywood-adjacent portion South Hollywood, with outlying areas given other names.

Next it was Hollywood's turn to fall in line. Encouraged by Colegrove's fate, Hollywood Mayor George Dunlop implemented a playbook virtually identical to the one Cole devised. "At a joint meeting of the directors of the Board of Trade and the City Trustees [last night]," the *Los Angeles Times* reported on November 16, 1909, "it was decided to call a public meeting at once and to push the plans for immediate consolidation with Los Angeles with the utmost vigor." Hollywood had only been autonomous since 1903, but it was already experiencing troubling developments that couldn't be fixed by its modest tax base. And the last thing messieurs Chandler, Sherman, and Whitley wanted—recall their huge investments in the Hollywood Hills—was a bankrupt town that would suffocate growth. The problem wasn't just a reliable water supply, but a dilapidated sewer system. Wedged against the Santa Monica Mountains, northern Hollywood was vulnerable to floods during heavy rainstorms. When its conduits overflowed, rivers of raw sewage swamped streets and front yards. In fact, Hollywood's inability to control its own effluence had been a continual point of contention for residents of Colegrove, who had the misfortune of living downstream. The Consolidation Committee pledged that L.A. would fix Hollywood's infrastructure problems, which would result in only minimal tax bumps for the town's 5,000 residents.

The vote to determine Hollywood's fate was held on January 24, 1910. It would have been an uneventful day if not for a scandal that turned heads and caused election officials at Precinct No. 30 to "gasp." Three well-dressed young women marched into the polling place, announcing that they were there to cast a vote for the annexation of Hollywood.

"But my dear young ladies," said a flushed official. "You can't vote."

"Oh, yes, we can," one of them replied, cheerfully disregarding the laws of the day. "We know exactly how to do it."

"Are you registered?" asked the precinct judge.

"Certainly," said another woman. "And christened, too."

This drew chuckles from the male clerks. Despite further pleas from the ladies, they would need to wait ten more years before their voices would legally count.

The election results were another one-sided affair, meeting with the approval of 6,224 L.A. voters versus 373 opposers. In Hollywood: 409 for, 18 against. With fanfare that resembled a wedding, a victory banquet brought together 250 guests from both sides of the civic aisle—librarians and high school principals, judges and city councilmen—to cheer the cities' union. The suddenly unemployed Hollywood mayor, George Dunlop, spoke for his constituents when he averred, "The highest consideration that influenced the people of Hollywood for the consolidation was the desire to participate in what they believed is destined to be the greatest city of modern times." George Alexander also gave a toast. "This is the pleasantest occasion I have experienced since I became mayor of Los Angeles," he said. He was one of many leaders who praised Hollywood's upstanding citizenry. "The highest class of intelligence," agreed R. D. Wade, a Los Angeles administrator. "The finest class of people in the county," echoed another speaker. One of the first things the L.A. City Council did was change the name of Prospect Avenue to

Hollywood Boulevard. Acknowledging Hollywood's predilection for piety, the council rebuffed various requests for poolroom and liquor licenses in the region. Perhaps no one was happier about the consolidation than the trio of Sherman, Chandler, and Whitley. In anticipation of a favorable election, Dunlop pointed to a healthy uptick in real estate sales over the last three months, far more compared to the prior twelve.

"I do not know how much more of Los Angeles County we shall annex," winked Mayor Alexander at the banquet. That very same day—February 18, 1910—Los Angeles held yet another annexation election for an adjacent territory. Located east of Western and Normandie Avenues, the East Hollywood Addition encompassed 11.11 square miles—almost triple Hollywood's 4.45 square miles—but was far less populated. Much of it included Griffith Park, the 3,000-acre mountainous sanctuary gifted to the city by Colonel Griffith J. Griffith. The acreage abutted miles of riverfront property along the Los Angeles River, with an eastern border hugging Santa Fe Railroad tracks along San Fernando Road (lying on the other side was Glendale, incorporated in 1906). Farther south, the East Hollywood Addition enfolded Ivanhoe and Edendale, two vestigial communities in the Silver Lake area whose names live on as a school, a street, a reservoir, and a post office.

On the morning of the election, newspapers published a statement from Mayor Alexander. Concerned about poor turnout from an election-weary populace, he tried to motivate voters by freezing city assets. "San Pedro harbor improvement bonds and other municipal matters of great weight have been held in abeyance until we could adopt East Hollywood," he warned. Allowing admittance would also secure an important link between Los Angeles and Griffith Park, a popular destination for pleasure outings that was in serious need of safety improvements. The mayor's scare tactics didn't really work; turnout was an anemic 3,633 in Los Angeles, with only 194 of those from East Hollywood. But once again, the outcome was never in question. Eight days after the election, the city attorney declared the territory part of L.A. and sent a certificate to the Secretary of State for verification.

No doubt the crown jewel of this new appendage was Griffith Park. It meant that Los Angeles was now home to the largest urban park in the nation. An all-day celebration was held on March 5, 1910, at the foot of the park's Mount Hollywood. After sitting through speeches by various pooh-bahs, 1,800 guests were treated to a picnic and live music. Adventuresome types were invited to go "mountain climbing"—these days, we'd simply call it hiking—up the Mount Hollywood trail, "which has been placed in excellent repair and offers an exhilarating climb."

Several days after one newspaper assured readers that annexation elections were done for several years, the *Times* broke news that "another election is in sight." Looking to merge with Los Angeles, the Arroyo Seco-adjacent districts of Bairdstown and Hermon filed petitions to piggyback on an April 14 special ballot for harbor bonds. The April 14 date was important to the Census Bureau; any new territories would have to be annexed before April 15 in order to be included in L.A.'s 1910 population figures.

In the end, the deadline was just too tight, and the two communities' fates would have to wait. It was just as well. The carousel of towns and territories wanting to join the City of Angels had become exhausting, resulting in nearly monthly elections and strained city resources. Now was the time to pause and take stock of just how far Los Angeles had come by the close of the twentieth century's first decade. At 101 square miles, it was the fifth largest city in America. And with a steady arrival of 30,000-plus newcomers each year, L.A.'s population had spiked to 319,198. This was still short of San Francisco's 416,912. But from 1900 to 1910, the city's growth soared 211 percent compared to San Francisco's twenty-two percent. For Chandler's Million Population Club to become a reality, the peddlers of paradise would need to do over the next decade what they had done so far: expand the metropolis that shouldn't exist through unceasing avarice, boosterism, and sheer force of will.

CHAPTER 13

The Big Ditch

"HE IS THE MOSES to whom we look to lead us out of the wilderness of any doubt as to the future of the [water] supply," wrote *Graphic* magazine. "The people believe in Bill Mulholland." The deification of L.A.'s water chief by print media only intensified after the passage of $23 million in aqueduct bonds in 1907. On July 1 of that year—not even three weeks after the election—the Water Board approved Mulholland "to make such trips as necessary in connection with your duties as an executive of the Los Angeles Aqueduct." The fifty-two-year-old superintendent took advantage of his granted freedom whenever he could. He still felt most at home in the field, away from incompetent department draftsmen and the "pinheads in Los Angeles" who tripped him up with red tape. Add to that the constant reprobation from unappreciative Angelenos: The homeowner in Boyle Heights who wrongly insisted that his drinking water contained diphtheria. The owner of a boiler company who demanded compensation to fix his well after a water crew blasted under his property. The spurious accusations of flawed water meters resulting in higher rates. Or any of the endless "complaints from old women." Mulholland often responded to these gripes himself, in letters or visits. As the architect of L.A.'s complex waterworks, he took every little slight personally, and thus only a personal response would do.

But now he didn't have time for such mundane affairs. Awaiting him was nothing less than the fourth largest civil engineering project in American history—a canal that would exceed the totality of the Roman aqueducts—all under the guidance of an autodidact intent on directly supervising its construction.

Reminiscent of L.A.'s miles of pipes, much of Mulholland's vision was mapped out in his head. Even for something as complex as the aqueduct, he would rely on his familiar habit of vocalizing what he wanted, or working out solutions in the dirt with a stick. Before departing for another trip to Owens Valley in November 1907, Mulholland approved the site of the San Fernando Reservoir in Sylmar, downstream from the future Cascades spillway that would mark the end of the aqueduct's 233-mile journey. He also settled on a reservoir and hydroelectric station to be built in San Francisquito Canyon, twenty-five miles north of the spillway. Money generated from the plant was projected to help pay down the aqueduct's costs. Years later, San Francisquito Canyon would play an ill-fated role in Mulholland's career and the lives of hundreds of canyon dwellers.

In Mulholland's defense, part of the tragedy that awaited him could be laid at the feet of his old friend Fred Eaton. The man who turned Mulholland on to Owens Valley in the first place planned to retire there one day, provided the townsfolk didn't string him up first. Back in 1905, Eaton had nabbed fifty miles of real estate along the Owens River, including 22,000 acres of ranchland known as Long Valley. It was, in Eaton's view, the ideal spot for a dam and reservoir. Mulholland agreed. But in the midst of working out details to transfer options from his name to the city of Los Angeles, Eaton decided to hold onto Long Valley and inflate his asking price. This was strictly a power play driven by pure greed. Los Angeles owned three quarters of the Owens Valley watershed and needed the final quarter from Eaton to build a catch basin near the intake of L.A.'s water. Even after Mulholland made a personal appeal, Eaton wouldn't release Long Valley for less than $1 million. Not only was this beyond the scope of Mulholland's budget, but it demonstrated blatantly bad faith. Mulholland wrote Eaton's adult son as much. "Since your father was acting as Agent for the City in the purchasing of lands at the time that you contracted with the State for this land," he conveyed, "such contract was made in view of having the City in prospect as an ultimate purchaser and that your price, in honor, should be scaled accordingly." But Eaton did not scale accordingly; he figured the longer the city dilly-dallied, the more valuable his property would become. Mulholland finally just threw up his hands, banking on the courts to secure the property: "When we want that power, we will condemn it." The courts never did warrant L.A.'s seizure of Long Valley. As more time passed, Bill's own bullheadedness got in the way of further negotiations with Fred, their friendship irreparably harmed. Consequently, instead of building a large reservoir near the aqueduct's headwaters, Mulholland would settle on the reservoir in San Francisquito Canyon—220 miles away but worryingly close to communities in the Santa Clara River corridor. One can't avoid thinking about the fateful machinations at play here: Eaton was doing to Los Angeles what Los Angeles had done to Owens Valley. When it was time for the bill to come due, karma would demand payment.

By December 1907, the first influx of aqueduct funds enabled work to properly commence. Mulholland's daunting checklist to construct the gravity-driven concrete channel brought its magnitude home: 280 miles of pipeline; six million pounds of dynamite; forty-three miles of tunnels; and 500 miles of roads to transport machinery, materials, and men through a mostly harsh desert landscape whose temperatures ranged from 120 degrees to below freezing. For his own transportation, Mulholland began shopping around for a personal automobile. Gen. Moses Sherman got wind of this and tried to sell him his. "It's as good as new, having only been used seven or eight months," he wrote. "It cost me $4,750.00. . . . You can get it for $2,500.00, and if you do not want to pay that much, then you shall name the price." Just as important were reliable beasts of burden to haul pipes in tight quarters where tractors couldn't go. Unsatisfied with the mangy mules picked out by the city, Mulholland assigned two councilmen with livestock experience to travel to Kansas City, whose Lathrop district was the "Mule Capital of the World." Two hundred sixty-one fine-looking mules were shipped on stock cars to the windblown outpost of Mojave, meeting with the Chief's satisfaction. "The best lot of mules ever brought across the Rockies," one of the councilmen beamed.

Mulholland's timeline of when the project would be completed varied, usually hovering around five years. Progress was often tied to the availability of capital. But because it was a municipal project that only sparingly contracted out work, Mulholland was able to control expenses. He proved to be an excellent steward of the city's money, his vigilance and resourcefulness drawing national attention. New York City's water commissioner, C. A. Shaw, marveled at Bill's progress compared to his own city's Catskill Aqueduct, which broke ground around the same time. Despite being seventy miles shorter and traveling over less challenging terrain, the Catskill Aqueduct would take four extra years to complete at eight times the price ($177 million versus $23 million). One big difference: Los Angeles chose to buy out private property early on, rather than waiting (and hoping) for courts to issue condemnation edicts, which would've dragged out the schedule and upped the costs.

The *Los Angeles Times* actively kept its readers abreast of the "Big Ditch," wowing them with engineering derring-do, which distracted from the miasma of unscrupulous land dealings well-covered by this point by other dailies. Harry Chandler had scribes send dispatches from the field. These accounts reinforced Mulholland's savant-like recall. "I never saw him make a note or refer to a note," reporter Allen Kelly observed, "yet at any point in the whole 250 miles he could show just where the line was located and tell the exact elevation as rapidly as a man can tell his own name and age." The prodigious project often required the use of untested equipment, such as a dredger coined "Big Bill" by the workers—a nod to Mulholland's high regard for the machine. Another new tractor was nicknamed by Bill himself. Enthralled by its amazing traction abilities, Mulholland allegedly remarked, "The damn thing looks like a caterpillar." The name stuck. The Chief ordered twenty-eight "caterpillar" tractors, but these early models were all rendered useless after sand clogged their gears. Meanwhile, the biggest excavation job was the five-and-a-half-mile Elizabeth Tunnel, billed as the world's second-longest aqueduct tunnel. Hard gneiss rock and granite were no match against the indurate Irish Moses. "I'm going into this as a man in the army goes into war because it would be cowardly to quit," Mulholland proclaimed, invoking jargon that must've warmed Gen. Harrison Otis's hawkish heart. "Nature is the squarest fighter there is, and I wanted the fight."

Left off local pages was reportage of hard living by the hired hands who occupied fifty-seven camps. Mulholland once surmised that, at any given time, a worker was drunk, asleep, or hungover. After being paid anywhere from two to seventy dollars a week, many laborers blew through their pay in a single night at nearby saloons. "Let me know when that's gone," one worker uttered to a bartender after handing over his paycheck. "Whiskey built the aqueduct," Mulholland conceded. But he didn't blame the men. Tunnel cave-ins, rockslides, falls, and blasting accidents were just some of the hazards on an extremely dangerous job, and the men needed an outlet. Many a night out ended in a barroom brawl. Those with money to spare played poker in backrooms or frequented brothels. Mojave was a notorious den of vice. The Los Angeles Board of Public Works appealed to Kern County to bust up its bordellos and bars, but the sheriff refused. The state finally passed a law that prohibited saloons from operating within four miles of worker settlements. After thirty taverns were forced to close, the men simply walked an extra mile to find more booze. And if they couldn't go into town for action, sometimes the action came to them. Come nightfall, one enterprising pimp/gambler was known to steer his horse-drawn wagon alongside the aqueduct, trolling the camps. Inside his gussied-up carriage, clients were offered either games of chance or a few minutes of "alone time" with the procurer's special lady.

Back in the trenches, a spirit of camaraderie prevailed. Mulholland was a taskmaster, but a generally well-liked one. Prone to rolling up his sleeves and joining his team in the dirt and grime, he hadn't changed much since rooting around a muddy L.A. River to save Christmas in 1889. "It has always been a great pride with me that I have been able to secure and retain the loyal devotion of my coworkers," he said. One way he kept his workers motivated was by dangling carrots. Shift bosses, motormen, miners, timbermen, and tunnel drillers could earn bonuses for completing more than an "average day's work" in twenty-four hours. Mulholland figured out that the extra cash expended moved up the project's timeline, thus saving the city money in the end. He also appealed to the men's egos through friendly competitions. The Elizabeth Tunnel owes its success to this practice. Mulholland assigned two different crews on either end of the mountainside. Whoever reached the middle first would earn a bonus on top of the daily bonuses they could already make. As a result, a job that was expected to take five years was completed in three-and-a-half. (The south crew earned bragging rights, by the way, but only because the north crew encountered more groundwater, which needed to be pumped out.) Even factoring in bonuses, Mulholland was able to shave twenty percent off the tunnel's budget. "With the completion of this tunnel, William Mulholland can sit back and twiddle his thumbs a little while," said one newspaper back in Los Angeles. Hardly. Dozens more tunnels were being excavated with unprecedented speed. Two of them broke international records that were held by tunnel drillers in Switzerland.

By the summer of 1910, Mulholland had completed almost twenty-five percent of his artificial river. He was bequeathed a new sobriquet, the "Goethals of the West," a nod to George Washington Goethals, the directing engineer of the in-progress Panama Canal. But Mulholland's momentum abruptly halted when a market correction dried up capital. He was forced to shed three quarters of his workforce and mothball the entire project until conditions changed. While the Chief waited out this financial drought, the Los Angeles oligarchy continued to pad its wealth. But it would soon be put to a deadly test.

CHAPTER 14

Explosive Changes

IT WAS THE LAST. "The last harvest on the last of the famous ranches in California!" the *Los Angeles Times* exclaimed. "The last crop to be garnered on the largest single wheat field in the State, before it is cut up!" And "the last time" cowboys would round up horses, now "vanished before the advance of civilization." In 1910, the newspaper began to trickle out more information about the former 47,500-acre property once owned by Isaac Van Nuys and optioned by, well, no one quite knew *who* yet. The *Times* still relied on euphemisms like "the management company" for the Los Angeles Suburban Homes Co.'s five principal investors, which included its own Harry Chandler and Gen. Harrison Otis. Only newspapers outside of Los Angeles, like *The Pomona Progress*, regularly roll-called Chandler, Otis, Gen. Moses Sherman, Otto Brant, and Hobart Whitley. (Investor Henry Huntington was not one of the principals.) Then, over the next few months, advertisements for the housing development suddenly identified Whitley as its General Manager. Interested parties were encouraged to write or telephone his office on Main Street.

If ever there was any doubt as to the syndicate's future success, they were quelled on June 1, 1910. Starting at six o'clock that morning, sales agents for the subdivision opened their doors to early-bird buyers interested in acquiring tracts in the waning wheatfield. As added urgency, parties had only thirty days to make an offer (after the thirty-day window, grain-harvesting season would begin and sales would not resume until the fall). The first day saw a stampede of buyers, evoking, noted one newspaper, the "land-hungry men and women at the Federal land

openings" of the homestead era. Real estate clerks were still field-
ing offers at midnight, setting "a new record for land selling."

Later that summer, the invisible hands of Chandler and Otis
teased more information about the erasure of the last frontier.
"The time has come when the [former] great ranches must support thousands of people," the *Times* said. "There will be an entire
town in the future," to be served by a major "asphalt boulevard"
running across the Valley, with proximity to unlimited water.
"The tunnel where the Owens River water will enter the valley
lies just above the fields that have never yet been watered." Pub-
licizing this new subdivision at the foot of William Mulholland's
aqueduct did yield one unintended consequence: the vilification
of Mulholland, who was lumped in with the wealthy land barons
by members of the Socialist party and Democratic League. The
Chief angrily denied that he was "in collusion with the leaders
of those syndicates." In truth, Mulholland viewed his relationship
with the syndicate members as "indifferent," even "unfriendly." He
was outraged that Valley parcels were being sold for such exorbi-
tant prices in order to build "rich men's country estates," and was
so confident of his innocence, he welcomed a full investigation.
The only tract he owned was 640 acres near far-flung Chatsworth,
which he had bought for his five children. Yet as the face and name
behind the aqueduct, there was a feeling that he somehow must
be guilty by association. Even today, casual students of Southern
California history mischaracterize Mulholland as the nefarious
brains behind the whole scheme. True, as a loyal civil servant he
toed the line with carefully crafted public stances. And he did indeed buy in to the aqueduct and deceive his share of farmers. But
it was Fred Eaton who concocted the "rape" of Owens Valley, city
officials who approved the plan, federal reclamation reps who betrayed Inyo County, and other people—like Chandler and company—who grew rich from the water. In an interview decades later,
none other than *Chinatown* screenwriter Robert Towne said he
had Harry Chandler in mind when he created the amoral king-
pin Noah Cross, not William Mulholland. Chandler's phlegmatic

personality bore no resemblance to the unctuous Cross, but he probably would've smiled at the comparison. Mulholland and Eaton notwithstanding, Chandler never objected when certain members of the media crowned him the true "Father of the Los Angeles Aqueduct."

Labor lawyer Job Harriman knew who the real foes were. As a mayoral candidate for the Socialist party, Harriman came down hard on Chandler and Otis. Besides using their newspaper as propaganda, they masterminded a capitalist cabal that stood to profit from taxpayers once the aqueduct opened. But any outrage among progressives was snuffed out on October 1, 1910. That's when Harriman and the city's pro-labor coterie suddenly found themselves on defense after an act of unspeakable horror visited *L.A. Times'* headquarters.

On the evening of September 30, Chandler was prepared to "put the paper to bed" sometime past midnight as was his custom. Earlier that day, someone deposited a suitcase packed with dynamite in an alleyway next to The Fortress (aka the *Times* building). The alley shared a wall that ran up to Chandler's and Otis's offices. At 1:07 A.M., The Fortress blew up in a giant fireball, reducing most of the building to rubble. Twenty-one employees were killed, dozens more hurt. Chandler was not among them. In a stroke of luck, his wife Marian had convinced him to come home early. (Reports differ on whether he left around 7 P.M. to attend the theatre with her, or whether she stormed into his office around 12:45 A.M. to drag him home.) Chandler was still up when the detonation rocked his house's foundation in nearby Bunker Hill. However, Chandler's secretary, J. Wesley Reaves, had the misfortune of taking over his boss's vacated desk when Harry went home. The explosion ripped off his head and limbs.

That same night, a bomb was placed against Otis's residence. In another lucky happenstance, the general was not home; he was in Mexico, and his house was spared when its occupants heard a strange ticking sound and called the police. The cops took the device to a park, where it discharged.

Two Union activist brothers, John and James McNamara—members of the International Association of Bridge and Structural Iron Workers—later confessed to the crime and their desire to "get General Otis." But in the smoldering hours after the bombing, the *Times* didn't need to wait for a trial to know who was behind the carnage. Otis rushed back to L.A. and made sure that his newspaper would still be published that morning, even if it was only four pages printed at another paper's facility. "UNIONIST BOMBS WRECK THE TIMES" screamed its headline. "They can kill our men and can wreck our buildings," wrote Harry Andrews, the paper's managing editor, "but by the God above they cannot kill the *Times*." The war between labor and capital had come to a head, and labor was the clear-cut loser. Job Harriman's prospects to become L.A.'s first Socialist mayor also died that night. His reputation was further sullied when he agreed to represent the McNamara brothers at their trial.

The tragedy permanently tattooed the *Times* leaders as vehement anti-unionists. In the immediate aftermath, Otis refused bodyguards, not wanting to look weak in the eyes of the murderers. The general rebuilt The Fortress to make it more imposing than ever, etching the phrase "True Industrial Freedom" into its façade. Chandler placed a copper box in a cornerstone of the building to memorialize the dead. The reverberations lasted over a hundred years and multiple generations of Otis-Chandler family ownership. After shooting down numerous attempts by its newsroom to unionize, *Times* management finally relented to their staff's right to organize in 2019.

Huntington, too, could now point to unionists as an anarchic force. Though he paid his trolley employees generously and treated them to many perks, he had long made clear that anyone who attempted to unionize would be fired on the spot. He was also known to employ strikebreakers and labor spies. Otis broadcast Huntington's beliefs in the *Times* on several occasions. "I believe in free labor, and shall employ no man who owes allegiance to a labor organization," Henry asserted in a column from 1904.

"There is not a union man on our payroll now. I cannot trust a union man because he is not a free agent." Privately, Huntington was even more emphatic. "Trade-Unionism," he wrote Otis in 1912, "has become a positive menace to our general prosperity to individual right and to the lawful pursuit of happiness."

The bombing also gave Mulholland license to claim the moral high road. One day after the McNamaras confessed their crime, the Chief spoke at a luncheon hosted by the City Club. He received a standing ovation from 300 members. Egged on by the crowd, Mulholland skewered Job Harriman, who, he pointed out, owned more land in Southern California than Bill's scrubby little patch in a corner of the Valley. He then pretended to forget the slogan of Job's failed mayoral campaign, "The Coming Victory." "Oh, what was it called?" Mulholland strained. "The Coming Calamity?" This brought the house down. He concluded with a now-famous bon mot that mocked Harriman's achievements against his own: "You might discredit me or disbelieve me if I were to say that the aqueduct will last as long as the pyramids of Egypt or the Parthenon of Athens," he quipped. "But I will tell you that the aqueduct will at least endure until Job Harriman is elected Mayor of the City of Los Angeles." Harriman would later bail the L.A. scene and establish the experimental socialist compound Llano del Rio in the high desert.

Despite the *Times* bombing, Chandler held to his maxim of "Forward, March!" His Suburban Homes syndicate didn't miss a beat subdividing its San Fernando Valley acreage into tracts and communities. On November 3, 1910, the *Times* published an advertorial under the header "The Sale of the Century." It promoted two "mammoth" auctions to unload 2,000 horses and mules left over from the former Van Nuys estate. In addition, fifty mowing machines, thirty hay rakes, twenty-five tank wagons, ten cultivators, six tractor engines, and hundreds of other farming items would be up for bid. The turnout at both auctions was a "scene to stagger the imagination." The Valley's last great agricultural fiefdom had a lineage that traced back to Isaac Van Nuys, his father-in-law Isaac Lankershim, and, before them, Pio Pico, the last governor of California under Mexican rule. Now, the purging was complete. When the *Times* proclaimed it "the beginning of a new empire and a new era in the Southland," for once, it wasn't hyperbole. General Manager Hobart Whitley announced that land sales would reopen for good just after the New Year.

The year 1910 was also a boon to Los Angeles's southern front. Ever since San Pedro and Wilmington joined the consolidation club in the summer of '09, the Shoestring Strip became L.A.'s hot new market. Real estate ads blanketed newspapers. A typical one read:

WHAT TO BUY? BUY REAL ESTATE
WHERE TO BUY? IN THE SHOESTRING STRIP
WHEN TO BUY? BUY NOW.
(LOW RATE OF INTEREST)

Among the selling points for this oblong corridor were its proximity to Los Angeles and the harbor, easy access to Huntington's electric rail lines, and a chance to get in at the bargain rate of $400 per acre. This figure was almost eight times higher than the $53 per acre that Suburban Homes Co. paid for its 47,500 acres in the sparse Valley. (Suburban Homes would soon list the lots for $150 to $600 per acre.) To put L.A.'s growth in perspective, recall that the first Otis-Chandler syndicate—the San Fernando Mission Land Co.—paid $35 per acre for its 16,450-acreage in 1903.

"IF YOU HAVE TEARS, BE SURE TO SHED 'EM NOW FOR THE UNFORTUNATE RICH" jeered a headline in the *Los Angeles Record*. Billing itself as "the only independent newspaper in Los Angeles," the populist periodical ran a series of articles that thumped the wealthy. Special attention was given to their obfuscation of financial assets, which grossly undervalued their net worth with the county assessor's office. After shaming *Los Angeles Express* owner Edwin T. Earl—part of the San Fernando Mission Land Co.—the *Record* cast a critical eye on the troika of Otis, Sherman, and Huntington (the stealthy Chandler slipped under the radar). All three reported their personal property to be worth $1,600 or less. In Sherman's case, the magnate's articles of value were listed as "$000," since he never filed statements with the county. "Gen. M. H. Sherman, who used to be a school teacher but was never in the army," the paper sneered, "HAS NO PERSONAL PROPERTY. That is, he is not DOWN for any on the assessor's books." As for Huntington, he "has picked up the furniture in his house, a few assortments of automobiles and a stable of supposedly fine horses for quite a bargain . . . he lives in simple style in a plain mansion on Oak Knoll, walks on simple Turkish rugs." In point of fact, Huntington's personal balance sheets from 1910 pegged his net worth at $50,483,000, which would make him a billionaire today. He also regularly fudged his financial records, possibly as a hedge against the Los Angeles City Council and the Board of Public Utilities. The agencies, frequently under pressure to create public railways, took a look at his books while exploring an acquisition of his Los Angeles Railway.

But Angelenos continued to have a soft spot for Huntington, who was well-known by virtue of his convenient trolley system. In a poll conducted by the *Record*, Huntington ranked as one of the Most Influential Citizens of Los Angeles, though many were wary of his sway on L.A.'s "city hall, court house, and county." Reader E. A. Wolfe summed up the public's mixed sentiments: "He has developed the country roundabout with his marvelous system of electric lines. He isn't any friend of mine, no sir . . . [but] he has played the most important role in the upbuilding of Los Angeles. When he came here this was a sleepy pueblo, now it is a great city with 300,000 souls, and Huntington got most of them here simply to see them dance and do his bidding." Beyond his railways, however, Huntington remained an enigma, letting his projects speak for themselves. "I never talk about my intentions until they become facts," he told one journalist. "What I am going to do must remain to be told by what I do do."

Mirroring the United States, Los Angeles was at a crossroads in 1910. The city had blossomed during an extended period of relaxed governmental oversight. Tax filers enjoyed no federal income tax, and syndicates took advantage of loose regulatory rules that goosed individual wealth. Citizens started demanding more accountability and a fairer society, leading to more liberal politics. Though candidate Eugene V. Debs of the Socialist Party of America never secured a single vote in the electoral college, he did increase his popular vote count for each of his five presidential runs from 1900 to 1920, the same year that the Nineteenth Amendment enshrined women's right to vote. (Job Harriman was his running mate in 1900.) "One cannot help noting from the reports of the public press all over the country the constantly growing tendency of the employe to seek to co-erce his employer into a more or less abject submission to his (the employe's) will," Huntington wrote Otis during the socialist movement, "by means of that irresponsible and impersonal mouthpiece called a labor leader."

As relics of the Gilded Age, Huntington, Otis, Chandler, and Sherman were, in the eyes of a growing faction, ripe for a reckoning. "M. H. SHERMAN A LOSER BY FIRE" read a cruel *L.A. Record* headline in 1910 after a conflagration wiped out one of Sherman's rail yards. The plutocrats were also proof that familiarity breeds contempt. Just as freeways would become an indispensable (and frustratingly overreliant) way to get around in the latter twentieth century, Huntington's trolleys filled that love/hate role in the early part of the century. By 1910, his streetcar system had reached 1,140 miles—one-third larger than present-day New York City's subway network. As *Record* subscriber E. A. Wolfe alluded to, the tycoon garnered respect, but also resentment for the power he held over an enslaved populace. Author Isaac F. Marcosson, who published the first definitive biography of Huntington in 1914, illustrated the reach of his empire with an apocryphal anecdote. In his book *A Little Known Master of Millions*, he quoted an exchange between a nameless mother and her daughter taking a trolley to the beach. The naive youngster starts the conversation:

"Whose street-car are we riding in?"
"Mr. Huntington's," was the reply.
Passing a park, the little one asked:
"What place is that?"
"Huntington Park."
"Where are we going, mother?" continued the girl.
"To Huntington Beach."
Arriving at the sea, the child, impressed by the sameness
    of all the replies, ventured one more query:
"Mother, does Mr. Huntington own the ocean or does
    that still belong to God?"

It is true that Huntington's specter haunts many of the automotive corridors that make up Greater Los Angeles's roadway system, including freeways. However, his trolley lines themselves often retraced routes forged by Americans settlers, Spanish missionaries, Mexican soldiers, and Indigenous societies. When Pacific Electric's Red Car opened through Cahuenga Pass in 1911, it provided a more accessible link between the San Fernando Valley and the coastal basin, but the route was a latecomer when viewed through the lens of transportation history. Railroads were merely faster means of conveyance alongside well-worn footpaths and wagon roads that had been utilized for centuries. Post-1911, the construction of Cahuenga Boulevard and, subsequently, the Hollywood Freeway (US 101) were the latest iterations to improve upon speed and safety through the pass.

Indeed, as Los Angeles continued to grow, even a thousand miles of trolley tracks weren't enough to get many Angelenos where they wanted to go. Gasoline-powered buses and jitneys—early rideshare vehicles—filled this void in the 1910s just as personal automobiles started to come down in price. By the 1920s, Los Angeles had more cars per capita than any city in the world. As an entrepreneur who prided himself on predicting trends, Huntington initially downplayed automobiles. In a letter from 1904, he mused to a business associate that he didn't see much of

a future for trackless, "trolleyless" cars. But then again, free-rang-
ing vehicles meant freedom of movement. Perhaps on principle
alone, the "peerless trolley king," as the papers called Henry,
could not embrace any mode of transportation that wasn't his,
or didn't deliver passengers to communities in which he had a
financial stake.

Nevertheless, Huntington did start to lessen his rail exposure
in response to shifting trends. Some of his actions were informed
by events leading up to the so-called Great Merger of 1911. E.
H. Harriman, his old Southern Pacific rival, died in 1909. Then,
on May 28, 1910, Sherman and Eli Clark sold their remaining
stock of Los Angeles-Pacific to SP. With the Octopus continuing
to strangle him, Huntington unloaded his fifty percent interest
in interurban lines that he co-owned with Southern Pacific. By
September 1, 1911, SP controlled virtually all inter-city traffic in
the Southland, including Henry's Pacific Electric and Los Angeles
Inter-Urban routes (which became the "new" Pacific Electric). In
return for giving up his interurbans, Huntington convinced SP to
divest of its forty-five percent interest in his intraurban Los Angeles Railway. By this point, LARy operated 222 miles of track and
continued as a reliably profitable operation. Shedding the mon-
ey-sucking interurbans also allowed Huntington to expand his
citywide system. Throughout the decade, he took over other trolley companies, even reabsorbing some former PE/LAIU routes
that SP had no need for. Just three years after the Great Merger,
LARy operated 386 miles and doubled its passenger load, trans-
porting 140 million people a year.

Huntington had another good reason to untether his trolleys.
Again, the interurban lines had always been intended to be a loss
leader, a mechanism to shuttle people to his new subdivisions. By
1910, that goal had largely been achieved. With the rising power
of trade unions and increasing governmental regulations around
private transit, Huntington was more than happy to delegate his
remaining city routes to underlings, allowing him to focus on his
utility and real estate companies. As he withdrew from the public

scene, the sixty-three-year-old oligarch built up an impressive collection of rare books and paintings. This new chapter of his life would come to define his legacy almost as much as his transportation empire helped define Los Angeles.

CHAPTER 15

The Road to Paradise

THE LOS ANGELES SUBURBAN Homes Company officially opened for business on January 9, 1911. Like its name inti-
mated, the development was pitched as a future suburb *of* Los
Angeles, not *outside* Los Angeles, with the company's letterhead
referring to it as "the Northerly Gates of the City." Besides its location only 4.5 miles northwest of L.A. city limits, the former
Rancho ex-Mission San Fernando dominion had plenty to offer: proximity to an aqueduct, scheduled to go online in 1913;
the impending arrival of Pacific Electric cars connecting the San
Fernando Valley to Hollywood; $500 discounts for owners who
made immediate improvements on their parcels; and the opening
of a signature "asphalt paved boulevard" across the Valley floor.
This would be no ordinary country ramble. Inspired by Mexico
City's Paseo de la Reforma and the broad boulevards of Europe,
the Valley's east-west thoroughfare would be the longest paved
street in California within an unincorporated area. Costing half-
a-million dollars, it would stretch fifteen miles and be framed
by ornamental trees and shrubs at Harry Chandler's insistence.
Though a Red Car trolley would occupy its center median, it was
to be one of the first roadways specifically designed to lure motor
cars at fast speeds—the "most perfect automobile speedway in
the world."

But what to call this magnificent motorway? As part of keeping a low profile, the Suburban Homes syndicate's controllers—
Chandler, Gen. Harrison Otis, Gen. Moses Sherman, Hobart
Whitley, and Otto Brant—reportedly had a handshake agreement not to name any prominent landmarks after themselves or

family members. But with the drawbridge now lowered on their 47,500-acre kingdom, some appeared to have a change of heart. The men settled on a name: Sherman Way. Intersecting this boulevard at its halfway point would be Hazeltine Avenue. Thus, Moses Hazeltine Sherman hit the trifecta. His surname graced the Valley's first major thoroughfare, while his middle name—also the name of his first daughter—furnished the offshoot. Actually, it was more like a quadfecta. The Valley's main north-south arterial was *also* named Sherman Way, divided into North and South. (In 1926, eleven years after the Valley joined L.A., the Los Angeles City Council ordered the name changed to Van Nuys Boulevard.)

Meanwhile, the east-west Sherman Way—since expanded several more miles between West Hills and Burbank—was laid out to connect to Suburban Homes' first three plats. They were billed as "the Wonder Cities of the Valley." The inaugural subdivision was called Van Nuys after Chandler's old acquaintance and the Valley's longtime custodian. Just west of that was Marian, a nod by Otis to his daughter and Chandler's wife. It was also Otis's idea to call the westernmost locality Owensmouth, a (wincing) wink to the Owens River's eventual new "mouth" in the San Fernando Valley. The general also concocted Vanowen Street, a portmanteau of Van Nuys and Owensmouth (or Owens Valley), and splashed his own name on Otis Avenue. Both streets live on, though Vanowen is by far the more consequential one.

Because he was already synonymous with his Hollywood holdings, Whitley declined any name dedications to avoid confusion. Brant had the least name recognition among the five principals, which was fine by him. Described by his son as "a retiring kind of guy," the title insurance executive steadfastly "would not let his company name anything after him, not even a street." As expected, Chandler also opted out of the naming sweepstakes. He rarely allowed his photo to be shown in the *Los Angeles Times* and even had set policies on how often his name could be mentioned in copy. Only later did he begrudgingly okay the dedication of

Chandler Boulevard, adopted as a Red Car-adjacent roadway by Los Angeles in 1926.

The first phase of tracts sold in Van Nuys was patterned after the Sale of the Century the previous November, when scores of livestock and farm equipment were sold off. General Manager Whitley formed a sales team headed up by W. P. Whitsett, an early booster of the Valley who turned everything "into money," according to Whitley. (Whitley paid him the ultimate compliment by naming Whitsett Drive in Van Nuys after him. Weirdly, this street became Valerio Street in 1917. Present-day Whitsett Avenue came later.) On February 22, 1911, 2,000 men, women, and children showed up for the sales bonanza. With Whitley serving as auctioneer, a couple hundred newly deeded owners blitzed through the acreage, arms aloft with stakes as if hunting down prey before plunging their markers into the hardened soil of their dream lots. Some measured a few thousand square feet; others were upward of ten acres, perfect for orchards or poultry farms. The syndicate sold $200,000 worth of homes in Van Nuys before the month was out, warranting breathless coverage in the *Times*: "Fifteen miles from the heart of the most rapidly growing city in the world, it lies today in the bosom of the largest and richest tract of undeveloped land near any great city of the globe." It was, as one full-page advert insisted, "The Town That Was Started RIGHT."

The same couldn't be said for Owensmouth. Despite the *Times* comparing it to "an eaglet bursting asunder the egg which nourished its embryonic life," the former barley field was more like a stunted nestling. Maybe it was always bound to disappoint after all the hype surrounding its founding by real estate agent Edwin Janss, hired by Whitley to handle sales. Each prospective buyer was gifted a plaster of Paris plaque depicting a stork holding a baby. It was inscribed with Owensmouth's "birthday" (March 30, 1912), spawning the phrase "Owensmouth Baby." To create excitement, Janss zoomed a 120-horsepower Fiat up and down Sherman Way, the car emblazoned with an "Owensmouth

Baby" banner. Barnstorming biplanes also brought crowds. For the main event, Janss promoted a race between his Owensmouth Baby Fiat and an airplane. Unfortunately, the showdown coincided with a Santa Ana windstorm. The devil winds whipped up turbulent dust clouds and jangled nerves, leading to its cancellation.

Janss did manage to sell $104,100 worth of property on the first day, but growth was sluggish thereafter. Suburban Homes controllers were miffed by Janss's propensity to overpromise and underdeliver. Whereas busy Van Nuys grew to such prominence that it eventually attained its own Civic Center (after annexing with L.A.), Owensmouth remained underdeveloped in relation to its Valley cousins. Part of that had to do with water. The community felt that its proximity to the headwaters of the Los Angeles River would continue to sustain it. Even when most of the Valley annexed with L.A., Owensmouth stayed the course, refusing to pay higher taxes to plug into the aqueduct while simultaneously limiting its prospects for growth. Not wanting to remain a baby town forever, however, it finally asked to be let into Los Angeles two years after the rest of the Valley had. But the self-abasement was not over. In 1931—following years of Owens Valley activists sabotaging the aqueduct—the name Owensmouth was extinguished after residents realized that its association with "stolen water" was not a good look. (Owensmouth Avenue remains.) The region is now known as Canoga Park, and includes portions of West Hills and Winnetka.

Marian was the last of the Wonder Cities along the spine of Sherman Way to be subdivided. Much of it overlapped with the "picnic land" that Chandler's children once thought a joke. Now, several years had elapsed and Papa was personally underwriting Marian's first general store, post office, and Pacific Electric depot. According to Whitley, Chandler owned "everything from Balboa [Boulevard] to the townsite of Marian." Like Owensmouth, however, its identity failed to take hold. The United States Post Office felt that Marian was too close in name to Marianna, Florida (established in 1828). The community became Reseda in 1921, named after a flowering plant genus.

As for Sherman Way, a typical modern-day motorist can scarcely make out much difference between it and Vanowen Street or Victory Boulevard or any other interchangeable east-west thoroughfare traversing the Valley. But the ballyhooed speedway did leave a legacy. Decades before Van Nuys Boulevard became a famous cruising destination, Sherman Way was the first patch of pavement in the Valley to celebrate car culture. After Janss's Owensmouth Baby stunt, it hosted auto races in 1912. It also had a neat gimmick that lead-footers found irresistible: no speed limit! "No speed cops will annoy you," promised a *Times* automotive reporter, who encouraged L.A. readers to motor into the Valley via newly opened Laurel Canyon Boulevard, a scenic alternative through the Santa Monica Mountains. Only later did maximum speed signs pop up on Sherman Way, but even these were cheeky. They read "100 miles per hour," a limit that even souped-up cars would be hard-pressed to clock. Nonetheless, the curious often lined Sherman Way to watch drivers give it a whirl, many returning home to rave about the heady new frontier of the Wonder Cities. In the end, Chandler and company earned a $5 million return from land abutting Sherman Way.

Coinciding with these sprouting suburbs, the Water Board conducted a comprehensive survey of Los Angeles's water needs in advance of the aqueduct. In a 1911 letter to the Chamber of Commerce, the commission issued its widely reported findings. Its "Conclusions" section was suspiciously rosy, aligning with the wishes of L.A.'s power elite. "We are especially indebted to William Mulholland," members added, "whose wide knowledge of local conditions and the water resources of the City has been of great service to us in arriving at the conclusions contained in this report." The board bumped his salary fifty percent to $15,000 a year—higher than the mayor's. Accounting for the incestuous relationship between the board, City Hall, and Mulholland, the commission's report could not be construed as truly independent. It reached five conclusions, summarized as such:

1. The City can never experience a shortage of water when the Los Angeles Aqueduct is completed.
2. All of the districts to which we have allotted surplus waters, should be annexed to the present City. This would not only eliminate many important legal questions involved, but would simplify the distribution of the water, and insure maximum economy in the administration, operation, and maintenance of the water system.
3. In case annexation cannot be immediately effected, we believe that water should not be furnished to any district, unless there is a reasonable assurance that it will ultimately become a portion of the City.
4. All districts should be required to pay in advance the cost of the main distribution conduits, which should be constructed by the City. These districts should also pay an annual charge for water to be continued until annexation or consolidation is effected.
5. The storage of waters below the terminus of the Aqueduct is vitally essential.

Points one and five might as well have been dictated by Mulholland himself. Summarizing points two, three, and four, the board's findings recommended fast-tracking the annexation of neighboring districts while withholding the sale of extra water to resisters—essentially, pressuring them to join "the City." These recommendations, codified by Los Angeles, would facilitate another frenzy of annexations over the next decade, when the city would bear down on San Francisco in population and the nation's number one ranking in square miles. But first, it would have to overcome an unexpected setback, a preview of anti-annexation antagonism that had taken hold northeast of Los Angeles.

"ANNEXATION GETS SOLAR PLEXUS BLOW" read the August 10, 1911, front page headline in the *South Pasadena Record*. As Chief Engineer Mulholland's worker bees battled nature's elements and unforgiving terrain to manufacture a river through the desert, South Pasadena—incorporated in 1888—was conducting its own water studies in the Arroyo Seco. "In excavating to construct the Arroyo bridge," the paper reported, "engineers are coming into an abundance of water there. Springs and wells at different parts of the city and vicinity show an extensive seepage." Hydrologists also pointed out that the nearby San Gabriel Mountains "are veritable reservoirs of water," the source of several independent companies that supplied South Pasadena with water. Adjacent Pasadena and Alhambra were also ignoring L.A.'s siren call to consolidate. An editorial cartoon in the South Pasadena newspaper pictured an alarmed old man named "Mr. Los Angeles" clutching the nozzle of a miles-long firehose labeled "Owens Valley Aqueduct." The frame drips with double entendres. Three prim lasses—Misses South Pasadena, Pasadena, and Alhambra—thrust empty cups toward him, waiting to get filled up. Under the title "The Proposal," Mr. Los Angeles says, "If you ladies want any Owens river water, you'll have to 'annex' me." But he can't get his nozzle to spew water. The ladies react to their impotent suitor with tittering embarrassment on his behalf. The comic was a comment on a recent meeting with the L.A. Chamber of Commerce, which left more questions than answers regarding local water politics. "What sentiment there was in favor of annexation to Los Angeles is growing less and less every day," the *South Pasadena Record* concluded.

The spirit of self-governance that characterized South Pasadena, Pasadena, and Alhambra bled into other old suburbs abutting the Arroyo Seco. Back in April 1910, there was momentum to annex Bairdstown and Hermon, but the election failed to materialize before the Census. Now, a year and a half later, the election was back on. This time it would include a cluster of communities making up the twenty-square-mile Arroyo Seco Addition. (Though South Pasadena, Pasadena, and Alhambra were unreachable for now, L.A. could at least nip at their heels.) While smaller Hermon was still in favor of annexation, Bairdstown and neighboring Belvedere were having reservations. Residents had seen how some taken-in districts were not getting their needs met by Angel City. Higher utility bills and carrying L.A.'s debt load also gave pause.

A week before the September 22, 1911, election, Bairdstown hosted a town hall to debate the annexation issue. George Dunlop, the former mayor of Hollywood, delivered an impassioned speech on behalf of the "pros," asserting that Hollywood was now enjoying better police and fire services and finer public schools under L.A.'s auspices. Other Arroyo Seco-adjacent districts also had a voice at the table. The meeting grew heated when R. H. Gowd of West Highland Park—which had gone rogue when Highland Park joined L.A. in 1895—leapt to the floor seven times to rail against annexation. Order was restored when he was threatened with expulsion, and newspapers reported that "those favoring annexation were greatly in the majority at the meeting."

But then election day showed up. "Unexpected Happens," lamented the *L.A. Times*. The shocking defeat was blamed on weak voter turnout in Los Angeles, and on a transitory statute that required a two-thirds passage within any districts up for annexation. Still, it was a razor-thin loss for L.A.; annexation came up only thirty-four votes short out of 6,045 ballots cast. As expected, precincts in Bairdstown and Belvedere failed to reach the sixty-six percent threshold. Annandale also came out strongly opposed. John P. Steele, who managed L.A.'s annexation task force, expressed concern that much of the prized Arroyo Seco Addition could conceivably fall to Glendale, South Pasadena or Alhambra unless L.A. redoubled its efforts and made another stab. Eventually, he predicted, all Big Three cities "are expected to be a part of Los Angeles."

Steele was patently wrong on that front, but his hint of an election do-over materialized on February 1, 1912. This time, Steele's team gerrymandered the Arroyo Seco Addition to guarantee victory. Only annex-friendly precincts were included on the ballot. Bairdstown, Belvedere, and a portion of Annandale were left off. Turnout was about 1,000 less than September's election, but favorable votes easily surpassed the required two-thirds majority. The newcomers brought L.A.'s total area to almost 108 square miles, nudging it ever closer to Philadelphia as the nation's fourth largest municipality by size. In addition to claiming much of the Arroyo Seco corridor, northeast Los Angeles now included Glassell Park, Mt. Washington, West Highland Park, York Valley, and parts of Annandale and San Rafael Heights. From its border with Pasadena to Point Fermin in San Pedro, Los Angeles measured thirty-two miles long. Equally important, its boundary was now contiguous with cities in the northeast. This placed L.A. in a legally sound position should it ever wish to unite down the line with, say, Eagle Rock (which had incorporated the year before), while casting an even larger shadow over Steele's targeted Big Three cities. "There is one subject which has ever been 'touchy' to all the old-timers in Pasadena," the *Times* acknowledged regarding the election, "and that is consolidation with Los Angeles." Indeed, whenever a particular policy matter divided Pasadena, councilmen there invoked consolidation with L.A. as a cudgel to get their way. "If you want to start something, just mention consolidation," observed the paper.

All the while, the Big Three were busy scooping up smaller communities of their own. Three of them were built by Henry Huntington's land development companies along his trolley routes—Dolgeville, Oneonta Park (named after Henry's hometown), and Oak Knoll. Each subdivision was laid out with a specific class of buyer in mind. Dolgeville had smaller lots for those of more modest means. Oneonta Park was for the upper-middle-class. And Oak Knoll was touted as the most exclusive neighborhood in the West. Where the Wonder Cities of the Valley were a relative bargain, Oak Knoll lots started at $5,000 an acre and climbed to $20,000 for ten acres. Entrée into these rarified addresses was reserved for Caucasians. Eventually, they were annexed by Alhambra (Dolgeville), South Pasadena (Oneonta Park), and Pasadena (Oak Knoll). Today, Oak Knoll is a stately enclave brushing up against the western boundary of San Marino, which initially subsumed it.

Borne out of Huntington's purchase of old Shorb Ranch (later, San Marino Ranch), San Marino has the vibe of a principality embedded in Los Angeles County, suggestive of the actual San Marino in Europe after which it is named. It was designed as a tax haven for Huntington and 500 industrialist neighbors—"the lowest tax rates of any city in the world," boasted one backer. Incorporated in April of 1913, San Marino's reputation as "Millionaire City" was a West Coast answer to Tuxedo, New York, whose "Gotham millionaires" included Mary Williamson Averell Harriman, the wife of Huntington's late rival, E. H. Harriman. So dominant was Huntington's imprint on the new town, his sprawling estate eventually accounted for one-third of its 2,500 acres. With no city hall and only one salaried city employee, "it has been suggested that H. E. Huntington declare his art galleries, museums and estates the official public places" of the town, the media reported.

Huntington had no intention of turning his estate into a civic square, but he had rechanneled his energies into a new life's journey. "When my home [in San Marino] is done, I am going to retire," he declared in 1910. Building out his collections for the budding Huntington Library and Gardens gave him more than just a purpose. Here was an opportunity to create an institution from the ground up, where the public could enrich its mind and spirit, much as his rail enterprises also served the common good. "All the great joy in life is in the creating," the closet artist said. "It is in the making of it that the real thrill comes." Huntington also found rejuvenation by remarrying. His new wife was Arabella Huntington, the sixty-one-year-old widow of Henry's uncle Collis. Some thought the union was a subconscious ploy by Huntington to enshrine his devotion to his uncle's memory. But both Henry and Bell, as he called her, had grown close over the years through business interactions. He admired her scholarly ways, which would no doubt help inform his pursuit of great works of art. Four days after their July 16, 1913, wedding, Henry exuded the excitement of a schoolboy in a letter to his sister Caroline. "I can never tell you how very happy I am," he gushed. "Bell is so sweet, good and kind, wishing one to have the best of everything, which is so entirely new to me. I am sure, my dear sister, I am going to be very, very happy in my new life." It was as if everything had been leading to this moment, and he was just "beginning to live."

While Huntington was enjoying a summer of marital bliss, Mulholland was edging perilously close to a breaking point. His beloved wife Lillie was battling uterine cancer. Owing to his aqueduct obligations in the field, he leaned on his older children to care for their mother and two preteen siblings. The waterway itself suffered various logjams of the technical, legal, and financial variety. Investigations further threatened to impede progress. Due to open in the spring of 1913, the project's inauguration kept getting pushed—from mid-May to mid-June to late-June to, finally, sometime later in the year. As the delays mounted, the fifty-seven-year-old Chief was still running the Los Angeles Department of Water. In those rare moments that he roamed City Hall, Old Bill spoke to friends of his insomnia. "The strain and responsibility have shattered my health," he confided. A physician prescribed forced amnesia. "Under my doctor's advice, I am trying to forget everything connected with the aqueduct," he said. That would prove impossible. Later in 1913, the aqueduct—and the hero behind it—was all anyone could talk about.

CHAPTER 16

Mulholland Delivers

THE FREESTANDING CORINTHIAN COLUMN soared 300 feet high. It was crowned by a thirty-foot-tall, goddess-like statue labeled Miss Los Angeles. From her tilted chalice flowed a continuous stream of water, glistening in the sun and under nightly colored lights as it cascaded down the monument. At the base of the column, four fountains pranced twenty feet in the air, and an interior grand stairway led to observation decks a la the Statue of Liberty.

At least, that's what the drawings promised.

It was to be called the Aqueduct Memorial Fountain, and it was to be a centerpiece of Exposition Park. Martin Neuner, the monolith's committee chairman, pointed out that most of the world's public sculptures commemorated martyrs, wars, and bloodshed. This one, however, would uplift, celebrating the city's greatest triumph under water chief William Mulholland, with the goal of laying the first cornerstone on the same day as the Los Angeles Aqueduct's debut. "The entire country travels to Europe to see its monuments," Neuner said. "Los Angeles will have something in this monument that will cause tourists to come from the old country here." But Martin never got to see his prediction come true. Unable to raise $500,000 in building costs, the project died.

By the time November 5, 1913, rolled around, however, no one seemed to care or notice. It was a beautiful sunny day, perfect conditions for the aqueduct's official coming out party. Completed in six years, the 233-mile engineering marvel was arguably the most ambitious water trough since the Suez Canal's completion in 1869 (Panama Canal wouldn't open until 1914). But whereas Suez was geared toward international commerce, coronated by kings and queens, Mulholland's canal was a river for the *people*. It professed to deliver 258 million gallons of liquid snow to the City of Angels every twenty-four hours. An anticipated 300,000 people were expected to attend the ceremony to see, with their own eyes, water crashing down the Cascades, the rocky cement spillway that marked the aqueduct's southern terminus. To handle the crush of attendees, Pacific Electric and Southern Pacific set up temporary railroad depots, and a giant dirt parking lot filled up with five thousand autos, one thousand motorcycles, and a clutch of wagons for those still getting around by horse and buggy.

In reality, "only" 40,000 spectators showed up, which was just as well. The Cascades were hemmed in by narrow Newhall Pass at the northern end of the San Fernando Valley. Early birds found spots along the banks of the conduit, jockeying to be among the first to feel the water's mist once the switch was flipped. Others brought drinking cups to sample Sierra's finest from faucets built into a pipeline. The carnival atmosphere bore the unmistakable stamp of Frank Wiggins, the Chamber of Commerce maestro who hadn't lost his gift of gimmickry for promoting Los Angeles. Everyone was handed an Official Program, which included maps of proposed water mains crisscrossing the San Fernando Valley (*hint hint* for homeseekers). Official Souvenir Pennants went for ten cents a pop. "Formal Opening Los Angeles Aqueduct," they read, each stamped with a seal of the Cascades ringed by flowers and oranges. Volunteers distributed 10,000 bottles to the first 10,000 attendees. The containers were filled with aqueduct water, compliments of San Fernando, "the Aqueduct City." Even San Pedro got into the act. Fifty miles away, naval warships in the harbor readied to fire mortars once the Owens Valley water was liberated.

At 11 A.M., a fifty-piece brass band warmed up the crowd until noon, when a motorcade of distinguished guests arrived from the Chamber of Commerce. The event was as much a celebration of the Big Ditch as it was for its architect. Cannon fire saluted

Mulholland's arrival, and he was heartily greeted by hat-waving well-wishers to the strains of "Hail to the Chief." Taking a seat alongside a happily bloated Gen. Harrison Otis, the Chief appeared gaunt and ill at ease. Six years of battling the elements in California's badlands had turned his skin leathery and brown, and his brow creased with deep lines as he squinted into the sun. Though he appreciated the recognition, he dreaded showboating events that smacked of political puffery. Not having his terminally ill wife by his side no doubt played into his anxieties; she had recently gone under the knife for surgery. With Lillie on bedrest, he was accompanied by his daughters Rose and Lucille.

Speakers included Congressman William Stephens, former Governor George Pardee, and Otis, who introduced Ellen Beach Yaw, a noted four-octave soprano nicknamed "Lark Ellen." Otis's *Los Angeles Times* had long championed the local soloist's career; in return, Miss Yaw regularly showed up at *Times* fundraisers and civic events amidst rumors that her relationship with the widowed general went beyond mere friendship. "Lift your voices in gratitude, a river is now here," she trilled, part of an anthem written for the occasion called "California, Hail the Waters!" Eyewitnesses were as much impressed by Yaw's pipes as they were by her ability to forge through a dusty gale, which "blew the ostrich plumes of her elegant chapeau across her face and threatened to muffle her voice." Her composition ended with a chorus:

> Hail the waters! Glorious waters!
> Heaven has blessed our land,
> Abundant waters now are here,
> Sent forth by God's own hand.

Though a predictable cliché by now, others at the lectern also trotted out biblical allegories to elevate the special occasion. Gen. Adna R. Chaffee, President of the Board of Public Works, resuscitated comparisons between Mulholland and Moses—not Moses Sherman, but the actual Moses. Both men succeeded at "smiting the rock" to quench the thirst of the faithful. Mayor Henry Rose concurred that the deific Irishman was "like the men of the Bible."

At last, it was Mulholland's turn to take the stage. A hush rippled through the crowd as the Goethals of the West ambled toward the grandstand. The Chamber of Commerce awarded him a silver loving cup, which he raised to his lips in an imaginary quaff of aqueduct water. He spoke briefly and from the heart, without notes. He made a point of invoking Fred Eaton. His estranged friend had offered a weak excuse for his absence, which at least avoided any awkwardness between the two codgers. "I am sorry that the man whom I consider the father of the aqueduct is not here, former Mayor Eaton," Mulholland intoned. "To him all the honor is due. He planned it. We simply put together the bricks and the mortar." After thanking his colleagues, his address continued along this humble path, casting himself as merely a glorified civil servant: "I have done nothing more than my duty." Gesturing to the rickety dais, he said, "This crude platform is an altar to consummate the delivery of this valuable water supply and dedicate to you and posterity forever a magnificent body of water." The crowd wasn't buying this living legend's self-effacement. Later that day, someone suggested he should run for mayor, to which Bill wryly replied, "I'd rather give birth to a porcupine backward."

At 1:15 P.M., the Chief unfurled an American flag, a signal that it was time to throw open the floodgates. Atop the Cascades, officials cranked iron valves to unleash the pent-up river. Onlookers leaned forward in anticipation, but they had to wait. The water had been held back near a tunnel. Finally, after an interminable two or three minutes, a burst of water raced down the spillway's 150-foot plunge. Pandemonium ensued, the roar of the stampeding crowd blending with that of the rapids. The release of water seemed to break an emotional dam within Mulholland too. He was reported to have slumped down with a sigh "that had a sob in it," and closed his eyes. Finally, a smile played across his face, and he threw his head back and laughed, freely and joyously. "Well, it's finished," he said, the realization finally hitting him. Beneath an explosion of fireworks, Rose and Lucille wrapped their arms around their father. It was at this moment that Mulholland uttered his immortal, ad hoc proclamation. It is unclear whether he directed it to his adoring public, who could scarcely hear him above the din, or to the mayor. But the message was for all.

"There it is," he shouted, gesturing to the rushing water. "Take it!"

"Thank you," said Mayor Rose.

Mulholland's Best Day Ever concluded that evening at the Hotel Alexandria, where an elaborate banquet was held in his honor by business leaders. After being presented with a parchment scroll that compared his "stupendous and daring" feat to the Roman aqueduct at Segovia, he was exalted for bringing the project in on budget with minimal casualties. (Though forty-three workers perished, this was considered low for such dangerous work.) Speeches were geared toward economic opportunities and what the aqueduct portended for the future of L.A. once its distribution lines were completed in a couple years. Money for maintenance, expenses, and bond interest would come from various sources—water sales for irrigation, an expanding tax base, and electricity-generating plants like the one being built in San Francisquito Canyon. Mulholland recalled the Water Board's edict from 1911. "We can only share our water with those that become permanently a part of Los Angeles," he said, "and in that way we guarantee the permanency of the institution of the aqueduct itself." Serenaded with huzzahs, he called for the continued annexation of L.A.'s neighbors. "The lands that are immediately contiguous and will soon be part of the city itself, come next." He then thanked city attorney W. B. Mathews for protecting him from all the agitators and, half-joking, keeping him out of jail.

"GLORIOUS MOUNTAIN RIVER NOW FLOWS TO LOS ANGELES' GATES" proclaimed the banner headline in the next day's *L.A. Times*, which lionized Mulholland as it recounted the day's festivities. A congratulatory telegram from President Woodrow Wilson was reproduced, as were the lyrics to Lark Ellen's "California, Hail the Waters!" Though Harry Chandler didn't speak at the dedication, his editorial agenda permeated the November 6, 1913, issue. One article pointed to the pleasantly high turnout of autos, resulting in a "busy, credible day for the Automobile Club," of which Chandler was a founder. The newspaper also promoted a souvenir booklet called *Pictorial History of the Aqueduct*, available for purchase at the *Times* offices. "From the standpoint of boosting Los Angeles," read the blurb, "no better service can be performed than for each man and woman in the city to send to some out-of-town friend a copy of the *Pictorial History of the Aqueduct*." It was a reminder that, while Eaton dreamed up the aqueduct, it was Chandler who envisioned and harnessed its potential in selling Los Angeles.

But the biggest news flash was an update on Mulholland's cancer-stricken wife. "WATER CURES SICK WOMAN," declared the headline. "Wife of Aqueduct Engineer Passes Danger With Torrent's Rush." The paper attested that, while Mulholland stood before the masses, he was "thinking of the bed of pain back home and wondering if in the hour of his triumph he would suffer a keen loss." Just after the water tumbled down the spillway, word reached Bill that Lillie had rallied. "Mrs. Mulholland was out of danger and . . . she would soon be on the way to recovery." In view of the Chief's already immortal status, what was one more miracle? Despite making for a feel-good nugget, Lillie did not regain her health. She would die a year and a half later at age forty-seven.

Ironically, the godlike glow around Mulholland belied the fact that he was not religious. "I believe in the golden rule," said the man who knew "most" of the Ten Commandments. "Conscience, progress, a chance for every man." He worshipped hard work but was suspicious of good fortune. His discomfort with his venerated status was understandable. Once one reaches the mountaintop, there's nowhere to go but down.

CHAPTER 17

The Latest Greatest Achievement

THE GESTURE WAS SYMBOLIC, but its intent was genuine. On November 12, 1914, Gen. Harrison Gray Otis handed Harry Chandler a "deed" to the *Los Angeles Times*. From now on, Otis was entrusting his son-in-law with "control and management" of the newspaper. In addition, Harry and his wife Marian would retain two-thirds' ownership of the *Times'* parent company, Times-Mirror. This official transfer of power had been a long time coming. While Otis would still lend his editorial voice to the *Times*, it was well-known Chandler had been managing the paper for years. He was also increasingly performing damage control.

Ever since the bombing of The Fortress by union activists four years earlier, the seventy-seven-year-old Otis had been acting more militant himself. The automobile that drove him to work flaunted an obscenely large replica cannon on the hood. After marching into his armed office in full Army regalia, he would often commence military drills to prepare for the next enemy attack. "The old general actually became senile," recalled a *Times* editor years later. "He would walk around the editorial office as if it were the Pentagon and say to the telegraph editor, 'Where are the dispatches from the front?'" After being told there were no dispatches—much less, a front—Otis would promptly fire the telegraph editor. Scenes like this played out numerous times. Chandler would pull aside the poor sap, tell him to visit the pub across the street, and stay there until Otis left the building. Chandler would then rehire the fired employee, and Otis seemingly forgot about it until he had cause to fire him again.

Additionally, Otis's puerile name-calling of adversaries was becoming tired, unbefitting a supposedly virtuous newspaper whose motto was "the proper medium for thinkers" in a city with increasingly diverse points of view. For decades, politicians who railed against the *Times*' beliefs did so at their own risk. But that was changing. When the paper's op-ed pages attacked Hiram Johnson, a progressive Republican running for governor in 1910, the candidate had no qualms about firing back against Otis in a campaign speech: "He sits there in senile dementia, with gangrened heart and rotting brain, grimacing at every reform, chattering impotently at all things that are decent, frothing, fuming, violently gibbering, going down to his grave in snarling infamy." He described the general as a "blot on the banner of Southern California . . . disgraceful, depraved, corrupt, crooked." Johnson would end up serving two terms as California governor, from 1911 to 1917.

Back at The Fortress, Otis's deed included a "letter of declaration" addressed to Harry and Marian that laid out his instructions for keeping the *Times* relevant. Dubbed the Ten Commandments, its ten points featured windy calls for patriotism, with orders to maintain "striking hard and deserved blows against . . . intolerable evils" while rejecting "the demoralization of human society." The *Times* published Otis's missive, calling it "a classic in the annals of journalism" that will be "read with world-wide interest."

Although Chandler and Otis shared conservative values, Harry was used to humoring the old man, as he likely did here too. For thirty years, Otis had fashioned the *Times* in his own blustery image. The taciturn Chandler continued to see the paper less as a bulwark of law and order and more as a tool to lure businesses, grow Los Angeles, and build his own empire. Sure, there would always be enemies. But where Otis smote them by wielding the pen as sword, Chandler did so by being the smartest guy in the room. Nonetheless, in a show of respect, the *Times*' masthead would continue to post Gen. Harrison Gray Otis as the paper's General Manager and President until his death, with Chandler the Assistant General Manager—undoubtedly how Harry liked it.

Gen. Moses Sherman cheered the promotion from the sidelines, predicting an even greater rise in fortunes for Harry and himself as he praised his friend's "wonderful brain." With L.A. about to enter a new phase of explosive growth, Harry's mental acuity would indeed serve them well.

In the spring of 1915, Los Angeles was preparing to annex three more districts. One was the Westside community of Palms. Located between Santa Monica and Los Angeles, the former bean field originally went by "The Palms" when it was founded in 1886, a reference to two palm trees swaying next to its Southern Pacific train depot (preserved and relocated to today's Heritage Square). While present-day Palms encompasses only two square miles between Venice Boulevard and the 10 and 405 Freeways, its original expanse measured 7.3 square miles. Palms' eastern border nuzzled the old Colegrove Addition, making it contiguous with Los Angeles, with a southeastern spur grazing today's Leimert Park. Like sections of Highland Park, a breakaway Palms chose not to be included on the annexation menu; this small district held out and merged with Culver City in 1917.

The second area up for annexation was Bairdstown, known today as El Sereno. The 3.3-square-mile neighborhood had already rejected unification with Angel City in the September 1911 election, then was left off the ballot in February 1912. Part of the problem with Bairdstown was that it was made up of four distinct neighborhoods— Rose Hill, Farmdale, Sierra Vista, and a smaller Bairdstown—each with differing views on the subject. But with the completion of the Los Angeles Aqueduct, communities that once shunned annexation had changes of heart. (Next-door Belvedere remained contrarian, becoming part of unincorporated East Los Angeles.) A recent straw poll revealed at least two-thirds of Bairdstown residents favored unification. For both Palms and Bairdstown, taking on L.A.'s bonded indebtedness now seemed a small price to pay for reliable water and sewer systems.

Then there was the biggest of the bunch: the San Fernando Valley. Immediately after the November 1913 christening of the

Cascades, the Annexation Commission sent surveyors through-out the Valley to establish boundary lines. In the interim, Valley residents conducted a poll that showed 681 voters in favor of join-ing Los Angeles versus 25 against, prompting their own annex-ation retinue to petition Los Angeles for admission. Newspapers were now flooded with "For Sale—Suburban Property" ads by developers flipping lots from Chandler's Los Angeles Suburban Homes Co. "The Padres of old and the Spanish Dons on these lands made good," declared one billing. "You can do better." In a typical listing from December 1914, one sales company promot-ed tracts at $350 an acre, perfect for irrigation, chicken-raising, or homebuilding: "ANNEXATION is the next step. . . . When this is all a part of the city of Los Angeles, with aqueduct water and city advantages—these prices will look very small." One month later, agents were charging $450 an acre in the same general area. "This land will be worth $1,500 to $3,000 an acre," the ad prophe-sied. Proximity to both Pacific Electric railway and Sherman Way was a value proposition, reflecting the changing transit habits of a populace caught between trolleys and automobiles. Within two decades, Valley land would indeed approach $3,000 an acre, translating to $100 million in estimated earnings for the Chan-dler syndicate.

In the summer of 1915, the *Times* prepped a four-page puff piece about the cash cow that was the Valley and the riches it would bring Los Angeles. Once again, Sherman was given ex-clusive editorial access. Chandler sent him a draft to peruse be-fore publication. "My dear General," he wrote, "Here is proof of a graphically written article in which Gen. Otis has prepared cov-ering our San Fernando deal from before the start of it until after the finish. He is anxious that you should read it over carefully and correct any errors you notice and offer any suggestions which occur to you." Just to cover his bases, Chandler also forwarded a draft of the article to co-syndicate member Hobart Whitley.

As usual, the person sweating it out behind the scenes was William Mulholland. Though the 233-mile aqueduct was completed in November of 1913, there was still the nagging issue of *getting* the water to Los Angeles households. Two months before the May 4, 1915, ballot vote for the annexation of the Valley and Palms (Bairdstown got pushed to a June election), the Chief was still scrambling to pipe the Sierra snowmelt into people's spigots. In order to get other Westside communities to follow Palms' lead to join L.A., it was important to demonstrate that mains ferrying water from the San Fernando Reservoir could be operational in newly added districts shortly before or after each election date.

Building this $2.6 million distribution network would occupy much of Mulholland's time through the early '20s, resulting in several reservoirs that are still around today. Upper and Lower Franklin Canyon Reservoirs near Beverly Hills were constructed first, requiring the excavation of a pipeline under the Santa Monica Mountains. It was bad enough that his wife Lillie died on April 28, 1915, one week before the annexation election. But Old Bill also couldn't escape a rising chorus of detractors, who pointed to the long delay between the aqueduct's opening and a fully functional delivery system as proof that his vision was misguided. The reliably cynical *Los Angeles Examiner* was already calling the aqueduct a bust, benefitting no one "except those having real estate for sale in the San Fernando Valley." Both the *Los Angeles Record* and the Independent Civic League called for Mulholland's salary to be slashed. But nothing could diminish the Chief's glow at City Hall. "I believe that if we paid Mulholland ten times his present salary and he lived to draw it 150 years, we would still owe him a great deal," one councilman said.

Nonetheless, on the eve of the election, the *Record* came out on the side of annexation. Despite grumbling about the sneaky syndicators getting fat off once barren land, the paper saw that the arrival of the aqueduct all but guaranteed the need to incorporate the San Fernando Valley. Both the city charter and a federal provision required that Los Angeles sell Owens Valley water only within city limits. Like a rat that must keep gnawing due to its continuously growing teeth, L.A. had no choice but to devour the Valley, as revenue from new taxpayers would help pay down the city's $24.5 million investment in the canal. Plus, there would still be surplus water, which would require even more customers. And the only way to get more customers? Grow, grow, grow!

The *L.A. Times*, meanwhile, was not taking any chances. Mulholland had rejected getting directly involved in previous campaigns to secure water bonds. This time, Chandler convinced him to publish an open letter to the citizens of Los Angeles in the Sunday edition before the election. "The proper thing to do is to extend the city's boundaries to cover such area as may be properly and adequately served with this water," Mulholland wrote. "I recommend that on the question of annexation, vote 'YES.'"

Since it was also a mayoral election (carried by Charles Sebastian), the final tally was robust. Out of 61,374 ballots cast citywide, sixty percent voted to annex the San Fernando Valley. Palms carried a sixty-five percent majority. The results were certified by the state on May 22, 1915. "GREATEST ACHIEVEMENT IN HISTORY OF THE CITY," the *Times* exclaimed about the Valley, the latest in a litany of exploits deemed the "greatest" in the last couple decades. Overnight, Los Angeles increased its size by a staggering 158 percent. The city had leapfrogged over Philadelphia, Chicago, and New Orleans, its 279 square miles now within spitting distance of the number one spot—New York's 286. The northern perimeter of the Valley included a jut that enclosed the Cascades spillway in Sylmar. From there, its upper border ran along today's 210 Freeway to Little Tujunga Canyon Road. Its easterly reaches resembled a serrated knife, stopping short of Sunland, Burbank (incorporated in 1911), Lankershim (North Hollywood), Universal City, and sections of today's Valley Village and Studio City. On the west, the Valley extended to the craggy hills of Bell Canyon and El Scorpion Park, hugging the path of Valley Circle Drive up to Chatsworth. The southern boundary was generally defined by the ridgeline of the Santa Monica Mountains (Mulholland Drive wasn't built yet), from present-day Woodland Hills to Cahuenga Pass. Because the affixed territory had to be adjacent to Los Angeles, Cahuenga Pass emerged as an important linchpin that connected the Valley to L.A. via Hollywood. Los Angeles, of course, already laid claim to the skinny Shoestring Strip, but the corridor through Cahuenga Pass was especially svelte. The pass's narrow canyon walls were hemmed in by mountainous territories on either side that had *not* been annexed by Los Angeles yet. At one point, the Cahuenga strip was more like a thread—only 223 feet wide! (A contemporary map shows this 223-foot section stretching from Woodrow Wilson Drive, across the front of Valley View Elementary School, to the northern lanes of Cahuenga Boulevard where it skirts the Hollywood Freeway.)

Notably, the old Encino Rancho and other small districts that had been excluded from the Los Angeles Suburban Homes Co.'s original 47,500 acres were now part of Los Angeles. So too were the 16,450 acres of the San Fernando Mission Land Co. That left only two "islands" within the San Fernando Valley. One was Owensmouth, the disappointingly half-baked burg that totaled about a hundred people. For the time being, it was to remain a "special irrigation district," a fancy way of saying it was allowed to remain unincorporated so that Mulholland and his crew could unfussily manage its waterworks near the source of the L.A. River. The other floater was the city of San Fernando. Incorporated in 1911, it rebuffed calls for annexation, thank you very much, doing just fine with a series of wells that nourished a thriving produce industry. Though there have been overtures to consolidate with Los Angeles in the years since, the 2.5-square mile indie town continues to rely on its own water, supplementing it, when needed, with supplies from outside agencies. (As recently as 2019, San Fernando's entire 24,000 populace received 100 percent of its supply from local groundwater.)

Even without San Fernando and the foothill communities near the Verdugo Mountains, the San Fernando Valley Addition was just plain huge. If the Valley were its own city in 1915, its

169 square miles would have ranked as the fourth largest in the United States, pushing Los Angeles (sans Valley) down to sixth. Yet for all its land, the Valley retained a frontier-era population density, averaging only nine people per square mile. The only region that resembled a city was Van Nuys. The Los Angeles City Council didn't even bother setting up a police station, relying instead on a troop of "rural police" patrolling on motorcycles.

Nevertheless, the months following annexation signaled emergent urbanism in the Valley's 64,000 subdivided acres. Lot prices continued climbing. Residential and commercial property accounted for tens of millions of dollars in sales. On May 29, 1915, J. A. Driffill, general manager of the American Beet Sugar company in Marian, was the first customer to receive Owens Valley water after Mulholland completed an irrigation culvert. And Sherman Way could now lay claim to the grandest boulevard in all of Los Angeles, reaching from Owensmouth to Lankershim. Motorists were coaxed into the Valley by its "Eighteen Miles of Roses," which lined the roadway four rows deep. Maybe the only person who didn't appreciate its panoply of 40,000 blossoms was Superintendent Frank Shearer of L.A.'s Parks Department. "There are twenty to one hundred blooms on each plant," he carped, daunted by his new detail. "These must be watered and cared for or they will die." He pushed to replace them all with palms.

In Owensmouth, Sherman Way intersected with brand-new Topanga Canyon Boulevard, the latest arterial sponsored by the Southern California Auto Club to help promote the Good Roads Movement, a federal and state campaign to improve rural roads as a way to spur growth. Complementing 1912's opening of Laurel Canyon Boulevard farther east, Topanga Canyon Boulevard offered western automotive passage through the Santa Monica Mountains. The lead-up to its May 30, 1915, launch was marked by hyperbolic overdrive. Its serpentine 14.3 miles through rugged chapparal would represent, as one newspaper pitched, "a marvelous wonderland that combines the rare beauties of a Switzerland, the picturesqueness of a Hawaii and the richness of a

Mexico" through the "Little Grand Canyon of Southern California." The *L.A. Times* devoted the front page of a Sunday edition
to its planned ribbon-cutting, marketing itself and the Auto Club
in its news section to promote a new 'Los Angeles Times' Scenic
Automobile Tour through Topanga Canyon. Chandler's presence
shone throughout, from his affiliation with the Auto Club to the
sale of maps available for purchase at the *Times* to his anonymous inclusion as a key player who bankrolled Topanga Canyon
Boulevard. "Members of the board of control of the Los Angeles
Suburban Homes Co. took up the matter of building this road,"
said George Hanna, a minor investor in the syndicate. "Today,
you see it completed largely through their efforts and also as a
result of large expenditures by them." "Them," of course, was
Chandler, Sherman, Otis, Whitley, and Otto Brant. It was a testament to their influence that the road got built at all. Initially,
Los Angeles County Supervisors deemed the task too remote to
justify its $140,000 price tag. Who was going to utilize a dusty
bypass from the gnarly bluffs of Malibu to the blistering fring-
es of the San Fernando Valley? But Chandler's group saw it as a
necessary investment with obvious marketing hooks. "BRINGS
SAN FERNANDO VALLEY NEAR TO THE OCEAN BEACH-
ES," touted a *Times* headline. As part of the *Times* Scenic Automobile Tour, Topanga Canyon Boulevard filled the final gap of
an ambitious circular route. A motorist could now loop all of Los
Angeles—coastal plain, San Fernando Valley, mountains. And,
like Sherman's old Balloon Route, it was a neat gimmick to funnel
visitors and homeseekers to Valley land that had been purchased
by Chandler, Sherman, and company. "Good roads add ten times
what they cost to property values," Whitley professed.

The boulevard's May 30 unveiling saw 1,500 vehicles participating in the scenic tour. Each motorist was handed a pennant
to mount on their car. "Every person in the Van Nuys-Owensmouth tract who has an auto should turn out and help celebrate
this canyon, which will provide an important link," *The Van Nuys
News* exhorted readers. "Do not fail to join the Van Nuys crowd."

Starting in downtown, the cavalcade traveled counter-clockwise into the Valley, turning left onto Topanga Canyon Boulevard from rose-lined Sherman Way. The Auto Club's famous scout car, Cactus Kate, led the way, driven by Club President Frank L. Baker, with lame-duck Mayor Henry Rose riding shotgun. The vehicles huffed up the thirty-foot-wide dirt road (later paved), climbing grades as steep as ten percent. As they neared unincorporated Topanga, drivers glancing over their shoulders could spot newly posted signs on the northbound lanes: "New City Limits of Los Angeles." The signs were installed by the Auto Club to mark the start of the San Fernando Valley.

In Topanga, motorists pulled over for a massive barbecue that was sponsored by the Suburban Homes Co. The menu included wild turkeys donated by local residents (wild turkeys were introduced to the Southland in 1908 by the California Fish and Game Commission; they also roamed parts of the Channel Islands since 1877). Lunch was accompanied by a parade, a cabaret, and a brigade of speakers that included Mulholland. By the end of the day, an estimated 5,000 motorists had sampled Topanga Canyon Boulevard. If true, the number would have represented almost one-fifth of all cars in Los Angeles in 1915. Clearly, automobiles were the key to future growth. In 1903, there were 300 "horseless vehicles" in L.A., more than any other city in the country. In 1915, there were 27,953, with L.A. County accounting for one-fourth of car ownership in the state.

Unlike northern Topanga Canyon and the inchoate Valley communities, thirty-year-old Palms was practically ancient by the time it joined Los Angeles. This presented familiar challenges in a region with fixed habits. Like the Arroyo Seco Addition or the Shoestring Strip, Palms had funky borders, informed by pockets that were or weren't opposed to annexation. Overnight, students who used to walk to the Palms schoolhouse now found themselves living outside the school's new Los Angeles address. In other cases, students living in L.A. found their old school "stuck" in a non-annexed section of Palms. Technically, pupils were not allowed to cross districts. A delegation from Palms took their grievances to the County Board of Supervisors to work out a solution. The fiasco put Palms' western neighbor on high alert. The seaside town of Venice (founded in 1905) lay in the pathway of L.A.'s relentless march westward. In a quirk of zoning, *its* high school sat in county territory. "Venice Warns Voters to Absorb Territory Before Los Angeles Swallows It," stated a newspaper's headline. Venice leaders called on its Chamber of Commerce to quickly call a special election to absorb Venice High School into its borders.

On June 7, 1915—one month after the Valley and Palms election—even more people cast ballots on the issue of annexing Bairdstown. The vote breezed through, with three out of four voters approving its admission to L.A. (Within two years, Bairdstown would change its name to El Sereno, or "The Serene.") Though only 3.3-square-miles, the little district took on outsize significance. Adding up the recent additions of the Valley, Palms and now Bairdstown, Los Angeles totaled 288.21 square miles. This number surpassed the magical 286 square miles held by New York City, making Los Angeles the largest city by area in the United States.

But was it?

After Bairdstown's inclusion carried L.A. to the top of the heap, newspapers suddenly downplayed the city's eclipsing of New York. An inconvenient truth was that New York's 286 square miles only counted its land. As a metropolis made up of islands, its actual area was 327 square miles when factoring in water acreage. (L.A.'s square miles did not demonstrably change when including water within its borders.) Starting in 1916, newspapers moved the mathematical goalpost, citing the revised figure of 327 square miles when invoking New York City. Nobody went on record to explain the change in calculations. But it's a fair assumption that L.A.'s boosters used the smaller, more achievable figure in 1915 as a ploy to motivate voters to the polls out of civic pride. Now that that milestone had been reached, a quiet reset was a convenient way to keep measuring Los Angeles against the behemoth back East.

Fortunately, with Palms now bound to Angel City, there appeared to be a contiguous path to overtake New York. Just as L.A.'s titans had gone west to seek their fortunes, all eyes focused on the vast western terrain that lay between the city and the ocean. Palms' northwestern extremity branched out like two stalks from a snail head, one poking into Westgate, the other touching Sawtelle. If Los Angeles could acquire those two districts, it would have more than enough territory to make up the forty-one square miles it needed to reclaim its status—this time, undisputed—as the largest city in America.

CHAPTER 18

A Hive of Annexation

IN THE SUMMER OF 1915, the *Los Angeles Express* announced that "the annexation bee buzzed merrily" throughout the communities west of Los Angeles. Other periodicals also invoked the "annexation bee" phrase as a shorthand for regions that were either seeking or fearing annexation by Los Angeles. Parts of Glendale had an "annexation bee in its bonnet." One locality worried that the bee would "sting" it. But the bee was mostly "hovering around Sawtelle and Westgate." Then, when leaders from those two districts met with the Annexation Commission in Los Angeles in August, the *Venice Vanguard* adopted a starker metaphor. It described the confab as a "Game of the Spider and Fly," with Los Angeles playing the role of the predatory arachnid, looking to ensnarl the two flies in its web.

Today, many Angelenos associate the Sawtelle district as the multi-block corridor along Sawtelle Boulevard known as Sawtelle Japantown. But Sawtelle has a deep, complicated history going back to the late 1880s. At the time, the hub of Sawtelle lay near the Soldiers' Home (aka the Veterans Affairs campus). The district began to creep southward as the Pacific Land Company subdivided 225 acres to sell to veterans. For Gen. Moses Sherman and Eli Clark, Sawtelle sat in a strategic zone between Los Angeles and the beach. After shrewdly swinging a right-of-way deal with Pacific Land's owners, they made the Soldiers' Home a must-see on their famous Balloon Route. On November 16, 1906, Sawtelle residents voted to incorporate. Excepting a cutout in the northeast to accommodate the VA property, it was bounded by Wilshire Boulevard on the north, Sepulveda Boulevard on the east, Pico Boulevard on the south, and Centinela Avenue on the west. Because it was its own municipality, Sawtelle—like Wilmington, San Pedro, and Hollywood before it—built a strong, proud identity that would not easily roll over for Los Angeles.

But water remained a concern. How much longer could Sawtelle rely on the limited supply of the independent West Los Angeles Water Company? In October 1915, after weighing the pros and cons, Sawtelle policymakers staved off consolidation with the big city. But they did leave the door slightly ajar. Next year, a proposition to amend the Los Angeles City Charter would be on the ballot. If passed, it would allow outside districts to access Los Angeles Aqueduct water. The proposition's outcome would determine whether Sawtelle could still go it alone or surrender to the spider.

Westgate, on the other hand, had a more transactional history and actively pursued coupling with L.A. Its modern legacy traced to 1839, when Governor Juan Bautista Alvarado of Mexico gifted Rancho San Vicente y Santa Monica to Francisco Sepulveda, a soldier who passed it onto his heirs. The land grant covered 48.5 square miles. Viewed on a contemporary map, its northwest wedge overlapped the Santa Monica Mountains National Recreation Area east of Topanga Canyon, including the southerly ravines branching off "dirt Mulholland." The eventual Mulholland Drive—both the dirt and paved portions up to Bel-Air's Roscomare Road—would serve as the divide between the Westgate Addition and the recently added San Fernando Valley. The rancho's eastern and southern contours extended as far as Beverly Hills (incorporated in 1914) and covered Century City, Westwood, and UCLA. Heading west—after dodging the Sawtelle district—its territory abutted Santa Monica and contained Brentwood, Westgate (the eponymous neighborhood), Pacific Palisades, and Rustic Canyon. Significantly, it also comprised three miles of beachhead, stretching up the coastline from West Channel Road to the Getty Villa.

In 1872, the Sepulveda clan unloaded the rancho to mining

magnate Robert S. Baker. Two years later, Robert and his wife Arcadia Bandini de Stearns Baker sold a three-quarter share to Nevada Senator John P. Jones. The parties subdivided their holdings to create the community of Santa Monica, which drew tourists, resorts, and businesses to what would be called the Gold Coast. On November 30, 1886, Santa Monica residents voted for cityhood. Its initial borders were Montana Avenue, 17th Street, and Pico Boulevard on the north, east, and south, with a dog-leg down to Venice Beach that encompassed the Ocean Park neighborhood.

But the incorporation of Santa Monica caused anxiety among Westgate inhabitants living next door to the beach city. Like Los Angeles, Santa Monica was looking to push out its borders. In 1897, Jones and the widowed de Stearns Baker founded the Santa Monica Land and Water Company. Most of their 50,000 acres lay in the Westgate region. By 1905, the company was marketing stately English manors and country villas in the vicinity of Brentwood. Playing off the popularity of Hollywood, Westgate Acres promised "the exact counterpart" to Hollywood, only better—proximity to cool ocean breezes and only 35 minutes from Los Angeles via trolleys. "Hollywood was a barley field only a few years ago," went one circular. "You know what it is today, and you can easily anticipate what Westgate Acres will be ten years hence." As with Sherman Way in the Valley, the subdivision offered a "regal highway" in the form of San Vicente Road (now Boulevard) with a Moses Sherman-owned electric streetcar down the middle. (It lasted until 1942.) One hundred thirty feet wide and adorned with ornamental trees, it promised to be "one of the finest automobile courses in the West." Also like Sherman Way, San Vicente drew racing contests, promoted by Santa Monica auto dealers. During one derby, 50,000 spectators crammed the throughway to watch speed demons from around the country compete for the top prize.

Though Sherman and Clark didn't have a stake in the new development, their earlier investment in Westgate put it on the

map. Among the first buyers in the region, they had already prof-
ited from subsequent Westside landowners who paid the partners
for the privilege of having their 180-mile-long Los Angeles-Pacific railway buzz past their properties. The LAP line, in fact, was
highlighted in Santa Monica Land and Water Co. ads. Prospective
buyers were instructed to "Take the Los Angeles Pacific cars to
Sawtelle. Our carriages will meet you at the BANK." New owners
were assured that "No lots in either Westgate or Westgate Acres
are more than five minutes' walk from electric cars." In one photo from around 1907, Sherman proudly stood in the middle of
a dozen well-appointed women and children who were family
members of sales agents. They were just one of many VIP groups
picked up in the Mermaid, his private coach, for special trips
along the Balloon Route.

It was Sherman's $6 million sale of the LAP franchise to E. H.
Harriman's Southern Pacific that later led to his falling out with
Henry Huntington. But Huntington did manage to carve out his
own modest slice of Westgate when he became a shareholder in
the Santa Monica Land and Water Co. He was especially interested
in the riparian Santa Monica Canyon, where his uncle Collis had
once purchased land to incorporate into the never-built commercial harbor that included his Long Wharf. By 1910, Henry named
his development Huntington Heights. Years later, farther up the
bluffs, the Santa Monica Land and Water Co. would open a subdivision of curvilinear streets and sunken utility lines in a corner of
Pacific Palisades. While Huntington was no longer involved with
the firm, its president, Robert C. Gillis, smartly cashed in on his
name anyway. The leafy enclave is still known today as Huntington Palisades.

Westgate's campaign to merge with Los Angeles—and ward
off Santa Monica—began in earnest during the "annexation bee"
summer of 1915. Two hundred people from the region packed
into an old post office building to close ranks around the issue.
In attendance were officials from Hollywood and San Pedro, who
spoke glowingly of their cities' seamless consolidations with L.A.

A city council member noted an inherent symbiosis: "It would create a splendid perpetual market for surplus aqueduct water, add largely to the municipality's revenues, and benefit the annexed territory immeasurably." William Mulholland also made an appearance. The water head echoed support for annexing the old rancho despite concerns about Rustic Canyon and Santa Monica Canyon. Nearly 8,000 acres of the rugged arroyos were not subdivided yet, making it difficult to figure out where to sink distribution pipes. However, so as not to hold up progress, he agreed to install mains and draw up provisional plans for residences. Representatives from the Los Angeles Country Club also sought assurances from Mulholland. The private club, established in 1897, had recently moved to its current location between Wilshire and Santa Monica Boulevards, just west of Beverly Hills. The club's concern? Making sure it got a discounted "irrigation rate" to keep its two 18-hole golf courses lush and green instead of being charged the higher "residential rate."

On April 24, 1916, the Westgate district conducted its own survey on annexation. The most demonstrative naysayer was Matt Wolfskill, owner of the 3,000-acre Wolfskill Ranch near today's Los Angeles California Temple in Westwood. Unlike his generous father John, who built the ranch and donated the land that became VA property in 1887, the junior Wolfskill was a known scoundrel whose wife also bucked conventions. When she wasn't winning sharpshooting competitions at Venice Beach, Mrs. Wolfskill exhibited very public meltdowns, including one that came after she drove drunk into a police car and a bus, sending passengers into "semi-convulsions." The judge at her hearing reprimanded her for her "shameless" smirking and sentenced her to a day in jail. Nonetheless, her husband's no-vote was in the minority, as 60 percent of Westgate residents favored joining Los Angeles. The outcome was heartily greeted by the L.A. City Council and the Annexation Commission, which lay the groundwork for a city-wide June 6 referendum.

The day before the vote, however, the Wolfskills again made

news. Matt Wolfskill filed a lawsuit in Superior Court, arguing that the election was illegal. His complaints were head-scratching, starting with the allegation that Westgate's annexation petition was fraudulent. "Electors who were not qualified were permitted to cast ballots," his attorney charged. Wolfskill also took issue with the fact that the "[Westgate] territory is largely a barren one"—an irrelevant point—and that it "includes nine square miles of the Pacific Ocean, which is not now nor ever has been inhabited." With money as no object, Wolfskill geared up for a long fight that legal experts said could drag on for years. Amid these court filings, Westgate was successfully voted into Los Angeles—29,014 to 23,479 among all voters. The results were ratified within days, and a judge quickly threw out the scion's specious claims. But this wouldn't be the last time anyone heard from Matt Wolfskill. Over the next two decades, he popped up in several scandals, including a Prohibition Era liquor bust at his ranch, a drunk-driving charge in Santa Monica that injured the other party, and the suspicious death of his wealthy sister, Edith Irene Wolfskill, whose decomposed body was found in a creek bed. As her only living heirs, Matt and his brother Ney were in line to inherit her fortune. Matt was uncooperative in the ensuing criminal investigation, her cause of death labeled "unknown."

With all the focus on the Westgate Addition, there was one other region seeking annexation that got scant attention in the run-up to the June 6, 1916, election: Occidental, a 1.4-square-mile tract named after Occidental College, its dominant landmark. Founded in 1875, the small liberal arts college was in need of a larger campus. In 1910, it purchased an unincorporated patch between Los Angeles and the community of Eagle Rock for its new home. Eagle Rock leaders assumed that the distinguished institute would establish its address within its borders, providing it with instant cachet after it voted to incorporate in 1911. But instead of joining the upstart city, the college preferred to be folded into L.A. Despite being spurned, Eagle Rock cashed in on Occidental College's proximity anyway when the new campus opened in 1914. The school was regularly highlighted in the *Eagle Rock Sentinel*, and Eagle Rock residents could choose to live in any number of developments that at least sounded prestigious—Occidental Terrace, Occidental Heights, and Occidental Annex. Meanwhile, the Occidental district's wishes were fulfilled when voters admitted it into Los Angeles on the same ballot that included Westgate. The add-on abutted Glendale and Eagle Rock and the old Arroyo Seco Addition (absorbed by L.A. in 1912). Combined, Occidental and Westgate brought Los Angeles's total size to 338 square miles. Even including New York City's water area, the City of Angels surpassed it by eleven square miles. It could now reclaim bragging rights as the largest city in America without any caveats or slanted math, a stunning development for a former pueblo that tallied less than fifty square miles some ten years earlier.

The June 1916 ballot revealed another consequential outcome: the defeat of a measure that would have allowed contiguous territories to petition Los Angeles for aqueduct water. This meant that Los Angeles could not sell its supply outside city limits, even through intermediary companies. This was a particular blow to Sawtelle. The town had gambled on a water-friendly verdict, but L.A.'s electorate spoke loud and clear, codifying the city's mantra of "No annexation, no water." Sawtelle had no choice but to reconsider the consolidation option.

The implications of the aqueduct proposition were foreboding. The borders of L.A.'s neighbors suddenly felt more porous than ever. As Los Angeles kept metastasizing, a reign of hegemony infected City Hall. After Mayor Charles Sebastian resigned for health reasons on September 2, 1916, the City Council responded to the leadership vacuum with a quiet coup that aligned with Harry Chandler's relentless expansionism. Council President Martin F. Betkouski promptly moved into Sebastian's vacant office and anointed himself the acting mayor, disregarding charter rules that called for the council to elect one. The *Los Angeles Times'* editorial section—whose masthead now declared that it

served "The Advancing City and Tributary Territory"—backed
up the council's agenda by asserting that the role of any new
mayor was to serve the council's interests. Candidates who were
not "in full sympathy" with the committee's hyper-growth man-
date need not apply. "All [Territories] Eventually Will Become
Part of Great Whole" a *Times* headline boldly averred. Betkouski
and his peers became obsessed with dissolving the lines between
Los Angeles city and Los Angeles County. "We should have city
and county consolidation," he pronounced, "and the first thing
to do is to annex the territory we wish to be included in the city
and county." Their model was L.A.'s eternal rival, San Francisco, whose city and county were already one and the same. But
the comparison was lopsided. San Francisco's city and county
measured only 46.5 square miles—two square miles *smaller* than
newly added Westgate and not even fourteen percent of L.A.'s
monstrous scale.

On September 21, Betkouski formed a task force with George
Dunlop, the former mayor of Hollywood who now headed up the
Annexation Commission. City agents canvassed neighborhoods
throughout L.A. County to educate people about the benefits of
merging, and "to invite citizens in these districts to organize local committees to co-operate with the work" of the annexation
committee. Once again, Mulholland was recruited to spread the
gospel, hopscotching across the county to preach about reliable
water and sewer systems. Besides its objective of "enlarging the
field of distribution of the aqueduct water and power" to pay
down L.A.'s bond burden, the campaign cited other "aims"—
most of them fatuous—that could only be achieved through the
synthesis of city and county. One aim was a desire for cartologi-
cal symmetry instead of the current hodgepodge of patches and
strips. Or, as the council put it, "the straightening out of the lines
of the city of Los Angeles to logical and uniform proportions as
a municipal unit." Apparently, no one thought to consider New
York, a city with famously messy borders that didn't seem overly
concerned with style points on its shape. Other aims included

a vague "elimination of local misunderstandings and jealousies" and a priority to "bring within the city the brains and capital that work by day in Los Angeles and sleep at night in Pasadena, Long Beach, and other nearby cities."

Alarm bells immediately sounded throughout L.A. County. "WARNING TO LONG BEACH" advised the lead to a *Long Beach Daily Telegram* article about Betkouski's imperialistic decrees. Farther north, Venice, having already dodged annexation when Palms fell to Los Angeles, found itself girding for another entrenchment after L.A.'s acting mayor—or was it acting despot?—wondered aloud why his city didn't control the entire county coastline. "Right now there is a piece of county lying between the recent Westgate annexation and the shoestring strip," Betkouski observed. "That particular section is absolutely cut off from the rest of the country. That entire section, including Venice, Ocean Park, Santa Monica, and the west beaches, should be joined to Los Angeles." Redondo Beach, Hermosa Beach, and Manhattan Beach were also singled out as fair game. In an eerie parallel to the Great War that had broken out in Europe, every district in the county was essentially Belgium to L.A.'s Germany. "The sooner we clean up all of these desirable annexations to the City of Los Angeles, the quicker we will be able to establish a consolidated city and county government," Betkouski concluded, assuring conjoined districts that they could maintain their own liquor laws.

But in another comparison to Germany, L.A.'s governing body made the mistake of overreaching. Angelenos didn't share their representatives' stated mission of conquering their neighbors while problems within their own borders were allowed to fester. The cadre's fall would come as quickly as its rise.

A water wheel along the Los Angeles River, circa 1870. Water was lifted out of the Zanja Madre, or Mother Ditch, and distributed to the pueblo of Los Angeles in wooden pipes.

Los Angeles Plaza, circa 1890. The building on the left belonged to Judge Agustín Olvera, later honored with Olvera Street. The sign on the center building says "L.A. City Water Co.," where William Mulholland had risen from a ditchdigger to superintendent.

LEFT: Gen. Phineas Banning, the Father of Los Angeles Harbor.

MIDDLE: 1891 photograph of San Pedro Harbor, which Banning used to monitor from his mansion's top floors. Here, two companies transfer lumber from docked ships to Southern Pacific trains bound for Los Angeles.

A poster celebrating Gen. Harrison Gray Otis's pet project, the opening of a federally backed "Free Harbor," complete with breakwater and trains steaming to and from Los Angeles. The city would annex San Pedro within ten years, giving L.A. a global seaport.

TOP: Young Henry Huntington, taking a cue from Napoleon Bonaparte as he perceives future greatness.

LEFT: Otis in 1899, shortly after his stint in the Philippines. When he wasn't bedecked with medals and epaulets, he was arming up at his *Los Angeles Times* Fortress, ready to wage battle with unions and other perceived "enemies of the city."

BOTTOM: Collis Huntington, left, and his nephew Henry, in early 1890s San Francisco.

Frank Wiggins pioneered the use of gimmicks to promote Los Angeles as "the garden spot of the world." Here, an elephant made out of walnuts dominates the Palace of Horticulture at the 1904 World's Fair in St. Louis.

Huntington, left, and Harry Chandler, right, enjoy a spin around Los Angeles in an early touring car. Chandler's vision of an automobile-based city would eventually push Huntington's streetcars off the scene.

RIGHT: Mulholland in the field, where he always felt more at home, away from City Hall "pinheads."

MIDDLE: Joseph B. Lippincott, Fred Eaton, and Mulholland in August 1906. It was Eaton who saw the promise of Owens Valley's water source, while Lippincott, a former U.S. reclamation agent, helped secure the water for L.A. via Mulholland's aqueduct.

The Los Angeles Water Board after signing off on the L.A. Aqueduct. Moses Sherman, center, would soon come under fire after revelations that he was part of a syndicate benefitting from the imported water.

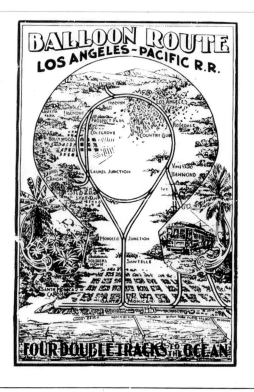

LEFT: A brochure for Sherman and Eli Clark's "Balloon Route," which advertised "101 miles for $1.00."

MIDDLE: Moses Sherman.

TO

Santa Monica	Ocean Park	Venice
Hollywood	Colegrove	Hermosa Beach
Laurel Canon	Sherman	Redondo
Playa del Rey	Soldier's Home	Manhattan Beach
Santa Monica Canon		Westgate

BOTTOM: A Balloon Route trolley from 1905. Besides being a major tourist draw, Sherman's Los Angeles-Pacific Railroad greased the wheels for L.A.'s westward development.

Henry E. Huntington: The Modern Colossus of Roads

He's the modern Colossus of Roads,
A magical bearer of loads,
And passengers grin when his cars they get in
To ride to their country abodes.

The real estate sharp never fails
To follow the Huntington "trails;"
He knows it means much to be in close touch
With the one who can stimulate sales.

Los Angeles finds it no task
In the light of his friendship to bask;
He's a man of affairs Who Does and Who Dares—
What more could the critical ask?

LEFT: By 1905, two out of three passengers rode a streetcar that was controlled by Huntington, prompting this cartoon from a local newspaper that hailed him as the man who tied all of Greater Los Angeles together.

BOTTOM: Pacific Electric Railway map from 1912, stretching from Orange County to the northwest San Fernando Valley. Most of the lines were built or absorbed by Huntington.

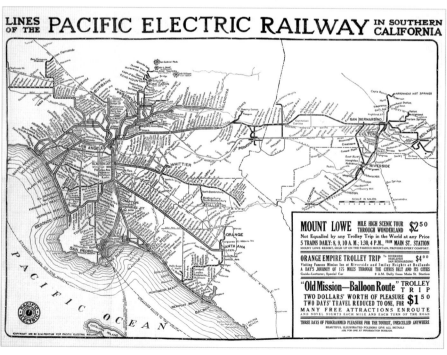

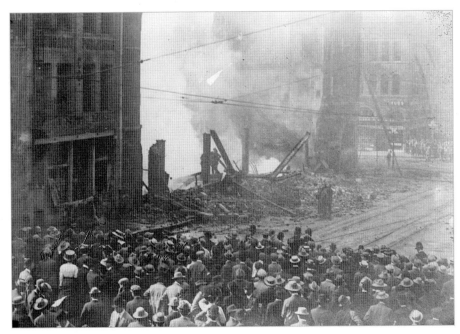

TOP: The morning of October 1, 1910, hours after labor activists dynamited the *Los Angeles Times* Fortress, resulting in dozens of casualties but sparing Chandler and Otis.

BOTTOM: Two years after the bombing, The Fortress was rebuilt, with Otis recommitting himself to "Industrial Freedom and the upbuilding of Los Angeles."

TOP: Two hundred miles to the north, workers begin to gouge out Owens Valley at the Los Angeles Aqueduct's headwaters. "Los Angeles Plots Destruction," mourned *The Inyo Register* in 1905.

BOTTOM: Mulholland incentivized aqueduct personnel with friendly competitions. The 5.5-mile Elizabeth Tunnel was built in record time, thanks to a years-long contest between a northern crew and a southern crew, which earned bragging rights by drilling to the middle first.

TOP: Some 40,000 people turn out to experience the onrush of water at the opening of the Los Angeles Aqueduct, November 5, 1913. Mulholland's signature project singlehandedly boosted L.A.'s population capacity another 700 percent.

BOTTOM: Officials crank open the floodgates at the top of the Cascades. "There it is," Mulholland hollered as the water roared downward. "Take it!"

Spurred by Chandler, the Southern California Auto Club helped drive L.A.'s expansion. The building of roads like Topanga and Laurel Canyon Boulevards to the newly annexed San Fernando Valley meant more money in the pockets of Chandler and friends.

Sherman Way linked "the Wonder Cities of the Valley" when it opened in 1912. By one supposed measure, it was the longest paved street in California.

Henry and his son Howard take in a baseball game played between employees of Huntington's Los Angeles Railway Co. LARy's Yellow Car system provided local service, tracing its origins to lines controlled by Sherman and Clark.

Huntington's private Red Car made the first trip over the hill into the Valley in 1911.

LEFT: Hollywoodland was the brainchild of Sherman and Chandler. The 1923 hillside subdivision was billed as a "white spot," a common designation for neighborhoods that included restrictive deed covenants.

BOTTOM: A Los Angeles guide from the 1920s warning against investing in "dark spots" defined by the "Negro race," while keeping the Fremont District white. The map bears the handiwork of an unknown party.

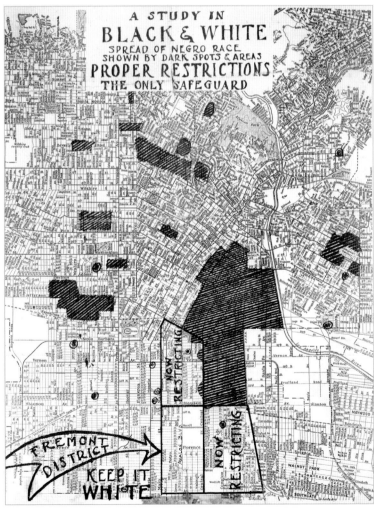

Mulholland (left), Sherman (second from left), and Chandler (fourth from left) next to a "Mulholland Highway" sign near its Hollywoodland terminus. Co-developer Sydney Woodruff (second from right) keeps his distance from Sherman after a falling out.

Sherman and Chandler with a caretaker at Tejon Ranch, where the friends owned 275,000 acres. By 1920, Chandler was reportedly the largest individual landowner in the United States.

Los Angeles gobbled up six cities in the 1920s, none larger than Venice, whose quaint but decaying canals were paved over for automobiles.

Barnes City was a circus town that also fell to L.A., though its legitimacy had long been called into question. Colorful founder Al G. Barnes allegedly counted monkeys among its electorate.

A tire factory—one of several—in Los Angeles's industrial zone in the 1920s. No single person did more to draw industry to L.A. than Chandler, aka the "Governor of Southern California."

A 1927 movie premiere at the Chinese Theatre, months after it opened. Chandler recognized the value of movie production to L.A. early on, even personally helping save Warner Bros. from insolvency.

A pamphlet for Edgar Rice Burroughs's community of Tarzana, its name derived from the author's own fictional character. The cover art plays off Burroughs's *Tarzan* adventure novels.

TARZANA
Home of *TARZAN*

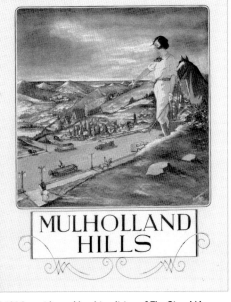

MULHOLLAND
HILLS

LEFT: The deification of Mulholland peaked in the mid-1920s, evidenced by this edition of *The Girard News* commemorating the opening of Mulholland Highway (Drive).

RIGHT: As with Huntington and Sherman, the Mulholland name was currency for realtors. The Mulholland Hills subdivision opened off his titular highway.

LEFT: Though the *Los Angeles Times* was L.A.'s biggest booster, Chandler was particular about who should be allowed access to the Land of Promise. A 1920 cartoon criticized the "unassimilated aliens" flooding in from Europe and Asia while Uncle Sam turned a blind eye.

BOTTOM: Later in his *Times* tenure, Chandler endorsed columns on eugenics. Taking a page out of Nazi Germany, the movement advocated sterilization for defective, simple-minded people and members of certain races.

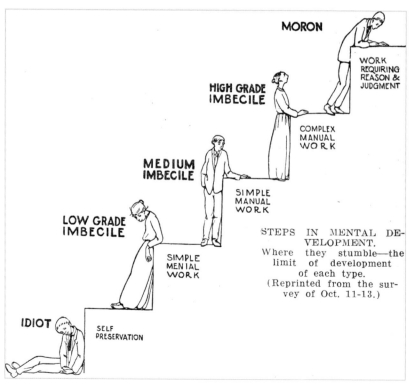

LEFT: Several years after his death in 1917, a group of statues honoring Otis was commissioned. They still stand today in MacArthur Park, minus the soldier figure, right, which was hit by a car.

RIGHT: Lavinia Graham Timmons, right, and her successor, Evelyn Champlin, headed the League of Women Voters of Los Angeles. After the ratification of the Nineteenth Amendment in 1920, women's voices finally counted in shaping L.A. policy.

If I am not on the JOB You can find me at the AQUEDUCT

A ubiquitous sign in Owens Valley, as up to 700 townspeople occupied the aqueduct in November 1924. A Los Angeles newspaper complained that the protest was "not good advertising" for the city.

TOP: Mulholland Dam at Lake Hollywood, 1925.

MIDDLE: Mulholland took pride in his namesake dam's ornate touches, including a row of grizzly bear heads beneath its curved arches.

BOTTOM: One year after Lake Hollywood's dam, Mulholland opened the similarly designed but much larger St. Francis Dam in San Francisquito Canyon.

The morning after the failure of the St. Francis Dam, whose death toll likely exceeded 500 people. Eerily, the remaining middle section resembled a giant "tombstone for flood victims."

After the St. Francis Dam catastrophe, skittish Hollywood residents called for the elimination of Lake Hollywood. Instead, its concrete barrier was reinforced with dense landscaping, creating a "psychological dam" for those below it.

TOP: Huntington at his San Marino grounds, pausing to admire the ducks and swans. The last chapter of his life was his most rewarding as he built out his gardens, library, and art galleries for public enjoyment.

BOTTOM: Huntington in later years at his estate.

Chandler was nicknamed "El Gran Benefactor" for his support of Olvera Street.

LEFT: Along with Chandler, Christine Sterling, right, was instrumental in creating Olvera Street. On July 4, 1929, she raised a California Bear Flag with former L.A. librarian Mary Foy, who observed a younger Mulholland studying engineering books under her watch.

RIGHT: Mulholland, Sherman, and Chandler aboard the *S. S. Sherman*, circa 1932, three agents of change for Los Angeles nearing the end of their reigns.

TOP: Built in 1863, Banning's Greek Revival-Victorian residence still stands, now part of the Banning Museum.

BOTTOM: Five years after his death in 1935, the Chief's legacy had firmly rebounded with the dedication of Mulholland Fountain. His granddaughter Patricia pressed a button that ignited illuminated fountains.

PART III

PARADISE FRAYED

CHAPTER 19

Consolidation Battles

AS HE APPROACHED HIS eightieth birthday on February 10, 1917, Gen. Harrison Gray Otis knew he was not long for this world. In addition to his creeping dementia, he had endured several heart attacks. Around this time, he bequeathed The Bivouac, his Mission Revival house in Westlake, to the County of Los Angeles, to be used "for the advancement of art in the West." (It became the Otis Art Institute two years later.) Then, he moved into Harry and Marian Otis Chandler's manse in Los Feliz, where a household staff catered to his myriad needs. He doted on his grandchildren, though he could be choleric in his enfeebled state. "I can't stand giggling girls!" he once cried when the peals of laughter became too much. On good days, he wandered the grounds in his worn Army uniform, weighed down with its medals of valor, or marched into the *Los Angeles Times* Fortress sporting an old Civil War slouch hat as he checked in on his Phalanx. The war in Europe was raging on, and it appeared just a matter of time before the United States got involved. The general kept himself battle-ready, no matter the capacity, even if it was from a bedside table firing off dispatches to the front.

Meanwhile, Los Angeles leaders maintained their crusade to acquire more territory, a movement abetted by Otis's own son-in-law and newspaper. Still intent on merging the city and county of Los Angeles into one jurisdiction, the City Council decided that the term "Annexation Commission" was too limiting. Thus, from late 1916 onward, the group was to be called the City and County Consolidation Commission. Council President and Acting Mayor Martin Betkouski had a dependable mouthpiece in the *Times*, which framed the "straightening out" of Los Angeles brought about by city/county consolidation only in positive terms while downplaying, ignoring, or misrepresenting opposing views. One article from September 1916 was subheaded "Words of Commendation Come to Councilmen from People Living in Outside Communities Who are Anxious to Join Los Angeles in Order to Reduce Expenses." The piece reported that Betkouski had received scores of letters from people in neighboring northeastern cities clamoring for consolidation. "Representatives of Pasadena . . . spoke very sympathetically of the movement," the paper rhapsodized in another story, quoting a Pasadena resident named Dean George A. Damon. But facts on the ground told a different story. The very next day, *The Whittier News* headlined: "PASADENA IS READY FOR FIGHT . . . DENIES SENTIMENT IN FAVOR OF CONSOLIDATION." Dean George A. Damon showed up in the article, claiming the *Times* had taken his quotes out of context and failed to mention that he was a member of the Los Angeles City Planning Association. F. E. Wilcox, president of the Pasadena board of trade, also cleared the air on behalf of Pasadena officials, who were "unalterably opposed to annexation to Los Angeles, or to city and county consolidation. . . . Pasadena has nothing to gain by going into Los Angeles." Similarly, the city council for South Pasadena took the position that it would not even broach the matter of consolidation "until asked to do so by a petition of citizens." No petitions ever emerged.

But the *Times* could afford to be dismissive of localized dailies like *The Whittier News*, dispensable fish wraps that couldn't hold a candle to its own power and subscriber base. By cherry-picking quotes and distorting narratives, the Chandler regime presented a respectable front that was more insidious than Otis's bloviating character assassinations and mudslinging. Combined with his wealth and influence beyond the newspaper, Chandler was now a formidable puppet master who effected change like no other force in Los Angeles.

By the start of 1917, the City and County Consolidation Commission introduced a new reason to meld Los Angeles into one governmental body: morality. During World War I, Russia and some European countries restricted alcohol consumption, while the U.S. curtailed exports to warring countries (and consumption among its own troops) to preserve grain for food manufacturing. Concurrently, the Anti-Saloon League and the Women's Christian Temperance Union were gaining political stature among progressive camps. Prohibitionists demanded a ban on all alcohol sales, which would ostensibly punish German Americans, who owned many of the nation's breweries. The temperance movement culminated with the passing of the Eighteenth Amendment and the subsequent National Prohibition Act in 1919. Against this backdrop, L.A.'s Consolidation Commission argued that immorality could be excised throughout the county if its plan came to fruition. "There was a time when the large cities were the centers of commercialized vice," the group stated. "As these cities have improved their moral reputations, there has been a tendency for small cities nearby to seek to capitalize into profits the forms of vice driven from larger cities." Consequently, the "evil influence" of unincorporated or smaller communities were "easily accessible to the young people of the entire area." Centralized law enforcement would vanquish these wicked zones, which currently "cannot be reached so quickly by the sheriff's office." The *Times* reduced the committee's main thrust to a laughable headline: "Morals Demand Consolidation."

On February 20, 1917, a special election was called in which Angelenos would decide two issues. "Group Owensmouth Annexation with Liquor Law," the *Times* commanded on the morning of the vote. Owensmouth had remained solo after most of the San Fernando Valley joined Los Angeles in 1915, still controlled by the county as a distribution hub for aqueduct water. With the system now online, Owensmouth conducted an internal vote in which 35 out of 39 voters opted to close "the hole in the doughnut" in this portion of the Valley, turning over its water operations to Los Angeles. The other ballot measure was dubbed the "Anti-Strong Drink Law," an ordinance that was backed by 25,000 signatures. It called for reduced hours for public liquor sales and the abolishment of hard alcohol in saloons, whose numbers were already more scarce compared to other American cities.

When the citywide results came in, the Owensmouth annexation squeaked by with a 50.8 percent majority that was partly attributable to voter confusion about its distribution role. At less than one square mile, L.A.'s newest member barely made a ripple on its boastful size. On the other hand, voters sent a very clear message on the drinking decree. It was dead on arrival. Perhaps sensing a countdown toward a nationwide ban, three out of every four Angelenos opted to keep the booze flowing. The one-sided outcome was also a strong statement against the formation of a single city and county entity and its proposal to scrub Greater Los Angeles of all vice.

On the heels of the Owensmouth addition, another territory containing important waterworks came up for annexation. However, where Owensmouth pumped water into Los Angeles, this one pumped it out. The so-called West Coast district was an oddly shaped 12.4-square-mile parcel of unincorporated land that occupied much of today's Westchester and Los Angeles International Airport. Its eastern border included the Angelus Vista neighborhood. On the west, it abutted a strip of land that belonged to the city of Venice, whose city limits blocked access to the coast. Directly below Venice's impervious shoestring, Los Angeles owned one coastal mile along Vista Del Mar, where it operated the Hyperion sewer plant. Just south of that, the city of El Segundo, which incorporated on January 18, 1917, owned the remaining beachfront up to Imperial Highway. Correspondingly, Hyperion—the disposal for *all* outfall sewage across the L.A. region and eventually the Valley—was boxed into a postage stamp-sized lot whose only access from the county (other than by sea) was a 420-foot-wide sliver between the southeast corner of Venice and the northwest corner of El Segundo. Clearly, losing this gap to either beachside city would be a catastrophic problem, shutting off Hyperion from the rest of Los Angeles.

Within weeks of El Segundo's establishment as a municipality, property owners in the West Coast region agitated the Los Angeles City Council to file an annexation petition, which resulted in a favorable April primary. The City and County Consolidation Commission fast-tracked the issue to get it on a June ballot. Though Angelenos didn't need much arm-twisting in this case, the *L.A. Times* did its part to underscore the urgency. "It is considered necessary that the city secure governmental jurisdiction over this stretch," it announced, "otherwise the frontage might be annexed to one of the small towns adjacent thereto, to the great embarrassment of the city in the discharge of its sewage."

It is ironic that the *Times* felt that Los Angeles was setting itself up for humiliation if it lost overland access to Hyperion. The effluent outlet had long been an object of derision. Opened in 1894, it was the end point of an evolving sewage system that diverted wastewater from the city's natural waterways. Over the years, it suffered from deferred maintenance and a limited capacity that was originally designed to handle thirty-one square miles and 250,000 people. It also lacked a treatment system, dumping raw refuse directly into Santa Monica Bay at present-day Dockweiler Beach. (Its conversion to a proper treatment plant would take decades.) Needless to say, the befouled water was hazardous for swimmers and fishermen. Ignoring calls not to fish by the outfall, Japanese crews were arrested for trawling within the contamination zone. In 1907, there were so many complaints of "sewer fish" sold at local markets, L.A.'s mayor enlisted the health department to crack down on scofflaws. Other times, untreated sludge burst through Hyperion's corroded pipes, once washing out Sherman's Los Angeles-Pacific tracks south of Playa del Rey. By 1908, the pier funneling wastewater pipes into the ocean was so rickety, beach residents pilfered its fallen stilts for firewood while a city engineer warned that the next giant wave would create "a large odoriferous splash" heralding its collapse. Finally, the

State Board of Health ordered Los Angeles to fix its sewer drain, and a county grand jury declared it a "nuisance." For the June 5, 1917, election, Los Angeles proposed a $5 million sewer bond to cover necessary upgrades on the same ballot that would decide the West Coast Addition, the two measures related.

The voting results were another telling snapshot of a changing city. As expected, the West Coast annexation carried easily, by a 2-to-1 margin. The new territory upped Los Angeles's area to 350 square miles, padding its lead over New York's 327. It also provided L.A. with a third tranche of ocean frontage, the newly acquired mile joining the harbor zone and the three miles added from the Westgate addition. But the sewer measure was roundly defeated. So were bonds for all other infrastructure projects. Voters seemed fed up with elected officials beholden to special interests, repudiating the "solid five" city councilmembers—all endorsed by the *Times*—who possessed the most power, including Martin Betkouski. What's more, the seemingly invincible president who sermonized for a moral society was morally bankrupt himself. Tagged "the Czar" by the *Los Angeles Record*, Betkouski was recently investigated by a grand jury for willful misconduct in a self-dealing land sale that netted him $56,000. With the Czar now out of the picture, the City and County Consolidation Commission lost its mojo in the new political environment, and talk of merging both administrations quietly went away. Within two years, the City and County Consolidation board dissolved, replaced by the City Planning Commission.

The *Times* may not have had its finger on the pulse of the public, but again, this hardly mattered to Chandler. Even before Mayor Charles Sebastian's retirement in 1916, Chandler had been grooming a replacement mayor to do his bidding. Frederic Woodman was the former president of the Harbor Commission, which Otis and Chandler helped create, and his rise in stature was buoyed by a series of favorable articles in the *Times*. On July 2, 1917, the first session of the new city council, Woodman delivered a message that reassured Chandler and the business lobby.

"The continued growth of the city demands that industrial enterprises should be encouraged," the mayor said. "The success of one is dependent upon the other, and it is our duty, as officials, to assure invested capital that it will be protected within the city to the fullest extent of the law." Woodman's not-so-veiled allusion to police "protection" against labor antagonists was elucidative. Starting in 1915, Chandler had helped install, through a series of complicit mayors, eight successive police chiefs who were hostile to unions. When the selection process of chiefs switched to a five-person commission in the mid-1920s, Chandler controlled most of them, too. Los Angeles was still very much "Otistown of the Open Shop."

Speaking of whom, by mid-July 1917, the man who had inspired the label continued to receive care at Harry and Marian Chandler's house. The United States had entered the World War in April, and the general furiously drafted a plan to end hostilities. On the morning of July 30, Otis awoke in his guest bedroom, sipped a cup of coffee, and opened the morning's delivery of the *Times*. The front page was steeped in war coverage. The Germans were advancing in Russia and the French launched a counterattack in Aisne. A Black maid named Lucy entered Otis's room with a tray of breakfast when the old man suddenly clutched at his heart. "Take the tray, Lucy," he wheezed. "I am gone." Death was almost instantaneous.

The funeral at the First Congregational Church had a solemn, regal air, with hundreds of *Times* employees paying tribute alongside family, friends, business leaders, and veterans. From the moment he bought a quarter share of the *Los Angeles Daily Times* in 1882, Harrison Gray Otis had seen more change in Los Angeles in his thirty-five years than the average person sees in two lifetimes—hadn't just seen it, but enabled it. His influential newspaper was as much an engine of commerce as any other industry in Los Angeles, helping drive the city's assessed valuation from $7.5 million in 1882 to $589 million in 1917. During that period, L.A.'s population rocketed from 12,500 to 500,000.

Russian artist Paul Troubetzkoy was commissioned to sculpt a triptych of bronze statues encapsulating Harrison's life, represented by a newspaper boy, a U.S. soldier hoisting a flag, and Gen. Otis himself perched on a rock, pointing westward. They were placed across from The Bivouac at Wilshire Boulevard and Park View Street. This being Los Angeles, a motorist eventually smashed into the soldier statue, which was carted away to the basement of Otis College. The other two statues stand sentry on a corner of MacArthur Park Lake. Their inscription reads: "General Harrison Gray Otis, 1837–1917. Soldier, journalist, friend of freedom. Stand fast, stand firm, stand sure, stand true."

The *Times'* leftist rivals gave Otis his proper due in their pages; however, just a year before his death, after another militant organizer was sent to prison in connection with the 1910 bombing of the *Times* building, the *Los Angeles Record* was still castigating Otis for the stain he left behind: "The man who brought all this labor hell on this town is Harrison Gray Otis, who for years distilled hate of the worker like venom and who made the big business interests of this city jump when he cracked the whip. . . . Hate begets hate, and anarchy begets anarchy, so Otis begot violence." The newspaper submitted that "Otis is waning, his power is gone." Technically, this was true as far back as 1914, after his famous Letter of Declaration deed to the Chandlers. But now it was official. Per the general's wishes, fifty-four-year-old Harry inherited the mantle of President and General Manager of the *L.A. Times*, with Marian Otis Chandler its Vice President and Secretary. Surpassing his father-in-law in power, Harry Chandler would continue to use the newspaper as a pulpit against labor, an instrument for his own profits, and a platform to raise the profile of Los Angeles. With a powerful oligarchy behind it, the city was well-positioned to achieve dizzying new heights in the postwar era, even as some citizens were coldly left behind.

CHAPTER 20

Growing Pains and Gains

THE OUTDATED HYPERION SEWAGE system wasn't the only facility ill-equipped to handle Los Angeles's meteoric growth. No sooner did the Los Angeles Aqueduct become fully functional than it started breaking down. In a bit of cruel irony, Los Angeles enjoyed above-average precipitation in the four years after the canal's completion in 1913. In February 1917, heavy rains wiped out an elevated pipeline in Antelope Valley, releasing precious snowmelt through ruptured steel walls. Water Bureau head William Mulholland also continued to hit a dead end in his bid to build a vast dam and reservoir in Long Valley. Fred Eaton, owner of the Owens Valley acreage and Bill's former colleague, rejected the latest offer of $500,000. "Fred, I'm asking you to appeal to reason," entreated the Chief, who had recently ascended to president of the American Society of Civil Engineers. Eaton wouldn't budge, holding firm at $1 million.

By May, as work on the main from San Fernando Reservoir was nearing completion, secondary conduits were springing leaks all over the San Fernando Valley. The *Los Angeles Times* was predictably mute on the issue, but the *Los Angeles Record* posted several photos of shoddy irrigation pipes. Frustrated farmers felt they were sold a bill of goods. "The entire water system here is the most inefficient piece of business I ever saw," said grower T. J. Walker, who filed suit against the Los Angeles Water Board. He showed a reporter written assurances from board members that he could plant beets, beans, and citrus trees—everything would thrive in this sodden wonderland. "There are lots of individuals in this territory who are going broke. I am desperate for water . . . they put in such leaky pipes that they are no sooner laid than the water has to be shut off, the pipe dug up and the leaks repaired." Porous joints were patched with tar, only to leak again. Walker had gotten so desperate that he asked the board if he could just lay in piping at his own expense. "This would be in addition to my taxes and everything I had already paid." Others tried jerry-rigging old pumps, only to find them unserviceable. "We relied on them, planted crops that demand lots of water," said another farmer, "and now we haven't got the water and don't see any signs of it coming. All we are sure of getting is more promises." Another owner sniped, "If we had known how the aqueduct water was going to disappoint us, we'd have planted 'dry crops' on those fields this year." The *Record* began referring to the aqueduct as the "Aqua Duck" (or, in a nod to Mulholland, "Bill's Ducky"). Scathing cartoons represented the Aqua Duck as a giant iron duck fashioned after L. Frank Baum's Tik-Tok man, with a patchwork of leaky rivets and cement shoes. A fat-cat bureaucrat fed Bill's Ducky "taxpayer dollars" while a Vaudevillian "Bill Mulholland" scrambled to mop up its spewing water.

Adding to Mulholland's problems, two avowed Socialists from the Aqueduct Investigation Board sought an injunction that would stop the import of Owens Valley water, calling it "unfit for human consumption." Their charge was bogus, echoing claims from a decade earlier when anti-aqueduct factions said the water contained typhoid. Nonetheless, the case went to trial. Mulholland was called to the stand to face cross-examination, which tested his notorious short fuse. He declared that thousands of people, including his own workmen, had been drinking aqueduct water for years with no ill effects. Hundreds of letters extolling its "excellent quality" had crossed his desk. "Where are you going to get pure water if we haven't it in the Owens River Valley?" he demanded. "If it isn't pure in the Sierras, where is it pure? There is not a water supply to any city of any size in the country that is as pure and free from contamination." When the plaintiffs' lawyer identified a creek that may contain polluted Owens Valley water,

Mulholland sarcastically replied, "Oh, I could point you to far more polluted sources than that." The attorney took the bait: "Really? And just what would those be?" Mulholland shrugged and suggested the attorney draw samples from beneath a riverside outhouse. "Or," he added, "you could roll a hog into the water with an apple in its mouth and take a photo of it."

Though Mulholland was ultimately vindicated, the trial did rekindle concerns over his autodidactic engineering ability and his dictatorial leadership within the water department. The court case also reignited bitter accusations that the titans who helped build the San Fernando Valley disproportionately benefitted. Harvey Van Norman, the superintendent of the aqueduct's operations, admitted that property owned by Gen. Moses Sherman and the estate of Gen. Harrison Otis lay in a part of the Valley with free-flowing aqueduct water while everyone else struggled with erratic flows.

As Mulholland scrambled to connect L.A.'s water grid to newly annexed households, Henry Huntington continued providing much of the area's natural gas and electricity. Just as Mulholland underestimated how long the Los Angeles Aqueduct could sustain a growing populace, Huntington was shocked (albeit pleasantly so) by how quickly the city's electrical needs grew. In 1914, his highly profitable Pacific Light and Power Company controlled one quarter of the power in the city of Los Angeles. That same year, the mogul observed that Greater L.A. had grown three years faster than he had estimated, forcing him "to develop power that we calculated would not be needed until 1917." Fast-forward to May of 1917, and the self-described "foresighted man" was about to cash in. With the approval of the Board of Public Service, Huntington merged PL&P with the Southern California Edison Company, creating the largest municipal power utility in the world. SCE took over ninety-five percent of PL&P's capital stock and $25 million of its debt. Huntington became SCE's largest shareholder at thirty-eight percent and received $12 million in preferred stock. Conversely, by acquiring

Huntington's prolific Big Creek powerhouse on the San Joaquin River, SCE became the fifth-largest electric company in America. (Big Creek still provides the overwhelming share of the company's hydroelectric production.) Edison also got a boost from the Huntington name, which was still prized currency in Southern California. "I am very proud to be so closely associated with one who has been such a factor in the development of this wonderful Southern California as has Mr. Henry Huntington," said John B. Miller, president of SCE. "Mr. Huntington has been the direct means of bringing more money to this community than any other person. He built the great Pacific Electric Railway system, which linked Los Angeles to the surrounding towns which became places of importance and the homes of thousands of prosperous people. . . . He is principal owner of the Huntington Land and Improvement Company . . . and he has many other interests interwoven with the very fibre of our financial and industrial life."

Consolidating PL&P with SCE nudged the sixty-seven-year-old Huntington one step closer to retirement. The free-market sage was tired of suffocating regulations. "We have too many laws by the tens of thousands," he once griped to a business group. "We are enslaved by laws. We are overwhelmed by them." A rash of health scares also took a toll. With the deal consummated, he boldly announced, "I am now out of business. I would like to sell all my interests and get clear of it." This was more wishful thinking, but he did manage to make good on delegating more responsibility to a team of trustworthy general managers. His legal adviser, William E. Dunn, steered Huntington's Los Angeles Railway through a particularly rough patch. The popularity of jitneys in the mid-1910s was a direct threat to urban railways. These unregulated, proto-Uber vehicles ran alongside Yellow Car tracks and picked off passengers with nickel rides; their operations were finally reined in by city ordinances. Meanwhile, private automobile ownership continued to eat away at Huntington's trolleys, thanks to the affordability of Model T Fords. Registered vehicles in Los Angeles numbered 47,000 in 1917, almost double from two years earlier, with access to over 2,516 miles of streets (a quarter of which were surfaced). Although LARy remained popular on certain routes, there was no getting around Huntington's liquidity problems. Bonds to expand his trolley to places like Boyle Heights dried up, and Henry received none of the cash due on his existing railroad bonds. As operating expenses increased, the California Railroad Commission forbade him from raising passenger fees. "Conditions have changed very materially," he wrote Dunn. "I do not want another foot of track laid or any franchise accepted until we can receive bonds for work already done." L.A.'s white-hot real estate market also started to wane. Huntington's rail empire had helped create a boom in the early twentieth century, contributing to some 500 new subdivisions a year. But in the mid-1910s, as more suburbs saturated the landscape, development slowed to about 200 subdivisions a year. Suddenly, Huntington's Land and Improvement Co. didn't always have enough cash on hand to pay back millions of dollars in loans.

On the plus side, Henry's marriage to Arabella in 1913 brought an infusion of wealth on top of his own. (When Collis Huntington died in 1900, he left Bell more than $50 million, making her one of the richest women in the country.) But despite their combined fortune, Henry and Bell kept separate bank accounts, and Huntington maintained his usual fiscal discipline in response to market instability. As his lieutenants restructured his assets to pay down debts, he tacked toward "enjoyment and fun" by building out his kingdom in San Marino. By 1917, his private library of rare books and manuscripts comprised over 50,000 volumes. Its crown jewel, purchased in 1911, made news across the world. "THE MAN WHO PAID $50,000 FOR THE GUTENBERG BIBLE," announced a headline in *The New York Times* on April 30. It was twice as much as any book had sold up to that point. "All the enormous energy which made him in his business days a genuine hustler is now concentrated on his collections," the newspaper noted. Huntington never actually read most of his literary gems, but that was beside the point. Outbidding other

millionaires for the world's most sought-after works was a supreme triumph for the boy in him, who saw erudite pursuits as
prerequisites to respectability. "I intend to go through my gram-
mer [sic] tomorrow and then commence it again the next day,"
he once wrote his sister at age twelve, "for I intend to go through
it again and again for I want to learn to talk correctly as I have
not learnt yet."

As an adult, Huntington could thank Bell for burnishing his
impressively refined palate. During their courtship, the two had
exchanged letters professing their love of British paintings. As
they settled into San Marino together, Bell's sophisticated taste
influenced his appetite for other priceless artifacts. He sought out
jewelry, sculptures, antiques, furniture from French monarchs,
and works from Medieval and Renaissance masters. In curating
these collections, Huntington had found his calling away from
the business world. It was now apparent that, in addition to his
growing library and gardens, he was going to need to build a
public art gallery. Coincidentally, at the same time Huntington
was assembling a paean to spirituality and high art, Harry Chandler was cornering the market on another engine of growth in
Los Angeles: pop culture.

CHAPTER 21

Fudge for San Francisco

ON NOVEMBER 2, 1917, film director D. W. Griffith returned to Los Angeles from Europe, where he, actress Lillian Gish, and other cast members were escorted to the front lines in battle-torn France to shoot scenes for his upcoming war epic, *Hearts of the World*. The motion picture pioneer owned a 147-acre plot in present-day Pacoima near the western flank of the San Gabriel Mountains that had hosted several of his western epics. Griffith Ranch was also, according to a plaque at the former site, "the inspiration for the immortal production, *The Birth of a Nation.*" But his little rustic studio had a big problem that saddled so many other communities—no source of water. Fortunately for Griffith, he had friends in high places.

Shot during the summer of 1914, *The Birth of a Nation* was a job juggernaut for Los Angeles and the Southland, which provided outdoor stages for the period drama. The film is commonly cited by historians for its innovative cinematic techniques that came to define modern moviemaking. When the movie was released on February 8, 1915, it smashed box-office records, despite calls for a boycott by the National Association for the Advancement of Colored People for its racist portrayal of Black characters. (The movie was originally called *The Clansman* and now bears the scar of helping resuscitate the Ku Klux Klan.) One person who took notice of the movie's popularity was Harry Chandler, who was already well-versed in the commercial prospects of this budding industry.

Like many millionaires of his time, Chandler wasn't an avid moviegoer. A typical two-reeler was a frivolous pastime for the

hoi polloi. But that was precisely the point. When an opportunity presented itself in late 1911, Chandler jumped on it. Looking
to escape Thomas Edison's oppressive patent wars, filmmakers
Al and Charles Christie got as far away as they could from New
York and, wooed by M. H. de Young of the *San Francisco Chronicle*, relocated to San Francisco. When word got out that the
Christie brothers were shooting a movie, Chandler kept track of
the weather in L.A.'s opposite number. It didn't take long before
gray, foggy skies impeded the brothers' progress (early silents relied on sunlight to illuminate their open-ceiling "indoor" sets).
Chandler immediately galvanized his cronies at the Los Angeles Chamber of Commerce into action. The board reached out
to the Christies with a weather report: warm with clear skies in
sunny Los Angeles. Within days, a chartered train relocated the
Christies' entire set and entourage to the City of Angels. Thanks
to Chandler, the Christies ended up staying and opened Nestor
Studios, considered to be the first motion picture studio in Hollywood. Studios began popping up like mushrooms throughout
Greater L.A.—fifty companies and counting over the next three
years. Suddenly, moviemaking had joined real estate, oil, tourism, agriculture, and manufacturing as another lucrative sector
of the Los Angeles economy.

Chandler, of course, charted all of this. Through the 1910s,
the puppet master pulled whatever strings he could to preserve
L.A.'s monopoly as a "picture town," even though he harbored
private disdain for the creative community's hedonism. In 1914,
the *Los Angeles Times* became the first newspaper in the country
to launch a regular motion picture column, which was written by
a female arts staffer, Grace Kingsley. Preceding *Daily Variety* and
The Hollywood Reporter by at least sixteen years, the articles were
dazzling reads, a heady mix of movie news, casting updates, juicy
scoops, and the business of Hollywood before "Hollywood" even
became a catchall for the movie industry. Chandler made sure
that snippets of Kingsley's column made it into the *Times'* special
Midwinter Editions. Well-heeled readers in the snowed-in East

and Midwest were greeted with this headline on January 1, 1915: "LOS ANGELES THE GLOBE'S MOVING PICTURE CEN-TER," followed by an enticing subhead that spoke to their wallets: "MILLIONS IN IT." The article name-dropped several rising pro-ducers who became cinematic royalty, including Thomas Ince, Jesse Lasky, and William Selig, who crowed that "the motion pic-ture industry is the fourth greatest industry in the United States." Kingsley added that "thousands of people are employed in the crowds," including, for *The Clansman*, "soldiers, negroes and Ku-Klux men, to the huge figure of 14,000."

Naturally, these actors—and movie folks in general—need-ed places to dine, dance, live, shop. When the movie columns weren't appealing to businessmen, they served as de facto guides for tourists or Angelenos-in-waiting: "Southern California is nat-urally suited to motion picture production, as its vast stretches of uncultivated foothill country, its big deserts and picturesque shore lines lend themselves ideally to the dramatic setting of great spectacular plays." Movie stars enjoyed motoring "along the beau-tiful Southern California boulevards." Actresses luxuriated in the pleasant year-round climate. Helen Ware got in "a swim before her day's work," Anna Pavlova tended to "posies in the early-morning sunlight," and Ina Claire took "long, delightful [horseback] rides in the Hollywood foothills." Fanny Ward was a true convert: "She declares she never wishes to go East again. She drives a car, swims, and plays tennis." In nearby Universal City, Carl Laemmle estab-lished his film studio in the hills of Cahuenga Pass. The public was invited to sit in bleachers and watch their favorite silent movie stars act in live scenes, with spectators encouraged to cheer the hero and hiss the villain.

In Los Feliz, just down the street from the Chandler resi-dence, movie fans flocked to the eastern terminus of Hollywood Boulevard to sneak a peek at a monstrous outdoor stage with rearing-elephant sculptures (an exact scale recreation formed the courtyard of the Hollywood & Highland mall when it opened in November 2001). The set was for the ancient Babylonian sequence in Griffith's follow-up movie, *Intolerance*. On October 17, 1916, 3,000 people sat "spellbound" at its Clune's Auditorium premiere, which landed on the *Times'* front page. "With 'Intolerance,' David Wark Griffith has made his place secure as one of the towering geniuses of the world," reported Harry Carr, who was in attendance. Besides finally revealing what "all those whopping, big and mysterious stage settings out on Hollywood boulevard" were for, Griffith had proven that movies deserved to be placed alongside "painting and sculpture and literature and music." Carr's copy reflected the editorial dictum of his *Times* boss. "Culture and the spiritual development of the community is vastly more important than economic development," Chandler told his team. Harry may have personally believed that, but the capitalist in him saw culture and spiritual development *as* economic development. Where Henry Huntington's gardens and library were philanthropic ventures, Chandler viewed enlightenment through the prism of profit-making institutions. Over the next ten years, he would help found several L.A. icons synonymous with cultural experiences, such as the Hollywood Bowl (classical music, religious services); the Coliseum (the Olympics, public speeches, artistic performances); Olvera Street (Spanish and Mexican heritages); and L.A.'s first commercial radio station, KHJ (opera, news, sermons from über-evangelist Aimee Semple McPherson). Looking to lure the brightest brains in science and technology to Southern California, he was also a key investor in the private research university Caltech in Pasadena. Now, Griffith's dual historical epics—*The Birth of a Nation* and *Intolerance*—had elevated a once lightweight medium into the realm of legitimized art, opening the door to commodify movies in a way that would appeal to wealthier conservatives.

All of which is to say, Chandler had high regard for D. W. Griffith. Shortly after the director's return from shooting *Hearts of the World* in the fall of 1917, the Los Angeles City Council responded to an annexation request from residents of Griffith Ranch by scheduling a special election for December 28. It would be an annexation election like no other. In the past, L.A.'s electorate cast ballots alongside those in the districts requesting entrée. Angelenos, it had long been felt, should have a stake in deciding whether a new community was a good fit for Los Angeles. Would the entrant be an asset or a strain on the city? What did its tax roll look like? Could William Mulholland even guarantee it water? For this election, however, only Griffith Ranch would vote. Technically, this was a legal application of California codes. Under the Annexation Act of 1913, if a majority of registered voters from a contiguous territory wished to latch onto a larger city, the larger city's council need only to set up an election in that micro-precinct. Several factors influenced L.A.'s shift to state policy. In some ways, the city was a stand-in for oligarchs like Chandler and Huntington, who needed constant streams of revenue to sustain their empires. New markets increased L.A.'s capitalization and impregnability. And with dozens of piecemeal territories on the horizon, the elimination of special elections—cumbersome, expensive, and annoying to voting-fatigued Angelenos—promised to streamline the annexation process. By switching to the state rules, a new city ordinance required only that a notice be placed in a local newspaper for four consecutive weeks before the election. Hence, after clearing the petition process, Griffith Ranch did not need "permission" from Los Angeles voters to join Los Angeles.

There was just one wrinkle. Occupying only 0.23 square miles of chapparal and fruit trees, the ranch was mostly populated by gophers and rattlesnakes, though Lillian Gish was known to hang out there with her pals on Sundays. It was the smallest proposed merger since L.A. started building out its original twenty-eight square miles. Nonetheless, on election day, the outdoor studio voted unanimously to join Los Angeles. That sounded impressive until it was revealed that only five people voted. Three of them sat on the ranch's election board—the minimum legal number— including a husband and wife who were presumably caretakers of the property. The others may have been "deputized" voters;

under L.A. laws, farmhands who spent much of their time on land under annexation consideration counted as electors. The state certified the election on February 16, 1918.

With relaxed guidelines in place, a pattern emerged among L.A.'s subsequent acquisitions: They got smaller. Prior to Griffith Ranch, there had been only two districts (Garvanza and Owensmouth) less than one square mile that had petitioned for annexation. But in 1918 alone, three more parcels under one square mile were taken in by the city: West Adams (a buffer preventing newly incorporated Culver City from snagging it), Ostend (a buffer against Long Beach on the San Pedro waterfront), and Orange Cove (not far from Griffith Ranch). The Valley's Hansen Heights was the only sizable territory to be added that year, 8.3 square miles covering much of today's Shadow Hills east of Hansen Dam, but it was more the exception than the rule. From 1918 to 1932—the latter year marking the point when Los Angeles acquired ninety-six percent of its present 468 square miles—there were *forty-one annexed districts* measuring less than one square mile. In addition to benefitting from a nimbler annexation process, these piecemeal specks were either the result of a particular district's desire to stave off a neighboring municipality or a reflection of the fact that the L.A. basin was simply running out of attainable land. Once causes for endless handwringing and pearl-clutching, annexations started to become blasé, their news buried on papers' back pages.

But that was decidedly *not* the case in Sawtelle. After Westgate consolidated with Los Angeles in June 1916, Sawtelle started having second thoughts about sitting on the sidelines. A coalition petitioned the Los Angeles City Council to set up a special election in Sawtelle for a redo. The final results showed 519 voters in favor of consolidation and 516 against. That's when the drama began. With such a slim margin, a handful of citizens cried foul. They retained a lawyer, Paul Schenck, who secured a temporary injunction as various judges opined on the validity of the election. The plaintiffs alleged several irregularities, including a discrepancy between the number of voters who signed the poll book versus actual voters. They also argued that L.A. should have called a *citywide* vote instead of relying on the new locals-only methodology, which wasn't in place for the initial election proceedings. (Truth be told, under the old system, the margin of victory would have been even greater since L.A. voters typically leaned pro-annexation.) Schenck figured out that the correct margin should have been 512 nays and 505 yeas, allowing Sawtelle to retain its status as a free-standing town.

Los Angeles City Attorney Albert L. Stephens wasn't buying the stall tactics of a few renegades. He cited the Secretary of State's certification of the election and a Superior Court decision that dissolved the injunction. "Los Angeles has a right to take over the city of Sawtelle," he asserted. And then, Stephens flexed. In the dark morning hours of February 8, 1918, the Los Angeles Police Department raided Sawtelle's government offices. Ten officers confiscated records and keys and locked them in a safe, which was hauled off to L.A. City Hall. Stephens also ordered the immediate disbanding of Sawtelle's police and fire departments. He even seized Sawtelle's official seal. "I did not want to take such drastic action," he said, "but we gave the Sawtelle officials more than two weeks to gracefully give up the ship. They refused and there was no alternative for Los Angeles." The invasion backfired. Los Angeles was now an occupying force in the eyes of most Sawtelle residents. The town's mayor, William Haas, vowed to forge ahead with city business, but he and his council were unable to conduct meetings in their City Hall—the LAPD had removed all the light bulbs. The representatives agreed to meet in each other's homes, a government-in-exile in a town under dual rule. As past-due bills piled up, the mayor shrugged and told collectors to contact Los Angeles since it had frozen Sawtelle's treasury. The feuding parties sought an appointment with the California Supreme Court to end the state of limbo. But that would take years. For the time being, Sawtelle residents would be forced to live double lives.

In 1919, Los Angeles scooped up five more tiny territories through local elections. The largest, West Lankershim, was a 1.17-square-mile breakaway section of independent-minded Lankershim. The other four were unincorporated pockets in San Pedro, shoring up the harbor region from Long Beach encroachment. Their consolidations further increased L.A.'s capacity to handle ever-increasing port traffic brought on by the end of the Great War and the opening of the Panama Canal. Since the first ship arrived via the canal in 1914, the Port of Los Angeles was now the third busiest industrial harbor in the world—an amazing turn of events for a seaport that wasn't even commercially viable until the early 1900s.

At the start of 1920, Los Angeles sat at 363 square miles—264 of them accrued over the past ten years. That year's Census placed it as the tenth most populous city in the union and number forty-four in the world. More importantly, Los Angeles had finally passed San Francisco in population—576,673 to 506,676. (The city included Sawtelle's 4,868 in its total.) Reflecting L.A.'s deep-rooted inferiority complex with its rival, the *L.A. Times* adopted a defensive stance after San Francisco newspapers "[took] another whack at Los Angeles because Los Angeles has been put ahead by the census returns." San Francisco was clearly "jealous" when it bellyached that it was only due to a flurry of annexations, and "not to legitimate growth," that L.A.'s population outpaced the Golden Gate city. The *Times* ascertained that the twenty annexed territories in the last ten years brought in only 11,197 people. Half the additions contained fewer than 100 inhabitants each. These sparsely populated areas were only absorbed because L.A. could not otherwise legally sell them aqueduct water. "Had Los Angeles been seeking mere population," the paper argued, "it would have endeavored to annex small areas containing cities instead of large areas containing in some cases only a few people to the square mile." The article name-checked Long Beach, Pasadena, South Pasadena, Alhambra, Glendale, Whittier, Vernon, Watts, Santa Monica, Venice, and Eagle Rock as neighboring cities with considerable populations, and "all are still separate municipalities."

But the *Times'* reassurance was disingenuous. Drunk on the "phenomenal" Census figures, another article in Chandler's newspaper boasted of an aggressive campaign, led by Chandler proxy Moses Sherman, to triple Los Angeles's size by dissolving the boundaries of all the adjoining cities it purported not to care about.

CHAPTER 22

Los Angeles, Inc.

AS NO STRANGER TO controversial appointments, it was inevitable that Gen. Moses Sherman, Harry Chandler's "spy," would pop up again on a civic committee advocating for the unfettered growth of Los Angeles. Nearly ten years had passed since his stint on the Water Board crashed and burned after accusations of self-dealing related to his holdings in the San Fernando Valley. In the interim, Chandler had risen to the most powerful man in Los Angeles. He and Sherman remained tight, heading up syndicates throughout Southern California. The partners had sunk $3 million into Tejon Ranch, 275,000 acres of oak-studded ranchland north of Los Angeles where they struck oil. They were also principal investors in the Imperial Valley and northern Mexico, where Chandler's Colorado River Land Company held various interests. By 1920, Chandler's real estate portfolio encompassed two million acres of land, making him the largest individual landowner in the United States. "It's just as well that Harry Chandler wasn't well when he came to California," jested *The Saturday Evening Post*, referring to his earlier sickly years, "for if he had been, the United States might have had to acquire China to provide scope for his activities."

All the while, Chandler's newspaper pumped out daily affirmations to bend public will in ways that benefited Harry and his friends. "It is a great thing to have a great newspaper like the Los Angeles Times (a wonderful man like Mr. Chandler) behind us, to help us," Moses conceded to Eli Clark, with whom he continued investing after divorcing Eli's sister, Hattie. Continuing a process that began fifteen years earlier, Sherman, in turn, suggested ways he could assist the *Los Angeles Times* in downplaying investments that might otherwise draw unwanted attention. "Please let me help a little in what was said," he wrote Chandler in a letter stamped "CONFIDENTIAL." "If what I have said herein could be done by you, I will be very glad." Another time, when the *Times* set up an interview with Sherman about his interactions with Southern Pacific, the general requested "the best and 'smoothest' reporter you have [to] come and see me." Chandler was happy to oblige.

Chandler equally benefitted from his relationship with Sherman. Moses provided comradeship, an astute business mind, and a reliable investment partner. Whenever Sherman sensed his buddy needed access to capital, he never hesitated to reach out. "Your perennial goodness and good will toward me brings me the biggest and deepest satisfaction that can come from a friend to another friend," Chandler replied in 1917 after turning down a $10,000 loan. "I can meet any obligation without using your kindly offered, free-from-interest loan, and for this we are both grateful."

Most importantly, Sherman remained a willing and stealthy envoy for Chandler, someone to head up committees that drove L.A.'s economy, even if, as with the Water Board, Sherman risked blowback while padding their bank accounts. His latest assignment was trotted out in a March 1, 1919, headline in the *Times*: "SHERMAN HEADS NEW COMMISSION." The "new commission" was actually an old one—the City and County Consolidation Commission—revived by Chandler ally Mayor Frederic Woodman and the City Council. "Gen. M. H. Sherman," the *Times* continued, "who has been untiring for years in his efforts to stimulate the growth and business of Los Angeles, was unanimously chosen permanent chairman of the commission." No mention was made of Sherman's getting forced off his previous post, which also had promised lifetime tenure.

So why did the commission to consolidate Los Angeles city and county make a comeback? Credit changing political winds. Thanks to the switch from citywide to local special elections, armies of pro-annexation petitioners could now knock on doors in contiguous cities, hoping to garner enough signatures for the Los Angeles City Council to set up a quick vote. When citizens' committees held town halls, agents from L.A. shamelessly picked up the tab for the gatherings. Though water, power, and sewage were the main reasons to surrender to Angel City, other issues popped up, too. Glendale residents tired of high telephone rates. Santa Monica and Venice worried about the loss of revenue that would result from cancelled liquor licenses once Prohibition kicked in on January 17, 1920. Underlying the insecurities of neighboring towns was a campaign by the *Times* that could best be described as a gentle indoctrination but was really an implied hostile takeover. Suddenly, the entire Greater Los Angeles region—defined as "from the mountains to the ocean running north and south, and from San Gabriel to the ocean, running east and west"—started being referred to as "natural Los Angeles" or "corporate Los Angeles." The idea was that island municipalities within L.A. were "really Los Angeles in all but names and government," so they might as well get on board before Los Angeles, Inc. forced their hand.

The notion of Los Angeles as a body politic reflected the tenets of G. Gordon Whitnall, L.A.'s first city planner. In the early 1910s, Whitnall was not much more than a callow left-winger who stumped for Job Harriman's failed mayoral bid in 1913. Yet his background as a Socialist informed his impressive career that followed. Employing strong organizational skills, Whitnall made the case for a more equitable city. In the old days, landowners living along major thoroughfares were responsible for road improvements. (Similar to how owners paid Sherman to route his railways past their properties.) Whitnall argued that it was "unfair to force property owners along these streets to stand the entire burden of the improvement along these streets, since they often run through districts of low property value." He proposed a standardized street system paid for by city-wide taxation, highways financed by the state, and strict zoning laws to regulate industry. All were eventually adopted. In 1920, Whitnall headed up the first City Planning Commission, a position he held for ten years. He also spearheaded the Los Angeles Regional Planning Commission, the first such county group in America. As the leader of both panels, perhaps it's not surprising that Whitnall reintroduced the idea of unifying city and county governance. "Thus far we have just 'happened,'" he said of Los Angeles. "We must now plan." L.A.'s willy-nilly growth, of course, was practically by design, a product of unbridled capitalism that drew derision from neighboring cities as what *not* to do. "Nobody ever PLANNED Los Angeles on a big scale," pooh-poohed a Burbank developer's missive. "She was just allowed to grow." In light of his socialist principles, Whitnall and Chandler made odd bedfellows. But Chandler was nothing if not pragmatic. He endorsed Whitnall's city/county amalgamation and made sure his paper gave it the full treatment.

On May 30, 1920, the *Times* unfurled a detailed, half-page map of what Los Angeles would look like in the year 1945. It was the first time the public laid eyes on the recommendations of Whitnall's planning department to create "order out of chaos." The territory was Napoleonic in scope. It imagined a 1,000-square-mile megacity, twenty-five miles east-west and forty miles north-south. The boundaries of every autonomous town— from San Fernando to Redondo Beach, from Santa Monica to San Gabriel—were completely melted away. Though underdeveloped northern Los Angeles County was not represented, the map did include illustrated insets of the Los Angeles Aqueduct and a typical hydroelectric plant, key features in "making this great development possible." Three million inhabitants would call Los Angeles home.

The planning commission was thirty-five years premature on its projected population. Los Angeles would not reach three million people until 1980, but then, the city never took in enough municipalities to get anywhere close to 1,000 square miles either. However, many predictions were pretty accurate. The map called for a Civic Center in northern downtown, a Union Station in the Plaza district, even a subway from Los Angeles to the coast via the Wilshire corridor. (It would take over a hundred years for MTA's D Line/Purple Line to be built, though it stopped five miles short of Santa Monica beach.) The mockup included an industrial zone between eastern Los Angeles and the harbor, with a "great truck boulevard" to haul freight to the warehouse district. This imagined thoroughfare would take shape decades later as the 710 Freeway, which carries more trucks than any other freeway in L.A. County. The proposal also envisioned an industrial stretch along the future path of Interstate 5, the second busiest truck route in the county. If readers squinted hard enough, a picture emerged of future freeways interlacing the map to fulfill Whitnall's "comprehensive system of highways . . . adequate in number and width to provide for the needs of a city of several millions." (Whitnall lived long enough to see the construction of L.A.'s freeway system . . . and experience its inadequacy. Little-traveled Whitnall Highway, part of the never-built Whitnall Freeway, lives on in the Valley.) One infrastructure project that remained a pipe dream was a network of dredged canals traveling inland from the San Pedro and Long Beach harbors, "so that ships can come well up into the industrial zone to receive and discharge cargoes." So much for waterfront property in L.A.'s Fashion District.

In a *Times* opinion piece titled "WORLD METROPOLIS HERE LOGICAL, INEVITABLE," Whitnall all but blamed the county's satellite cities should Los Angeles fail to realize its future greatness. "The life of these [smaller] cities is inseparably bound up with the life of Los Angeles," he maintained. "Los Angeles' problems are their problems and theirs are ours. Their citizens and ours intermingle in a maze of interrelated business and social intercourse." He praised those communities that were already circulating petitions to join L.A., while gently chiding opposing municipalities as interlopers going against the "natural process" of creating a "natural Los Angeles." Despite Whitnall's call to arms, autonomous cities mostly yawned. In 1920, three minor districts were added to Los Angeles, totaling only 0.5 square miles. In 1921, no territories were added. There were rumblings about water-law amendments on the horizon. If implemented, the changes would offer a lifeline to parched towns across the county.

Though Los Angeles was not growing outward during this two-year span, it was at least growing in stature. As the 1920 Summer Olympics got underway in Antwerp, the *Times* reported that several participating athletes from L.A. "have stuck the name of Los Angeles right into the world's eye." For the last year, Chandler stoked a movement to position L.A. as the host city of an upcoming Olympiad. His point person was real estate guru Billy Garland. Smart, charming, and connected, Garland was the perfect ambassador to sell Los Angeles to the International Olympic Committee, and he made repeated trips to Europe to regale its representatives. But he had several hurdles to overcome. Most Europeans had only a vague notion of Los Angeles. With the continent in shambles after the war, financial arrangements to transport hundreds of athletes halfway around the world seemed a herculean task. After all, Los Angeles didn't even have a large-scale venue to host events.

Chandler aimed to fix that. As Garland campaigned overseas, Chandler manned an eight-person commission known as the Community Development Association. Its purpose was to raise funds for special events and institutions that would boost the city's prestige. The committee convinced the Los Angeles City Council to sponsor a $900,000 bond measure to finance a stadium in Exposition Park known as the Los Angeles Memorial Coliseum. Its initial 75,000-seat capacity would make it the largest arena in the United States. "As the largest city in the Western Americas, we must do things in the largest way in the Western Americas," the Chamber of Commerce announced. The bond vote would be part of a primary election on August 31, 1920. "Feel confident that if Los Angeles coliseum is approved by voters," cabled Garland from Europe, "its unequalled facilities for carrying on this great international event will land it."

The bond failed, its 65.1 percent yeas falling just short of the sixty-six percent needed to carry. Mayor Meredith P. Snyder called its defeat "a calamity." He condemned Angelenos for their anemic showing—only a quarter of all registrants bothered voting—and vowed to have the city resubmit the bond proposition in November. But others preferred to move on. Not trusting the public with a "do-over," the Community Development Association worked out an agreement to lease the land from Los Angeles, build the stadium, then rent it out to the city and county for ten years, with revenues helping pay off $1 million in construction loans. Architect John Parkinson, later known for codesigning Los Angeles City Hall and Union Station, drew up blueprints. And just like that, construction of the Coliseum began on December 21, 1921, and wrapped on May 1, 1923. The timing was propitious. Having already been passed over for the 1924 and 1928 Games, Los Angeles was awarded the 1932 Olympics three weeks before the Coliseum's completion. Improbably, it was another high-stakes gamble that paid off.

At the same time that the Coliseum was coming together, Chandler was on a bender of drawing other endeavors to Los Angeles. Sitting on over fifty boards of directors, the mogul had unrivaled access to business opportunities and investment capital. Many of his relationships were cultivated at the prestigious Los Angeles Athletic Club. Those who wanted to keep in good stead with Harry were pressured to invest in projects he believed in. Given his golden touch, few had reason to dodge him. After World War I, Chandler met an engineer named Donald Douglas through a mutual acquaintance. Though he had secured a U.S. Navy contract to deliver three planes, Douglas was having trouble raising money. "I am not sure whether you know anything about building airplanes or not," Chandler told him, "but Los Angeles needs more business enterprises." Chandler loaned him $1,500, then convinced a fraternity of wealthy friends to kick in another

$13,500 so that Douglas could build his fleet. The Navy was so impressed with the product, it ordered twenty-five more planes from Douglas. Chandler's down payment led to the formation of the Douglas Aircraft Company, a key producer in the Southland for the next seventy-five years. "[Chandler] was really the chap who made the town progress," Douglas recalled years later.

Around the same time as Douglas's venture, Chandler cajoled fifty associates into investing $20,000 each in the newly created California Greatwestern and Interstate Air Route Corporation. Its aim was to dominate the aircraft industry in every capacity. "If the plans are developed," a spokesman announced, "Los Angeles will be to the air what New York or Liverpool is to the sea or what Chicago is to the rail transportation." Southern California did indeed emerge as a leader in aerospace and aviation. When the United States Postal Service announced that it was starting airmail delivery, Chandler quickly organized Western Air Express, preemptively blocking San Francisco from becoming a West Coast hub. Western was awarded the nation's first airmail contract in 1925. It lived on as the popular passenger carrier Western Airlines before merging with Delta in 1987.

Chandler also sat on the local board for the Goodyear Tire & Rubber Company. Parlaying his influence as chair of Greatwestern and Interstate, he convinced the Akron, Ohio, firm to purchase a 380-acre field in Los Angeles to construct its airships. But what Chandler was really after were Goodyear tires. He was, after all, a founder of the Automobile Club of Southern California. He was also an investor in oil and gasoline companies, and an early exponent of highways to the city's suburbs, where he still owned land. Securing $7 million in startup funds, he persuaded Goodyear to build a massive tire plant in the car capital of the world. The City Planning Commission directed Goodyear to the site of the former Ascot Park raceway in South Los Angeles, located in Whitnall's newly created industrial zone along the Shoestring Strip. When the $20 million plant opened in 1920, it was hailed as the largest industrial building in the West, employing several thousand people and eliciting an open letter from Goodyear's chairman crediting Chandler for the company's success. Goodyear's prosperity beckoned three more major tire manufacturers to the region in the 1920s, including B. F. Goodrich. Following a natural evolution—after all, tires need cars—Chandler also convinced the heads of Ford, General Motors, and Chrysler to set up assembly plants in the Southland. For his part, Whitnall used the establishment of the tire factories to push for more annexations in districts between downtown and the harbor. Prospective companies are "impressed with Los Angeles' water supply," he told the *Times*, "and therefore want their factory inside the city limits."

By 1923, Los Angeles had vaulted to second in the nation in the issuance of building permits, closing in on New York City. It seemed as if every civic improvement, program, or policy somehow led back to Chandler. As they motored to homes built on lots that were once owned or co-owned by Harry, suburbanites were living reminders of his tire, gas, oil, automotive, and real estate interests. He inspired a slew of nicknames. The Los Angeles Realty Board, which counted Sherman as a member, honored Chandler with a "Most Useful Citizen" award. *Newsweek* called him the "Midas of California." Republican allies dubbed him the "Governor of Southern California"—a discordant yet fitting label. For a man who shunned the spotlight, Chandler remained knee-deep in political affairs, easily the most influential non-politician in the state. Bolstered by favorable tailwinds that he helped create, Chandler's net worth reached a level that made him, by one *Times* estimation, the eleventh richest man in the world. Of course, few titans achieve their status with a clean record, and history tends to uncover blemishes.

Chandler's genial façade continued to mask the Machiavellian image in the mirror. As early as the 1880s, when he ingeniously manipulated newspaper subscriptions to enrich himself, Chandler proved adept in the art of subterfuge and playing one side against the other. For decades, his self-serving behavior was buried under layers of deception, with the *Times* providing effective cover. But he couldn't hide from all his morally dubious transactions. In 1915, during the Mexican Revolution, Chandler was indicted by a federal grand jury on charges of conspiring to recruit American troops to protect 800,000 acres in northern Mexico, where his investments included oil, cotton, and the Colorado River delta. (Chandler acquired the land under corrupt Mexican President Porfirio Díaz, who was forced out of office in 1911. "If he has been a despot," Chandler said cavalierly, "he has been a wise and benevolent despot.") Chandler was acquitted as a suspected revolutionary, but his holdings inspired a change to the Mexican Constitution in 1917, empowering the government to confiscate foreign-owned properties and ban new foreign investments near the border. That same year, the *Times* mysteriously toned down rhetoric against the Communist uprising in Russia. Many suspected it was because Chandler had swung a deal with Vladimir Lenin's Bolshevik party to drill for oil in Siberia. But after Lenin allegedly reneged on the agreement, Chandler's paper went back to bashing unionists as Reds and socialists. William Randolph Hearst's *Los Angeles Examiner* was quick to call out Chandler's hypocrisy, tweaking him with the charged headline "Chandler Denies He Is a Bolshevik Fiscal Agent."

But Chandler was used to pot shots from yellow journalism. As the 1920s unfolded, he was in the unique position of being Los Angeles's greatest benefactor and beneficiary. It was as if he and the city had become a singular force, their fortunes rising in lockstep through magnetic cohesion. Even annexations picked up again. In 1922, several centrally based regions (La Brea, Manchester, Melrose, Angeles Mesa, and Rimpau) added five more square miles to the city. Meanwhile, that old bugaboo Sawtelle was still making news. After four confusing years of dual governance, the California Supreme Court invalidated the 1918 election result that folded Sawtelle into L.A., holding that balloters were not informed that they would be paying "a proportionate share of [L.A's] bonded debt." At last, Sawtelle residents were legally unshackled from Los Angeles . . . only to quickly regret it. Faced with depleting water and no money for improvements, townsfolk held *another* consolidation election in July of 1922. This time, the favorable vote took for good. Sawtelle added 1.82 square miles to Los Angeles, plugging an important hole on the Westside. Chandler's vision of a grand metropolis was nicely falling into place.

But the *Times'* fundamentalist president was also wary of an emerging existential threat, something closer to home that could unravel decades of progress and prosperity. Having helped create a West Coast Eden, Chandler would turn his discriminating eye on who should be granted access to this earthly paradise—and who should be excluded.

CHAPTER 23

HARRYMOSESLAND

ON THE EVENING OF December 8, 1923, Angelenos living in the coastal basin could peer northward and witness an awesome spectacle. Perched on a hilltop near Griffith Park were thirteen letters made of sheet metal—each fifty feet high, thirty feet wide, and painted white—brightening the night sky through the magic of 3,700 twenty-watt light bulbs. The letters lit up in three sequences: First "HOLLY," then "WOOD," then "LAND," then, finally, "HOLLYWOODLAND" all at once. "HUGE ELECTRIC SIGN BLAZONS NAME OF DISTRICT ACROSS SKY," blared the *Los Angeles Evening Express*. "This gigantic sign, the largest in the world, vies with the stars in the luminous beauty."

The idea of the sign was Harry Chandler's. The letters and the land under it were the property of Gen. Moses Sherman. The men were advertising their latest venture, a subdivision in the Hollywood Hills called Hollywoodland. The sign's nocturnal premiere must have come as a great relief to the longtime partners, as the entire project almost fell apart several times. Not only did the development succeed, but the sign itself—later shortened to Hollywood—emerged as a visible icon to celebrate Los Angeles, taking its place alongside the Statue of Liberty, the Egyptian Pyramids, and the Great Wall of China among the world's most instantly recognizable landmarks.

The germ for Hollywoodland was planted in 1905, when Sherman and Eli Clark purchased 640 acres of wilderness straddling Beachwood Canyon for $10,000. The parcel came to be known as the Sherman and Clark Ranch; the brothers-in-law leased a portion of it to the Los Angeles Stone Co., which quarried rock in the area now known as Bronson Canyon. For years, Whitley Heights and today's Outpost Estates and Hollywood Heights were the only subdivisions in the Hollywood Hills. When Hollywood joined Los Angeles in 1910, these residential districts were brought in, too. Sherman and Clark continued to sit on the undeveloped land until 1922, a year in which local conditions were ripe for building. Los Angeles's housing sector was not keeping up with its population, a growing percentage of whom were employed by the motion picture industry. Movies had become big business, a $100 million machine that drew forty million Americans to theaters every week. Eighty percent of all movies were made in and around Los Angeles. The actors, directors, and producers who cranked them out desired hillside homes that were high above the riffraff but close enough to Hollywood, where many worked and played. Fortuitously, the Sherman and Clark Ranch sat squarely above the flats of Hollywood, occupying the mountainous southeast corner of the old Rancho Providencia. Los Angeles had long sought the unincorporated domain, which was bounded by Universal City on the west, Griffith Park on the east, and present-day Forest Lawn Drive on the north.

Unfortunately, Los Angeles wasn't the only suitor. Burbank abutted Providencia's San Fernando Valley border from the north and was undergoing its own annexation conquests. As the head of Los Angeles's annexation committee (the "county" nomenclature had been dropped again), Sherman was well-positioned to effect the fusing of Providencia and Los Angeles. If successful, this unification would allow his subdivision to access L.A.'s amenities. Thus was born the Hollywoodland syndicate. Besides Sherman, Chandler, and Clark, it included two experienced real estate men: Sydney Woodruff, head of construction planning; and Tracy Shoults, head of sales. Shoults had recently worked with Chandler on the upscale Windsor Square tract, leaving quite the impression. "The most wonderful salesman I ever knew in my life," Chandler told Sherman, adding that he was even better than Hobart Whitley. Each syndicate member put up

$25,000 to break ground.

Word of the subdivision's opening hit newspapers on March 31, 1923. Much of the copy was lifted from a press release sent out by Shoults. With his reputation as a heavy hitter, Sherman's involvement was a strong selling point. "It was confidence such as [Sherman's] that gave Southern California railroads, and vision that foresaw the future beauty of what is today named Hollywoodland," the *Hollywood Daily Citizen* stated. The first thing built were ornate stone gates—mined from Bronson Canyon—that lent the new tract a "You Have Arrived" gravitas. Beyond this entryway was a quaint little village featuring a grocery store, beauty salon, and filling station, with an English stable at the end of Beachwood Drive. Stone-quarried staircases connected tiered paved roads through woodsy hills. Plots started at $2,000, many with majestic views of the city. Upholding Hollywoodland's stately air, buyers had a choice of four old-school architectural styles to confect their dream aerie: English Tudor, French Normandy, Spanish Revival, or Mediterranean. As the nation's first themed hillside subdivision, Hollywoodland was a stark departure for Sherman, whose previous housing projects were often clustered around his railways and geared for the middle class. In fact, most advertisements denigrated the types of neighborhoods he had helped build. "Will your family enjoy a delightful home in the clean, pure mountain air of Hollywoodland, with its wonderful climate, broad open spaces and plenty of 'elbow' room?" asked one ad. "Or—will you live in a 'dwelling' in the flat, uninteresting houses-in-a-row sections of the City, your family's freedom hampered by this maelstrom of human existence?" For Valley residents who bought ho-hum dwellings in the flat houses-in-a-row along Sherman Way, here was an all too literal call to action to improve their lots in life.

On July 2, 1923, Sherman conveyed to Chandler how pleased he was to have Shoults on their team. The veteran real estate broker was a font of "wonderful ideas" for Hollywoodland, informed by twenty-five years of promoting subdivisions throughout the Southland. The general was so appreciative of Shoults, he planned "to give a nice party to him and his wife and a few of their friends . . . either this week or next." But the party never happened. Four days later, while working in his Hollywood-land realty office, Shoults dropped dead from a heart attack. He was only fifty years old and left behind a wife and two-year-old daughter. His premature death spooked Sherman, who was mere months from turning seventy. "I am getting to be an old man. (I have not many more days left on earth)," he penned Clark. "I will soon go the same way that Mr. Shoults has." Indeed, losing Shoults greatly compounded Sherman's stress. The sales whiz had attacked his job with a cheery vigor, and served as a direct conduit to office-mate Woodruff. By contrast, Woodruff was a dour engineer with a sketchy background who had moved around the country to avoid threats of lawsuits. Sherman viewed his new, hands-on role with Woodruff as penance for the way he treated Clark when they were starting out. "You know," he wrote his ex-brother-in-law, "when we were doing such wonderful work building railroads, I did not praise you enough (I want you to know that I feel very sorry that I did not praise you more, when you worked so hard, and when you did such wonderful work). I do not want to make this mistake with Mr. Woodruff."

But as the summer wore on, Sherman's faith in Woodruff cratered. "Woodruff is spending money faster than it comes in," he complained to Chandler. After Shoults's passing, sales of homesites slowed, reducing available revenue to pay for construction costs. Woodruff told Sherman he needed an infusion of $100,000 to keep the project on schedule but refused to put up any capital himself despite being a partner. "This is all wrong," Sherman continued to Chandler. "He wants to make all manner of expensive improvements and he wants it to come out of my pockets (If you were in my place and saw a great army of men there drawing big salaries and no money to pay them with, you would feel bad about it)." Part of Sherman's concern was that he was already highly leveraged due to other investments with Chandler, both on the hook for millions of dollars in notes connected to Tejon Ranch and the Colorado River Land Co. Feeling "old, worn out and sick," Sherman was intent on not financially burdening his family. "Please let's not buy any more land," he begged of Chandler. "Please let's go 'slow' (Let's try and pay our debts)." Meanwhile, Sherman's relationship with Woodruff reached a new low when the angry foreman threatened to quit and stormed out of a meeting in which Sherman asked for itemized expense reports. This ended their ritual of riding horses through Hollywoodland to monitor its progress. "The reason I have not been horseback riding at Hollywoodland, of late," he told Chandler, "is because he worries me. . . . He tells you things, that I say that are not so and makes me unhappy." Sherman saw only one solution: "I want him to do all of his talking to you."

But while Sherman was bogged down by day-to-day drama, Chandler was busy with bigger-picture items, like pressuring the city council to nullify petitions by groups opposed to the subdivision, and strongarming the county to pave Beachwood Drive. (Shoults had pitched the idea of having Beachwood connect to the Valley through a tunnel under the Santa Monica Mountains. The proposal fizzled out after Shoults's death, leaving the legacy of an orphaned Beachwood Drive in Burbank.) But these were rote affairs for Chandler. His greatest contribution to Hollywoodland had been in the works for months. And it all started on a whim.

In the spring of 1923, Chandler commissioned a twenty-six-year-old designer named John Roche to create a brochure for Hollywoodland. Roche sketched a mélange of homes, streets, and bridle trails. He then innocuously scribbled "Hollywoodland" under the peak now known as Mt. Lee, never intending for an actual sign on the face of the mountain. When Roche showed his work to his boss, Chandler was captivated by the signage. What if there really *was* a hillside sign promoting Hollywoodland that could be seen all over Los Angeles? Could Roche look into something like that?

Later in life, Roche recalled that he conducted his own

feasibility study by heading out to Wilshire Boulevard, where he calculated that the letters should be at least fifty feet tall to be visible from that distance. He took his sign specs to Chandler's *Los Angeles Times* office late one night. "Do it," came Chandler's reply. Such was Chandler's power that Roche never had to go through environmental reviews or pull permits, an impossibility in today's world. "We just put it up," he said. "We didn't have engineers or anything." Working with a team of Mexican laborers armed with pickaxes and shovels, Roche anchored the thirteen letters to telephone poles hauled up by mules. "We did things then by guessing and by God." The sign was built in sixty days at $21,000. It made its debut—sans lightbulbs—on September 3, 1923. The illuminated version of HOLLYWOODLAND was still three months off.

While the sign may have started off as a gimmick, its conspicuous placement did seem to have an impact on sales. "The week-end of September 15th more persons visited Hollywoodland than on its opening date late this spring," Woodruff told journalists. "More than 500 motor cars passed through the entrance portals into Hollywoodland on Beachwood Drive." Sales agents were so "swamped with live prospects," many transactions had to be completed over a series of days. That same month, at the first Hollywoodland Jubilee, 200 people convened over a barbecue steak dinner. Chandler brought in Mulholland to assure folks that the subdivision would get aqueduct water. The Chief touted a new reservoir that would open nearby—Lake Hollywood—whose location in Weid Canyon was secured by Harry. Tickled that so many "picture people" were snatching up lots, Sherman began to see the light at the end of the tunnel. "It will be the most valuable property in Los Angeles County for residences," he enthused to Chandler.

Indeed, it did not take long for the Hollywoodland sign to become something more than a billboard for a subdivision. By December of 1923—the month of its first illumination—it attracted legions wishing to get up close to the world's largest sign.

The *Los Angeles Express* perceptively captured the public's awe, likening it to a movie marquee: "It has become a veritable 'show place' in a land which has long been counted as the 'show place of the world.'" In 1932, when depressed actress Peg Entwistle committed suicide by symbolically jumping off the "H," the sign further solidified its link to moviedom. In 1949, after years of deterioration, the "LAND" portion was removed, leaving only "HOLLYWOOD." This made perfect sense, as the sign's connotative evolution was complete. Without any sort of campaigning by Chandler or the film industry, the world had naturally alighted on the sign as a metaphor for hopes and dreams (including the shattered kind), a canvas projecting back our feelings in the way that the Berlin Wall, decades later, was not just a wall, but a symbol of Cold War oppression.

Not coincidentally, the Hollywoodland sign's unveiling roughly coincided with the official annexation of Providencia. A small election board in the region, assisted by Sherman, voted itself into Los Angeles on October 10, 1923 (ratified by the state on February 4, 1924). Hollywoodland and the pending Lake Hollywood area comprised much of its 4.82 square miles. Its absorption capped the most prolific one-year period in the annals of L.A. annexations. The additions were all over the map, filling in holes to the north and east, and continuing the build-up of the greater Fairfax and Hancock Park regions between Wilshire Boulevard and Melrose Avenue. Half of the fourteen newcomers were less than one square mile. One patch was so tiny, only one qualified resident submitted a "yes" vote after its three-member election board signed the petition. The largest strand was the Laurel Canyon Addition. Its 13.57 square miles encompassed not only rural Laurel Canyon, but most of the Santa Monica Mountains from Cahuenga Pass East to just beyond Beverly Glen on the west, where tractors were terracing hillside subdivisions. Taking a cue from the Hollywoodland sign, several realtors spelled out their residential tracts with hilltop letters, albeit far cheaper, scaled-down versions. Outpost, Beverly Crest, and Bryn Mawr were just some of the neighborhoods blazoned with signs.

Two other coups for Los Angeles in 1923 were the acquisitions of Burbank-adjacent Lankershim (now North Hollywood; 7.64 square miles) and, sandwiched between Glendale and Pasadena, Eagle Rock (3.17 square miles). For both locales, access to aqueduct water was the deciding factor. "They're getting thirsty," a writer in the *Times* taunted about the remaining holdout cities in Los Angeles County. "Let them parch awhile. They'll have to come in." Not necessarily. The following year, Sacramento drafted a bill that permitted California cities to vote on forming their own metropolitan water districts. If an MWD were established in Los Angeles, it would usher in a new era of water politics, with far-reaching implications for the growth of Los Angeles and the sovereignty of those cities embedded within it.

CHAPTER 24

Moving Mountains

AFTER LOS ANGELES FINALIZED the purchase of Weid Canyon for water storage, William Mulholland drafted plans for the construction of Lake Hollywood. He had scouted the ravine way back in 1912, believing its elevated spot east of Cahuenga Pass to be "so situated as to be able to furnish a gravity supply [of water] to the fast-growing hill section of Hollywood." By 1923, Mulholland had captained L.A.'s water needs for 37 years. Championed by the *Los Angeles Times*, business advocates, and grateful Angelenos, his folk hero status was set in stone. But the year would also prove to be an inflection point in his storied career. Two years shy of seventy—an age when most civic employees were well into retirement—Old Bill was about to face an onslaught of new hardships that would stymie someone even half his age or better educated.

The first materialized when Mulholland's designs for Lake Hollywood went public. Unlike the earthen barricades of his other, smaller reservoirs, it would be his first curved arched concrete dam. It would also be the first dam built directly above a heavily populated area. This greatly concerned the Hollywood Chamber of Commerce, which termed the structure "dangerous to life and property." A breach from an earthquake could submerge Hollywood in billions of gallons of water. Other opponents called on the county to conduct additional safety studies. Mulholland predictably slammed petitions for legal injunctions. "The Weid Canyon Dam, as it will be constructed by the Water Bureau, will be strong enough to hold its reservoir filled with molten lead," he pontificated. "If the proposed Weid Canyon dam should break

or weaken in the slightest detail, it would establish a world's record since there has never been a recorded instance of a dam of
that mighty type failing in any degree." Once again, the engineer
was given carte blanche by Los Angeles officials, who had long
determined that this "common-sense genius [was] infinitely better educated for his profession than any graduate of engineering
schools." Construction of the $1.25 million dam began in August
1923. "Lake Hollywood is rapidly becoming a reality," hailed Sydney Woodruff in the *Times* seven months later, after its first seventy-five feet of foundation were laid.

Shortly thereafter, Mulholland and his crew broke ground
on the St. Francis Dam, thirty miles north of Lake Hollywood.
Again, the San Francisquito Canyon site—situated along Los
Angeles Aqueduct conduits between Castaic and Antelope Valley—was not Mulholland's first choice to marshal Owens Valley
water. But Fred Eaton continued to play hardball, spurning offers
to unload his Long Valley property, which would've allowed for
a reservoir near the aqueduct's intake. Mulholland publicly responded by downplaying Long Valley, which served to discredit
Eaton. This only fueled more resentment. "The attempt to minimize the importance of this storage to the Aqueduct scheme has
failed to depreciate its value," Eaton vented to a Los Angeles official. "My company is prepared to wait." Eaton warned that when
the time was right, he would "enlighten the Public on the subject
so it will know what Long Valley storage means to the Aqueduct
Project"—loaded words that would come to haunt Mulholland's
St. Francis Dam.

The design of the St. Francis was a larger version of the dam
at Lake Hollywood. While both stood about 200 feet, the St.
Francis was thicker and wider, with a nearly quarter-mile service
road traversing its crest. The levee's heft was necessitated by the
reservoir's twelve-billion-gallon water capacity—five times greater than Lake Hollywood's. Unlike the Hollywood dam, however,
St. Francis's construction coasted through planning commissions. Its location in a remote corner of L.A. County assured that

it would receive far less scrutiny.

One month after work began on the St. Francis Dam, in the early morning of May 23, 1924, an explosion ruptured the Los Angeles Aqueduct. Forty ranchers from Owens Valley and Mojave had ignited a box of dynamite 190 miles north of Los Angeles. Concrete was hurled up to 2,000 feet, unleashing thousands of gallons of water while knocking out L.A.-owned telephone and power lines. No lives were lost, though the ranchers threatened to kill Mulholland if he dared show up. Not only did the Chief show up, but he issued a threat of his own, snarling that he "half-regretted the demise of so many of the valley's orchard trees, because now there were no longer enough trees to hang all the sons of bitches who live there." As the city scrambled to track down the saboteurs, Harry Chandler's *Times* was quick to indict William Randolph Hearst for inciting the mob. "HEARST PAPER FANS FLAMES" read a *Times* headline in the May 23 late edition. It was a reference to several articles in the mogul's *San Francisco Call* over the preceding weeks that had focused on the heartrending plight of Owens Valley, which had become infertile scrubland since the aqueduct went in. Hearst's rag had characterized the ranchers "as hapless victims of the grasping greed of Los Angeles which had robbed them of their life's blood, water," the *Times* protested, myopically. In addition to inspiring dynamiters, the *Times* claimed that several men wrote letters to the *Call* telegraphing their acts of terrorism, though this was never proven.

As Owens Valley ranchers suffered up north, residents endured sporadic water service back in Angel City. It was now obvious that Mulholland's canal was not the magic bullet that it was sold as. Sabotage aside, snowpack from the Sierra Nevada was inconsistent from year to year. Rates of growth projected that the aqueduct would prove inadequate within ten years. What hedges did Los Angeles have besides dwindling groundwater and an overburdened L.A. River polluted by urban and agricultural run-off? At a city-sponsored summer luncheon, Mulholland was forced to address the status of lawsuits brought by disgruntled

Angelenos who were experiencing water problems. Things grew heated when a Mr. Volney Craig of the San Fernando Valley stood up and challenged the Chief, prompting a shouting match. Two hundred guests came to Bill's defense, drowning out the homeowner with thunderous applause that lasted several minutes.

Meanwhile, the May 23 aqueduct blast turned out to be a prelude to a far bigger flare-up six months later. On November 16, 1924, 100 people stormed the gates of a spillway near Lone Pine, diverting water into the fallow Owens River bed at a rate of 2,182 gallons per second, or $10,000 a day. The protestors refused to move from their post. The sheriff of Inyo County urged Governor Friend William Richardson to send in the state militia. Fearing that the use of force would spark an all-out civil war, the governor stood down. In Los Angeles, the Water Bureau countered with harsh words and threats of litigation. "It is now planned to sue for damages each man in the group of raiders," Mulholland said. "Interference with a public utility is a serious matter, of greater importance than robbing the mails." But what L.A. officials termed as "anarchy," Owens Valley residents saw as retribution. "If we can call state-wide attention to the city's treatment of our ranchers, we may get justice," said a spokesman of the group. Indeed, as civilian occupation of the aqueduct dragged on, Los Angeles found itself playing the role of the heavy. Press coverage extended as far away as Paris and tended to sympathize with the farmers. Even entertainer Will Rogers remarked on the "valley of desolation" that was now Owens Valley: "Los Angeles had to have more water to dilute its orange juice, and for its Chamber of Commerce to drink more toasts to its growth, and more water for its geraniums to delight the tourists." For the first time, the Water Board floated the idea of compensation to Owens Valley inhabitants, offering enough water to irrigate 30,000 acres of farmland. The proposal was met with mixed response, but it did set a precedent of remedial measures—many forced through jurisprudence—between Los Angeles and Owens Valley that continue to the present.

Over the next several days, it seemed as if everybody in Inyo County had joined the takeover. In Bishop, store owners posted placards in their windows that read, "If I am not on the JOB, You can find me at the AQUEDUCT." On November 19, Los Angeles sent a battery of attorneys and agents to Inyo County, seeking warrants for the arrest of hundreds of guerillas. Even the *Los Angeles Record*, no friend of Old Bill and his "Aqua Duck," called for the resistance to disperse: "The entire situation is causing Los Angeles enormous damage. . . . The news of the affair is going over the world. It is NOT GOOD ADVERTISING for Los Angeles." An armistice was finally called on November 20, by which point the seizure had reached 700 occupiers. Though Los Angeles regained authority over its dominion, Owens residents had won in the court of public opinion. The *Record* insisted that Mulholland resign. "He speaks insultingly of the people of Owens valley and of their community," the paper argued. "He has FOSTERED HATRED between the counties of Los Angeles and Inyo." Mulholland's perceived crimes contributed to the present hostilities, including years of bungled opportunities to offer an olive branch to the ranchers, and his inability to build a reservoir in Long Valley. The only solution was to become less dependent on Owens Valley through "the formation of a gigantic water district including most of the cities of Southern California." Such a plan already appeared to be gaining momentum.

In the early 1920s, metropolitan areas across America—from Boston to Omaha to San Francisco—were either exploring or implementing their own metropolitan water districts (MWDs) through legislation. As public agencies, MWDs were different from city-run water departments in that they served multiple municipalities within a wider region. To join a water confederacy, a city need only figure out how to fund its pro rata share of expenses and vote itself in. An MWD in the L.A. metro region would solve a host of problems. By removing water as a pretext for annexation, Los Angeles would no longer feel compelled to consume its neighbors to service its now $84 million in debts;

it would receive its share of water along with others. Every municipality that entered into an agreement with the MWD would be represented on its board, further reinforcing their autonomy. Just as important, Mulholland had settled on another source that could supplement the Owens Valley watershed: the Colorado River, where the federal government was preparing to build Boulder Dam (later Hoover Dam) in a glen between Nevada and Arizona. Mulholland envisioned a 242-mile Colorado River Aqueduct serving the counties of Riverside, San Bernardino, Orange, and Los Angeles, each sharing in its construction, maintenance, and bounty under the MWD's auspices.

It all seemed win-win until a 1924 bill by state legislators bumped against the imperiousness of L.A.'s power brokers. "Most of the Angeleno delegation at Sacramento voted against it and aided in defeating it," deplored *The San Bernardino Sun*. After the bill was amended to address concerns by the Los Angeles City Council, the measure failed again anyway. Tellingly, council representatives did not reflect the views of everyday Angelenos, who later voted out those members who opposed an MWD. That left Mulholland as the most prominent non-elected official weighing in on the issue. Emulating the affairs at the state's capital, he too suddenly pivoted. The city, he said, was not interested in a socialist-type junta controlling the fate of its water: "Los Angeles city can put this [aqueduct] through alone without a metropolitan district plan such as was defeated in Sacramento." He haughtily suggested that if cities in San Bernardino, Orange, and Riverside Counties needed Colorado River water, they could simply follow the lead of other thirsty towns that were swallowed by L.A. "Those cities were annexed to Los Angeles, and they are getting Owens River water," he stated. This did not go over well in San Bernardino or Santa Ana. "We aren't ready to be annexed to Los Angeles," the *Santa Ana Register* editorialized. "We aren't ready now and we hope never to be." Santa Ana was thirty-five miles south of L.A., to say nothing of more distant cities in the Inland Empire and beyond. Since acquired territories needed to be contiguous, the Chief's proposed consolidation would have had Los Angeles tacking on about 9,000 square miles, or seven Rhode Islands. It would take several more years before Mulholland—and Los Angeles officials—would come around to an MWD draft that met with their satisfaction.

In the meantime, as if his ego needed more of a boost, Mulholland was regaled with two honorary dedications during a three-month stint starting at the end of 1924. On Saturday, December 27, Los Angeles celebrated the grand opening of Mulholland Drive (alternately, Mulholland Highway or High Way), twenty-five miles along the spine of the Santa Monica Mountains between Cahuenga Pass and Calabasas. The Mulholland Highway Festival was the city's biggest commemoration since the aqueduct's arrival at the Cascades eleven years earlier—another Mulholland-centric pageant. The events were related. The Los Angeles Aqueduct had enabled the annexation and residential development of once "worthless hills," as press for the highway festival called them, in the regions formally known as Providencia, Laurel Canyon, and Westgate. Previously, homebuilders in the canyons had formed associations to finance access to their subdivisions via north-south arterials. What was missing was an east-west axis to tie them all together. The coalition raised $1 million for such a highway. "It is a living monument to the man who made the city of Los Angeles possible—William Mulholland—by bringing the waters from the eternal snows of the high Sierras to us," said one journalist, "and he has made possible the city of millions which is to follow." Mirroring other savvy developers who had leveraged the Mulholland name for over a decade, the Merrick & Ruddick company touted their new subdivision Mulholland Hills, an area straddling the ravines north of Coldwater Canyon Avenue and Franklin Canyon Drive. Fittingly, both streets provided automotive passage for Mulholland's team to service the Franklin Canyon Reservoirs. The canyon routes were also the first links between Beverly Hills and the San Fernando Valley's main drag, Ventura Boulevard, which meant that the

"Mulholland Hills lie directly at the most important intersection of the entire Mulholland High Way."

The dedication of Mulholland Drive kicked off at 11 A.M. with the esteemed engineer christening his roadway in Calabasas. (The roadway's actual engineer was DeWitt L. Reaburn, who also worked on the aqueduct.) In photos from the event, the Chief looked characteristically put out by all the fuss. In lieu of a champagne bottle—this was during Prohibition, after all—he smashed a bottle filled with Los Angeles Aqueduct water over an oversize golden key held by Mayor George Cryer. As Mulholland inserted the key into a golden lock, it unfurled a flowery chain that was strung across the highway, whereupon "thousands of men, women and children . . . broke into a deafening cheer." The fanfare came fast and furious: An official caravan rumbling through the road's western portal. Daredevil pilots buzzing the skies. Actor Tom Mix staging a Wild West show produced by Universal Studios. And, just down the hill, parades marching along Ventura Boulevard from one end of the Valley to the other, sponsored by booster groups and the Auto Club.

That afternoon, organizers dialed up the occasion for Hollywood, an easy southerly jaunt from Mulholland Drive's Cahuenga Pass egress. As crowds greeted the convoy at Vine Street, artillerymen from the Great War pumped rifle shots into the air. The Shell Oil Company, no doubt delighted to be endorsing a new motorway, donated 1,000 gallons of gasoline for airplanes to circle the Hollywood Bowl and shower an audience of Hal Roach's *Our Gang* production with roses. By nightfall, the program mimicked a lavish movie premiere—apropos since this portion was choreographed by Cecil B. DeMille. As searchlights canvassed the sky, a star-studded costume carnival raged at Vine's junction with Hollywood Boulevard, one of the earliest known events to thrust "Hollywood & Vine" into the local lexicon. Natalie Kingston performed her seductive Peacock Dance and Betty Blythe, star of *The Queen of Sheba*, reenacted her "Baghdad Number." As the fluttering divas flanked Old Bill, he looked as if he might die of humiliation. An estimated 100,000 people partook in the day-night gala, while 32,000 motorists test-drove Mulholland Drive. The only buzzkill came when a rumor spread about another attack on the aqueduct. "The rumors come directly from the [Owens] valley," Mulholland maintained. Owens Valley officials vehemently denied any sabotage; they blamed Bill for fomenting false reports as a way to further smear upstate ranchers during a high-profile moment.

Nonetheless, the over-the-top opening of Mulholland Drive was just the latest example of what Los Angeles did so well: throw itself a party. Celebrating civic progress didn't just bring together Angelenos, but also, as one paper put it, "notified the world that Los Angeles prospers." Described as the longest scenic mountain boulevard in the world lying entirely within city limits, the highway boasted a spectacular vista of the San Fernando Valley, the "fruit basket and vegetable garden of Los Angeles," per the Van Nuys Chamber of Commerce. "People now come to look at the Valley, and after taking one glance, remain to live." No Valley locale benefitted more than Girard (today's Woodland Hills). Founded in 1922 by developer Victor Girard, who purchased 2,886 acres from Chandler's Los Angeles Suburban Homes Co., the neighborhood sat at a plum spot. Its newly terraced subdivision could be accessed by both Mulholland Drive *and* Topanga Canyon Boulevard, two mountainous corridors that intersected in Girard. As a bonus, Victor Girard also published his own newspaper. On the morning of the December 27 highway coronation, *The Girard News* ran an eight-page spread devoted to the current event's significance. Many of Victor's advertorials oversold the importance of Mulholland Drive to Los Angeles— for example, the roadway did not directly lead to a "material increase" of industries within one year's time—but one prediction hit the bullseye: "Photographs of and from the highway, as well as descriptive stories will be published far and wide," *The Girard News* said. "The story of the San Fernando Valley and its highway will be broadcast to the leading thinkers of the United States and foreign countries, and the value of such advertising as reaped for the valley will be inestimable." Indeed, sweeping views from Mulholland Drive of both the Valley and the coastal plain still thrill, especially at night. "One scarcely knows where the stars leave off and the twinkling city lights begin," gushed Sydney Woodruff in one circular. In subsequent decades, the mystical roadway beckoned generations of necking teenagers, hot-rod racers, shutterbugs, and celebrity home buyers. Filmmaker David Lynch titled a critically acclaimed movie after it.

But for now, Mulholland the man was all the buzz. The centerpiece of *The Girard News* spread was a mammoth photo of his mustachioed face gazing sternly at the reader. Under the headline "The Modern Mahomet!," Victor Girard, Billy Garland, and a parade of paladins exalted Mulholland with a stanza that sealed his Caesar-level apotheosis:

> He Saw the Mountain and Cut It Away.
> He Is Los Angeles' Master Mind of Progress.
> He Is the Locomotive of Mental Energy.
> He Is the Gate-Builder of a New Empire of Wealth.
> He Is a Living Monument of Vision.
> He Is the Wise Man of Opportunity.
> He Came. He Saw. He Conquered.
> He Is William Mulholland!

Over the next few years, the western front of Mulholland Drive would extend another thirty miles from Topanga Canyon Boulevard to Ocean Highway (today's Pacific Coast Highway). Aside from an eight-mile section west of Encino that retains a dirt surface, the city rushed to pave the entire route. This created another marketing opportunity for automobile ownership. By 1925, Los Angeles registered 500,000 vehicles, solidifying its status as the car capital of the world. Like the Topanga Canyon-oriented loop that opened ten years earlier, sightseers were invited to drive an even more exhilarating circular route:

Imagine! Fifty-five uninterrupted miles of scenic splendor from the Hollywood Bowl to the Pacific Ocean on the broad shoulders of L.A.'s signature mountain range! Cruise south on the coastal highway, turn left on newly paved Sunset (née Beverly) Boulevard, through posh Brentwood, Beverly Hills, and downtown before returning to Cahuenga Pass—144 miles in all!

The eastern extremity of Mulholland Drive was another story. Vague and disjointed, it was meant to extend five miles beyond Cahuenga Pass. Maps envisioned the graded motorway skirting Lake Hollywood, snaking through Hollywoodland, and stopping in the upper reaches of Griffith Park at a junction with eventual Mt. Hollywood Drive (now closed to automobiles). But only a 0.75-mile spur of what's called Mulholland Highway ever got surfaced, most notably a quirky stretch in Hollywoodland in which east- and westbound lanes were built at different levels, its retaining wall mined from the Bronson Canyon quarry. In a publicity photo from March 1924, Chandler, Mulholland, Woodruff, and Gen. Moses Sherman awkwardly posed in front of a brand new Spanish Revival house next to a large wooden sign that read: "This Is Mulholland Highway."

The other four miles of today's Mulholland Highway exist in spectral form as hiking trails or fire roads, labeled on maps as either Mulholland Trail or Mulholland Highway. Given that Mulholland Highway was meant to be a cornerstone of Hollywoodland, it's odd that this portion was never fully realized. What accounted for this? A common myth is that the city "ran out of money" when the Great Depression hit in 1929. In reality, the project was simply abandoned in 1927 after a bitter dispute. On one side were Chandler, Sherman, and Woodruff, controllers of the Hollywoodland syndicate. On the other was W. I. Hollingsworth, a wealthy speculator who owned hundreds of acres of unimproved land in the former Providencia district abutting Hollywoodland. Hollingsworth argued that Chandler and company deviously excluded themselves and Hollywoodland property owners from contributing $1 million in assessments to complete the roadway. They did this by gerrymandering an "Improvement Zone" that *excluded* the boundaries of Hollywood-land—the main beneficiary of a Mulholland Highway—and instead saddled Hollingsworth with the bulk of expenses, even though most of his property lay over the hill in present-day Forest Lawn Hollywood Hills cemetery. When the deep-pocketed Hollingsworth threatened to sue, the Los Angeles City Council dropped the whole idea of completing Mulholland Highway like a hot potato.

Around the same time as the dedication of his titular highway west of Cahuenga Pass, Mulholland was putting the finishing touches on the dam for Lake Hollywood. Over the next few months, the reservoir filled with water primarily drawn from the aqueduct, creating a wooded lake that remains an alpine gem. On March 17, 1925, Mulholland reaped his reward—the second time in three months that his name was memorialized on a civic monument. "CITY HONORS MULHOLLAND" read the headline in the next day's *L.A. Times.* "Dedicates New Dam in Name of Engineer." The date was not a coincidence; it was also St. Patrick's Day, giving the city an excuse to link the achievements of its own patron saint, the Belfast-born Mulholland, with that of Ireland. The Ancient Order of Hibernians, the oldest Irish Catholic organization in America, was on hand to offer blessings.

Photos revealed an assemblage of dignitaries joining Mulholland along the dam's decorated roadway. The guest of honor was cited for his "wisdom" and "genius." But this affair was noticeably lacking Hollywood star wattage. A smattering of applause greeted the biggest celebrity of the day—a German Shepherd named Strongheart. The heroic canine actor "showed the delicacy of his dramatic instinct by barking in a polite parlor falsetto." The liturgy ended with an appearance by Arabelle W. Hurlburt, whose great grandfather, William Wolfskill (he of the combative grandson, Matt Wolfskill), allegedly planted the first oranges in Southern California. Donning a flapper dress and cloche hat, Hurlburt parted an American flag to reveal the dam's bronze tablet. In jutted block lettering, "WM MULHOLLAND" is identified as the Chief Engineer. Under it, in a faint inscription that looks like an afterthought: H. L. Jacques, Engineer in Charge of Construction.

Despite the present luminaries, the dam easily outshone them all, striking in its grace, accented by a row of ornamental grizzly bear heads and Roman aqueduct-style arches. Even Old Bill couldn't resist a little humble brag. "My associates are in the habit of twitting me on the appearance of all the work I have done elsewhere," he quipped. "They say it looks like an old woman's apron—an object of utility, but not of beauty. But in this job, I think I may take a little pardonable pride." The dam properly consecrated, Mayor Cryer cranked a giant control valve, releasing the first plume of reservoir water into the city mains.

Accounting for Mulholland's immortal status by this point, all that was missing was a statue in his likeness. But even that was in the works. The first record of its planning was a blurb in the *Los Angeles Record* on New Year's Eve, 1924, when the city was still humming over Mulholland Drive: "Somewhere between Cahuenga pass and Calabasas, on a commanding point of the new Mulholland drive, a heroic statue of William Mulholland . . . will stand soon." Sponsors had already commissioned the artist: Sally James Farnham, a renowned female sculptor in a male-dominated field. But by the spring of 1925, updates disappeared. The City of Angels moved on, understandably distracted by other pursuits. The statue's stalled momentum was a troubling metaphor for the white-haired engineer, spelling an end to his glory days. Not too long after his dedications, his most vocal critics would be clamoring to strip his name off Mulholland Drive and demolish Mulholland Dam. Like a god who fell from the sky, the water messiah would be sentenced to the shame of living out his remaining years as a mortal man.

CHAPTER 25

Beauty and the Baron

OF THE SIX KINGPINS whose collective efforts helped grow Los Angeles, only Henry Huntington spent a good chunk of his life basking in the serenity of a true retirement. Long hours toiling over railways, utilities, subdivisions, cost sheets, contracts, and mergers and acquisitions gave way to tending his personal Shangri-La. "Nowhere on earth is there a place so dear to me as Southern California, and my home here," he remarked about his estate in 1919. "I always come back to San Marino." The thought of sharing his earthly paradise with the public gave him great pleasure. "People do not have a proper appreciation of beauty," he once said. "There's nothing in the world as exquisite as one single rose."

Whenever Henry and his wife Bell left the grounds, it was usually to acquire art in New York or even in Europe, where owners were desperate to sell off masterpieces to pay down debts incurred by the war. Back at home, Huntington and landscape architect William Hertrich continued expanding his 130-acre garden, now a buffet of themed subgardens—from rose to Japanese to cactus to tropical. In 1923, Huntington completed a library to house his rare books and manuscripts. That same year, he created the Huntington Foundation at San Marino, offering up his gardens and library for public enjoyment and scholarly research. On May 11, 1923, the state Senate adopted a resolution recognizing Huntington's contributions, a portion of which read, "This benefaction is in its extent, and in its educational and artistic value to the American people, one of the greatest gifts of an individual to a State or nation known in all history." In a photograph from this era taken on his veranda, the bushy-mustached mogul, propped in a wicker chair, looks like a dapper Southern gentleman posing for a painter, perhaps a reflex from all the portraits he had commissioned of himself over the years. The picture invites the viewer to imagine one of his thirteen grandchildren—his most precious treasures—clambering onto his lap.

Of course, Huntington's life wasn't devoid of stress. He still owned interests in dozens of enterprises, still sat on boards of directors and tussled with knockers. He also retained ownership of the Los Angeles Railway (LARy), which his son Howard had overseen in various capacities since being demoted as GM after his nervous breakdown. Sadly, Howard's health had been steadily declining since 1911, and he died of a stomach ulcer on March 27, 1922. He was only forty-six and left behind a wife and six children. "The shock has been great but I keep myself busy here, with the many things that are of interest to me," the senior Huntington wrote an art dealer in New York five days later. "I am glad that I have the comfort of work—the building up of the Library and Art Gallery which now absorbs a great deal of my time." In that same letter, Huntington disclosed that "The Blue Boy arrived safely," a reference to the famous Thomas Gainsborough painting that Henry bought at auction for $850,000 the previous November. Anticipating the opening of his art museum, Huntington correctly appraised it to be "an attraction to future generations here."

Despite being surrounded by ethereal beauty inside and outside his mansion, Huntington kept getting unwelcome visits from the real world, like the grim reaper riding up to his porte cochère. On July 24, 1924, Henry contacted his most trusted confidant, attorney William E. Dunn, who managed his business affairs: "Mrs. Huntington has been seriously ill, and although she is better now, she is still quite sick." Death took Arabella Huntington three weeks later. She was eventually laid to rest in a Grecian mausoleum being built near the main house. One year later, on August 22, 1925, Huntington absorbed another blow when Dunn himself died of a stroke. After his cremation, all LARy streetcars came to a halt for one minute to honor his importance to their operations.

Huntington was hardly the picture of health himself, a kind of negative inversion of the flexing lad depicted in his beloved *Blue Boy*. Already weakened by personal loss, he grew increasingly incapacitated by various ailments, including a problem with his prostate that required surgery at a Philadelphia hospital in late 1925. Post-op, his physician assigned him a live-in nurse, a Miss McTavish. The nurse's iron fist became a running joke in Henry's letters to friends. In April 1926, he wrote Joseph Duveen, a legendary British art dealer, that he "went down stairs yesterday for an hour, and would have staid [sic] longer if the ogress who presides over me had not been on the watch." Confined to his bedroom and forbidden from hosting guests, the antsy Huntington invented new nicknames for Miss McTavish. "Miss Maybe is as much a tyrant as ever," he told Duveen a month later, though he admitted she's "a wonderful nurse" who played a mean game of Hearts. As Huntington rallied, "maybes" turned to "yesses" and he was again allowed visitors, who included oil tycoon John D. Rockefeller, the prince and princess of Sweden, and shipbuilder Homer L. Ferguson.

Huntington was particularly close to the Ferguson family, even becoming pen pals with Homer's young daughter Elise. In the summer of 1926, the Fergusons came out from the East Coast to stay as extended houseguests, prompted in part by Elise's dream to visit Huntington's magical-sounding kingdom. It was the fulfillment of a promise Henry had made one year earlier, when he had responded to Elise's latest letter with such achingly tender care, it transcended his avuncular relationship with the girl and seemed almost as much about his own love for his adopted hometown in sustaining his spirit in his twilight years:

My dear Elise:

I hope, too, that you may some time come out here to see not only the paintings, but also many other lovely things in California. There are beautiful things everywhere, but it seems to me we have more here than in any other part of the world. Just now the roses are at their best: how would you like to see a white rose bush climbing a tree for over a hundred feet? I can show you that. Then there are roads with rose covered fences that stretch sometimes a mile. . . .

I am glad you like The Blue Boy. He must have been a fine little fellow, and although we know little about him, he looks as if he did a lot of good in the world as he grew up. He will be here waiting for you, and also a beautiful little Scotch boy, painted by Raeburn, and I want you to meet him too.

My kindest regards to your mother and father, but my love to you.

Affectionately yours,
Henry Huntington

Following the Fergusons' visit in 1926, Huntington suffered another prostate-related setback. He returned to Philadelphia for a second surgery in May 1927. "There is very little danger of it not being successful," he assured a friend. But complications ensued, and he died in Philadelphia on May 23, 1927. He was seventy-seven years old. A private train carried Huntington's body back to Southern California, where flags flew at half-mast. Mourners met his black sheathed car as its bell tolled through San Marino. Upon its completion, Henry was interred next to Arabella in the mausoleum.

The value of Huntington's estate was pegged, conservatively, at $40 million. His board of trustees announced a $2 million endowment to the Collis P. & Howard Huntington Memorial Hospital (better known as Huntington Hospital) and an $8 million trust fund for scholarships and fellowships of American and English history. Through his foundation, his collections of art, books, and manuscripts were bequeathed to the public. His death also made news in London, but for different reasons. Many patrons were still stung by the loss of *The Blue Boy* and other English artwork. A shrugging *Daily Telegraph* was at least glad that the late magnate intended to share his paintings with the citizenry: "Very few private collectors on this side of the Atlantic have been able of recent years to resist the inroads of Mr. Huntington's agents, armed as they were with carte blanche for the victory. This is why so many of our treasures in art and literature have found their way to the handsome pavilions in California."

Material assets aside, wrapping Huntington's legacy into one tidy package was an elusive task. "Probably no man in Southern California saw the possibilities of this great southland as did Henry E. Huntington," wrote the *Pasadena Evening Post*. "Bringing every city within a radius of 50 miles into direct and immediate communication with Los Angeles, the growth of this vast metropolitan section can be laid at the door of this great empire builder." Variations of the statement "No single individual has done so much to promote the phenomenal growth of Southern California"—in this case, uttered by directors of Henry's real estate arm—were pronounced by numerous parties, even if they were equally true about Harry Chandler.

As notes of sympathy poured in from around the world, Chandler did not feel compelled to make a personal statement; he had more than expressed his admiration through private exchanges in which he praised his fellow visionary's "lasting monument" at San Marino, and thanked him for his "aggressive railway building," which had "done more than anything else to make [Los Angeles] attractive to tourists and homeseekers." All the same, Chandler's voice can be inferred through a *Los Angeles Times* tribute on May 24, which credited Huntington for nourishing progress and enlightenment, a fusion that the *Times* president concurred was important for any big city. "Others have made millions in Southern California," the paper intoned, "but no other has dedicated so many of those to the public service. Mr.

Huntington was one of those who held that the educational—the cultural—development of Southern California should keep pace with the industrial development." In the same breath, Chandler's idealized vision for Los Angeles of efficient highways to the ex-urbs could be gleaned from a passage that read like an epitaph for Huntington's railways: "Those [cultural] treasures will remain intact when the last of the lines of railroad he builded will have been abandoned to make way for a new form of transportation." Indeed, an inaugural segment of the Arroyo Seco Parkway, the city's first freeway, would open about ten years later.

Huntington would have agreed with Chandler's viewpoint, sensing early on that the Los Angeles metropolitan area he had helped shape was changing in ways that were now out of his control. It's one of the reasons he found such happiness in building his institution. It was a place where he could still be the master of his domain, leaving an imprint that would outlive his railways and other capitalistic ventures while assuaging his sensitive soul. (The museum now houses 45,000 pieces of art; the library, 11 million items.) "I have been approached regarding a biography, but I do not want that," he once said. "This library will tell the story. It represents the reward of all the work I have ever done."

CHAPTER 26

White Spots

IN 1925, THE FORMER railroad tent city named after Gen. Moses Sherman was feeling the heat. Five more tracts had recently annexed with Los Angeles, including Santa Monica Canyon and Martel. The latter was just the latest adjunct to encroach on the border of Sherman, now hemmed in by Beverly Hills on the west and Los Angeles on the north, south, and east. The time seemed ripe for the unincorporated community to surrender its borders as so many had already done. But when the issue was decided by Sherman residents in a 1924 election, many longtimers were not ready to dissolve their identity. One person who sided with them was seventy-one-year-old Moses Sherman.

It might seem peculiar that someone who played such a pivotal role in L.A.'s expansion would draw the line at Sherman. But Sherman the businessman had reasons to preserve the town in his name. Besides possible sentimental reasons, he was concerned about saddling Shermanites with L.A.'s debts and higher property taxes. The locale also had the luxury of relying on its own water through the Sherman Water Company, although pro-annexationists declared the company's wells "unfit for human consumption," having been tainted by cesspools oozing from homes in the hills. In the end, the election returns resulted in a razor-thin majority against annexation. The virtual 50-50 vote betrayed the electorate's split personality, one that fell on both sides of Los Angeles's infamous blue laws.

Thanks to its unincorporated status, Sherman acquired a reputation during the Prohibition Era as a hotbed for liquor-fueled nightclubs and underworld gambling dens. One contingent of Sherman was bent on shielding the town from L.A.'s vice squad. Other habitués argued that it was in desperate need of an image makeover. In the summer of 1925, in a compromise of sorts, townsfolk voted to upgrade its name without necessarily changing its character. East Beverly and Beverly Park received consideration as ways to piggyback off the allure of Beverly Hills. After much debate, West Hollywood won out. Realtors had already been referring to that appellation for years to emphasize its proximity to world-famous Hollywood. But the change wasn't without controversy. "It's not right to change the name of our town," one resident admonished. "We should have proper respect for our founder, Gen. Sherman, who still owns property here and is interested in the improvement of the town." Not only did the name West Hollywood stick, but so did its reputation for good times. Loose county oversight famously led to the flourishing of the Sunset Strip. By the time West Hollywood finally incorporated in 1984—by then, a popular district for LGBTQ+ residents— the city's repute as a haven for inclusiveness and permissiveness was firmly entrenched.

Interestingly, the success of Sherman/West Hollywood in staving off Los Angeles probably helped Beverly Hills remain autonomous as well. Around the time of Sherman's annexation vote in 1924, the Rodeo Land and Water Co., which managed Beverly Hills's water (and counted Henry Huntington as a board member), insisted that merging with L.A. was the only way to avert a water crisis. The alternative didn't look good. People complained that the town's water had "laxative qualities," and the formation of the Southern California Metropolitan Water District was still a few years off. Proving the power of celebrity, anti-consolidationists created an advocacy group called the Beverly Hills Eight, a band of movie stars who included Will Rogers, Harold Lloyd, Rudolph Valentino, and power couple Mary Pickford and Douglas Fairbanks. The entertainers cavorted door to door throughout Beverly Hills, handing out autographed glossies while persuading homeowners that water problems could be managed without

giving in to Los Angeles. Housewives and hubbies properly flat-
tered, the town voted to preserve its independence after working
out a water-share deal with neighboring West Hollywood. The
towns' common border offered another advantage, as West Hollywood created an eastern buffer between Beverly Hills and Los
Angeles. Years later, the Beverly Hills Eight were honored with a
bronze and marble obelisk called "Celluloid," which stands on a
traffic island in Beverly Hills that remains aggressively uninviting
to pedestrians.

Meanwhile, Moses Sherman factored into two other Los Angeles developments in the 1920s. After seeing his name swapped
out for West Hollywood, he simply lent it to a new subdivision
two years later: Sherman Oaks. The general had held onto the
unimproved 1.5-square-mile tract for years. Procured for a song
from the Los Angeles Suburban Homes Co., of which he had an
interest, lots now went for $780 an acre. "I think they are going to
make a great success in Sherman Oaks," Moses wrote his friend,
Arnold Haskell, about his sales team. "There is great fun in 'doing things.'" Sherman Oaks now occupies eight square miles of
prime real estate, most of it in the foothills of the southern San
Fernando Valley.

Sherman also played a part, albeit a largely forgotten one, in
the run-up to the biggest annexation story of 1925. Even more
than prideful Westside stalwarts Sawtelle and Santa Monica,
Venice was sui generis among Southland cities since its founding
in 1905. Accepted narratives impart that visionary entrepreneur
Abbot Kinney came up with the idea of creating a "Venice of
America" along the coast. However, those accounts are inaccu-
rate. On July 16, 1902, Sherman and Eli Clark sold 100 lots at
auction in Playa del Rey, where their Ballona Lagoon resort was
a popular stop on the Balloon Route tour. The *Los Angeles Times*
announced that their new subdivision would include waterways
between residences and be called "Venice of America." Unlike
the later Venice under Kinney, Sherman's Venice was designed as
a "millionaires colony of villas." In an update on July 31, 1904, the

Times reported that sidewalks and utilities were going in at the Venice of America tract, also called Venice Park, which was accessible via the partners' Venice Short Line spur. In addition, four parallel canals, each 1,100 feet long, were laid out perpendicular to the Pacific Ocean. They were named after Sherman and three of his real estate associates (Linnie, Howland, and Carroll). Coincidentally, in the same July 31 *Times* issue, Kinney announced plans for a new subdivision in former Ocean Park, where he had just taken sole ownership of land north of Venice Park. Kinney designated his community "Venice"—clearly appropriating the other Venice that had been in the works for two years. In fairness, however, both men appear to have been inspired by the Canal of Venice exhibition at the 1893 World's Fair in Chicago.

Nonetheless, Kinney's genius in realizing *his* reimagined Venice cannot be denied. Dredging worthless swampland, he built three miles of bridged canals through a residentiary and commercial district, highlighted by a Grand Canal that connected Sherman's Venice Park with his own Venice. (Worried about being upstaged, Kinney rushed to complete his plans before Henry Huntington could finish Naples, another navigable community in Long Beach.) Though he intended to lure intellectually curious adults with symphonies, lectures, and self-improvement symposiums, it was the lowbrow fare that brought people in. The thriving amusement zone, nicknamed the Coney Island of the Pacific, was located between residences and the shoreline. It became the most attended tourist spot in Greater L.A., its picture postcards beguiling out-of-towners with a gallery of roller coasters, pleasure piers, dancehalls, and gondolas, wherein gondoliers crooned in Italian as they plied the canals.

By 1925, 25,000 people called Venice home, making it one of the most populous municipalities in the county. Many property owners were people of color, drawn by inclusive regulations. But even before Kinney died in 1920, the city's canals had fallen into disrepair—fetid, slimy, expensive to maintain. In this new age of the automobile, the creaky conduits were seen as a hindrance to civic progress. People tired of the inconvenience of relying on trolleys and walkways (as romantic as they sounded) to get around. Plus, the town was broke, powerless to hire more police to patrol its legendary bacchanalia. In light of all this, Venice officials set a special election for October 2, 1925, to decide whether to consolidate with Los Angeles.

At a town hall meeting debating the issue, a hydraulic engineer named F. C. Finkle played into anti-annexationists' fears. "You will not lose your identity if you annex to Los Angeles," he said wryly. "Your identity will be recognized just as San Pedro's and Hollywood's has been." Finkle pointed out that the only time Los Angeles Harbor is not called "Los Angeles Harbor" is when a bootlegger is busted there. That's when it's demeaned as "San Pedro Harbor." Similarly, "When a twelve-story building is erected in Hollywood, it's 'Los Angeles.' But when a dope party is uncovered in the movie colony it is always 'Hollywood.'" Another anti-annexation voice, Judge Fred H. Taft, dispelled the notion that newbie Angelenos will reap higher property values; his experience was that the opposite was true, and he reeled off cities with higher average real estate prices: Santa Monica, Pasadena, Glendale, Beverly Hills, Alhambra, Burbank, Inglewood, and South Pasadena. Another group passed around a petition calling for Venice to join forces with its northern neighbor, a lesser-evil proposition. "Consolidation of Venice and Santa Monica as one united municipality will mean the utmost protection for Santa Monica Bay District interests," said Dan Dillon, a Venice landowner. "Annexation Means Slavery," one Venetian business insisted on a store window sign.

On the morning of October 3, all the ballots were counted. "VENICE VOTES TO ANNEX TO LOS ANGELES" read the headline in the *Los Angeles Record*. The spread was 3,310 to 2,215. The only precinct out of Venice's nineteen districts to reject consolidation was the amusement zone. The City of Angels tacked on 4.1 square miles, much of it prized beachfront, bringing its grand total to 415 square miles. Venetians celebrated the best way they knew how: with "a gigantic parade throughout the city and by general merrymaking." Unfortunately, under L.A. ordinances, dancing on Sundays was now taboo. The ban had an immediate chilling effect, stanching revenue from thousands of pleasure seekers who normally flooded Venice ballrooms at the end of the workweek. Locals were irate. Wouldn't it make more sense to encourage Angelenos to spend their hard-earned dollars in Los Angeles instead of a rival beach city? Two couples from Venice lampooned the law by staging a photo that made the papers. The duos danced on the sidewalk border of Los Angeles and Santa Monica, where the pastime was permitted. Standing on the Santa Monica side was a harmonica-playing police officer providing musical accompaniment. On the Venice side stood a stern LAPD cop, clutching a placard that read "NO SUNDAY DANCING."

Frustrated Venetians found allies in pro-business groups and at Los Angeles City Hall. Councilman Pierson M. Hall of the downtown district declared that many blue laws aimed at "so-called moral conduct" were outdated. People were sick of "busybodies [telling] them what they should and should not do." A prominent waitress union backed a campaign to resume Sunday revelries. "Many waitresses who are off that day cannot attend dances on other days," reported the *Venice Vanguard*. A proposition to allow Sunday dancing in Venice was included in a Los Angeles election on April 30, 1926. It easily passed, aided by a "late afternoon rush of housewives to the polls" who voted with their feet. In its own modest way, the measure helped fortify Venice's reputation as a mecca for self-expression that continues to this day.

However, not all rights were so easily earned. Even if they resided in Venice, Black residents were not welcome at Venice's ballrooms, reflecting broad discrimination policies against people of color in the 1920s. Though Los Angeles had more integrated businesses than other cities in the U.S., dance clubs, bowling alleys, ice rinks, public pools, and many restaurants had "No

Negroes" signs or mandates. Shunned from Angel City, African Americans spent Sunday nights at Caldwell's dance hall in Santa Monica at Third and Pico. But even that was short-lived. Santa Monica council members subsequently adopted a resolution that banned Sunday night dancing at Caldwell's, "as a result of complaints from numerous white residents of that section." That same year, L.A.'s district attorney uncovered a horrific Ku Klux Klan "torture plot" that targeted Black residents living along Central Avenue, a rising African American entertainment corridor. "Negroes informed of the plot against them have armed themselves," reported the *Los Angeles Express*. "They are badly frightened." By methodically picking off Black residents, the Klan hoped to ignite race riots. "The Ku Klux Klan has steadily gained in power," warned the *California Eagle*, a prominent African American newspaper. "This is a dark picture indeed."

And it would only get darker. As Los Angeles evolved into an industrialized metropole, its population grew more varied. Southern Blacks joined Jewish and Catholic immigrants from southern and eastern Europe among those drawn to L.A.'s economic opportunities. A similar pattern played out in other U.S. cities, coinciding with a rise in xenophobia from Anglo-Protestants who resented "foreigners" threatening to take their jobs and move into their neighborhoods. The KKK capitalized on these fears. Its membership swelled to six million by 1924, by which point the organization achieved mainstream acceptance in conservative circles—hosting picnics, sponsoring charities, informing politics. On December 27, 1924, the same day that *The Girard News* splashed the opening of Mulholland Drive across its masthead, an adjacent headline read "Klanmen Visit Eight Churches." Fifteen Knights "in full regalia" had swooped into nine San Fernando Valley chapels unannounced during Sunday services and presented ministers with Christmas cards that contained $25 checks payable to the church. "Enthusiastic applause greeted the gift in every instance," the paper reported. The hooded heroes also donated $250 to the American Legion Hospital Fund. The hate group also played a key role in pushing through the John-son-Reed Immigration Act of 1924, which established strict quotas from non-Western European nations. John Clinton Porter, a senior member of the Klan's L.A. chapter, rode his white supremacy platform all the way to the mayor's office in 1929.

All of this was discomfiting on its own, but it was magnified by the casual way in which nativism was framed by the media. While nickel weeklies like *The Girard News* had limited readership, the *L.A. Times* reached hundreds of thousands of eyeballs a week via subscriptions and newsstands. As the newspaper's arch-conservative president, Harry Chandler increasingly gave space to divisive articles under the guise of civic welfare. In the summer of 1923, readers woke to the headline "COMMUNISTS IN DRIVE TO AROUSE NEGRO HATRED." Written by free-lancer Fred R. Marvin, who built a cottage industry around the menace of Communism, the piece tidily conflated ideology and race to create a double-headed boogeyman to counter white Christian democracy. Moscow agents were allegedly embedded "within colored churches," where they enlisted Blacks to subvert America. Marvin's thinking wasn't so radical at the time. Looking for scapegoats to explain rising tension and violence among American laborers, U.S. Attorney General A. Mitchell Palmer and Bureau of Investigation chief J. Edgar Hoover had been warning of communist infiltration among Black people since 1919. The only solution, in Marvin's view, was segregation, with one unifying goal: "The negro masses must get out of their minds the stupid idea that it is necessary for two groups to love each other before they can form an alliance against their common enemy."

The same week as Marvin's piece, Chandler's beliefs rang loud and clear in a *Times* editorial titled "THE SOUL OF THE CITY," which pinned L.A.'s success to the white race. "It is one thing to be prosperous and enterprising," the essay preached. "It may be another to be morally clean and mentally just." Where once the city attracted people like Chandler—"eager pilgrims whose faces are turned toward Los Angeles . . . mainly the descendants of

American pioneers"—it was a slippery slope down to the squalid, alien slums rife with crime and commies that defined parts of Chicago and New York. The piece also noted that Los Angeles could at least take pride that it has "no vast foreign districts in which strange tongues are ever heard. The community is American clear to its back-bone." In order to stay that way, it was imperative to sell the city as a "white spot," a hard-earned distinction in the wake of America's post-WWI malaise: "During that period the Los Angeles district was the only white spot on the 'money map' of the country. . . . Los Angeles is still the white spot on any industrial map that may be drawn. May it also prove to be a white spot when character-building is being charted."

"The White Spot" was a common stamp of approval among business and finance groups in the early 1920s, borne out of the industrial maps referred to by the *Times*. These regularly updated graphs displayed not just which American cities had thriving business conditions, but which *sections* of each city. White sections, per map legends, were good for business; "black and darkly shaded areas" were bad. This was a sly inversion of normal, run-of-the-mill maps in which areas highlighted in shades of gray tend to draw one's focus, while white or unshaded areas recede in relevance. Instituting this contrarian scheme lent itself to other lexical euphemisms of "white spots," like the aforementioned juxtaposition of "white" and "character-building," which implied a superior white race. Newly arrived, home-seeking Midwesterners need only read between the lines. (Or simply view one racist map that unequivocally warned against the "SPREAD OF NEGRO RACE SHOWN BY DARK SPOTS & AREAS.") White Spot maps also disincentivized investment in the darker areas, locking in their undesirability. Along that same spectrum, the charts presaged the redlining of "risky areas" on color-coded real estate maps. Like a scarlet letter, neighborhoods marked in red—typically home to large Black populations—were not worthy of government-backed loans as part of a federal program to spur home ownership.

Racial covenants in the 1920s reinforced the divide in home ownership that was formulating in Los Angeles. A typical resolution adopted by realty boards stated that sellers "shall not sell or lease property in districts now occupied by the white or Caucasian race to members of any other race." The policy was prompted by neighbors concerned about depreciating home values, as anyone who was "other than the white or Caucasian race in any residential district creates antagonism and bitter feelings." Racial exclusivity became as commonplace in real estate ads as picturesque views or good schools. "Restrictions just sufficiently high to secure desirable neighbors," read the copy for a new Highland Park tract, which redundantly added, "Also restricted to the Caucasian race only." From Silver Lake to Crestview to the San Fernando Valley, Los Angeles was flush with "whites only" subdivisions in the mid-1920s. One development called Western Avenue Crest—between Western and Normandie Avenues in South Los Angeles—held a contest on opening day that promised $25 first-place prizes to prospective owners competing in the following brackets: Happiest Smile, Reddest Red-headed Girl, Fattest Bald-headed man, Slenderest Girl, Tallest Man, Most Beautiful Blonde, and Fattest Man with a Red Moustache. The contest's categories (signaled by "blonde" and "red" hair) were limited to those who could buy lots: "Men and women of the white or Caucasian race only are eligible to enter." Just south of Western Avenue Crest lay Goodyear Park, a massive industrial parcel dominated by the Goodyear factory that Chandler had lured to Los Angeles. Several square miles emanating from the plant were "perpetually restricted," per the De Witt-Blair Realtor Co. "The white race alone can live or have business establishments in Goodyear Park. This is done to protect your home."

Hollywoodland—Chandler's and Sherman's crown jewel—was the most high-profile subdivision to include Caucasian ownership in its deeds when its world-famous sign went up in 1923. The following year, Hollywoodland developer Sydney Woodruff spearheaded the Greater Los Angeles Association, a business lobby whose motto was to "keep the white spot white . . . and make it whiter than ever." In a move that bore the markings of another Chandler masterwork, a literal "white spot" subsequently appeared on the slope beneath the Hollywoodland sign. Like its larger companion, the highly visible dot—thirty-five-feet in diameter and painted on some sort of canvas—was illuminated at night like a beacon. "Biggest electric sign in the world is supplemented by blazing disc that blazons forth claim of business supremacy" read a newspaper caption accompanying a photo of the solid white circle. Hollywoodland associate George R. Hannan crowed about the subdivision's $2.5 million in home sales. "Los Angeles and Southern California are in the midst of the most prosperous era of history," he said, led by "the 'white spot' of Hollywoodland." (Located, conveniently, near Hollywood Boulevard, the "Great White Way.")

THE PAINTED spot amidst Mt. Lee's chaparral eventually faded away due to the elements. The Hollywoodland sign also lost its luster once its namesake community became established. After the Hollywoodland syndicate dissolved, the signage remained the property of the M. H. Sherman Co., which owned its mountain perch. But its maintenance was a financial burden. Light bulbs kept burning out or were rumored to be purloined by thieves during the Great Depression. Four letters fell down from storms in 1938, resulting in "HO----OODLAND." The sign eventually went dark, and in 1944, the Sherman company donated the eyesore to Los Angeles. After the city moved to tear it down, the Hollywood Chamber of Commerce took over its operation. The commission removed the "LAND" portion so that it simply promoted Hollywood itself, an ingrained metonym for L.A.'s motion picture ecosystem and all its attendant dreams and glamour.

Though the lit-up sign and "white spot" flickered off by the 1930s, their implications cast long shadows that were felt across Los Angeles for generations. Housing policies propagated by realtors continued to favor, to borrow Chandler's term, "descendants of American pioneers." Recalling nineteenth-century homestead land grabs, suburbanites in the 1920s had a base from which to build equity and pass their prosperity onto generations of family. Black and Latino residents were left to languish in the margins, joining low-income workers on the wrong end of the era's ever-increasing wealth gap. California Senator Hiram Johnson blasted the *Times* in 1924 for showing "the utmost contempt and hatred of ordinary citizens. They are ever on the side of privilege and entrenched dishonesty." Johnson, who had made a blood sport out of attacking Gen. Harrison Otis, was also the first prominent Republican to call out Chandler's pernicious influence. "With his enormous wealth, his multifarious connections and his disreputable newspaper, he has established himself as a petty tyrant, ordering and directing public officials and private citizens alike."

But the populace responded with a collective shrug. Whether it was a flashy movie premiere, a maiden scenic highway, a new annexation, or an exclusive white spot subdivision throwing open its portals, most Angelenos were distracted by a constant barrage of shiny new objects as the city marched toward one million people and the 1932 Olympic Games.

CHAPTER 27

A Circus Atmosphere

THE IMAGE THAT MADE the morning papers on February 3, 1926, was an incongruous thing, like seeing a penguin waddling past a cactus. For there was William Mulholland, head of the Municipal Water Bureau, stiffly posing for a photograph with a black umbrella fanned over his head. The Chief hated umbrellas in his hands because they sent the wrong message. Umbrellas repelled water; he embraced it. But that didn't stop R. F. Del Valle, president of the Water and Power Board, from gifting his friend the item in light of recent rains, then alerting news photographers to memorialize the moment. Mulholland took it all in stride. "As one, who for [forty] years has been held responsible for providing an adequate water supply for the people of Los Angeles, I have come to regard a rain as something to be warmly welcomed rather than shunned," he said. "I am always happy to take a ducking in a soaking rain, for during the wetting process I am comforted by the knowledge that the city is gaining a most precious supply of water."

Water had always occupied permanent residence in Mulholland's brain, but lately it had been keeping him up at nights. Old Bill found himself in the familiar role of publicly reassuring the city he had everything under control while privately worrying that he did not. By 1926, Los Angeles had finally joined the Million Population Club as coined by Harry Chandler. That year, the city acquired an additional twenty-three square miles, adding 25,000 more people. But it was also coming off three straight years of only half its normal rainfall. The Los Angeles Aqueduct was at peak capacity, and the Colorado River Aqueduct, projected to provide for ten million people, had not even broken ground yet. Meanwhile, the Southern California Metropolitan Water District Act was mired in legislative limbo. If there was a silver lining, it was that Mulholland and L.A. lawmakers had finally agreed in principle to the MWD, which would serve Los Angeles (with Mulholland still running point) and its vicinity. At last, Los Angeles County cities would have a tool to preserve their independence without having to play footsie with their powerful neighbor. Burbank, Santa Monica, Beverly Hills, Pasadena, Glendale, Whittier, Long Beach, and Huntington Park were among the first to buy in to the agency. On this front, Mulholland, who just two years earlier had suggested L.A. consume most of the Inland Empire, could now breathe a sigh of relief.

But the possibility of an MWD indirectly created new conundrums. Newly empowered Burbank, Glendale, Culver City, and Santa Monica now actively sought to expand their own borders. Residents in sparsely populated locales wedged between L.A. and another city were suddenly forced to make decisions about their own destinies: Which side would be more advantageous to join, if at all? The Verdugo Mountains community of Sunland fell into this category. After neighboring Tujunga achieved cityhood in 1925, some Sunland residents courted Tujunga, others flirted with Los Angeles, and still others insisted on staying unattached. Regardless, Los Angeles was not content to simply cede territory to adjacent towns that might impede its geographic contiguity. Nor did it want to be frozen out of the county's few remaining desirable pockets. These tug-of-wars triggered what would become the last burst of meaningful annexations in Los Angeles history.

The first dominos fell along the Shoestring Strip in early 1926. When it incorporated in 1907, the town of Watts was little more than a depot on Henry Huntington's Pacific Electric route to Long Beach. For years, it was the butt of Vaudeville jokes, the way Cleveland would later become a punchline for comedians. But with the arrival of factories in the early 1920s, Watts crammed 20,000 residents into two square miles, a vibrant stew of working-class immigrants. Like Venice, it was one of the few places where African Americans and Latinos could own property in Greater L.A. But Watts was ill-equipped to handle its surging masses, and quickly found itself drowning in debt. Despite opposition from merchant groups and the KKK (still holding sway), city officials petitioned to merge with Los Angeles, going so far as to preemptively change street names to conform with L.A.'s numbered system—for example, switching out Main Street for 103rd Street, and so on. There was just one legal hiccup holding Watts back: It didn't share a border with Los Angeles. That all changed on March 18, 1926, when Green Meadows, a 3.5-square-mile parcel between Watts and the Shoestring district, came under the wings of Angel City. Shortly thereafter, on April 3, Watts voted to consolidate. Los Angeles now had access to another industrial hub within the shoestring corridor. The city also inherited bizarre sculptural towers that artist Simon Rodia had been building out of found objects since 1921. Completed in 1954, Rodia's obsession became the iconic Los Angeles landmark known as Watts Towers.

Farther north, Sunland held a special election on June 23, 1926. Citizens voted 328 to 221 to attach to Los Angeles via the old Hansen Heights appendage. A few months later, another Verdugo Mountains district, Tuna Canyon, voted 140 to 17 to join L.A. Although Sunland and now-La Tuna Canyon brought in only 2,225 new residents, together they added 13.6 square miles to Los Angeles. More importantly, by folding La Tuna Canyon and Sunland into its borders, L.A. stymied land-hungry competitors Burbank and Glendale from creeping northward while blocking Tujunga from growing westward and southward. As Sunlanders rejoiced at Monte Vista Park to mark their new status as Angelenos, several peeved residents tried to negate the annexation. Their lawsuit contended that, after declaring their intention to hold an election, Sunland officials had failed to submit a petition to Los Angeles within the requisite thirty days. Further, the unhappy bloc argued that a petition to annex with Tujunga—*their* preferred partner city—was filed in time, and their election results were unanimous: 22 to 0 to join Tujunga. (The twenty-two voters accounted for only one percent of Sunland's total population.) Los Angeles officials dismissed the renegade results and ratified the "real" election in August. But like the Sawtelle debacle before it, it would take years for Sunland's legal challenges to play out. "Village Residents Not Sure Where They Live," read a newspaper headline that summer. "Complex Question Up to the Courts."

A circus-like atmosphere hovered over another annexation war in 1926, only this one involved an actual big top. In the 1920s, the Al G. Barnes Circus had entered its third decade of dazzling audiences across America. In the summer of '26, the *Chippewa Daily Herald* praised the colorful Barnes as "the last of the veteran showmen who have been before the American public the last 30 or 40 years" now that "Barnum & Bailey and most of the Ringling Brothers have gone." When the ensemble wasn't touring, it hunkered down in Southern California. "The late Abbot Kinney of Venice was responsible for me bringing the circus to winter in California in the beginning," Barnes explained. "That was back in 1910 and we used to winter at Venice." Kinney let the troupe live rent-free in return for weekend performances, and Pacific Electric Railway Company furnished barns and pens for the circus's menagerie of 4,000 wild animals, another quid pro quo arrangement. "When we were putting up billboard paper in the various towns advertising the circus attractions, we also used to put up posters advertising the advantages of living in California," Barnes said. As his train crisscrossed the country, its coaches were blazoned with the names of Southland cities like Venice, Santa Monica, and Los Angeles. "I also instructed all employees of the circus, about 1,000 of them, to tell people about the wonders of California. I believe we were responsible for bringing thousands here."

In 1923, Barnes moved to a larger site east of Centinela Avenue along Washington Boulevard, where he built the popular Barnes Circus Zoo. Its location next to Culver City, incorporated six years prior, was fortuitous. Studios there employed Barnes's workers for circus movies and rented his horses, elephants, and primates. Then, on February 3, 1926, Barnes City was born. The impresario installed friends as the town's board of trustees and helped get his brother, running under the "circus ticket," elected mayor. Despite its big-sounding name, the two-square-mile municipality was "never a community," in the words of historian Daniel Prosser. "It was instead a legal device to protect a circus and zoo from attempts to regulate its activities." Its population of 2,500, however, included a sizable contingent of homeowners who did not work for Barnes or his zoo. They insisted that the election to incorporate Barnes City was rigged. Among their accusations, Barnes didn't follow proper procedures, and almost half the electors were transients who worked for the circus but didn't live in Barnes City. What's more, other balloters were monkeys who "voted" in their cages. The dissenters' grievances made it all the way up to the California Supreme Court.

Judges mandated a new board of trustees, then invalidated the February election altogether. The circus city was ordered to de-incorporate and revert to the county, where Culver City and Santa Monica salivated at the thought of carving into territory that would soon be back on the market. To block those two cities, Los Angeles quickly approved a consolidation petition signed by the Barnes City residents not on Barnes's payroll. The fateful election was held on September 14, 1926, a date when the circus would be in Nevada on a summer tour. That didn't stop Al Barnes from sending 200 employees back to cast votes, though most were ineligible to do so because they were unregistered. Ultimately, a majority of non-circus, human inhabitants elected to join Los Angeles by a 261 to 153 count. That was the end of Barnes City, which existed for all of seven months. The former town makes up much of today's Del Rey neighborhood, while a breakaway section was absorbed by Culver City. As for Barnes, he still made out okay. After subdividing his land, he moved his circus colony to a 300-acre compound in Baldwin Park in 1927 before selling the whole operation two years later.

One group that kept a watchful eye on the Barnes City an-nexation election were residents of Mar Vista, formerly Ocean Park Heights. Located in the zone west of Palms and east of Santa Monica and Venice, Mar Vista owed its existence to Gen. Moses Sherman, thanks to a Venice Short Line depot that put it on the map in 1902. The district had recently rejected overtures from Santa Monica to come into its borders, preferring to hold out for Los Angeles. Mar Vista's pro-annexation caucus purposely scheduled an election one week after Barnes City's fate would be decided. Eugene Rittenhouse, a Mar Vista businessman who ran a beach chair and umbrella rental outfit at Venice Beach, spoke for many who wished to see "a continuous stretch of Los Ange-les territory from Broadway to the sea through which will run the Venice Short line, Venice Boulevard and many other arter-ies leading from various parts of Los Angeles to the beach." The creation of an uninterrupted belt would bring bus and streetcar control solely within Los Angeles, resulting in cheaper fares and ease of transit, which would lead to more Angelenos heading to the beach.

On September 22, 1926, Rittenhouse got his wish. Mar Vista voted by a 2-to-1 margin to merge with Los Angeles, contributing another 3,000 people and five square miles. (Though there would be fourteen incremental Mar Vista additions between 1946 and 1974, all were footnotes that merely filled in the edges of the orig-inal tract.) Westside residents were no longer cut off from the big city, and hailed the moment with a huge parade that included a 100-car convoy through Mar Vista. The event drew revelers from Venice and Barnes City—two areas defined by their festive spir-it—which may have had something to do with the rowdy affair lasting well into the night.

Leave it to that killjoy William Mulholland, however, to ruin the fun. After the binge of annexations, the water oracle grum-bled to officials about slapdash growth. Back in 1905, under the newspaper headline "TITANIC PROJECT TO GIVE CITY A

RIVER," he had promised that the Owens Valley aqueduct would accommodate up to two million Angelenos. In 1927, after culling twenty-two years of data (and L.A.'s fickle rainy seasons), he downgraded that figure to 1.5 million people, a threshold that was fast approaching. He also announced that the $100 million Colorado River Aqueduct would not start flowing until 1939, around the same time a newly planned 105-mile northerly extension of the Los Angeles Aqueduct to Mono Lake was scheduled to open. Sizing up local options, he noted with irritation that Venice's wells were nearly bone dry after its brain trust had promised they'd last much longer. Finally, at a City Council meeting on August 2, 1927, Bill's hair-trigger temper snapped. "There is a limit to our water supply," he scolded the council. "We have reached it." Ironically, it was the expected approval that month to annex the Wiseburn district—a mere speck at eighty-nine acres—that appeared to finally do him in. Mulholland believed that the wee ribbon of land near Imperial Highway was the first step toward bridging the gap between Los Angeles and Hawthorne (incorporated in 1922) until the cities shared a border. Once that will have occurred, Hawthorne was prepared to hold a consolidation election, having already submitted its intentions with L.A. councilmembers. If Hawthorne was absorbed, who's to say other contiguous communities as far south as Redondo Beach wouldn't follow suit? "The people would have the right to demand water," Mulholland said of this forty-square-mile region. Convinced he was being set up to fail, he lobbied to get the council to prohibit any further annexations for the next ten years. The motion was debated but not adopted. Nonetheless, Mulholland's remonstrance was a wake-up call. From the time he delivered his lecture until the opening of the Colorado River Aqueduct and Mono Lake extension in 1939 and 1941, Los Angeles did not add any territories greater than 262 acres, save for one exception in 1932. As Mulholland predicted, Los Angeles was able to bring its population up to 1.5 million citizens in those intervening years simply from growth within its existing borders.

Not everyone appreciated Mulholland's "solemn warning," as newspapers characterized it. A businessman named William P. Maurer sent a letter to the council that blamed Mulholland for padlocking L.A.'s sprawl. "The water department appears to have bungled the [water] conservation program at the source of supply and the transportation of that supply," he wrote. "The city does not get half the water it should be getting from that source." Maurer picked at Mulholland's one sore spot—his failure to build a reservoir at the headwaters in Owens Valley, which was rooted in his decades-long feud with old partner Fred Eaton. In 1905, Eaton had offered his 22,000-acre Long Valley ranchland for $220,000. Mulholland rejected it. Eaton upped his price to $1 million and held firm. By early 1928, however, his health was in serious decline. Mulholland paid him a visit, only to find a half-paralyzed, rambling old man ravaged by rheumatoid arthritis who wasn't up for business talk. Back in Los Angeles, Mulholland authorized the Water Board to bid $800,000 for the acreage. But even with his Land and Cattle Company in receivership, Eaton still stood pat at $1 million. For the umpteenth time, Mulholland had had enough. He vowed never to buy Eaton's land until the stubborn septuagenarian was "six feet underground."

To save face from his latest thwarted negotiations, Mulholland reiterated his claim that a Long Valley reservoir was unnecessary. He also placed blame on Owens Valley residents, who filed an injunction suit that tied up any serious discussions in the 1920s. Though a proposed 150-foot-tall dam could store 340,000 acre-feet of water, Mulholland now dismissed it from an engineering standpoint. "A dam 150 feet high will leak," he scoffed, despite the fact that seven concrete dams in the U.S. exceeded 300 feet at that time. Perhaps Mulholland was alluding to his own experience. Two years earlier, he unveiled his latest engineering sensation—the 205-foot-tall St. Francis Dam in San Francisquito Canyon, seventeen miles north of Los Angeles city limits. The dam leaked almost from the day it opened, its drip-drip-drip akin to a ticking time bomb set to explode.

CHAPTER 28

Mulholland Falls

THE LOS ANGELES AQUEDUCT, the Cascades, Mulholland Dam at Lake Hollywood, even Mulholland Drive—all were given the VIP treatment when they opened as tributes to William Mulholland. But the debut of the St. Francis Dam and reservoir, arguably one of the water superintendent's most impressive and important works, was devoid of splashy spectacles. The *Los Angeles Times* was the only newspaper to give its quiet opening extensive coverage, burying it on inside pages. "WATER POURING INTO RESERVOIR, NEW SAN FRANCISQUITO BASIN TO STORE VAST SUPPLY," read the headline on March 20, 1926. Los Angeles's low-key approach reflected the sensitivity around the dam. Unlike its smaller cousin at Lake Hollywood, the St. Francis Dam sat directly on the Los Angeles Aqueduct, which had been sabotaged by activists in 1924, the dam's first year of construction. Despite a $10,000 reward by the city of Los Angeles, no one in Owens Valley outed the perpetrators. Since then, several more sections of aqueduct pipeline were blown up in Inyo County. At the request of Mulholland, Police Captain Herman Cline issued "shoot to kill" orders to rifle-carrying patrolmen if the bombing continued. There were even rumors afoot about plans to detonate the St. Francis Dam. Downplaying its completion was an act of prudence.

The seventy million gallons that flowed into the reservoir in its early days were a mere drop in the bucket. At full capacity, Mulholland observed, its twelve billion gallons would double the combined storage of the six principal reservoirs serving Los Angeles. Plugging a V-shaped gorge, the St. Francis Dam—1,225 feet across its crown, 150 feet wide at the base—held back a four-mile lake. But from the moment it came fully online on May 4, 1926, a sense of doom pervaded the Santa Clara Valley communities downstream from the dam. Like the monolithic Weeping Rock in Utah's Zion National Park, the structure always seemed to be crying in the form of "tears" dribbling down its face. "If the leaks in the dam continue, it will be over with us soon," warned a Saugus resident to a postal worker. Others relieved their stress through gallows humor, with one local telling another, "See you again, if the dam don't break." Mulholland was aware of the cracks and had his crews patch them up, only to see new ones form. "Like all dams, there are little seeps here and there," he later said. But when muddy groundwater formed at the foot of the dam, alarm turned to panic. It suggested that water was percolating under its now-compromised foundation, and prompted Tony Harnischfeger, the dam's keeper, to place an urgent call to the Bureau of Water. On the morning of March 12, 1928, Mulholland and his assistant Harvey Van Norman headed out to the site. After a cursory inspection, the Chief found the water to be "clear as glass"; it only looked muddy because it came into contact with the ground. The men were back in L.A. in time for a late lunch.

That evening, two minutes before the stroke of midnight, the dam gave way with an ear-splitting roar. Harnischfeger was the first to lose his life as a tsunami of water, steel, and concrete careened down the canyon. Back in Los Angeles, the phone rang in the Mulholland household. Bill's daughter Rose answered. It was Van Norman. The dam was gone. She woke her father, who stumbled out of bed in shock. "Please, God, don't let people be killed," he said, over and over. "Please, God, don't let people be killed."

There were heroes in the darkness. The telephone operator, thirty-eight miles away in Santa Paula, who risked certain death by remaining at her post to ring households to evacuate. The family of four who clung to a mattress and rode out the flood. The motorcyclist who outraced a sixty-foot wall of water, rousing neighbors, Paul Revere-style. But most victims were asleep and never had a prayer.

The harsh light of daybreak revealed a swath of devastation, sixty miles long, two miles wide. Bridges and trees were gone, replaced by a coat of sludge encasing snapped telephone poles, parts of houses, dead livestock, and bloated corpses. At least 431 people were killed, a number surely higher when accounting for undocumented harvest workers in Piru, Fillmore, Saticoy, and Santa Paula. Boy Scout troops fanned out across the ruins, placing little flags on the deceased to alert officials. Bodies were found at the river's estuary at Ventura Beach, some washing up as far as San Diego. Others were entombed under thirty feet of silt, never to be found excepting skeletons that revealed themselves decades later. It remains the worst man-made disaster in the history of California.

A platoon of police officers and emergency personnel from Los Angeles descended on the scene, but their presence only served as a reminder that it was Los Angeles that caused this calamity. Irate residents yelled at them to go home, threatening their lives. The failed dam spoke of the big city's arrogance, its casual disregard for human life that stretched clear up to Owens Valley. Needless to say, Mulholland was public enemy number one. Wasn't he the one who swatted away neighbors' concerns about the leaks? One woman whose Ventura County home was caked in mud—one of 12,240 houses ruined—placed a blood-red painted sign in her front yard: "KILL MULHOLLAND."

Later that day, Mulholland and Van Norman trudged out to the dam site, or what was left of it. The dam's left and right walls had collapsed where they had been anchored to the rock, leaving behind a protruding concrete stub in the center that the *Los Angeles Express* noted looked eerily like a "tombstone for flood victims." As photographers framed the two men surveying the debris, the imposing "tombstone" loomed behind them. In one shot, Mulholland had the lost, faraway look of a man still trying to process the magnitude of it all, wondering where it went wrong. In another, he climbed a dusty trail away from the site. He

looked frail and defeated, his body pitched forward as if carrying
the weight of the world on his back. As one writer succinctly put
it, "The tragedy of the people in the canyon and the Santa Clara
Valley is the tragedy of William Mulholland."

Death threats continued to hound Mulholland after he returned home, necessitating twenty-four-hour armed guards at
his house on St. Andrews Place. He faced even more scrutiny
outside the home. Summoned to a Coroner's Inquest, he was
asked to speak on the record for a nine-person jury that included
five engineers who would determine if he was criminally liable.
His testimony made riveting front page news. Reporters wrote
that he walked to the stand with feeble steps and, stricken by pal-
sy, held up a trembling hand to take the oath. "On an occasion
like this, I envy the dead," he rasped. As Deputy District Attorney Edward Dennison interrogated him, the veteran engineer
was still struggling to comprehend what had happened, falling
back on his penchant for curses and wizardry. "The break has all
the appearances of a hoodoo," he said. When asked if he would
ever build the dam in the same location again, he remarked, "It's
in a place vulnerable to human aggressiveness." Was Mulholland
implying sabotage? "I have a suspicion," he said, "but it is a very
serious thing to make a charge that I don't even want to utter
without having more to show for it."

Mulholland's inferences that the same militant ranchers
who had damaged the aqueduct might have detonated the dam
drew a contemptuous open letter from Inyo County. "We vigorously resent the linking of the name of Owens Valley with the
great disaster," wrote the Bishop Chamber of Commerce. "The
self-aggrandizement of a small political ring embodied in the
Bureau of Water and Power, unfortunately continued in power, is the sole cause." The letter went on to portray the agency
as "murderous," just the latest example of an "attitude that has
prevailed in some quarters never willing to be fair or just to us."
Unbowed, Harry Chandler's *L.A. Times*—for decades, Mulholland's staunchest defender—ran with the dynamite allegations

anyway, a "whodunnit" involving parties who either observed or overheard zealots from Owens Valley plotting to blow up the edifice. "DAM WAS NOT DYNAMITED" countered the rival *Los Angeles Record* in a shrieking front-page headline. That conclusion came after jury members had a chance to visit the dam site and pick through the bedrock. In fairness to Mulholland, he admitted he had no facts to back up his theory, ultimately pinning the blame on someone else: himself. "We must have overlooked something," he said. "Fasten it on me if there was any error of judgment—human judgment!"

An array of hydraulic experts, dam employees, and civilian witnesses also didn't hesitate to fasten the fiasco on Mulholland. Ultimately, the jury cleared the aging engineer of criminal culpability: "The destruction of this dam was caused by the failure of the rock formations upon which it was built, and not by any error in the design of the dam itself or defect in the materials on which the dam was constructed." Historians have also tended to exonerate Mulholland. Geological engineers point out that the science of dam-building was not as advanced then as it is now. Mulholland would not have known, for instance, that ancient landslides weakened the slate rock that buttressed the wings of the dam. The physics of uplift were also not fully understood, contributing to the structure's susceptibility to tilt forward from saturated water underneath it. On the other hand, Mulholland did not keep up with newer techniques employed by engineering peers that could have fortified the dam. Others fault him for desiring to build a replica of the dam at Lake Hollywood—a curved gravity type—when a safer design may have been better suited to the topography of San Francisquito Canyon. On this front, the coroner's jury did not hesitate to knock Mulholland off his pedestal. "The construction and operation of a great dam should never be left to the sole judgment of one man, no matter how eminent," it concluded. The State Legislature agreed. The following year, it passed the California Dam Safety Program, requiring that all state dams and reservoirs be subject to procedural review to prevent failures and protect lives.

Over the next few months, the city of Los Angeles paid out $15 million in restitution to affected residents and $5,150 for each dead body and its burial. Mulholland offered to resign from his post. Water commissioners accepted his tender, but to take some sting out of his humiliation, they retained him as a consultant on the Colorado River Aqueduct project. It was an anticlimactic denouement for a man who was so instrumental to the rise of Los Angeles, one whose profile would arguably be the first to be chiseled into the city's own Mount Rushmore. Starting with the Los Angeles City Water Co. in 1886, Mulholland's reign as L.A.'s water head lasted forty-two years. In 1902, when he took over the newly created municipal water department, the utility served 23,780 customers in a city of 85,000 people. Only 141 miles of main pipelines had been laid down. Twenty-six years later, L.A.'s waterworks served ten times more customers in a city of over one million people. Augmenting the 233-mile aqueduct were 2,900 miles of mains—enough to stretch from Los Angeles to Bangor, Maine—making it the largest city-run water market in the world.

By the end of 1928, a new era had dawned. The Swing-Johnson Bill authorized the building of Hoover Dam (necessary for the viability of the Colorado River Aqueduct), Van Norman took over as Mulholland's successor, and the Southern California Metropolitan Water District, at long last, opened for business. Even without the St. Francis disaster, Mulholland's career seemed to reach a natural completion point. The man who had famously not taken a true vacation for thirty-five years now had nothing but time. And only time would tell how Los Angeles would reconcile his complicated legacy.

CHAPTER 29

Past vs. Present

ONE YEAR AFTER THE St. Francis Dam saga, William Mulholland's legendary vitality had given way to a shuffling gait. Much of his physical decline could be explained by advancing age—he was now seventy-three-years-old—but friends and family also attributed it to a life that had lost its central purpose. Confined to the margins, he no longer benefitted from regenerative expeditions into the field and suffered from sleepless nights. "It was that damned dam that killed him," said his chauffeur, George Bejar.

Mulholland wasn't the only surviving paradise keeper engaged in a slow dance with mortality. In letters between them, Gen. Moses Sherman and Harry Chandler were now more inclined to kibitz about their personal welfare than business affairs. Sherman had long complained of stomach ailments, sciatica, rheumatism, and bladder trouble. Now, at age seventy-five, his health issues had compounded to the point of occasional immobility, a source of embarrassment to him. Unable to attend a meeting that included oil baron Edward Doheny, Sherman wrote Chandler, "Please [do] not tell people I am 'sick.' Please tell Mr. Doheny . . . that I have another 'engagement.'" On a doctor's advice, he took on a full-time nurse to give him a twice-daily bladder wash, a procedure that is as uncomfortable as it sounds. But his bladder became inflamed, requiring painful trips to San Francisco, where an expert recommended surgery. "My children are doing a great deal of worrying about their father," Moses confessed to Harry. "They are very anxious for me not to work so hard, as I have been doing, for years; also, you have told me the same thing. . . . I want so much to live and be useful." Even

Sherman's fake teeth, installed by a leading dentist, were unco-operative. "I am not able to use the excellent teeth he made for me, very much," he wrote Arnold Haskell. "They hurt me so. . . . You see, the false teeth improve my looks so much (They make me look younger); I am very sorry that I cannot wear them, more than I do."

Though a relative spring chicken at sixty-four, Chandler countered the ravages of age by trying to capture the fountain of youth. After obsessing over how many times the words "milk" and "honey" were mentioned in the Bible, the puritanical pub-lisher devoted himself to a breakfast of milk and honey, gath-ered from family cows and bee farms in the hills behind his Los Feliz estate. This was often followed by an apple for lunch and bread and milk for dinner. Privately, he expressed a desire to live at least as long as his parents, who died at the ripe old ages of ninety-two and ninety-four years old, almost as long as Moses (the biblical one). To ensure his longevity, Chandler—and his *Los Angeles Times*—became apostles of a crack doctor who touted the transplanting of goat glands by grafting them into men's scrotums. Hailing from a small town in Kansas, Dr. John R. Brinkley claimed that goat hormones cured over twenty-sev-en ailments—from skin disease to insanity—as well as sexual dysfunction. With the aid of a local anesthetic, procedures took place twenty minutes after the removal of glands from young bil-ly goats' severed testicles. "The glands become absorbed by the human glands, and the man is renewed in this physical and men-tal vigor," Brinkley attested. Chandler was so taken by the doc's cutting-edge practices, he invited him to Los Angeles to set up his own shingle. Intrigued as he was, Harry was hesitant to go under the knife himself. He managed to find guinea pigs, though, paying four *Times* employees $750 to receive the transplant in re-turn for guaranteed lifetime employment. (Disturbingly, beloved *Times* editor Harry Andrews died four years after his procedure, a period that coincided with a protracted illness.) Chandler even worked on Sherman. "He was trying to get the general to take it," Dorothy Chandler, Harry's daughter-in-law, recalled years later. "And the general was yelling back at him. He thought it was a lot of no-good foolstuff." Chandler finally saw the light after the *Times*' health columnist knocked some sense into him. Still, Brinkley did just fine without Harry or Moses as patients. Thanks to years of prominent mentions in the *Times* and a wealthy clientele, the quack's net worth climbed to $20 million at its peak. "It was really Chandler who made me famous," he said before he died in 1942.

Coupled with his longing to recapture his salad days, Chandler was prone to wistful memories of the hopeful invalid who set foot in Plaza de Los Angeles for the first time. Was it really almost half a century ago that he got kicked out of that boarding-house for coughing? He expressed sadness at how much the former pueblo had changed. But a chance encounter with a socialite named Christine Sterling brought a meeting of the minds. She too was disappointed at the way the Plaza district's Spanish and Mexican roots had been all but wiped out. The torch of L.A.'s glorified colonial past, stoked by Helen Hunt Jackson's novel *Ramona* in 1884, was all but a flicker now. If anyone could keep the flame alive, it was Chandler, who helped finance the popular Mission Play at the San Gabriel Mission Playhouse. And so, Chandler and Sterling hatched a plan to refurbish and preserve the birthplace of Los Angeles—including the 115-year-old Plaza Church and Avila Adobe, the city's oldest residence—while creating a Mexican marketplace that would double as a tourist magnet. After getting rubber-stamped by the City Council, Chandler hit up Sherman and other investors to convert an old alley into Paseo de Los Angeles, more commonly known as Olvera Street. Plodding around the Old Plaza's brick-stone walkways in soft Mexican huaraches, Chandler became a regular presence in the area, earning him the nickname "Gran Benefactor de la Ciudad."

Olvera Street, however, exposed an unfortunate dichotomy. The street's 1930 Easter Sunday opening coincided with the government's "Mexican Repatriation." From 1929 to 1936, upward of one million Mexicans and Mexican Americans were deported to Mexico. As journalist Gustavo Arellano put it decades later, "People seemed happy to glorify dead Mexicans . . . it was only the living ones they wanted to get rid of." Those with Mexican heritage provided ready-made scapegoats during the Great Depression, blamed for hogging welfare programs, stealing jobs from unemployed white workers, and "overrunning" the city. This created awkward optics. By mid-1931, as Los Angeles's celebration of its Mexican filiation was in full swing, 75,000 Mexican people from Greater L.A. had already been loaded onto Mexican-bound trains.

To his credit, the Gran Benefactor denounced the repatriation program. Aside from the humanitarian toll, Chandler felt it was bad for Southern California's economy, with his *Times* offering backhanded compliments to the deportees: "Railroad authorities assert they must have Mexicans for section work and track maintenance, for they have proved singularly suitable in resisting the heat which white men cannot endure." Farmers also faced collapse, as "the Mexicans are especially adapted to the harvesting of vegetable crops of the so-called stop and knee variety." The Depression may have highlighted it, but the dynamics of brown labor were nothing new. "Nativism and anti-immigrant sentiment can be very vocal and violent while at the same time the basic functioning of the American West has always required immigrant labor," notes Jessica M. Kim, a historian of U.S. and Mexican relations. "Both can be true at the same time."

Olvera Street did achieve Chandler's primary goal as a popular tourist spot, even if the *Los Angeles Record* called its neatly packaged nostalgia for Old Mexico just another "gadget" in a city synonymous with Hollywoodized fantasies. Meanwhile, Mexican American families who managed to stave off deportation now faced another slap in the face. Also in 1931, the state Assembly voted to segregate public schools in California, separating children of Mexican and Spanish descent from "white races." Los Angeles officials opposed the bill, wary of Jim Crow-type laws that would lead to segregation of other public facilities. Fortunately, the discriminatory measure was defeated, avoiding a nightmarish scenario in which Mexican Americans could get arrested for commingling with Caucasian customers at Olvera Street's Mexican restaurants.

If Olvera Street cast one eye on the past, the recently opened Los Angeles City Hall, a mere quarter mile south, pointed toward the city's future. The stepped pyramid, Art Deco monolith employed the same architect, John Parkinson, who was behind the previous record-holder for L.A.'s tallest building, the Continental Tower. At first glance, City Hall's twenty-eight stories seemed rather excessive to house municipal departments, which occupied only four floors. But the design team saw the unused capacity as a bet on the city's untapped growth. At the building's 1928 dedication, choreographed by MGM Studios and directed by movie theater impresario Sid Grauman, the Official Program played into this theme, applauding "a forward-looking people, determined to win a happy community Destiny . . . always climbing upward." Proving that L.A.'s origin story had room for two contrasting narratives, special recognition was given to "the men of action who aroused the drowsing pueblo from its peaceful laziness, [and] said 'Let us build here a city!'" Years later, thanks to television series like *Dragnet, Superman*, and *Perry Mason*, Los Angeles City Hall was beamed into millions of living rooms, securing its place among the most recognized buildings in the world. It also attained special status by virtue of its 454-foot height, the sole exception to L.A.'s 150-foot limit that dwarfed other structures until the city charter's height restriction was lifted in 1958.

AS THE 1920s drew to a close, Los Angeles boasted three landmarks—City Hall, Olvera Street, and the Hollywood Sign—that firmly established a sense of place and identity. Chandler had a direct role in the latter two and helped secure City Hall's location across the street from the *Times* Fortress as part of the new Civic Center. As the U.S. plunged into an economic depression, Los Angeles was well-positioned to weather the storm. Indeed, the city had shed the traits of a growth stock, slave to the vicissitudes of market forces as occurred during the real estate crash of 1887 and the Panic of 1893. Now, it correlated to a value fund, boasting a wealth of diversified industries upon which much of the world was dependent. No longer focused on expanding its borders, it had settled into a mature metropolis, preparing to host the 1932 Olympics and getting on with managing the assets in its sizable portfolio.

One order of business was what to do about Venice's decrepit canals. Opinions were split on converting them to roadways. By 1929, there were 124 cars registered for every 100 families in Los Angeles—a better than 1:1 ratio. Improved automotive accessibility in and out of Venice would help businesses and drive more tourism. But residents along the canals worried that home values would plummet, and resented paying into a fund to pave over them. After drawn-out court battles, Los Angeles emerged victorious. In July of 1929, the city began to fill in all the waterways that had been excavated by Abbot Kinney. Venice's newspaper commended the city for "sacrificing sentiment on the altar of progress." But in doing so, Los Angeles was also sacrificing Venice's wonderful oddness to progress, a concern raised in more recent times in cities like Portland, Austin, and Santa Cruz, where gentrification-weary denizens have commanded, "Keep [city name] Weird." After all, what was Venice without its signature canals? Ironically, the extant canals in Venice are the six channels south of Venice Boulevard built by Moses Sherman's Venice Park syndicate, separate from Kinney's old grid.

The year 1929 also saw several neighborhoods trying to class up their names. Well before the San Fernando Valley joined Los Angeles, the centrally located outpost of Zelzah was a whistle-stop on the Southern Pacific line. But in a symbolic photo from '29, Mayor John Porter was on hand to witness the removal

of the depot's "Zelzah" sign, replaced with "North Los Angeles."
(The new name didn't even last as long as Zelzah did. North Los
Angeles became Northridge in 1938.) Across town, residents in
Sawtelle resumed their identity crisis. For years, the townlet famously contested the results of its 1918 election to consolidate
with Los Angeles until court decisions led to its surrender in
1922. Seven years later, in a ploy similar to Zelzah's attempts to
glom onto L.A.'s allure, Sawtelle voted to switch *its* name to West
Los Angeles. "If this keeps on we will have communities known
as 'North-Northwest by West Los Angeles,' and 'West-Southwest
by West-three-Points Los Angeles,'" gibed *Times* reporter Harry
Carr. In the years since, West Los Angeles has come to define not
just former Sawtelle, but a vast geographical area that extends as
far east as Century City and Rancho Park.

Folks in Runnymede also sought a name change, but they
weren't interested in derivations of Los Angeles. Their preferred
reference point was Hollywood royalty. In 1919, Edgar Rice Burroughs, author of the adventuresome *Tarzan* novels, purchased
550 acres in the southwest San Fernando Valley that used to be-
long to Gen. Harrison Gray Otis, who had carved it out of the Los
Angeles Suburban Homes Co. After subdividing the land, Burroughs sold lots in "Tarzana" in 1923. Brochures showed the ape
man riding a wild male lion—inspired by the cover art for *Tarzan
and the Golden Lion*—above the phrase "TARZANA: Home of
TARZAN." Sales agents held open houses that promised "fresh-
kill Jungle Barbecue" served by Tarzan, autographed photographs
of Burroughs, and (wink wink) the tract's imprimatur as a "white
spot." Located between Tarzana and Reseda, Runnymede applied
for a post office in 1927. But the postmaster told the community
that it would need to abandon its name due to a conflict with another Runnymede. That led to an agreement between Tarzana and
Runnymede to synthesize the districts and call the whole thing
Tarzana. Tarzana got its post office in 1930, but the mythological
hero behind the name—more popular than ever thanks to Hollywood—got no love from the local library. As late as 1969, the Los

Angeles library system didn't stock Tarzan books because they were "devoid of literary value."

A more serious matter was unfolding in actual Hollywood. It was not forgotten by anyone that the design of Mulholland Dam at Lake Hollywood was identical to that of the St. Francis Dam, a fact reconfirmed at the coroner's inquest. Even before the St. Francis catastrophe, residents below the Hollywood dam were already nervous about it towering over their neighborhood. Now they filed motions to have experts test its structural viability. In the early 1930s, the dam was deemed "safe," though several engineers found deficiencies, including insufficient drainage and a lack of protections against uplift. Once again, Mulholland's autodidactic pedigree suffered another blow. The Water and Power Board came very close to tearing the whole dam down, with Mayor Porter even signing off on draining Lake Hollywood for a smaller reservoir that would eliminate the lake's "menace to the city." But new water chief Harvey Van Norman offered an alternate plan that appeased litigious locals: reinforcing the face of the stepped dam with 300,000 cubic yards of earth and dense landscaping. The present Mulholland Dam reflects this conversion to a "psychological dam," as the press called it, while still preserving the fanciful bear heads and arches along its crest. Not surprisingly, the city kept William Mulholland as far away as possible from discussions about the dam. If anything, he was fortunate to still have his name attached to it. Besides the indignity of almost seeing his eponymous edifice torn down, there had been rumblings of renaming Mulholland Drive because of taint from the St. Francis Dam disaster. The engineer's name had already been erased from Mulholland Park in Montebello, Mulholland Hills near Beverly Crest, the community of Mulholland (now Pacoima) and Mulholland Street (parts of present-day Foothill Boulevard), although these weren't for reasons related to the tragedy.

As Old Bill lingered in the shadows, Sherman was already there. Increasingly bedridden and anxious, he continued to seek the nation's finest doctors to repair his disorders. "I am going to the John [sic] Hopkins (Baltimore)," he wrote his daughter in 1929, "in regard to my bad Bladder trouble (I suffer a great deal of pain, from it)." Sherman had recalled that Chandler's father-in-law, Gen. Otis, had had a successful procedure at Johns Hopkins in 1908, and was hoping a miracle could be performed on himself. With Mulholland and Sherman sidelined, Chandler, hypochondria notwithstanding, was more potent than ever. But on the brink of Los Angeles's finest hour, the *Times* titan almost saw his life come to a grisly and abrupt end before those of his two depleted friends.

CHAPTER 30

The Peak and Passing of the Patriarchy

IN 1930, LOS ANGELES held onto the top spot as the largest city in the U.S. by area and ranked fifth most populous with 1,272,037 inhabitants. An almost equal number of people had moved into Los Angeles County during the 1920s. It was the largest internal migration the nation had ever seen. "One long drunken orgy" is the way L.A. historian Carey McWilliams described the frenzied decade. Years of campaigns targeting prospective homeowners had paid off. One out of three Angelenos owned the dwelling they lived in, besting homeownership in San Francisco (twenty-eight percent), Boston (nineteen percent), and New York (thirteen percent). Where Pacific Electric's Red Cars once shuttled people to all parts of L.A. County—ridership peaked at 109,185,650 passengers in 1924—the rise of the automobile sealed its death warrant. It's no coincidence that, outside of the San Fernando Valley, most new subdivisions from 1924 to 1930 were located in the Santa Monica Mountains, Verdugo Mountains, San Gabriel Mountains, and San Rafael Hills. The freedom and navigability offered by vehicles led to a sprouting of foothill communities like Hollywoodland, Beverly Crest, Encino, Sunland, and Flintridge, all largely inaccessible to streetcars or featuring steep, curvy grades.

Now entering his third decade as the *Los Angeles Times'* official or unofficial President and General Manager, Harry Chandler and his paper continued to paint Los Angeles as a shining refuge during dark times. His latest boosterism gimmick—started in 1925—was the "Make a Friend for California" contest. Local business owners were encouraged to have employees send letters throughout the country to expound on the virtues of Los Angeles. Chandler provided companies with a press kit of sorts, which included stats and a template letter. The best letter would receive a prize. On the news side of things, his *Times* remained a bullhorn for partisan agendas. "There's only one way to cover a union story," he once reproached a *Times* reporter, "and that's the *Times'* way." Labor strikes remained a rare occurrence in Los Angeles. "The reason is because it has the *Los Angeles Times*," he boasted. In shades of his late father-in-law, Gen. Harrison Otis, Chandler told his young grandson, Otis Chandler, that he kept a ten-gauge shotgun in his office: "If those damn unionists come to blow up the *Times* again, I'm ready for them!"

Beyond the paper, Chandler remained L.A.'s apex dealmaker and influencer. When Jack Warner and his Warner Bros. were on the verge of bankruptcy after producing the seminal but pricey talkie *The Jazz Singer*, Chandler lent them money to save the studio. When close friend Herbert Hoover needed someone to help the nation get back on its feet after the stock market crash, it was Chandler whom the president appointed to the National Business Survey Conference. Harry even came to the aid of his archrival William Randolph Hearst. When banks threatened to take over the publisher's San Simeon castle during the Great Depression, Harry stepped in and assumed the mortgage. Helping his friends (and frenemies) was not a strain for Chandler. His estimated net worth ranged between several hundred million to half a billion dollars. That Chandler was "many times a millionaire" wasn't in and of itself a concern to the *Los Angeles Record* as much as the fact that "he hasn't a lazy bone in his body." Indeed, Chandler's wealth, work ethic, and access to the most powerful people in America made him an indominable force, a kind of one-man monopoly outside the reach of anti-trust laws. "It is Chandler's unflagging activity that makes him dangerous to all progressive projects."

Like other magnates, Chandler's megafortune made him a target, especially during desperate times. In September 1930, gangsters out of Chicago kidnapped a Western Union night manager named W. R. Finch, tied him to a tree in Benedict Canyon, and tortured him by twisting a cord around his neck until he gurgled out the combination of the safe at the branch office. Two other prominent men were also abducted and forced to buy their way to freedom. Though they were too scared to talk to investigators, the District Attorney's office found out that Chandler was next on the mob's hit list. He and his family were assigned twenty-four-hour protection while suspicious characters near his house and office were rounded up and interrogated. After the *Los Angeles Express* broke the story in November, Chandler was forced to put out a statement. Not wanting to look weak or worried, he minimized the situation and even lied about having bodyguards for several weeks: "I know nothing about the supposed plot to 'kidnap' me beyond the fact that, a few days ago, I received information from an apparently reliable source that something of the kind was contemplated by a group of gangsters from outside the city. Such reports are not uncommon, and, beyond taking ordinary precautions, I did nothing about it." After a junior member of the outfit confessed to their crimes, indictments were handed down and Chandler was free to resume his already well-insulated life behind his secluded estate and the *Times*' Fortress.

Though organized crime worked with corrupt city officials to control rackets like prostitution and bootlegging in Los Angeles, it was a disorganized bunch that didn't really coalesce until the 1940s and '50s under Jack Dragna. For now, the lack of a strong mob presence was another distinction separating L.A. from Chicago or New York. With one million visitors expected to pour into the City of Angels for the 1932 Olympics, it was important to maintain a safe and sunny image. Relatedly, the city organized an extravaganza called La Fiesta de Los Angeles in September 1931 that was, for all intents and purposes, a dry run for the Olympic Games. Under the leadership of booster extraordinaire

Billy Garland, La Fiesta was a ten-day citywide birthday party commemorating 150 years since L.A.'s founding. With the flags of Spain, Mexico, and the California Republic flapping in the wind, every day brought heavily hyped events—many requiring admission—whose scale would not just rival Olympic meets, but provide opportunities to work out logistical kinks. One hundred thousand attendees packed into the Los Angeles Memorial Coliseum for a gigantic Sunday mass led by an ecclesiastical delegate from Rome. Aquatic events were staged at "all beaches from Long Beach to Santa Monica," just as they would for next year's Summer Games. And 500 synchronized planes and fireworks put on an aerial ballet presaging the Olympiad's opening and closing ceremonies.

Predictably, Hollywood had a role in the dress rehearsal. Douglas Fairbanks and Mary Pickford led a cast of thirty silver screen stars in re-enactment pageants that was hailed as a "billion dollar turnout." Playing a caballero, Fairbanks romped in on a horse at the Old Plaza, followed by a procession of other Anglo actors impersonating Indians, vaqueros, Spanish soldiers, and Franciscan fathers. Even Mayor John Porter got in on the action, dressing as a ranchero. Fairbanks and Pickford subsequently headed up the Olympics' Welcoming Committee, lining up friends like Charlie Chaplin and Marlene Dietrich to put on shows that boosted ticket sales.

When it ended on September 13, 1931, the Sesquicentennial celebration proved that Los Angeles had what it took to pull off the Olympics. The city generated 18,000 temporary jobs and grossed $500,000 in receipts from 500,000 paying customers during the worst economic crisis in American history. Though the festival garnered only a slim profit, that was beside the point. "While money making is not and should not be the chief end and aim of this celebration, it is worth noting that expenditures made upon it are quite likely to be returned several fold," wrote the *L.A. Times*. "Such affairs are the best sort of advertising." Isadore B. Dockweiler, president of the La Fiesta Association, couldn't resist tweaking the naysayers. "We were told it could not be successful in the face of the so-called depression throughout the country, and we were advised to abandon the idea of the celebration at this time," he said. "Los Angeles, through its cooperation on every hand, gave the lie to the depression talk."

Dockweiler's sentiments were echoed by Chandler. Mere days before Dockweiler's quote, the *Times* editorialized that "much of the depression is psychological." The newspaper was deep into its second year of reporting on stories that refused to acknowledge material conditions for the nation's collapsed economy. "DEPRESSION CHARGED TO PESSIMISM" announced a July 1930 headline attributed to the president of RCA-Victor Co. "'CHEER-UP' CAMPAIGN HAS BEEN LAUNCHED TO DISPEL PSYCHOLOGY OF DEPRESSION" read another headline a year later, referring to a movement to "dispel the gloom" by the Shriners of America. But all the cheerleading in the world couldn't change the facts on the ground. By 1932, unemployment in California was at twenty-eight percent. "Hooverville" shantytowns dotted the landscape. Farm income was slashed in half from 1929, and building permits dried up because few had money to buy homes. Unable to raise travel funds for their athletes, nations across the globe called for canceling the Olympics. Even local pride was fading. One night, jobless Angelenos smashed store windows that hawked Olympic pennants, while unemployed marchers called for "Groceries, not Games" at the state capitol. With the biggest moment in Los Angeles history in jeopardy, Chandler took the unprecedented step of publishing a full-page personal letter in the *Times* on New Year's Day, 1932. Addressed to "Our Readers and Patrons," his "Message for the New Year" was a clarion cry to keep the faith. "The future is one to which California can look toward with serenity and confidence," it began. Over the next two paragraphs, he made the case that L.A. residents had an ace in the hole. They were living, he reminded them, in paradise. And the pull of paradise was as strong as gravity, everlasting and unalterable.

The Times has seen this community battered many times before by financial hurricanes. It has always emerged bigger and stronger. It is no more possible to stop Los Angeles than to push back the rising sun. Our real wealth has been untouched.

Not a ray of sunshine has been struck from our climate; not an inch from the height of our mountains; not a wave withheld from our beautiful seacoast. . . . Everything that held out a lure to bring people to Southern California is still here. The Westward trek to the Land of Promise may have been checked; but it has not been stopped.

The letter was signed in cursive, "Harry Chandler."

Though his *Times* was not alone in rekindling the Olympics, Chandler's esprit de corps for Los Angeles was infectious. He had already pulled the 1932 Summer Games out of the jaws of defeat once before. Several years earlier, the Community Development Association, alarmed by rising costs, had been all set to withdraw L.A. as the host city. Then Chandler walked into the meeting and worked his magic. Billy Garland recalled, "Had it not been for the arrival, a few minutes later, of one of the most enthusiastic members and sponsors of the Games, Mr. Harry Chandler . . . the Tenth Olympiad would never have been held in Los Angeles." Gradually, as more nations committed to sending athletes, momentum shifted. By June 1932, thirty-six nations were "in." The Games were on.

If there was one disappointment for Chandler, it was that Gen. Moses Sherman would not be able to join him in a private box for the opening ceremonies, or at any of the events for that matter. The general was confined to a hospital for several weeks. When he was released in mid-August, he convalesced at his new home in Newport Beach in Orange County. The salty ocean air was a daily balm for the frail baron, whose business affairs were now handled by his confidant Arnold Haskell. By this point in his life, Sherman's idea of excitement was to flip open the newspaper and peruse the Shipping News. There, he could keep tabs on the comings and goings of the *Gen. M. H. Sherman.* The steamer operated out of Los Angeles Harbor, delivering cargo to far-flung ports of call as part of the Arrow Line. The S.S. *Sherman* represented the last seaworthy vestige of Moses's tenure as president of the Los Angeles Steamship Company, of which Chandler owned a share. At its peak, the line offered passengers round trips to Hawaii. A victim of the economic hard times, the company soon went belly-up.

Back in Los Angeles County, the City of Angels prepared to welcome the world. It is impossible to overstate just how big a roll of the dice this was for the city's fortunes. Beginning in 1896, the modern Olympics had been held in seven European cities whose ages could be measured in centuries, if not millennia: Athens, Paris, London, Stockholm, Berlin, Antwerp, Amsterdam. The only time the Olympiad took place in the United States—St. Louis in 1904—it was so awful, most historians have consigned it to the ash heap of history. As if a second go-around in the Americas wasn't bad enough, Los Angeles might as well have been an archipelago in the South Pacific as far as Europe was concerned. Dismissing the city as a second-class Podunk, London's *The Observer* grumbled that holding The Games there "raises a truly tremendous problem for the other nations who have got to find their way to this remote corner of the earth." Like an underdog athlete looking for any slight to motivate their performance, the Los Angeles Olympic Committee was determined to not just prove the skeptics wrong, but to show that Los Angeles was a major player on the world stage.

Fortunately, it made a great first impression. As 1,300 athletes trickled in to Los Angeles before the July 30 Opening Day, they were given red carpet treatment at the first-ever Olympic Village. Constructed over 321 acres in Baldwin Hills, a few miles west of the Coliseum (alternately, Olympic Stadium), it truly was a self-contained village. Male athletes were lodged in 550 two-bedroom bungalows with access to a post office, library, cinema, and restaurants. (Female athletes were housed at the luxe Chapman Park Hotel.) High on privacy and low on stress, the complex ensured a frictionless experience for the world's most elite competitors. "There never has been anything to compare with the arrangements made in Los Angeles," observed Carl Diem, Germany's organizer for the 1936 Games, after touring the Olympic Village. His biggest hope for Berlin was "to follow this wonderful model that the organizing committee has made for us." It also helped that L.A.'s postcard-perfect climate lived up to its billing. Daytime temperatures hovered around seventy-seven degrees, several degrees below normal. Foreign correspondents raved about L.A.'s weather, unexpected modernity, and top-notch facilities, which included the Rose Bowl, Grand Olympic Auditorium, Griffith Park, and a Coliseum-adjacent aquatics stadium. Just as Chandler had reassured, the Land of Promise need not worry. It would sell itself.

Though the Olympic Village would be torn down after the Games, such campuses are now the norm. Other innovations also entered the Olympiad canon. Where previous Games were held over a period of weeks or months, Los Angeles locked in the sixteen-day schedule. The city's motion picture industry— employing elite technicians, producers, and image-makers— informed many of the rituals now taken for granted: the use of photo-finish cameras; award-winning athletes climbing tiered podiums, which played up their celebrity; and media hubs linking photographers and wire services with up-to-the-minute feeds, a precursor to what would later be termed "video village." On a local level, the city permanently changed the name of 10th Street to Olympic Boulevard.

On August 14, 1932, 105,000 spectators packed the Coliseum for the elaborate closing ceremonies. The United States led all nations with forty-one gold medals, well ahead of runner-up Italy's twelve. But the fact that the Tenth Olympiad exceeded everyone's wildest dreams during such tumultuous times felt as if everyone won. "The greatest Olympic Games the world has ever known" trumpeted a London newspaper on August 17, upending that city's earlier dire predictions. Despite a lackluster showing, Germany continued its lovefest with Los Angeles. "We came here with 100 young men and women who will return home with one of the most beautiful memories of a nation and a people in their souls," gushed Theodore Lewald, a representative for the upcoming Berlin Games. "There was no rain, only a continuous shower of friendship and attention." He promised "a return of the kindness and hospitality we received." (Adolf Hitler would indeed present the Germans as a peace-loving people, but only by temporarily suppressing the Third Reich's intolerance of Jews and imperialistic agenda.) Two decades after World War II, Los Angeles and Berlin became sister cities.

Another country that would soon emerge as a reviled foe of the United States was equally magnanimous. Heading into the Olympics, relations with Japan were strained after U.S. Secretary of State Henry L. Stimson criticized Tokyo's aggression in China. But American goodwill washed all that away. "We do not care now what your Secretary, Mr. Stimson, says about us," vowed Tadaeki Yamamoto, leader of Japan's squad. "Our Japanese men know your men now. We admire them. Japan is now closer to you. We will take back the word." Clearly, the good vibes didn't stick. If the Olympics demonstrated anything, it was that heads of state excelled at corrupting friendships between foreign individuals. Then again, the Japanese team experienced a similar hypocrisy during their stay in Los Angeles. Occasionally, they were stopped at L.A. establishments with "No Mexicans" signs. The Japanese athletes had been mistaken for Mexicans. Set against the segregationist policies in place for people of color, the *Times'* observation that "race prejudice has been completely tramped to death by the running and jumping feet of the Olympics" rang particularly hollow.

While the human drama made for good copy, the Games' balance sheet was far more important to the business community.

Here too Los Angeles came out a winner, boasting a $1 million profit ($23 million in today's dollars). Additionally, 500 financiers from Europe, Latin America, and Asia registered with the Chamber of Commerce to establish beachheads in Los Angeles for international trading. Wall Street took notice of it all. "In an era of world-wide depression, the games have been remarkably successful from any point of view," *The New York Times* wrote. "For crowds and gate receipts, Los Angeles has set a new Olympic standard." One can imagine the pleasure Chandler must have taken reading passages like "the laurels go to Los Angeles" in domestic and foreign news. Over five decades, Chandler had experienced—and helped orchestrate—an improbable metamorphosis. The former dusty outpost was no longer a pretender or contender. It had finally and irrefutably achieved the level of global legitimacy it had long sought. An *L.A. Times* editorial recapping what the Games meant for Los Angeles was practically infused with a long sigh of relief from its sixty-eight-year-old patriarch:

> She can rest on the sidelines and let the newspapers of the world speak for her. But Los Angeles can glow with appreciative pride at the tributes showered on the Games in the millions of special articles, descriptions, illustrations, editorials and cartoons appearing in columns circling the globe.

The worldwide accolades left a lasting impression, factoring into the International Olympic Committee's decision to award Los Angeles the Games in 1984 and 2028. For the Thirty-fourth Olympiad, the Coliseum will have the distinction as the first stadium in the world to host three Summer Games.

Meanwhile, if there was a saving grace for the ailing Sherman, it was that he was still alive during L.A.'s proudest moment. Looking back upon his life's work, he could take pride in the part he played to get it there. On September 9, 1932, mere weeks after the closing ceremonies, Sherman finally passed away at his home. His career was saluted on the front page of the next day's *Times*, which called him "an outstanding leader in the economic progress of Southern California" and an "important factor in [the] rise of Los Angeles." The article was filled with tidbits that only a close friend like Chandler would know, such as the fact that Sherman, perhaps sensing it was his last Christmas, distributed up to 2,000 presents the previous December, "having his clerks, stenographers and helpers buying, wrapping, distributing remembrances to all old-time citizens and families with whom he had ever had contact." He was survived by his ex-wife Hattie and daughters Hazeltine and Lucy. (His adopted son Robert died in 1930.) In a metaphorical coincidence, the paper pointed out "that on the day Gen. Sherman's life journey ended, the *M. H. Sherman* . . . also reached journey's end and put into her home port at San Pedro."

In fact, the deck of the *M. H. Sherman*, docked in Pedro, appears to be the setting for the last known photograph taken of Sherman, Chandler, and Mulholland, the final prophets of paradise. It's an amateur snapshot; the shadowed head of the photographer juts into the bottom frame while the upper half reveals a "City of Los Angeles" lifebuoy hanging from the railing of the ship's quarterdeck. In the foreground, the trio stand shoulder to shoulder in three-piece suits. By the end of their lives, the sum total of their years building up the city would form its own Sesquicentennial. "We are not quitters," Sherman was fond of saying. "We are all stayers."

Though the date and circumstances of this photo are unknown, it was likely taken within a year of Sherman's death—perhaps early 1932. Looking disoriented and in some discomfort, the general squints open-mouthed into the sun, his rotten teeth clearly visible, no doubt a more practical option at this stage than the pricey veneers that continually bothered him. To his right is Mulholland, almost unrecognizable. His onetime commanding frame, thick and sturdy as an oak tree, is spindly and diminished. His face is crooked, with erstwhile twinkling eyes now dim and askew, as if the result of a small stroke. The photo lends credence to a statement made by Lillian Darrow, an employee of the Water Bureau, who swore that "his face aged twenty years" after the St. Francis Dam disaster. But there is still a hint of Old Bill's famed vitality in his hands—large hands made for work, sweat and grime, hands that saw more action manufacturing Los Angeles than any other pair in the last fifty years. With his left thumb sportingly crooked in a coat pocket, his right hand, gnarled and calloused, firmly grips his fedora as if clenching a claw hammer.

And then there's Chandler, loyal to the end, positioned behind Sherman's left shoulder so that his fading crony is literally framed front and center on his namesake vessel. "You are my best friend," Moses had written him once during a dark moment. "You love me and I know you will help me." Yet there is also an air of impatience in Harry's posture, the way his weight is shifted to his right foot as he leans in for the snapshot, as if not fully committed, his lips forming a tight horizontal line that is neither a smile nor a frown. "Take the picture, please," his body language implores. A folded folio peeks out of his pocket. Perhaps the day's itinerary typed out by his secretary. Compared to the other two retiring gentlemen, Chandler still had places to go, things to do, history to be made. As a restless city awaited his appointments, he didn't want to fall behind.

EPILOGUE

ON AUGUST 14, 1932, the same day as the closing ceremony of the Olympic Games, the Metropolitan Water District announced the sale of the first tranche of $220,000,000 voter-approved bonds to build the Colorado River Aqueduct. W. P. Whitsett, last seen shilling property in Van Nuys, was the MWD's chairman of the board. The aqueduct promised 20,000 construction-related jobs during the Great Depression and, when completed, the capacity to comfortably boost Los Angeles's population well beyond its current 1,470,516. The city had already added 2,300 people earlier in the year when it took in Tujunga. The secluded, communitarian-minded town had rebuffed consolidation efforts in 1930 and 1931. Increasingly in need of amenities, however, it finally joined L.A. in 1932, even if longtime residents accused newer ones of bringing in ringers from outside the town to push the vote through (718 to 659). No one realized it at the time, but Tujunga's 8.7 square miles were the last sizable territory Los Angeles would ever absorb. Since 1932, the overwhelming majority of the city's 200-plus annexations have measured less than 100 acres each. (For various administrative reasons, Los Angeles has actually given *back* modest acreage to cities like Burbank, Beverly Hills, and Vernon.) Over the span of its history, Los Angeles annexed or consolidated 298 tracts of land to account for its 468 square miles. In an uncanny parallel, that is the same number of square miles L.A. once owned in Owens Valley to secure its water. In other words, to reach its current size, Los Angeles built a second Los Angeles in size farther north. The city even got around to acquiring Long Valley to build a reservoir dam—William Mulholland's decades-long white whale—after its owner,

Fred Eaton, finally cracked.

Like so many others, Eaton fell on hard times during the Depression. He lost $200,000 after the bank where he did business went under, then lost Long Valley to foreclosure when he couldn't pay the notes. In December 1932, the city of Los Angeles purchased his ranchland for its appraised value, well below the $1 million bar he had stubbornly set. Weakened by a stroke, he moved in with his son in L.A. and called for his old chum Bill Mulholland. The two had not spoken in five years, but the Chief didn't hesitate to come over. According to Eaton family members, Mulholland greeted him with a "Hello, Fred," and the two hugged and broke down in tears.

Eaton died on March 11, 1934. Though he and Mulholland had patched things up, his death fulfilled Mulholland's angry pledge in 1928 to outlive his estranged friend. Nevertheless, Eaton's passing shook him, reminding him of his own mortality. He confided to his daughter Rose that he had been dreaming of Fred. The men appeared young and vigorous, "yet I knew we were both dead," he said. Later that year, Mulholland's own decline was hastened by a fall that broke his arm and a stroke that rendered him unable to speak. Newspapers went on a Mulholland death watch, pumping out "NEAR DEATH" headlines.

Resting in his bed on July 22, 1935, just shy of his eightieth birthday, he awoke for a moment and gave orders to a ship's lookout—perhaps reliving his days at sea as a teenage British Merchant Naval officer—before drifting off to the hereafter. He left behind five children and their families. While the city no longer blindly worshipped him, most Angelenos still held a place in their hearts for all he had done. Thousands pilgrimaged to his open casket at City Hall. Public buildings lowered their flags, 10,000 workers on the Colorado River Aqueduct paused in silence, and reverential statements were issued. Mayor Frank Shaw pointed to the Los Angeles Aqueduct as an accelerant to "the development of Los Angeles." The *Los Angeles Times* ran a multi-page pictorial recapping Mulholland's career. In keeping with the paper's practice of ignoring inconvenient facts—and preserving the Chief's legend—its obituary completely omitted the St. Francis Dam disaster. However, lawyer and Catholic community pillar Joseph Scott addressed the issue head-on in City Hall's rotunda, where he delivered a stirring eulogy that spotlighted Mulholland's accountability. "In these days of alibi artists and buck passers," he said, "this venerable chieftain's humble but lofty self-sacrifice should read a lesson in intellectual honesty and moral stamina that should not be forgotten by the rest of us." Most of all, Mulholland was remembered for his tireless devotion in service to Los Angeles. "A man's worth is measured by his importance to society," Mulholland had once said. "I never wanted to be wealthy. . . . All I did want was work." Mulholland's one request on his headstone was that it acknowledge his role in building the Los Angeles Aqueduct. "Well done, good and faithful servant," decreed Reverend Franklin L. Gibson. Five years later, the engineer's memory was enshrined with the William Mulholland Memorial Fountain at the corner of Los Feliz Boulevard and Riverside Drive, which also features a commemorative "aqueduct garden." Though it falls well short of the once envisioned 300-foot-tall aqueduct monolith, the site at least features prancing fountains with colored lights.

Coincidentally, sharing the *Times'* front-page coverage of Mulholland's funeral was an article about approved plans for Union Station, the long-awaited terminal for three major railways. Architectural drawings showed an elegant Spanish Revival citadel, slated to open in 1939 in northern downtown. It was yet another iconic project advanced by Harry Chandler, who owned property in the area and facilitated the razing of the original Chinatown in the name of progress. "Chinatown is doomed by the march of the greater Los Angeles Civic Center and the Plaza union depot," the *Times* declared. The paper's unsympathetic view toward a long-persecuted minority group dovetailed with another development in 1935, when Chandler started publishing features that supported eugenics. Up until 1941, writer Fred

Hogue hosted a regular *Times* column called "Social Eugenics" that promoted selective breeding in order to eliminate defective people from society—typically those of color, low economic stature, or of "insane" or "feeble" minds. "The number of happy morons . . . living on the dole is a marked contrast to the overworked and unhappy producers who have to provide not only for their own families but for those of the morons as well," went one screed. Eugenics had already gained notoriety in Nazi Germany to justify the extermination of Jews, deemed a threat to the Aryan race. "Hitler, with the support of the German people, is an exponent of sterilization of the unfit," Hogue chirped in the *Times* in 1939. "He seeks large families where the bloodstream is pure, and no children where there is an infected bloodstream." In addition to publishing Hogue's missives, Chandler was a trustee of the Human Betterment Foundation, which promoted compulsory sterilization laws in California. In 2021, Caltech, an early recipient of Chandler's largesse, stripped his name from its dining hall. Five other benefactors also had their names and honors removed. All subscribed to eugenics' "morally reprehensible" tropes, which the university noted "already had been discredited scientifically during [their] time."

Chandler had exhibited disturbing views on race as far back as 1915, when the *Times* published an article called "Our Vanishing American Race," which fretted over the prolific birthrates of "negroes and aliens." His advocacy of eugenics reinforced the insular atmosphere of his *L.A. Times*, which was increasingly out of touch with not just Los Angeles, but the nation. In 1937, Washington correspondents voted the newspaper the third worst in the country "in terms of fairness and reliability." Chandler was blistered by media critic George Seldes for lacking any qualities that could be "interpreted even vaguely as humanitarian, altruistic, liberal or progressively intelligent," his paper seemingly more interested in not offending its elite roster of advertisers. By 1941, Chandler suffered the ignominy of seeing William Randolph Hearst's *Los Angeles Examiner* and *Los Angeles Herald* surpass the

Times in daily circulation, which stalled at around 300,000. That same year, Harry's son Norman Chandler took over as president and publisher, perpetuating the Otis-Chandler dynasty. The daily maintained a narrow readership of clubby Republicans who didn't want to be challenged by impartial news that pierced their societal bubbles, and GOP pols who looked to the *Times* for guidance on how to vote on legislative issues. By contrast, the paper's eventual reputation as an outlet for smart, nonpartisan journalism and Pulitzer Prize-winning investigative stories didn't begin until Norman's son Otis Chandler took over in the 1960s. Otis was named after his great-grandfather, Harrison Gray Otis, providing a fitting bookend as the *Times'* fourth and final publisher in the Otis-Chandler lineage.

On June 5, 1944, Harry and Marian Chandler marked their fiftieth wedding anniversary. Three months later, Harry died of congestive heart failure. The last of L.A.'s kingpins was eighty years old. Despite his preoccupation with biblical living and immortality, he didn't come close to matching his parents' ages at death, but he did live long enough to see his seven surviving children grant him nineteen grandchildren and two great-grandchildren. Services were held at the First Congregational Church. "A tall and rugged oak has fallen in the forest," intoned the minister, Dr. James W. Fifield Jr., whose free-market teachings lent him the nickname "The Apostle to Millionaires." He continued:

> Harry Chandler was a man of extraordinary vision. He saw the Greater Los Angeles and set in motion causes which would result in its reality. . . . He saw the long-range effects of aqueduct water, harbor, city planning, tourist trade, cultural institutions, educational development, and under all a sound business economy to support it.

Time magazine credited Chandler for doing more to grow Los Angeles than anyone in the city's history. Years later, in an article for the *Atlantic Monthly*, writer David Halberstam posited

that Chandler, and by extension Gen. Otis, "did not so much foster the growth of Southern California as, more simply, invent it."
Even Norman's wife Dorothy Chandler, who helped establish the
Los Angeles Music Center, conceded that the *Times* was merely
an adjunct for her father-in-law: "I think of Harry Chandler not
as a publisher but as a land developer, a dreamer, a builder. His
mind wasn't on the newspaper." One thing that did occupy his
mind was the destruction of any traces of how he accumulated
his wealth. Per his directive, Marian burned all his papers upon
his death.

IN THE decades after Chandler's passing, the road to paradise
grew increasingly hectic. Following national trends, post-WWII
prosperity was marked by white flight to L.A.'s suburbs. Even
here the original industrialists' handiwork greased the wheels for
decentralization. Phineas Banning had built a popular railroad
to the harbor, opening up the Shoestring Strip and South Bay for
commercial and residential development. The electric railways
of Gen. Moses Sherman and Henry Huntington carved out a
honeycomb of neighborhoods upwards of thirty miles from the
original Plaza district. Chandler led the charge to the San Fernando Valley, and his vision for an auto utopia, defined by wide
boulevards, highways, and freeways, hastened the exodus. As a
city more improvised than planned, L.A.'s reputation as a "young
and noisy giant of the West" was not all that fundamentally different from Silicon Valley's "move fast and break things" mantra
generations later. Its scattershot grid mirrored the philosophy of
a Bay Area architect named Charles H. Cheney, who drafted the
state's first urban planning legislation in 1915. "A city plan should
be prepared from the economic standpoint first," Cheney's report concluded, "the social or human standpoint second, and
the aesthetic point last." Cheney even went so far as to criticize
any planners who put the human element first. As late as 1971,
the blueprint laid down by ancient transit routes produced "a

detailed sketch for the whole of Los Angeles that exists today," as pointed out by Reyner Banham in his seminal book *Los Angeles: The Architecture of Four Ecologies.*

But as a host of problems made clear, that sketch was unsustainable. Freeways that were once glorified were now lambasted by social and environmental activists, resulting in court-ordered shutdowns of freeway construction in the 1970s and '80s. Epic traffic jams and diesel-belching trucks contributed to chronic smog. Los Angeles was a city of faded dreams, symbolized by the Hollywood Sign, whose letters were tumbling down the hillside and in need of a rebuild. By the early 1990s, L.A. was awash in record crime, rampant police corruption, and a continual spiral of shuttered factories that included General Motors, Lockheed, and Chandler's beloved Goodyear Rubber plant.

Fed up with ineffective, bloated bureaucracy, a groundswell of residents in Hollywood and the San Fernando Valley looked to break away from Los Angeles. Their beefs were reminiscent of early annexed districts that felt underserved compared to those with stronger ties to City Hall. But in a citywide general election on November 5, 2002, registered voters slapped down Hollywood's and the Valley's secession movements. (On its own, the Valley would have ranked as the sixth largest city in the nation in 2002.) For all its problems, most people felt that gouging out large chunks of L.A. was to strip away its soul. "That's selfish of Hollywood, wanting to separate," said a renter in Hollywood named Aaron Michelson. "I always thought that Los Angeles was the sum of its parts."

But was it? Writer Dorothy Parker once described Los Angeles as "seventy-two suburbs in search of a city." Nowadays there are over 200 recognized neighborhoods, including some 100 neighborhood councils, just within Los Angeles. For context, in the decades after its founding in 1781, L.A. still adhered to Spanish Governor Felipe de Neve's decree that pueblos measure "four square leagues," or twenty-eight square miles. Typical of the Walking-Horsecar Era (pre-1800 to 1890), Angelenos could

walk between their homes and occupations. Even those residing in the Plaza's four corners were still part of one community.
The onset of electric railways initiated urban sprawl, although
the first wave of territories to be annexed—Highland Park, San
Pedro, and Hollywood, among them—had already forged their
own identities and business districts. It wasn't until the automobile became the preferred mode of transportation that the idea
of Los Angeles as a collective community began to falter. This
was especially evident after the annexation of the San Fernando Valley, where many subdivisions were only accessible by car.
Van Nuys notwithstanding, most neighborhoods lacked a true
commercial center and common spaces where neighbors could
spontaneously interact. New homeowners complained of feeling
lonely. One early suburbanite, a middle-aged woman, lamented,
"None of the people round here call on each other and not a single neighbor has invited us in. . . . We don't know anybody and we
don't see much sign of neighboring." This sense of distrust spread
down the block. "I don't know what [my neighbor's] name is, and
I have never cared to find out," said another housewife. These
comments could just as well be uttered today, as the existential
sense of isolation that pervaded L.A.'s earliest auto-centric residential neighborhoods is still all too common.

And yet, as a municipality that was largely manufactured
into being, the City of Angels has a knack for reinventing itself.
Or at least borrowing from the past to chart its future. In 1990—
eighty-nine years after Huntington established Pacific Electric
and twenty-seven years after the last Red Car was torn from its
tracks—LA Metro launched the Blue Line (now A Line) from Los
Angeles to Long Beach. "What we are trying to do is re-rail Los
Angeles," acknowledged a Los Angeles Transportation Commission executive at its opening. "To re-create the old Red Car system." Metrolink, serving Greater Los Angeles, similarly retraced
Huntington's interurban railways. Even the city's current subway
system has an antecedent in Pacific Electric, whose Hollywood
Subway route burrowed through downtown's Belmont Tunnel in

the 1920s. All told, LA Metro and Metrolink operate roughly 675 miles of railway in the metropolitan region, or about half the total miles PE achieved at its peak.

Building a robust multimodal network that also includes more bus and bike lanes goes beyond reducing car dependency. It fits into a grander scheme known as the "15-Minute City." Adopted by the Los Angeles City Council in 2023, the concept revisits old patterns of municipal development centered around walkable, mixed-used districts, in which basic necessities can be attained within a fifteen-minute stroll or bike ride of one's home. Several facets of the 15-Minute City were rolled out during the Covid-19 pandemic, part of ongoing quality-of-life changes to the national urban landscape that included the removal of street parking for outdoor restaurant dining; "road diets" to promote traffic calming and slow living; the conversion of streets to pedestrian plazas; more green belts, tree canopies, and parks; more residential units clustered near transit stations; and, in a bid to make housing more affordable, the erasure of zoning laws that require new residential buildings to meet parking minimums (mandatory parking leads to fewer available units, resulting in higher rents). Forget "suburbs in search of a city." Twenty-first-century Los Angeles is a city embracing its disparate suburbs. G. Gordon Whitnall, L.A.'s first urban planner, embraced the idea that "real community pride" was the key to livability. Viewing communities as "units," he espoused "not one great whole, but a co-ordination of many units, within each of which there shall be the most ideal living conditions [and] the most ideal conditions for business or industry."

Whitnall never got to fully witness his vision, but then, how could he? L.A.'s Gilded Age-reared oligarchy was driven by an "economic standpoint first" ethos of unregulated expansionism, one that denied non-white races access to said units while simultaneously viewing them as vital cogs in the economy. Against this backdrop of structural racism, it's perhaps no wonder that people of color make up eighty-seven percent of the most distressed neighborhoods in present-day Los Angeles. In December of 2020, the Los Angeles City Council formed the LA Civil Rights Department to help level the playing field. "We just need more resources going towards those communities first," says David Price, Director of Racial Equity. "That's what equity is. To stop the bleeding and then to begin repair. To stop the lasting effects of policies from the late nineteenth century, early twentieth century." The result is a city that is continually fixing outdated or inequitable practices once championed by the Otis-Chandler trust.

Besides resuscitating non-automobile transit and more walkable neighborhoods, L.A.'s approach to water infrastructure is also a throwback to an earlier time. For ninety years, Mulholland's Los Angeles Aqueduct—and the Second Los Angeles Aqueduct, which opened in 1970—provided up to sixty percent of the city's annual water. But federal air pollution standards and restitution edicts have compelled L.A.'s Department of Water and Power to share its supply with Inyo and Mono Counties. (L.A.'s usurping of Owens Valley would be all but impossible these days, thanks to stricter annexation laws for local governments.) Reliable provisions from the Colorado River Aqueduct are also imperiled, owing to megadroughts and Western states squabbling over water rights. And massive river dams are proven disasters to the environment. Consequently, Los Angeles County officials have harkened back to those inglorious days when Mulholland used to wade through murky zanjas, figuring out how to extract every last drop within the L.A. basin.

Since 2018, the county's Safe Clean Water Program has spent over $1 billion to capture stormwater and create more permeable surfaces to recharge groundwater. In Los Angeles, officials hope to recycle 100 percent of the city's wastewater by 2035, further dampening the need for imported water. Hydrologists have also considered inflatable dams on the Los Angeles River. The temporary barricades, already used on the San Gabriel and Santa Ana Rivers, are another way to catch storm runoff. A seventy-foot water wheel would draw the impounded water out of the river to replenish aquifers north of downtown. It's a page right out of 1859, when a newly built water wheel diverted water into the Zanja Madre near the same location. Somewhere the ghost of Old Bill is experiencing déjà vu. The hectoring water conservationist, who famously unsnarled the L.A. River to save Christmas in 1889, would probably appreciate the back-to-basics ingenuity behind the waterway's reconfiguration in order to rescue his beloved city once more.

On the other hand, one can't help wondering how the officious sextet of Mulholland, Chandler, Otis, Huntington, Sherman, and Banning would fit into the rubric of modern-day Los Angeles. None could influence today's melting pot of four million souls as they once did; the world is a different place, what with carbon reduction mandates, social awareness, and reparations of past deeds, not to mention layers upon layers of red tape. All reigned during a hubristic era of Big Ideas, when white privilege and an eagerness to conquer nature fueled many entrepreneurial exploits. Theirs was a Los Angeles striving for global respect at breakneck speed. At a time when most Angelenos—and America—celebrated Prometheus figures, their boldness of vision elevated the pueblo of their youths to the megalopolis of their deaths. Whether or not these titans created a literal paradise misses the point. Like Shangri-La, Eden, or even Hollywood, paradise will always exist as long as humankind keeps dreaming. For that reason alone, Los Angeles was always destined to be.

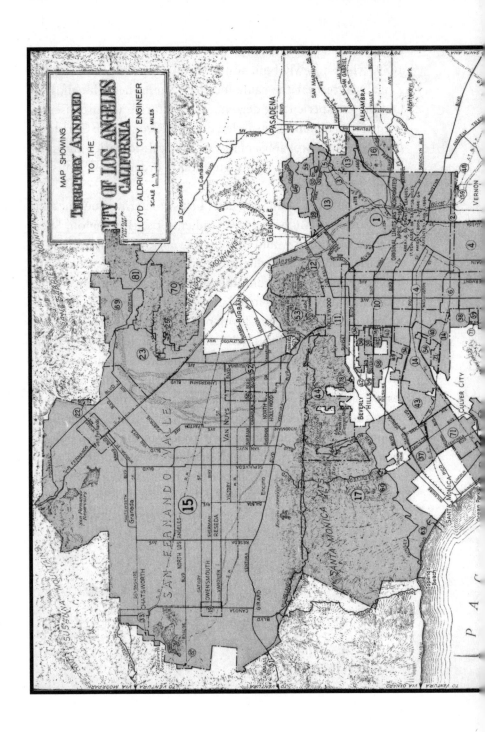

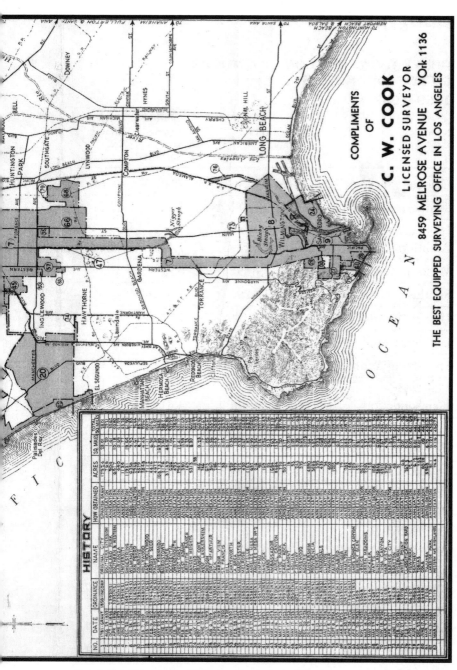

Boundaries of Los Angeles, 1932, when the city had achieved ninety-six percent of its current 468 square miles.

APPENDIX

ANNEXATIONS AND CONSOLIDATIONS: CITY OF LOS ANGELES 1859–1932

Name	Ratification Date	Annexed Area (sq. miles)	Total Area (sq. miles)
Original Pueblo	Sept. 4, 1781	28.01	28.01
Southern Extension	Aug. 29, 1859	1.20	29.21
Highland Park Addition	Oct. 18, 1895	1.41	30.62
Western Addition	Apr. 2, 1896	6.71	37.33
Southern Addition	Apr. 2, 1896	3.47	40.80
University Addition	June 12, 1899	1.77	42.57
Garvanza Addition	June 12, 1899	0.69	43.26
Shoestring Addition	Dec. 26, 1906	18.64	61.90
*San Pedro Consolidation	Aug. 28, 1909	4.61	66.51
*Wilmington Consolidation	Aug. 28, 1909	9.93	76.44
Colegrove Annexation	Oct. 27, 1909	8.72	85.16
*Hollywood Consolidation	Feb. 7, 1910	4.45	89.61
East Hollywood Annexation	Feb. 28, 1910	11.11	100.72
Arroyo Seco Annexation	Feb. 9, 1912	6.90	107.62
San Fernando Valley Annexation	May 22, 1915	169.89	277.51
Palms Annexation	May 22, 1915	7.30	284.81

Name	Ratification Date	Annexed Area (sq. miles)	Total Area (sq. miles)
Bairdstown Annexation	June 10, 1915	3.40	288.21
Westgate Annexation	June 14, 1916	48.67	336.88
Occidental Annexation	June 14, 1916	1.04	337.92
Owensmouth Annexation	Feb. 26, 1917	0.77	338.69
West Coast Annexation	June 15, 1917	12.41	351.10
West Adams Addition	Feb. 13, 1918	0.59	351.69
Griffith Ranch Annexation	Feb. 16, 1918	0.23	351.92
Hansen Heights Annexation	Apr. 11, 1918	8.30	360.22
Ostend Annexation	July 11, 1918	(under 1 acre)	360.22
Orange Cove Annexation	Nov. 13, 1918	0.23	360.45
West Lankershim Annexation	June 17, 1919	1.17	361.62
Dodson Annexation	July 23, 1919	1.05	362.67
Fort MacArthur Annexation	Aug. 6, 1919	0.56	363.23
Peck's Addition Annexation	Sept. 10, 1919	0.45	363.68
Harbor View Annexation	Sept. 25, 1919	0.17	363.85
St. Francis Annexation	Feb. 26, 1920	0.05	363.90
Hill Addition Annexation	Sept. 10, 1920	0.11	364.01
Chatsworth Addition	Nov. 19, 1920	0.34	364.35

Name	Ratification Date	Annexed Area (sq. miles)	Total Area (sq. miles)
La Brea Addition	Feb. 28, 1922	1.53	365.88
Manchester Annexation	Mar. 2, 1922	0.33	366.21
Melrose Annexation	June 16, 1922	0.67	366.88
*Sawtelle Consolidation	July 13, 1922	1.82	368.70
Angeles Mesa Annexation No. 1	July 27, 1922	0.99	369.69
Angeles Mesa Annexation No. 2	Oct. 5, 1922	0.34	370.03
Rimpau Addition	Oct. 5, 1922	0.14	370.17
Hancock Addition	Jan. 18, 1923	0.26	370.43
Evans Addition	Jan. 18, 1923	0.13	370.56
Laurel Canyon Annexation	May 16, 1923	13.57	384.13
Ambassador Addition	May 16, 1923	2.63	386.76
*Hyde Park Consolidation	May 16, 1923	1.20	387.96
*Eagle Rock Consolidation	May 17, 1923	3.17	391.13
Vermont Annexation	May 17, 1923	0.03	391.16
Laguna Annexation	May 17, 1923	0.08	391.24
Carthay Addition	May 17, 1923	0.38	391.62
Agoure Annexation	Dec. 20, 1923	0.02	391.64
Rosewood Addition	Dec. 20, 1923	0.62	392.26
Lankershim Annexation	Dec. 29, 1923	7.64	399.90
Providencia Annexation	Feb. 4, 1924	4.82	404.72

Name	Ratification Date	Annexed Area (sq. miles)	Total Area (sq. miles)
Cienega Addition	Feb. 13, 1924	0.93	405.65
Annandale Annexation	Feb. 23, 1924	0.68	406.33
Clinton Addition	May 31, 1924	0.15	406.48
Wagner Addition	Sept. 8, 1924	0.94	407.32
Fairfax Addition	Sept. 8, 1924	1.88	409.20
Holabird Addition	Jan. 3, 1925	0.01	409.21
Danziger Addition	Jan. 8, 1925	0.12	409.33
Hamilton Addition	Jan. 30, 1925	0.44	409.77
Martel Addition	Apr. 28, 1925	0.23	410.00
Santa Monica Canyon Addition	Apr. 28, 1925	0.17	410.17
Beverly Glen Addition	Oct. 26, 1925	0.81	410.98
*Venice Consolidation	Nov. 25, 1925	4.11	415.09
Green Meadows Addition	Mar. 18, 1926	3.57	418.66
Buckler Addition	May 10, 1926	0.20	418.86
*Watts Consolidation	May 29, 1926	1.69	420.55
Sunland Addition	Aug. 5, 1926	6.01	426.56
Tuna Canyon Addition	Nov. 18, 1926	7.67	434.23
Mar Vista Addition	Mar. 5, 1927	4.98	439.21
*Barnes City Consolidation	Apr. 11, 1927	1.81	441.02
Brayton Addition	June 11, 1927	0.08	441.10
Wiseburn Addition	Feb. 10, 1928	0.14	441.24
White Point Addition	Nov. 27, 1928	0.01	441.25
Classification Yard Annexation	Feb. 17, 1930	0.41	441.66

Name	Ratification Date	Annexed Area (sq. miles)	Total Area (sq. miles)
Viewpark Annexation	Apr. 17, 1930	0.02	441.68
Sentney Addition	Aug. 1, 1930	0.01	441.69
Tobias Addition	Dec. 22, 1930	0.01	441.70
Cole Addition	June 17, 1931	0.09	441.79
*Tujunga Consolidation	Mar. 7, 1932	8.70	450.49

*Indicates a city

Total Square Miles from Founding to 1932: 450.49
Total Square Miles, Present: 468.87

SOURCE: Los Angeles County Department of Public Works

ACKNOWLEDGMENTS

Inventing Paradise was informed by my previous nonfiction book, *Freewaytopia: How Freeways Shaped Los Angeles.* Researching the latter work was a reminder of how much freeways and the general growth of Greater Los Angeles were spurred by the actions of the core group contained in these pages. The question of "how did we get here?" was one I wanted to continue to explore. In their own humble way, *Inventing Paradise* and *Freewaytopia* bridge the pre- and post-freeway eras, forming a continuum about Los Angeles that spans some 150 years.

Although much of this book relies on newspaper archives, I am indebted to a number of research institutions and the people behind them. The Sherman Library in Corona del Mar houses a treasure trove of records pertaining to Moses Sherman and his peers. Head librarian Jill Thrasher, and her predecessor Paul Wormser, provided invaluable insight into Sherman's personal and business lives. Ditto David Sanborn at the Banning Museum in Wilmington, where the legacy of Phineas Banning has been meticulously preserved. Thanks also to Clay Stalls, the Reader Services Department, and the entire staff at the Huntington Library in San Marino, whose mother lode of materials truly brought Henry Huntington, Harry Chandler, Harrison Gray Otis, and other key figures to life. The digital files and ephemera at the University Library at California State University, Northridge, especially the Catherine Mulholland Collection, were paramount in flushing out the minutiae and human element behind William Mulholland's triumphs and tragedies. My thanks to David Sigler.

On a broader scope, I am incredibly grateful to an array of individuals whose historical insights helped frame events in this book. Those who took the time to converse with me include Capri Maddix, David Price, and Mark Pampanin at the Los Angeles Civil + Human Rights and Equity Department (aka LA Civil Rights); Jessica M. Kim, author and Associate Professor of the History Dept. at CSUN; columnist Gustavo Arellano of the *Los Angeles Times*; Josh Stevens, urban-planner journalist and author of *The Urban Mystique: Notes on California, Los Angeles, and Beyond*; Akiela Moses, Interstate Resources Manager at the California Department of Water Resources; Sandy Freund, a member of the American Institute of Certified Planners; and Steven P. Erie, author and Professor Emeritus of Political Science at UC San Diego. Special thanks to Abraham Hoffman, author and Adjunct Professor of History at Los Angeles Valley College. Abe was instrumental in turning me on to obscure but vital publications with regard to water politics and accounts of early Los Angeles.

This book is my fifth tour of duty with Santa Monica Press. One reason I keep coming back for more is that I have been spoiled by the support, guidance, and professionalism of publisher Jeffrey Goldman and his entire editorial and graphics team (special shout-out to the inimitable Amy Inouye). As always, I owe everything to my wife and two children. With quotidian lives that are far more interesting than my own, they provide loving counterbalances to the solitude of writing and keep this dad-and-husband's feet firmly planted in the real world.

SELECTED BIBLIOGRAPHY

BOOKS

Ainsworth, Ed. *Memories in the City of Dreams: A Tribute to Harry Chandler: Gran Benefactor de la Ciudad.* Los Angeles: Ed Ainsworth, 1959.

Alef, Daniel. *Harry Chandler: Man With the Midas Touch.* Santa Barbara: Titans of Fortune Publishing, 2009.

Ansell, Martin R. *Oil Baron of the Southwest: Edward L. Doheny and the Development of the Petroleum Industry in California and Mexico.* Columbus, OH: Ohio State University Press, 1998.

Babcock, Gwendolyn Garland. *The Ancestry of Harry Chandler.* San Marino, CA: Gwendolyn Garland Babcock, 1990. Published for internet, 2005. www.babcockancestry.com/books/chandler/photolinks/010b-ChristmasAtTheChandlers1932.shtml.

Balderrama, Francisco E. *In Defense of La Raza: The Los Angeles Mexican Consulate and the Mexican Community, 1929 to 1936.* Tucson: University of Arizona Press, 1982.

Banham, Reyner. *Los Angeles: The Architecture of Four Ecologies.* Berkeley; Los Angeles; London: University of California Press, 1971.

Banning, Phineas. (Dictated to Edward P. Newkirk.) *Settlement of Wilmington. San Francisco, 1883*; Berkeley: Bancroft Library, 1938.

Berges, Marshall. *The Life and Times of Los Angeles: A Newspaper, A Family and A City.* New York: Atheneum, 1984.

Bonelli, William. *Billion Dollar Blackjack: The Story of Corruption and the Los Angeles Times.* Beverly Hills: Civic Research Press, 1954.

Bowman, Lynn. *Los Angeles: Epic of a City.* Berkeley: Howell-North Books, 1974.

Boyarsky, Bill. *Inventing L.A.: The Chandlers and Their Times.* Santa Monica: Angel City Press, 2009.

Braudy, Leo. *The Hollywood Sign.* New Haven; London: Yale University Press.

Brock, Pope. *Charlatan: America's Most Dangerous Huckster, the Man Who Pursued Him, and the Age of Flimflam.* New York: Three Rivers Press, 2008.

Carr, Harry. *As You Were Saying: A Contribution to Our Chief.* Los Angeles: Times-Mirror Press, 1934.

Clare, Nancie. *The Battle for Beverly Hills: A City's Independence and the Birth of Celebrity Politics*. New York: St. Martin's Press, 2018.

Crump, Spencer. *Ride the Big Red Cars: How Trolleys Helped Build California*. Los Angeles: Trans-Anglo Books, 1962.

Davis, Margaret Leslie. *Dark Side of Fortune: Triumph and Scandal in the Life of Oil Tycoon Edward L. Doheny*. Berkeley; Los Angeles: University of California Press, 1998.

Davis, Margaret Leslie. *Rivers in the Desert: William Mulholland and the Inventing of Los Angeles*. New York: HarperCollins Publishers, 1993.

Davis, Mike. *City of Quartz: Excavating the Future in Los Angeles*. New York; London: Verso, 1990.

Deverell, William F. and Sitton, Tom. *Water and Los Angeles: A Tale of Three Rivers, 1900-1941*. Oakland: University of California Press, 2017.

Deverell, William F. *Whitewashed Adobe: The Rise of Los Angeles and the Remaking of Its Mexican Past*. Berkeley; Los Angeles: University of California Press, 2004.

Easlon, Steven L. *The Los Angeles Railway Through the Years*. Sherman Oaks, CA: Darwin Publications (Reprint), 1973.

Eberts, Mike. *Griffith Park: A Centennial History*. Los Angeles: Historical Society of Southern California, 1996.

Faragher, John Mack. *Eternity Street: Violence and Justice in Frontier Los Angeles*. New York: W. W. Norton & Company, Inc., 2016.

Fogelson, Robert M. *The Fragmented Metropolis: Los Angeles, 1850-1930*. Berkeley; Los Angeles: University of California Press, 1993.

Friedricks, William B. *Henry E. Huntington and the Creation of Southern California*. Columbus: Ohio State University Press, 1992.

Gage, Beverly. *G-Man: J. Edgar Hoover and the Making of the American Century*. New York: Viking, 2022.

Gottlieb, Robert and Wolt, Irene. *Thinking Big: The Story of the Los Angeles Times, Its Publishers and Their Influence on Southern California*. New York: G. P. Putnam's Sons, 1977.

Grabar, Henry. *Paved Paradise: How Parking Explains the World*. New York: Penguin Press, 2023.

Halberstam, David. *The Powers That Be*. New York: Knopf, 1975.

Hawthorne, Christopher (Editor). *Past Due: Report and Recommendations of the Los Angeles Mayor's Office Civic Memory Working Group.* Los Angeles: Huntington-USC Institute on California & the West, 2021.

Hendricks, William O. *M. H. Sherman: A Pioneer Developer of the Pacific Southwest.* Corona Del Mar, CA: Sherman Library & Gardens, 2018.

Hobbs, Charles P. *Hidden History of Transportation in Los Angeles.* Charleston: The History Press, 2014.

Hoffman, Abraham. *Vision Or Villainy: Origins of the Owens Valley-Los Angeles Water Controversy.* College Station, TX: Texas A&M University Press, 1981.

Ingersoll, Luther A. *Ingersoll's Century History, Santa Monica Bay Cities.* Los Angeles: Luther A. Ingersoll, 1908.

Irwin, Lew. *Deadly Times: The 1910 Bombing of the Los Angeles Times and America's Forgotten Decade of Terror.* Guilford, CT: Lyons Press, 2013.

Kahrl, William L. *The Politics of California Water: Owens Valley and the Los Angeles Aqueduct, 1900-1927.* Berkeley; Los Angeles: University of California Press, 1976.

Kim, Jessica M. *Imperial Metropolis: Los Angeles, Mexico, and the Borderlands of American Empire, 1865-1941.* Chapel Hill: The University of North Carolina Press, 2019.

Krist, Gary. *The Mirage Factory: Illusion, Imagination, and the Invention of Los Angeles.* New York: Broadway Books, 2018.

Loomis, Jan. *Images of America: Brentwood.* Charleston; Chicago; Portsmouth, NH; San Francisco: Arcadia Publishing, 2008.

Loomis, Jan. *Westside Chronicles: Historic Stories of West Los Angeles.* Charleston: The History Press, 2012.

Marcosson, Isaac F. *A Little Known Master of Millions: The Story of Henry E. Huntington.* Boston: E. H. Rollins & Sons, 1914.

McDougal, Dennis. *Privileged Son: Otis Chandler and the Rise and Fall of the L.A. Times Dynasty.* Cambridge, Mass.: Perseus Publishing, 2001.

McWilliams, Carey. *Southern California: An Island on the Land.* Salt Lake City: Peregrine Smith Books, 1946, 1973.

Molina, Natalia. *How Race is Made in America: Immigration, Citizenship, and the Historical Power of Racial Scripts.* Berkeley; Los Angeles; London: University of California Press, 2014.

Mulholland, Catherine. *The Owensmouth Baby: The Making of a San Fernando Valley Town.* Northridge, CA: Santa Susana Press, 1987.

Mulholland, Catherine. *William Mulholland and the Rise of Los Angeles.* Berkeley; Los Angeles: University of California Press, 2000.

Myers, William A. and Swett, Ira L. *Trolleys to the Surf: The Story of the Los Angeles Pacific Railway.* Glendale, CA: Interurbans Publications, Inc., 1976.

Newmark, Harris. *Sixty Years in Southern California, 1853-1913.* New York: The Knickerbocker Press, 1916.

Petroleum in California: A Concise and Reliable History of the Oil Industry of the State. Los Angeles: Lionel V. Redpath, 1900.

Poole, Jean Bruce and Ball, Tevvy. *El Pueblo: The Historic Heart of Los Angeles.* Los Angeles: The J. Paul Getty Trust, 2002.

Reisner, Marc. *Cadillac Desert: The American West and Its Disappearing Water.* New York: Penguin Books, 1987.

Robinson, John W. *Los Angeles in Civil War Days, 1860-1865.* Norman: University of Oklahoma Press, 2013.

Roderick, Kevin. *The San Fernando Valley: America's Suburb.* Los Angeles: Los Angeles Times Books, 2001.

Roman, James. *Chronicles of Los Angeles: Exploring the Devilish History of the City of the Angels.* New York: Museyon Inc., 2015.

Siegel, Barry. *Dreamers and Schemers: How An Improbable Bid for the 1932 Olympics Transformed Los Angeles From Dusty Outpost to Global Metropolis.* Oakland: University of California Press, 2019.

Sitton, Tom. *Grand Ventures: The Banning Family and the Shaping of Southern California.* San Marino, CA: Huntington Library Press, 2010.

Sitton, Tom and Deverell, William (Editors). *Metropolis in the Making: Los Angeles in the 1920s.* Berkeley; Los Angeles: University of California Press, 2001.

Standiford, Les. *Water to the Angels: William Mulholland, His Monumental Aqueduct, and the Rise of Los Angeles.* New York: HarperCollins, 2015.

Stanton, Jeffrey. *Venice California: 'Coney Island of the Pacific.'* Los Angeles: Donahue Publishing, 1987.

Stargel, Cory and Stargel, Sarah. *Vanishing Los Angeles County.* Charleston: Arcadia Publishing, 2010.

Starr, Kevin. *Material Dreams: Southern California Through the 1920s.* New York: Oxford University Press, 1990.

Thorpe, James. *Henry Edwards Huntington: A Biography.* Berkeley; Los Angeles: University of California Press, 1994.

Titus, Roger L. and Bunte, Jim. *Destinations: How Trolleys and Postcards Helped Create the Southern California Dream*. Rancho Cucamonga, CA: Gem Guides Book Co., 2008.

Twelve Pioneers of Los Angeles. Los Angeles: Times-Mirror Printing & Binding House, 1929.

Wakida, Patricia (Editor). *LATITUDES: An Angeleno's Atlas*. Berkeley: Heyday Books, 2015.

Walker, Jim. *The Yellow Cars of Los Angeles: A Roster of Streetcars of Los Angeles Railway and Successors from the 1890s to 1963*. Glendale, CA: Interurbans Publications, 1977.

Weingarten, Marc. *Thirsty: William Mulholland, California Water and the Real Chinatown*. Los Angeles: Rare Bird Books, 2015.

Wilkman, Jon. *Floodpath: The Deadliest Man-Made Disaster of 20th Century America and the Making of Modern Los Angeles*. New York: Bloomsbury Press, 2016.

Williams, Gregory Paul. *The Story of Hollywood: An Illustrated History*. Los Angeles: BL Press LLC, 2005.

Wilson, Ben. *Metropolis*. New York: Doubleday, 2020.

Yoch, James J. *On the Golden Shore: Phineas Banning in Southern California 1851-1885*. Wilmington, CA: Friends of Banning Park, 2002.

Zimmerman, Tom. *Paradise Promoted: The Booster Campaign That Created Los Angeles*. Santa Monica: Angel City Press, 2008.

ARTICLES, REPORTS, AND MAGAZINES

15City. www.15minutecity.com.

Bray, Stephen D. "Harry Chandler," *American Newspaper Journalists, 1926-1950*, edited by Perry J. Ashley, Gale, 1984. Dictionary of Literary Biography Vol. 29. Gale Literature Resource Center.

Chamberlain, Lisa. "The Surprising Stickiness of the '15-Minute City,'" Common Edge. January 25, 2022. www.commonedge.org/the-surprising-stickiness-of-the-15-minute-city.

Cheney, Charles Henry (Editor). *What City Planning Commissions Can Do*. San Francisco: The California Conference on City Planning, June 1915.

County of Los Angeles, www.lacounty.gov.

Denig, James. "The Proposed Nicaragua Canal," *United States Naval Institute Proceedings*, Vol. 65, No. 437, July 1939.

Didion, Joan. "Letter from Los Angeles," *The New Yorker*. February 26, 1990.

Dumke, Glenn S. *The Growth of the Pacific Electric and Its Influence Upon the Development of Southern California to 1911*. Thesis, Occidental College, 1939. (Unpublished.)

Fernandez, Tyron, Christina Martinez, Timothy Yo. "History of Los Angeles Planning," Urban Planning: Los Angeles. www.urbanla.weebly.com.

"Forest Lawn Memorial Park – Hollywood Hills Master Plan," City of Los Angeles. February 2011. www.planning.lacity.org/eir/ForestLawnMemPrk-HlwdHillsMP/DEIR/index.html.

Fulton, William. "'Those Were Her Best Days': The Streetcar and the Development of Hollywood Before 1910," *Southern California Quarterly*, Vol. 66, Issue 3, October 1984.

Guinn, J. M. "How the Area of Los Angeles City Was Enlarged," *Annual Publication of the Historical Society of Southern California*, Vol. 9, Issue 3, January 1914.

Hirschfeld, Andy. "The 15-Minute City: How Walkability Is Gaining a Foothold in the U.S.," *YES!* Magazine. May 5, 2021. www.yesmagazine.org/economy/2021/05/05/15-minute-city-walk.

"Historic Los Angeles: Wilshire Boulevard When It Was Residential," Wilshire Boulevard Houses. www.wilshireboulevardhouses.blogspot.com/2013/04/2401-wilshire-boulevard-please-see-our.html.

Ionescu, Diana. "Downpours Yield 33 Billion Gallons of Captured Stormwater in L.A. County," Planetizen. January 19, 2023. www.planetizen.com/news/2023/01/121086-downpours-yield-33-billion-gallons-captured-stormwater-la-county.

Kelly, Kate. "Phineas Banning, Father of the L.A. Harbor," *America Comes Alive!* www.americacomesalive.com/phineas-t-banning-father-of-the-l-a-harbor.

King, Peter H. "As Chandler Dynasty Evolved, So Did Power in L.A.," KCET.org. October 9, 2018. www.kcet.org/shows/inventing-la-the-chandlers-and-their-timesas-chandler-dynasty-evolved-so-did-power-in-l-a.

Mallory, Mary. "A Street by Any Other Name," *Toluca Lake* Magazine. March 1, 2021. www.tolucalake.com/2021/03/a-street-by-any-other-name.

McCarthy, John Russell. "Water: The Story of Bill Mulholland" serial, *Pacific Saturday Night* Magazine. 1937-1938.

Meares, Hadley. "Infernal Machines: The Bombing of the Los Angeles Times and L.A.'s First 'Crime of the Century,'" KCET.org. April 25, 2014. www.kcet.org/history-society/infernal-machines-the-bombing-of-the-los-angeles-times-and-l-a-s-first-crime-of-the-century.

"Porter Ranch Then & Now," Chatsworth-Porter Ranch Chamber of Commerce. www.chatsworthchamber.com/porter-ranch-then-now.

Prosser, Daniel (Contributor). *SurveyLA: Los Angeles Citywide Historic Context Statement: Pre-Consolidation Communities of Los Angeles, 1862-1932*, Prepared for City of Los Angeles Dept. of City Planning Office of Historic Resources, July 2016. www.planning.lacity.org/odocument/232b11bd-19fd-4781-93f8-704d17b0aebc/Pre-ConsolidationCommunitiesofLosAngeles.pdf.

Quinton, J. H., W. H. Code, Homer Hamlin. *Report Upon The Distribution of the Surplus Waters of the Los Angeles Aqueduct*, Los Angeles, 1911. www.calisphere.org/item/ark:/86086/n2ft8kmd.

Roderick, Kevin. "Part One: LA and Its Owens Valley Water," LAObserved. November 4, 2013. www.laobserved.com/archive/2013/11/sfv.php.

Ruffing, Russell C. *Venice Canals*, Historic American Engineering Record, HAER No. CA-124, February 1992. www.venicenc.org/assets/documents/5/committee62f19969923a9.pdf.

The Saga of the Sign: The Rise, Ruin and Restoration of Hollywood's Biggest Name, Hollywood, CA: Hollywood Sign Trust, 2018.

Spitzzeri, Paul R. "The White Spot and a Black Stain: The 'Greater Los Angeles Association Weekly Bulletin,'" The Homestead Blog. May 5, 2021. www.homesteadmuseum.blog/2021/05/05/the-white-spot-and-a-black-stain-the-greater-los-angeles-association-weekly-bulletin-5-may-1924.

Stone, Erin. "The '15-Minute City': A Strategy To Reduce The Traffic, Pollution and High Housing Costs in LA," LAist.com. July 21, 2022. www.laist.com/news/climate-environment/can-l-a-be-a-15-min-city-some-angelenos-think-so.

Taylor, Frank J. "It Costs $1000 to Have Lunch with Harry Chandler," *The Saturday Evening Post*. December 16, 1939.

Testa, Stephen M. "The Los Angeles City Oil Field: California's First Oil Boom During the Revitalization Period (1875-1900)," Petroleum History Institute. 2011.

Waldie, D. J. "How the All-Year Club Sold the L.A. Summer," KCET.org. August 11, 2017. www.kcet.org/shows/lost-la/how-the-all-year-club-sold-the-l-a-summer.

"Who's Who—And Why: An Effectively Transplanted New Englander," *The Saturday Evening Post*. June 5, 1926.

Zack, Michele. "Altadena's Beginning as Mecca for the Ill," Altadena Heritage. www.altadenaheritage.org/altadenas-beginning-as-mecca-for-the-ill.

Zuniga, Erik. "Old Chinatown and the Present Union Station: Transportation, Land Use, Race, and Class in Pre-WWII Los Angeles," California Historical Society, March 1, 2022. www.californiahistoricalsociety.org/blog/old-chinatown-and-the-present-union-station-transportation-land-use-race-and-class-in-pre-wwii-los-angeles.

NEWSPAPERS

Burbank Review
California Eagle
Chippewa Daily Herald
The Daily Outlook
The Daily Telegraph
The Girard News
Hollywood Daily Citizen
Illustrated Daily News
The Inyo Register
(London) Daily Herald
(Los Angeles) Daily News
Los Angeles Evening News
Los Angeles Examiner
Los Angeles Express
Los Angeles Herald
Los Angeles Post-Record
Los Angeles Record
Los Angeles Times (LAT)
Long Beach Daily Telegram
Long Beach Press-Telegram
Monrovia Daily News
The New York Times
The Observer
Pasadena Evening Post
The Pomona Progress
Sacramento Record-Union
Sacramento Union
St. Louis Daily Globe-Democrat
St. Louis Post-Dispatch
The San Bernardino Sun

The San Diego Union-Tribune
The San Francisco Call
San Francisco Chronicle
The San Francisco Examiner
San Pedro News-Pilot
San Pedro Pilot
Santa Ana Register
South Pasadena Record
The Van Nuys News
Venice Vanguard
The Ventura County Star
The Whittier News

NOTES

As a general rule, precedence is given to singular accounts from specific sources, or those that proved particularly noteworthy. Facts attained from multiple sources (see Bibliography and Newspapers) are not always noted. Due to the divergence and unreliability of old records, the author occasionally arrives at certain figures (e.g., election results, streetcar miles, budget numbers, population during non-Census years) based on an aggregate of sources and scholarly guidance.

Historical rain and temperature records were derived from the online sites Los Angeles Almanac and Extreme Weather Watch, and from Los Angeles Weather Bureau archives in the *Los Angeles Times*.

Historical annexation records were drawn primarily from "Annexation Map of the City of Los Angeles, Board of Public Works Engineering Department; John C. Shaw, City Engineer, 1928"; "Map Showing Territory Annexed to the City of Los Angeles, California; Lloyd Aldrich, City Engineer, 1935"; "Map Showing Territory Annexed to the City of Los Angeles, California; Homer Hamlin, City Engineer, 1916." An interactive annexation map hosted by the Los Angeles County Department of Public Works' digital database proved extremely helpful: www.dpw.lacounty.gov/mpm/cityannexations.

Census-year population numbers were taken from the U.S. Census Bureau.

Introduction

7   **a city that should not exist:** Various, including "Los Angeles: The City That Shouldn't Exist: How Engineers Will Solve L.A.'s Water Problem," The University of Southern California Andrew and Erna Viterbi School of Engineering, www.youtube.com/watch?v=XfYIJJrho74.

7   **twelve million in its metropolitan region:** Los Angeles Metro Area Population 1950-2023," Macrotrends.net, www.macrotrends.net/cities/23052/los-angeles/population#:~:text=The%20current%20metro%20area%20population,a%200.1%25%20increase%20from%202020.

7   **Indigenous peoples lived comfortably:** Guinn, "Los Angeles City," *Historical Society*, 173.

7   **Mexican-American War:** Encyclopedia Brittanica, www.britannica.com/event/Mexican-American-War/Invasion-and-war.

8   **"The Father of Los Angeles Harbor":** "History of the Port of Los Angeles," The Port of Los Angeles, City of Los Angeles, www. portoflosangeles.org/about/history.

9   **"enemy of the city":** Gottlieb and Wolt, *Thinking Big*, 133.

9   **"quickly developed the fixed idea":** McWilliams, *Southern California*, 274.

9   **"Land lust tempted me":** Taylor, "It Costs $1000," *Saturday Evening Post*, 64.

10 **"Keep your money rolling"**: Dumke, *Pacific Electric.*
12 **adding a wishful "Esq."**: Video lecture by William Deverell, director of the Huntington-USC Institute on California and the West, "The Founder and the Future: Becoming Henry Huntington," The Huntington Library, October 23, 2019.
12 **"I am just beginning to live"**: Letter from Henry Huntington to Caroline Densmore (Huntington) Holladay, The Huntington Library, July 20, 1913.
12 **"my water"**: C. E. Kunze, "Hidden Hand Felt in Valley," *Los Angeles Record*, June 18, 1927.
12 **"I am not going to die"**: Letter from Moses Sherman to his daughters, Sherman Library, February 17, 1912.
13 **"We have the advantage of 'climate'"**: Letter from Moses Sherman to Sarah (Pratt) Carr, Sherman Library, December 2, 1908.
13 **"There's nothing like this Southern California"**: Thorpe, *Henry Edwards Huntington*, 178.
13 **"man-made end"**: Taylor, "It Costs $1000," *Saturday Evening Post*, 8.

Chapter 1: The Father of the Harbor
17 **"pitiful compensation"**: Guinn, "Los Angeles City," *Historical Society*, 174.
17 **Starting in the 1860s**: Ibid.
17 **whose heirs would establish Hancock Park**: Windsor Square-Hancock Park Historical Society, www.web.archive.org/web/20100423114912/http://www.wshphs.org/windsor.html.
18 **"our hero"**: This and other excerpts from Banning's memoir: Phineas Banning, *Phineas Banning—Settlement of Wilmington.*
18 **"Some native tribes"**: Yoch, *Golden Shore*, 74.
19 **"Bay of the Smoke"**: Patt Morrison, "L.A.'s Port Could Have Been in Santa Monica. Here's How San Pedro Won Out," LAT, November 30, 2021.
19 **"Banning was always thinking about transportation"**: Author interview with Michael Sanborn, April 2023. Sanborn pointed out that Banning also built the first stagecoach line to Ft. Tejon, California.
20 **a contract to build Camp Drum**: Yoch, *Golden Shore*, 17.
20 **"forever in a hurry"**: Ibid., p 19. Quote attributed to Maj. Edward D. Townsend in the army's Adjutant General's Office, per Michael Sanborn.
20 **Twenty-six people were killed**: D. J. Waldie, "Horrible Catastrophe! Disaster in Civil-War-Era Los Angeles," KCET.org, June 6, 2017, www.kcet.org/shows/lost-la/horrible-catastrophe-disaster-in-civil-war-era-los-angeles.
20 **Banning was absolved**: Robinson, *Civil War*, 116.
20 **"always hold himself in readiness"**: Phineas Banning, *Phineas Banning—Settlement of Wilmington.*
21 **"crazy old coot"**: "A Queer Habitation," *St. Louis Daily Globe-Democrat*, October 14, 1883.
22 **She had died during childbirth**: Yoch, *Golden Shore*, 32.
22 **America's rail industry grew**: Adam Burns, "Railroads and Westward Expansion (1870s)," American-Rails.com, April 21, 2023, https://www.american-rails.com/1870s.html.
23 **The conglomerate offered**: Crump, *Red Cars*, 28.

24   **"the grandest affair"**: "Los Angeles Centennial," *Sacramento Record-Union*, September 7, 1881.

24   **"rich costumes"**: Ibid.

24   **"spirit of his race"**: "Centennial," *Sacramento Record-Union*.

24   **Hell-Hole of the West**: McDougal, *Privileged Son*, 13.

24   **"Where the Indian worshipped"**: "Centennial," *Sacramento Record-Union*.

24   **the California press also denigrated Chinese immigrants**: "Mob Rule," *Los Angeles Daily Star*, October 26, 1871.

24   **the massacre of nineteen Chinese people**: Bowman, *Los Angeles*, 197.

25   **"A Chinaman never dreams"**: "The Heathen Chinee [sic]," LAT, December 8, 1881.

25   **He doted on his three adult sons**: Author interview with Michael Sanborn, December 2021 and April 2023.

26   **"Do not forget"**: Yoch, *Golden Shore*, 27.

26   **"fine appreciation of the fine arts"**: Letter from Phineas Banning to Hancock Banning, The Huntington Library, May 27, 1884.

26   **"My dear Uncle Hancock Banning:"** Ibid.

26   **"Los Angeles Harbor"**: "World's Paradise," *Los Angeles Express*, December 29, 1888. The *Express* was one of the first newspapers to refer to "Los Angeles Harbor" before the name was official.

27   **The carriage ran over him**: Sitton, *Grand Ventures*, 148, and Yoch, *Golden Shore*, 45.

Chapter 2: Men of Brains, Brawns, and Guts

28   **Harry Chandler's L.A. story**: Various, including Babcock, *Harry Chandler*.

29   **"I felt that if my picture"**: Ainsworth, *Memories*, 8.

29   **"Get out of here, you son of a bitch!"**: Ibid., 9, and "Who's Who," *Saturday Evening Post*, 52. Both sources infer that Van Nuys called Chandler a "son of a bitch."

29   **Chandler had socked away $3,000**: Ainsworth, *Memories*, 9.

29   **Harrison Gray Otis strode into the offices**: Joe Mozingo, "Visionaries and Scoundrels Made the Los Angeles Times, Which Returns to Local Ownership After 18 Years," LAT, June 17, 2018.

30   **"gallant and meritorious conduct"**: "Eliza A Otis," *Magazine of Poetry: A Quarterly Review*. October 1892: 375. Print. Vol. IV, No. 4. Buffalo, New York: Charles Well Moulton.

30   **"It is the fattest land"**: Mozingo, "Visionaries and Scoundrels," LAT.

30   **Otis borrowed $5,000**: Ibid.

30   **"'Los Angeles wants no dudes'"**: Didion, "Letter," *New Yorker*.

31   **Santa Fe Railroad launching the first direct route from the East**: "Down the Decades with Los Angeles," LAT, December 4, 1941.

31   **One study determined**: Michele Zack, "Altadena's Beginning as Mecca for the Ill," Altadena Heritage, altadenaheritage.org/altadenas-beginning-as-mecca-for-the-ill.

31   **"mecca for sick pilgrims"**: Patt Morrison, "Go Ahead and Rub L.A.'s Winter Sunshine in People's Faces. We've Been Doing It Forever," LAT, January 11, 2022.

31   **Lummis set out for Los Angeles**: Bowman, *Los Angeles*, 209.

31 **By the time he arrived in L.A.:** McDougal, *Privileged Son*, 19.
31 **"lungers":** Morrison, "Go Ahead," LAT.
31 **"I joined the staff December 5th, 1885":** Harry Chandler, "Harry Chandler, 'Oldest Employee,' Has Seen This City Transformed," LAT, December 4, 1941.
32 **switched to the *Times*:** Gottlieb and Wolt, *Thinking Big*, 122.
32 **sabotaged the competition:** Additional anecdotes from "How Chandler Got His Start," *Los Angeles Record*, March 5, 1924.
32 **the *Tribune* quickly went under:** Carr, *As You Were Saying*, 8.
32 **"Why, Harry bought the type yesterday":** Taylor, "It Costs $1000," *Saturday Evening Post*, 60.
33 **"Harry Chandler of the *Los Angeles Times*":** W.E.W., "Just a Little of This & That," *The Van Nuys News*, October 17, 1930.
33 **dropped to a single dollar:** McWilliams, *Southern California*, 118.
33 **120,000 in 1887 alone:** Siegel, *Dreamers and Schemers*, 7.
33 **Acres that went for $100 a year:** Ibid.
34 **"fattest newspaper in the country":** McDougal, *Privileged Son*, 33.
34 **"Very Finest Speculation" and "Large Profits":** Numerous advertisements in LAT and *Los Angeles Herald*, 1887.
34 **"Magnolia—Keep your eye on this town":** Magnolia advertisement, LAT, April 29, 1887.
34 **"Ramirez!":** Newmark, *Southern California*, 575.
34 **"payable at the counter":** Various LAT editions, 1886-1888.
34 **wiping out $14 million in assessed value:** Siegel, *Dreamers and Schemers*, 7.
34 **"the height of the infection":** Newmark, *Southern California*, 572.
35 **a desperate few who committed suicide:** Ibid., 583.
35 **he collected on the unpaid debts:** Taylor, "It Costs $1000," *Saturday Evening Post*, 60.
35 **"the most important city":** Siegel, *Dreamers and Schemers*, 9.
35 **eighty-seven miles of paved streets:** Ibid., 8.
35 **the University of Southern California:** University of Southern California, www.about.usc.edu/history.
35 **Occidental College:** Occidental College, www.oxy.edu/about-oxy/our-history.
35 **France was excavating a shipping canal:** Denig, "Nicaragua Canal," *Naval Institute Proceedings*.
36 **he died at age fifty-four:** Yoch, *Golden Shore*, 45.
36 **"a pioneer":** "Gen. Phineas Banning: Death of a Pioneer of Los Angeles County," LAT, March 10, 1885.
36 **"He saw in the distance":** "Captain Winfield Scott Hancock, Phineas Banning & the SS Ada Hancock," Civil War Talk, February 15, 2021. Banning's obituary appeared in the *Los Angeles Herald*, March 19, 1885.
36 **"indebted [to the] wheel-horse":** "Local Brevities," *Los Angeles Herald*, August 19, 1879.
36 **Los Angeles's population had soared to 50,395:** C. Mulholland, *William Mulholland*, 38.
36 **More people now resided *outside* L.A.'s twenty-nine square miles:** "Population," Los Angeles Almanac, www.laalmanac.com/population.

37   **signed a thirty-year lease:** C. Mulholland, *William Mulholland*, 21.
37   **breakouts of dysentery, cholera, and typhoid:** Various, including McDougal, *Privileged Son*, 9.
37   **Houses on fire:** C. Mulholland, *William Mulholland*, 54.
37   **small wriggling fish:** Ibid., 31.
37   **fish would flop into the machine:** Mozingo, "Visionaries and Scoundrels," LAT.
37   **the company announced that it would charge extra:** C. Mulholland, *William Mulholland*, 34.
37   **"bathing should be encouraged":** Ibid.
38   **300,000 daily gallons needed:** Ibid.
38   **The first "motor carriage":** "Huntington Land Company," LAT, May 11, 1897.
38   **L.A.'s first streetcar line:** Easlon, *Los Angeles Railway*, 5.
38   **its inaugural cable car line:** Ibid.
38   **San Francisco opened the world's first:** "Cable Car History," San Francisco Municipal Transportation Agency, www.sfmta.com/getting-around/muni/cable-cars/cable-car-history.
38   **"It must anticipate":** Friedricks, *Henry E. Huntington*, 7.

Chapter 3: The Teacher and the Autodidact

41   **he claimed to pay more in taxes:** Nathan Masters, "How the Town of Sherman Became the City of West Hollywood," KCET.org, December 1, 2011, www.kcet.org/shows/lost-la/how-the-town-of-sherman-became-the-city-of-west-hollywood.
41   **"Looking for some cheap ostriches":** Letter from Moses Sherman to Col. Marble, Sherman Library, 1890.
42   **"We might build":** Friedricks, *Henry E. Huntington*, 7.
42   **the Panic of 1893:** Jessica Pearce Rotondi, "Why Did the Gilded Age End?," History.com, January 19, 2022, www.history.com/news/gilded-age-end-reasons.
42   **settled in 1874 by wealthy Midwesterners:** "Pasadena History," Pasadena Chamber of Commerce, www.pasadena-chamber.org.
43   **he received a gold watch:** C. Mulholland, *William Mulholland*, 42.
43   **"jumped out of bed":** "The Water Supply," LAT, July 16, 1890.
43   **"I never had my shoes off":** Wilkman, *Floodpath*, 25.
43   **"the city would have to go back":** "Water Supply," LAT.
43   **self-professed autocrat:** Josh Stephens, "The Engineer: William Mulholland and the Search for Water in Los Angeles," Los Angeles Review of Books, June 27, 2015, www.lareviewofbooks.org/article/the-engineer-william-mulholland-and-the-search-for-water-in-los-angeles. Mulholland's exact quote is: "I have tendencies that are absolutely autocratic and at times unreasonably domineering."
44   **"It was a beautiful, limpid little stream":** Weingarten, *Thirsty*, 17.
44   **"The world was my oyster":** Davis, *Rivers*, 258.
44   **"studious":** C. Mulholland, *William Mulholland*, 32.
44   **"I went to school":** McCarthy, "Water," *Pacific Saturday Night*, February 12, 1938, 31.

44 **"When we were down six hundred feet"**: Weingarten, *Thirsty*, 31.
45 **"None of your goddamn business"**: Standiford, *Water*, 38.
45 **"Mr. Perry says you're the foreman"**: Ibid.
45 **"the size and character"**: C. Mulholland, *William Mulholland*, 64.

Chapter 4: The Nephew
47 **"make the grass grow"**: "Huntington Is an Obstructionist," LAT, April 17, 1896.
48 **"The Southern Pacific of Kentucky"**: "The Huntington Gall," LAT, April 6, 1896.
48 **"free harbor" and "free community"**: Ibid.
49 **"socialist freaks"**: "Perils of America," LAT, November 10, 1906.
49 **"born mob leaders"**: Mozingo, "Visionaries and Scoundrels," LAT.
49 **"leeches upon honest work"**: Ralph E. Shaffer, "The Ghost of Harrison Gray Otis: History, Unions and a Late-Night Ruckus Outside the L.A. Times Building," *DT News*, February 5, 2018, www.ladowntownnews.com/opinion/the-ghost-of-harrison-gray-otis/article_20c2e188-086b-11e8-8735-ff895732896d.html.
49 **"Otistown of the Open Shop"**: McDougal, *Privileged Son*, 45.
49 **L.A.'s labor costs**: Ibid.
49 **"if the Government do not build"**: Letter from Henry Huntington to Collis Huntington, The Huntington Library, April 7, 1893.
50 **"I wanted to get into someplace"**: Friedricks, *Henry E. Huntington*, 22.
50 **"I do not think"**: Ibid., 23.
50 **"He said he was thinking"**: Ibid., 22.
51 **"I am glad to hear"**: Ibid., 24
51 **"I cannot tell you how gratified"**: Ibid., 26.
52 **"[Huntington] is possessed"**: "Killing of Babes," *San Francisco Chronicle*, April 23, 1895.
52 **"so constructed as to prevent"**: "Ordinance No. 2866," *The San Francisco Call*, February 2, 1898.
53 **"WHEN WILL HUNTINGTON ACT?"**: *The San Francisco Examiner*, January 31, 1898.
53 **"Street-Car Murders"**: "The List of Street-Car Murders," *The San Francisco Examiner*, January 31, 1898.
53 **twenty-nine more people had been killed**: Ibid.
53 **a gory cartoon**: "There Is a Reaper Whose Name is Huntington" cartoon, *The San Francisco Examiner*, February 2, 1898.
53 **"ground the little tot"**: "Another Baby Murdered by a Fenderless Car," *The San Francisco Examiner*, January 31, 1898.
53 **an accompanying article**: "Picked Up by a Fender and Saved," *The San Francisco Examiner*, January 31, 1898.
53 **"The law in the case"**: "The Law in the Case Has Been Disregarded for Two and a Half Years," *The San Francisco Examiner*, January 31, 1898.
53 **"'The Examiner' is Compelled"**: "The Law Invoked to Stay the Murder of Children," *The San Francisco Examiner*, February 1, 1898.
53 **an illustration of an officious mustachioed man**: Ibid.

54 **"Hearst had an infallible instinct":** Gray Brechin, "William Randolph Hearst: Unfinished History," FoundSF, 1994, www.foundsf.org/index. php?title=William_Randolph_Hearst.

54 **the *Examiner* resorted to simply invoking Octopus:** The "Octopus" was used primarily in *San Francisco Examiner* articles from 1895 to 1898, though others also used the epithet.

54 **"Judge Conlan's Decision":** "Huntington Freed -- His Company Scored," *The San Francisco Examiner*, July 17, 1898.

55 **"I feel as if I could remain here":** Thorpe, *Henry Edwards Huntington*, 178.

55 **"There is no limit":** Ibid.

55 **convert a fleet of locomotives:** Ansell, *Oil Baron*, 33.

55 **"People will inevitably seek":** Isaac F. Marcosson, "A Modest Master of Millions," excerpted from Marcosson's book in the *Los Angeles Times*, February 8, 1914.

55 **"He has not been looking well":** Thorpe, *Henry Edwards Huntington*, 129-130.

56 **"Whatever may be said":** "The Iron Trade Booming," *Los Angeles Express*, November 6, 1897.

56 **"The shock of his death":** Friedricks, *Henry E. Huntington*, 152-153.

Chapter 5: Sherman's March Westward

57 **It was April 1, 1896:** All accounts of the first electric railway to Santa Monica from "To the Sea," LAT, April 2, 1896.

57 **"Sherman's march to the sea":** Ibid.

58 **"From the late 1800s":** Author interview with Josh Stephens, May 2023.

58 **"It must be borne":** "How Nephew Waxes Rich," *The San Francisco Examiner*, April 19, 1896.

59 **"pioneers of interurban transportation":** Mary Mallory, "Hollywood Heights: Hollywoodland Opens March 31, 1923," *The Daily Mirror*, March 27, 2023.

62 **Rosedale Cemetery:** "Angelus Rosedale Cemetery," www.AngelusRosedale. com.

Chapter 6: Gen. Otis, Freedom Fighter

63 **"corpse defacer":** Gottlieb and Wolt, *Thinking Big*, 24.

63 **"moral leper":** "Moral Lepers Cleaned Out," LAT, January 23, 1906.

63 **pro-bestiality:** Mozingo, "Visionaries and Scoundrels," LAT.

64 **"Chandler saw that speculation":** Fulton, "'Best Days,'" *Southern California Quarterly*, 239.

64 **"Every good citizen":** Gottlieb and Wolt, *Thinking Big*, 124.

65 **"the garden spot of the world" and "sanatorium of the universe":** Frances A. Groff, "Frank Wiggins, Glad-Hand Artist," *Los Angeles Herald*, November 1, 1910.

65 **"California on Wheels" train:** "Coming West," *Los Angeles Herald*, April 2, 1890.

65 **"Oranges for Health, California for Wealth":** Hadley Meares, "Sunkist Skies of Glory," Curbed Los Angeles, May 24, 2018, www.la.curbed. com/2018/5/24/17350622/los-angeles-history-promoted-boosters-ads.

65   **850-pound elephant made out of California walnuts:** Paul R. Spitzzeri, "Greater Los Angeles and the World's Fair of 1893," The Homestead Blog, July 7, 2017, www.homesteadmuseum.blog/2017/07/07/greater-los-angeles-and-the-worlds-fair-of-1893.

65   **"The Filipinos are without doubt":** Gottlieb and Wolt, *Thinking Big*, 22.

65   **"ignorant, misguided and bumptious natives":** Ibid.

65   **put in his resignation, received an honorable discharge, and was hailed a conquering hero:** Ibid., 23.

66   **Free Harbor Jubilee:** Accounts and quotes sourced from "San Pedro Day," LAT, April 27, 1899, and "The Great Fight for a Free Harbor and How It Was Won," LAT, April 28, 1899.

69   **the general was known:** McDougal, *Privileged Son*, 45.

69   **kids hunted jackrabbits and adults once attended bullfights:** Guinn, "Los Angeles City," *Historical Society*, 175-176.

69   **One of the few townships:** Ibid., 176.

70   **There was also the issue:** C. Mulholland, *William Mulholland*, 84-85.

70   **"I know a good old man. . . ." exchange:** Ibid.

70   **random homes with meters:** Ibid., 83.

70   **"For more than two years" exchange:** Ibid., 84.

70   **"Let the arid wastes":** "Growth-Progress-Promise," LAT, April 4, 1889.

71   **218-foot Chronicle building:** Peter Hartlaub, "The Cliff House Was Once a Colossal Victorian Mansion – That Met a Dramatic End," *San Francisco Chronicle*, April 29, 2023.

71   **"I don't know what we'll do":** C. Mulholland, *William Mulholland*, 90-91.

71   **Continental Tower:** "Continental Building," Los Angeles Conservancy, www.laconservancy.org/learn/historic-places/continental-building.

71   **a civic ordinance:** Nathan Masters, "L.A.'s Changing Skyline: A Brief History of Skyscrapers in the City of Angels," KCET.org, May 23, 2012, www.kcet.org/shows/lost-la/l-a-s-changing-skyline-a-brief-history-of-skyscrapers-in-the-city-of-angels.

71   **"broad and harmonious":** Ibid.

71   **"dark walled-in streets":** "Sold on Future of Los Angeles," LAT, December 28, 1924.

71   **"A building 150 feet high":** Colin Marshall, "Los Angeles in Buildings: City Hall," KCET.org, October 18, 2017, www.kcet.org/shows/lost-la/los-angeles-in-buildings-city-hall.

Chapter 7: Tracking the Future

74   **"BALLOON ROUTE – LOS ANGELES-PACIFIC R.R.":** Advertisement, LAT, February 1, 1901.

74   **"Kite-Shaped Track":** Advertisement, LAT, February 1, 1901.

74   **the Balloon Route was *the* premium route:** Balloon Route information primarily drawn from: Balloon Route brochures, The Huntington Library; Balloon Route Excursion Souvenir, The Huntington Library; "Superior Transportation Facilities," *Los Angeles Herald*, September 3, 1905; Victoria Bernal, "The Balloon Route: A Tourist's Trolley Trip Through Early-1900s Los Angeles," KCET.org, June 9, 2016, www.kcet.org/shows/lost-la/the-balloon-route-a-tourists-trolley-trip-through-early-1900s-los-angeles.

76   **"the best-known proper noun":** Myers and Swett, *Trolleys*, 34.

76   **its wholesome origins:** There are numerous websites and books devoted to the inspiration of the word Hollywood. The two most prevalent are the woman on the train who had an estate named "Hollywood" and the wild holly berries in the hills. These accounts include their own variations.

76   **"dream of beauty":** Hadley Meares, "How One Ohio Native Became the 'Mother of Hollywood,'" Curbed Los Angeles, February 20, 2014, www.la.curbed.com/2014/2/20/10142088/hollywood-history-daeida-wilcox-beveridge.

76   **"Mother of Hollywood":** Ibid.

77   **ability to "hypnotize" investors:** Weingarten, *Thirsty*, 70.

77   **"the finest suburb of Los Angeles":** Hollywood Ocean View Tract advertisement, LAT, October 11, 1903.

78   **Disembarking passengers were greeted:** "Progress of Hollywood," LAT, April 26, 1903.

78   **"The Tract That Made Hollywood Famous":** Hollywood Ocean View Tract advertisement, LAT, October 18, 1903.

78   **the structure held militaristic import:** Hadley Meares, "Sign of the Times II: Outpost Estates and the Importance of Mythmaking," KCET.org, January 25, 2013, www.kcet.org/history-society/sign-of-the-times-ii-outpost-estates-and-the-importance-of-mythmaking.

78   **"strictly accurate historically":** "The Treaty of 1847: Correction of an Error Relative to the Place of Signing," LAT, July 13, 1917.

78   **To create urgency:** Fulton, "'Best Days,'" *Southern California Quarterly*, 244, and Gottlieb and Wolt, *Thinking Big*, 147.

78   **According to Arnold Haskell:** Transcript of interview with Arnold Haskell by Mel Lesser, The Huntington Library, April 17, 1962.

79   **"Let's call it Hollywood":** Ibid.

79   **"light refreshments":** Fulton, "'Best Days,'" *Southern California Quarterly*, 244.

79   **"Behold what God hath wrought!":** Williams, *Hollywood*, 36.

79   **"hill-climbing contest":** "Progress of Hollywood," LAT.

79   **"The guests departed":** Fulton, "'Best Days,'" *Southern California Quarterly*, 244.

80   **"City of Homes":** Various Hollywood newspaper advertisements, including LAT, December 17, 1904.

80   **Whitley banked $26 million:** Ibid., 251.

80   **Ocean View made a tidy sixty percent profit:** Judson A. Grenier, "Harry Chandler," *Dictionary of American Biography, Supplement 3: 1941-1945.* Reproduced by South Bay Historical Society, January 29, 2005, www.sunnycv.com/steve/ar/mm3/chandler.html.

Chapter 8: A Right to Water

82   **"I had found gold":** "Are There More Oil and Gas Wells in LA Than Movie Stars?," EcoWatch, March 6, 2015, www.ecowatch.com/are-there-more-oil-and-gas-wells-in-la-than-movie-stars-1882017660.html.

82   **"Beautiful Homesites—All Oil Rights Included":** Petroleum Gardens advertisement, *Long Beach Press-Telegram*, January 20, 1923.

82   **one quarter of the world's petroleum output:** Rachel Schnalzer, "'A Parallel Hollywood Story': How L.A.'s Oil Boom Shaped the City We Know Today," LAT, December 8, 2021.

82   **1.6 billion gallons of recoverable crude:** Los Angeles Times Editorial Board, "Editorial: L.A. Is Right to Phase Out Oil Drilling, but Communities Can't Wait 20 Years," LAT, August 15, 1922.

82   **"menace" to water tables:** C. Mulholland, *William Mulholland*, 91-92.

83   **L.A.'s daily per capita water usage:** Ibid., 72.

83   **"If cleanliness is next to godliness":** Ibid.

83   **helped found Pasadena:** Sid Gally, "Pasadena History: Judge Eaton Essential to City's Formation," *Pasadena Star-News*, January 25, 2015.

83   **"sixth white child":** "Pioneer of City Expires," LAT, March 13, 1934.

84   **"killing Wiggins":** Transcript of William Mulholland Presentation to Sunset Club, "The Water Supply of Southern California," CSUN University Library, November 14, 1904.

84   **"a Limburger cheese factory":** Rollin Hu, "Charles Hatfield: The Moisture Accelerator of the 20th Century," *The Johns Hopkins News-Letter*, June 16, 2023.

84   **"I do not make rain":** Weingarten, *Thirsty*, 79.

85   **hired Hatfield to seed the clouds:** Merrie Monteagudo, "From the Archives: A Rainmaker Named Hatfield Came to San Diego 50 Years Ago," *The San Diego Union-Tribune*, January 18, 2022.

85   **to inspire *The Rainmaker*:** Christopher Klein, "When San Diego Hired a Rainmaker a Century Ago, It Poured," JSTOR Daily, December 12, 2015.

85   **buried on a sunny winter's day in Glendale:** Ibid.

85   **the Chief pointed out:** C. Mulholland, *William Mulholland*, 103.

85   **"If they can take":** Ibid., 104.

85   **opting to stay in L.A.:** Ibid., 24.

86   **"It is big":** Ibid., 120.

87   **"The city could not disclose":** William Mulholland, Transcript from Court Records, CSUN University Library, November 24, 1913.

87   **"The supply that will be obtained":** Transcript of William Mulholland Presentation to Sunset Club, "The Water Supply of Southern California," CSUN University Library, November 14, 1904.

88   **"TITANIC PROJECT TO GIVE CITY A RIVER":** LAT, July 29, 1905.

88   **"Los Angeles' water supply":** Ibid.

88   **"Water, living water":** "Coming—A River of Delight," LAT, July 30, 1905.

88   **"Then will Los Angeles county":** "Titanic Project," LAT.

88   **"a mighty earthquake":** Ibid.

89   **"Back to the headwaters":** Ibid.

89   **"It has not been cut out":** Transcript of William Mulholland Presentation to Sunset Club, "The Water Supply of Southern California," CSUN University Library, November 14, 1904.

89   **"a few thousand years ago":** "Titanic Project," LAT.

89   **"Los Angeles Plots Destruction—Would Take Owens River, Lay Lands Waste":** *The Inyo Register*, August 3, 1905.

89   **"There is something romantic":** "All Praise the Water Board," LAT, August 4, 1905.

89 **"50,000 acres of water-bearing land"**: "Titanic Project," LAT.

90 **"locoed millionaire"**: Ibid.

90 **"everyone is happy"**: Ibid.

90 **"I do not believe"**: Ibid.

90 **"canny old Scotch woman"**: Ibid.

90 **"I said that I had taken a flyer"**: Ibid.

90 **"I never saw a fellow"**: Ibid.

91 **"the spy"**: Davis, *Rivers*, 103.

91 **"When I go back"**: Ibid., 23.

91 **"[The water] is a hundred- or a thousand-fold"**: Les Standiford, "What Would Mulholland Do?," LAT, April 14, 2015.

91 **"The law is intended"**: "Good Grace of Government," LAT, July 29, 1905.

92 **"Judas B. Lippincott"**: Hoffman, *Vision or Villainy*, 103.

92 **"the very lands"**: Marc Weingarten, "This Is the Battle That Made Los Angeles – And a Great Newspaper War,"Salon, February 7, 2016, www.salon.com/2016/02/07/this_is_the_battle_that_made_los_angeles_and_a_great_newspaper_war.

92 **aiming to hunt him down**: Weingarten, *Thirsty*, 113.

Chapter 9: She Has But Just Begun to Grow

95 **"Before you girls die"**: Transcript of interview with May Goodan by James Bassett, The Huntington Library, January 4, 1973.

95 **"Papa's *really* crazy"**: Ibid.

96 **"It was necessary"**: William Mulholland, Transcript from Court Records, CSUN University Library, November 24, 1913.

97 **"The ranchers say"**: Weingarten, *Thirsty*, 100.

97 **"The purchase was made"**: "Great Porter Ranch Sold to Syndicate," LAT, October 23, 1903.

97 **the actual suburb called Porter Ranch**: Porter Ranch advertisement, LAT, September 13, 1963.

98 **"flushing the system"**: McDougal, *Privileged Son*, 41.

98 **six million gallons of water**: "Meter Is the Remedy," LAT, August 4, 1904.

99 **"Fudge for Cry-Baby Lowenthal!"**: LAT, July 31, 1905.

99 **"Everybody is laughing"**: Ibid.

99 **"placing himself in the attitude"**: Didion, "Letter," *New Yorker*.

99 **three million gallons a day**: "No Other Source Than Owens River," LAT, September 3, 1905.

99 **"mass exodus"**: Weingarten, *Thirsty*, 134.

99 **"barely enough"**: "Business Interests Favor Water Plan," *Los Angeles Herald*, September 7, 1905.

99 **"If you don't get the water now"**: Davis, *Rivers*, 31.

100 **"an ample supply"**: Letter from William Mulholland to W.J. Washburn, Los Angeles Chamber of Commerce, CSUN University Library, June 5, 1906.

100 **"Adjacent towns will soon be knocking"**: "For Greater Los Angeles," LAT, August 11, 1905.

100 **"The vote on the water bond"**: "The Water Bond Election," *Los Angeles Herald*, August 16, 1905.

101 **"Let me tell you":** "Mulholland, He Wants to Yell," LAT, September 8, 1905.

101 **"proudest"** and **"This is our birthday":** "Surveyors Soon to Be in Field," LAT, September 8, 1905.

101 **"Viva Los Angeles!":** LAT, September 8, 1905.

101 **"Los Angeles joyously announces":** Ibid.

101 **"Timorous, ignorant, penurious":** Ibid.

101 **an editorial cartoon:** "Magnificent Chorus of Voters Shouts for Owens River Project," LAT, September 8, 1905.

102 **"Mulholland was a gentleman":** Ibid.

102 **"The brunt of the [water] campaign":** "Pueblo to Metropolis," LAT, December 4, 1931.

104 **"toss pebbles into the sea":** "Annexation by a Hair," LAT, November 13, 1906.

105 **"her schoolhouse on one side":** "Consolidation or What," LAT, December 28, 1906.

105 **"I tell people":** Sheryl Stoleberg, "In Search of an Identity," LAT, January 1, 1989.

105 **"We're like in limbo":** Ibid.

105 **a tragic incident in 1984:** Allan Parachini, "A Paramedic Program Breakdown Brings Tragedy to 'Valley of Death,'" LAT, July 1, 1984.

105 **"valley of death":** Ibid.

106 **"medical desert":** Bryant Odega (@BryantOdega), "The way our community gets treated you'd think the city forgot we even existed," July 30, 2023, 8:30 pm, www.x.com/BryantOdega/status/1685855531926208512; Jacqueline Fonte (@JacFonte),"We don't call it the valley of death anymore but it is part of LA's medical desert," July 30, 2023, 10:28 pm, www.x.com/JaqFonte/status/1685885034421739521.

106 **"Now that the plan":** "All Are Eager for Annexation," *Los Angeles Herald*, November 14, 1906.

106 **"Water! Water! Water!":** "Real Estate Men Feast and Boost," *Los Angeles Herald*, January 25, 1907.

Chapter 10: Huntington Goes All In

107 **Otis's own health took a turn:** McDougal, *Privileged Son*, 44.

107 **The charred tree still clings to life:** "Palm Garden," The Huntington, www.huntington.org/palm-garden.

107 **"The people of San Francisco":** Letter from Moses Sherman to Harry Chandler, Sherman Library, August 10, 1906.

108 **"EVERYBODY KEEP COOL":** *Los Angeles Herald*, April 20, 1906.

108 **"completely outside the natural pathway":** Ibid.

108 **"appreciate again the delicious sunshine":** Ibid.

108 **"This is the longest state":** Ibid.

108 **"I know well":** Letter from Harriet Sherman to Moses Sherman, Sherman Library, ca. 1906-1907.

108 **"The journey is soon over":** Letter from Moses Sherman to Harriet Sherman, Sherman Library, June 2, 1907.

108 **autograph seekers confusing him for a thespian:** Hendricks, *M. H. Sherman*, 28-29.

109 **"I need a long vacation":** Letter from Moses Sherman to Sarah Carr, Sherman Library, May 7, 1907.

109 **"You are growing constantly":** Letter from Harriet Sherman to Moses Sherman, Sherman Library, June 9, ca. 1906-1907.

109 **"I know how":** Letter from Moses Sherman to Harry Chandler, Sherman Library, September 15, 1906.

110 **Moist no tears:** Ella Wheeler Wilcox poem "Resolve" quoted in letter from Harriet Sherman to Moses Sherman, Sherman Library, March 24, 1907. Harriet substituted "Moist" for "Waste."

110 **"had not maintained conjugal relations":** Thorpe, *Henry Edwards Huntington*, 173-174. Mary's brother Edward H. Prentice also testified that the spouses "had not maintained conjugal relations for the past six years."

110 **"given her husband any excuse":** "Mrs. Huntington Gets Divorce in Seven Minutes," *St. Louis Globe-Democrat*, March 23, 1906.

110 **$2 million trust fund:** Thorpe, *Henry Edwards Huntington*, 174.

110 **boarded a passenger ship for Japan:** Ibid.

110 **"intense nervousness":** Ibid., 166.

110 **"For my own part":** Friedricks, *Henry E. Huntington*, 71.

111 **"I am a foresighted man":** Crump, *Red Cars*, 238.

111 **"[Dad] is certainly buying":** Friedricks, *Henry E. Huntington*, 59.

111 **"His forehead showed intuitiveness":** Thorpe, *Henry Edwards Huntington*, 159.

112 **"twenty different kinds" of ears:** J. A. Fowler, "How Your Ears Tell How Long You Will Live, What You Are Fit For and All About Your Character and Disposition," *The San Francisco Examiner*, July 5, 1903. Huntington's No. 13 ear classification is the author's own observation based on pictures.

112 **"Can Triple Huntington Millions":** Thorpe, *Henry Edwards Huntington*, 159.

113 **"Fabulous is leniency":** Message from Henry Huntington to Isaias W. Hellman, The Huntington Library, June 18, 1903.

113 **"Huntington Came Within an Ace":** "Near Two Millions Paid for Traction," LAT, April 19, 1903.

113 **"Henry E. Huntington: The Modern Colossus of Roads":** *Los Angeles Evening News*, October 16, 1905.

114 **it was estimated that 100,000 out of 150,000 passengers:** Thorpe, *Henry Edwards Huntington*, 189.

114 **"well-grounded report":** "Busy Day for Mr. Huntington," *Los Angeles Herald*, August 22, 1905.

114 **"Would you believe it":** Ibid.

114 **"Much to my surprise":** Friedricks, *Henry E. Huntington*, 83.

114 **"There can be but one head":** Ibid., 84.

114 **"mental breakdown":** Ibid., 83.

115 **"I would not like to have my name":** Letter from Henry Huntington to Allen P. Nichols, The Huntington Library, December 1906.

115 **"willingness to permit":** Letter from Allen P. Nichols to Henry Huntington, The Huntington Library, December 1906.

115 **In 1892, federal courts granted:** Steve Kilgore, "Los Angeles Land Covenants, Redlining; Creation and Effects," LAPL Blog, June 22, 2020, www.lapl.org/collections-resources/blogs/lapl/los-angeles-land-covenants-redlining-creation-and-effects.

116 **"Buy Where Huntington Buys!":** Pasadena Villa Tract advertisement, *Los Angeles Herald*, December 31, 1905.

116 **all seventeen cities:** Friedricks, *Henry E. Huntington*, 82.

116 **"Huntington Park?":** Ron Harris, "A Family Mirrors Roots of Black L.A.," LAT, August 22, 1982.

117 **"Wherever the Huntington railways":** Gottlieb and Wolt, *Thinking Big*, 145.

118 **"All right, Huntington":** Friedricks, *Henry E. Huntington*, 80.

118 **"So far as Mr. Harriman":** Letter from Henry Huntington to Harry Chandler, The Huntington Library, December 13, 1906.

118 **"Things seem to be coming":** Letter from Henry Huntington to Moses Sherman, The Huntington Library, May 11, 1900.

118 **after the general's condition required a visit to a Northern California sanitarium, Henry regularly checked in:** Letter from Henry Huntington to Moses Sherman, The Huntington Library, August 1, 1900.

118 **note of sympathy and, later, a bouquet of flowers:** Thank-you letters from Henry Huntington to Moses Sherman, The Huntington Library, September 18, 1900, and January 21, 1901.

119 **"The reply [by Sherman] is said to have been discourteous":** "Moses and Eli to Harriman," *The Daily Outlook*, March 19, 1906.

119 **"My dear Mr. Chandler":** Letter from Henry Huntington to Harry Chandler, The Huntington Library, December 13, 1906.

120 **"I don't think Sherman":** Ibid.

120 **"My dear Andrews":** Letter from Moses Sherman to Harry Andrews, Sherman Library, June 30, 1906.

121 **"I should certainly feel":** Letter from Henry Huntington to Harry Chandler, The Huntington Library, December 13, 1906.

Chapter 11: Here, There, Chandler

122 **"I must admit":** Letter from Harriet Sherman to Moses Sherman, Sherman Library, ca. 1906.

122 **"I do enjoy working":** Letter from Moses Sherman to Harry Chandler, Sherman Library, April 13, 1908.

122 **"Harry, it is not the money":** Ibid., September 1908.

122 **"Please be sure and tear this up":** Letter from Moses Sherman to Harry Chandler, Sherman Library, June 22, 1906.

122 **"I must confess":** Letter from Henry Huntington to Harry Chandler, The Huntington Library, December 31, 1906.

122 **"anything published that makes Los Angeles":** Ibid.

123 **"WHY BE AFRAID OF $3.20 A YEAR?":** LAT, June 9, 1907.

123 **each household would owe only $3.20 per year:** Ibid.

123 **"deficient in intelligence":** "Forward, March!," LAT, June 13, 1907.

123 **"politics and water don't mix":** Wilkman, *Floodpath*, 50.

123 **"Why, I'd sooner skin a dead dog"**: McCarthy, "Water," *Pacific Saturday Night*, October 23, 1937, 32.

123 **"One of the streams"**: "All Praise the Water Board," LAT.

124 **"MILLION POPULATION CLUB"**: LAT, June 13, 1907.

124 **"Most Valuable Citizen in Los Angeles"**: W. E. W., "Just a Little," *The Van Nuys News*.

124 **"We have it in sight now"**: "Million Population Club," LAT.

124 **"put the [morning's] paper to bed"**: Transcript of interview with May Goodan by James Bassett, The Huntington Library, January 4, 1973.

125 **"I hope you will not return"**: Letter from Moses Sherman to Harry Chandler, The Huntington Library, August 24, 1907.

125 **"from morning until night"**: Letter from Moses Sherman to Sarah Carr, Sherman Library, November 14, 1908.

125 **"development of this locality"**: Ibid., December 2, 1908.

126 **"We will have a whole lot of fun"**: Letter from Moses Sherman to Harry Chandler, Sherman Library, February 7, 1909.

126 **"He was a great catalyst"**: Transcript of interview with Arnold Haskell by James Bassett, The Huntington Library, December 11, 1972.

126 **including one for $3 million:** "Who's Who," *Saturday Evening Post*, 52.

126 **"Sell the ranch to Harry Chandler"**: Babcock, *Harry Chandler*.

126 **The general mailed back a reply:** Letter from Moses Sherman to Harry Chandler, Sherman Library, sometime between December 1908 and June 1909. The inference is that Sherman is responding to a tactic presented by Chandler.

126 **"It seems to me now"**: Ibid.

127 **"GEN. SHERMAN MUST RESIGN FROM THE WATER BOARD"**: *Los Angeles Post-Record*, April 27, 1909.

127 **"A member of the water board"**: Ibid.

127 **The *Record* also published open letters to new mayor George Alexander:** Articles between April and June 1909, including "His Master's Voice" cartoon, *Los Angeles Post-Record*, May 11, 1909.

127 **"Moses in L.A. Bullrushes"**: *Los Angeles Record*, June 2, 1909.

127 **in favor of removing Sherman:** "Mayor Removes Gen. Sherman," *Los Angeles Record*, July 20, 1909.

127 **"resign under fire"**: "City Attorney on Sherman's Rights," LAT, July 10, 1909.

128 **"I was very foolish"**: Letter from Moses Sherman to Harrison Gray Otis, Sherman Library, August 15, 1909.

128 **Sherman was finally sacked:** "Removes Sherman from Water Board," *Los Angeles Express*, January 20, 1910.

128 **"He had inside information from Moses"**: Author interview with Abraham Hoffman, April 2023.

128 **"Father was the one"**: Transcript of interview with May Goodan by James Bassett, The Huntington Library, January 4, 1973.

128 **"He wasn't a man"**: Transcript of interview with Arnold Haskell by James Bassett, The Huntington Library, December 11, 1972.

128 **"a partial list"**: "Syndicate Buys Lankershim Ranch," LAT September 24, 1909.

129 **thirty shareholders, each contributing:** Gottlieb and Wolt, *Thinking Big*, 145.

129 **largest land transaction ever recorded in Los Angeles County:** Roderick, *San Fernando Valley*, 48.

129 **"It was stated yesterday":** "Great Lankershim Ranch Sold, Local Syndicate to Subdivide," LAT, September 24, 1909.

129 **"The syndicate will build":** Ibid.

129 **"significant business gains":** "Significant Business Gains," LAT, August 31, 1909.

Chapter 12: Ready Suitors

131 **"deplorable conditions":** "Ships and Rails," *San Pedro News-Pilot*, July 27, 1931.

131 **Only after proprietors were reassured:** Ibid.

132 **"I believe traffic will grow":** "Enthusiastic Gathering of Friends of the Bond Issue," *Long Beach Daily Telegram*, August 24, 1909.

132 **vehicles flew consolidation pennants and soused citizens buzzed through town with consolidation pins:** "'Antis' Hiding in Their Hole," LAT, August 11, 1909.

132 **"A man-made harbor":** Taylor, "It Costs $1000," *Saturday Evening Post*, 8.

133 **"the man-made end" and "the God-made end":** Ibid.

134 **"At a joint meeting":** "For Immediate Consolidation," LAT, November 16, 1909.

135 **if not for a scandal:** All quotations and accounts of January 24, 1910, voting incident from "Hollywood of the Foothills Enters Greater Los Angeles," LAT, January 25, 1910.

135 **a victory banquet:** "Hollywood Is Banquet Host," *Los Angeles Herald*, February 19, 1910.

135 **"The highest consideration":** "Annexation Cause of Large Banquet," *Los Angeles Express*, February 19, 1910.

135 **"This is the pleasantest occasion":** Ibid.

135 **"The highest class of intelligence":** Ibid.

135 **"The finest class of people":** John J. Gosper, former Secretary of Arizona Territory, quoted in "Vote to Consolidate Hollywood with Los Angeles, Is Urgent Plea," *Los Angeles Herald*, January 23, 1910.

136 **the council rebuffed various requests:** "Hollywood Is Royal Host," LAT, February 19, 1910.

136 **uptick in real estate sales:** "East Hollywood Solid for Annexation Now," LAT, February 17, 1910.

136 **"I do not know":** "Annexation Cause," *Los Angeles Express*.

136 **"San Pedro harbor improvement bonds":** "Urges Big Vote for Annexation," *Los Angeles Herald*, February 18, 1910.

137 **An all-day celebration:** "Hundreds Feast in Griffith Park," *Los Angeles Herald*, March 6, 1910.

137 **"mountain climbing":** "East Hollywood Will Celebrate," *Los Angeles Express*, February 28, 1910.

137 **assured readers that annexation elections were done:** "Urges Big Vote," *Los Angeles Herald*.

137 **"another election is in sight":** "Election News," LAT, February 25, 1910.

137 **would have to be annexed before April 15:** Ibid.

Chapter 13: The Big Ditch

138 **"He is the Moses":** Quoted from *Graphic* magazine by McCarthy, "Water," *Pacific Saturday Night*, January 15, 1938, 28.

138 **"to make such trips":** C. Mulholland, *William Mulholland*, 153.

138 **"pinheads in Los Angeles":** Ibid., 154.

138 **The homeowner in Boyle Heights:** Letter from William Mulholland to Mr. Visnel, responding to complaint by Visnel, CSUN University Library, October 2, 1906.

138 **The owner of a boiler company:** Letter from Pioneer Boiler and Machine Works to William Mulholland, CSUN University Library, December 9, 1907.

138 **The spurious accusations of flawed water meters:** C. Mulholland, *William Mulholland*, 103.

138 **"complaints from old women":** McCarthy, "Water," *Pacific Saturday Night*, January 15, 1938, 32.

139 **vocalizing what he wanted, or working out solutions in the dirt with a stick:** Weingarten, *Thirsty*, 160.

139 **"Since your father was acting":** C. Mulholland, *William Mulholland*, 169.

140 **"When we want that power":** Kunze, "Hidden Hand," *Los Angeles Record*.

140 **"It's as good as new":** Letter from Moses Sherman to William Mulholland, CSUN University Library, September 17, 1907.

140 **"Mule Capital of the World":** "Lathrop History," City of Lathrop, Mo. Official Website, www.cityoflathropmo.org/lathrop-history.html.

141 **"The best lot of mules":** "Select Mules for Aqueduct," LAT, April 17, 1909.

141 **"I never saw him make a note":** McCarthy, "Water," *Pacific Saturday Night*, January 15, 1938, 33.

141 **"Big Bill":** C. Mulholland, *William Mulholland*, 168.

141 **"The damn thing looks like a caterpillar":** Ibid. While Mulholland and his crew may have noticed the tractor's similarity to a caterpillar and called it as such, the claim that he inspired the tractor's official name may be apocryphal. Caterpillar's website has an alternate origin story: www.caterpillar.com/en/company/history/1920.html.

141 **ordered twenty-eight "caterpillar" tractors:** Weingarten, *Thirsty*, 156.

142 **"I'm going into this":** McCarthy, "Water," *Pacific Saturday Night*, January 15, 1938, 33.

142 **"Nature is the squarest fighter":** Weingarten, *Thirsty*, 160.

142 **a worker was drunk, asleep, or hungover:** Ibid., 151-152, and Author interview with Abraham Hoffman, April 2023.

142 **"Let me know when that's gone":** Weingarten, *Thirsty*, 151.

142 **"Whiskey built the aqueduct":** Ibid.

142 **After thirty taverns were forced to close:** Ibid., 152.

142 **Inside his gussied-up carriage:** C. Mulholland, *William Mulholland*, 173. ("Alone time" quote the author's own.)

143 **"It has always been a great pride":** Ibid., 231.

143 **friendly competitions:** Weingarten, *Thirsty*, 155.

143 **The south crew earned bragging rights:** Ibid., 166-170.

143 **"With the completion of this tunnel":** "Aqueduct Bores, Smiles Long, To be Joined Today," *Los Angeles Herald*, February 26, 1911.

Chapter 14: Explosive Changes

144 **"The last harvest":** "Last Vast Harvest on Greatest Ranch," LAT, August 14, 1910.

144 **newspapers outside of Los Angeles, like *The Pomona Progress*:** Los Angeles Suburban Homes Sites advertisement, *The Pomona Progress*, May 23, 1910.

144 **"land-hungry men and women":** "Record Sales in the Valley," LAT, June 2, 1910.

145 **"a new record":** Ibid.

145 **"The time has come":** "Last Vast Harvest," LAT.

145 **"in collusion with the leaders":** Transcript of William Mulholland speech at City Club at Westminster Hotel, CSUN University Library, December 2, 1911.

145 **"indifferent"** and **"unfriendly":** Ibid.

145 **"rich men's country estates":** McCarthy, "Water," *Pacific Saturday Night*, February 12, 1938, 30.

145 **he welcomed a full investigation:** C. Mulholland, *William Mulholland*, 207-208.

145 **the "rape" of Owens Valley:** Quote attributed to W. A. Chalfont in McCarthy, "Water," *Pacific Saturday Night*, December 4, 1937, 33. The analogy of "rape" in relation to Owens Valley has appeared in print for decades.

145 **Robert Towne said he had Harry Chandler in mind:** McDougal, *Privileged Son*, 2.

146 **"Father of the Los Angeles Aqueduct":** "Harry Chandler, Famed Publisher of Times, Dies," *Long Beach Press-Telegram*, September 24, 1944, and McDougal, *Privileged Son*, 468.

146 **The explosion ripped off his head and limbs:** "Los Angeles," JD Supra, www.jdsupra.com/post/fileServer.aspx?fName=79c0cfa3-c914-4efc-92c9-85370217cbd4.pdf.

146 **The cops took the device to a park, where it discharged:** Darrell Kunitomi presentation of *Los Angeles Times* history at Los Angeles Public Library, November 10, 2022.

147 **"get General Otis":** Hadley Meares, "Infernal Machines," KCET.org, April 25, 2014, www.kcet.org/history-society/infernal-machines-the-bombing-of-the-los-angeles-times-and-l-a-s-first-crime-of-the-century.

147 **"UNIONIST BOMBS WRECK THE TIMES":** LAT, October 1, 1910.

147 **"They can kill":** "A Plain Statement," LAT, October 1, 1910.

147 **"I believe in free labor":** Friedricks, *Henry E. Huntington*, 137.

148 **"Trade-Unionism":** Letter from Henry Huntington to Harrison Gray Otis, The Huntington Library, December 1, 1912.

148 **the Chief spoke at a luncheon:** All quotes and accounts from transcript of William Mulholland speech at City Club at Westminster Hotel, CSUN University Library, December 2, 1911.

148 **"Forward, March!":** LAT, June 13, 1907.
148 **"The Sale of the Century":** Advertisement, LAT, November 3, 1910.
149 **"the beginning of a new empire":** "Forerunner New Empire," LAT, November 5, 1910.
149 **"WHAT TO BUY?":** Shoestring Strip advertisement, *Los Angeles Herald*, January 6, 1910.
149 **"IF YOU HAVE TEARS, BE SURE TO SHED 'EM NOW FOR THE UNFORTUNATE RICH":** *Los Angeles Record*, August 20, 1909.
150 **"$000"** and **"Gen. M. H. Sherman":** Ibid.
150 **"has picked up the furniture":** Ibid.
150 **In a poll conducted by the *Record*:** "Judge Wilbur is Most Influential Citizen Says the Prize-Winner," *Los Angeles Record*, August 3, 1909.
150 **"city hall, court house and county":** Ibid.
150 **"He has developed the country":** Ibid.
150 **"I never talk about my intentions":** Friedricks, *Henry E. Huntington*, 68.
151 **"One cannot help noting":** Letter from Henry Huntington to Harrison Gray Otis, The Huntington Library, December 1, 1912.
151 **"M. H. SHERMAN A LOSER BY FIRE":** *Los Angeles Record*, February 3, 1910.
152 **"'Whose street-car are we riding in?'":** Marcosson, *Master of Millions*, 23-24.
152 **he didn't see much of a future for trackless, "trolleyless" cars:** Letter from Henry Huntington to G. E. Miles, The Huntington Library, March 1, 1904.
153 **"peerless trolley king":** "If You Have Tears," *Los Angeles Record*.

Chapter 15: The Road to Paradise
155 **the former Rancho ex-Mission San Fernando dominion had plenty to offer:** Various newspapers, including Los Angeles Suburban Homes Co. advertisement, *The Pomona Progress*, May 23, 1910.
155 **"asphalt paved boulevard":** Los Angeles Suburban Homes Co. advertisement, *Los Angeles Herald*, December 25, 1910.
155 **longest paved street:** McDougal, *Privileged Son*, 68.
155 **Costing half-a-million dollars, it would stretch 15 miles and be framed by ornamental trees and shrubs at Chandler's insistence:** "Who's Who," *Saturday Evening Post*, 52, and "Our Beautiful Sherman Way," *The Van Nuys News*, April 19, 1912.
155 **"most perfect automobile speedway":** Los Angeles Suburban Homes Co. advertisement, LAT, December 25, 1910.
156 **"a retiring kind of guy":** Noel J. Stowe, "Development in the Californias: An Interview with David Otto Brant," *California Historical Society Quarterly*, Vol. 47, No. 2, June 1968.
156 **rarely allowed his photo to be shown:** Taylor, "It Costs $1000," *Saturday Evening Post*, 62.
156 **set policies on how often his name could be mentioned:** Ibid.
157 **turned everything "into money":** Letter from Hobart Whitley to W. P. Whitsett, CSUN University Library, January 31, 1912.

157 **"Fifteen miles from the heart":** "Fact and Comment," LAT, February 26, 1911.

157 **"The Town That Was Started RIGHT":** Van Nuys Public Auction advertisement, LAT, February 21, 1911.

157 **"an eaglet bursting":** "Stork's Happy Call to the Golden Valley," LAT, March 31, 1912.

158 **Santa Ana windstorm:** C. Mulholland, *Owensmouth Baby*, 32.

158 **$104,100 worth of property:** Nathan Masters, "Canoga Park at 100: A Brief History of the Birth of Owensmouth," KCET.org, April 4, 2012, www.kcet.org/shows/lost-la/canoga-park-at-100-a-brief-history-of-the-birth-of-owensmouth.

158 **its association with "stolen water" was not a good look:** Author interview with Abraham Hoffman, April 2023.

158 **"everything from Balboa":** C. Mulholland, *Owensmouth Baby*, 87.

159 **named after a flowering plant genus:** Mark Tapio Kines, "Reseda Blvd.," L.A. Street Names, www.lastreetnames.com/street/reseda-boulevard.

159 **"No speed cops will annoy you":** Fred Flint, "Motor Jaunt to Calabasas," LAT, February 26, 1911.

159 **many returning home to rave:** Fulton, "Best Days," *Southern California Quarterly*, 244.

159 **Chandler and company earned a $5 million return:** "Who's Who," *Saturday Evening Post*, 52.

159 **"We are especially indebted":** Quinton, Code, and Hamlin, *Surplus Waters*, 20.

159 **bumped his salary fifty percent to $15,000 a year:** C. Mulholland, *William Mulholland*, 181.

159 **higher than the mayor's:** Author interview with Abraham Hoffman, April 2023.

159 **It reached five conclusions:** Details taken from Quinton, Code, and Hamlin, *Surplus Waters*, 19-20.

160 **"ANNEXATION GETS SOLAR PLEXUS BLOW":** South Pasadena coverage and "The Proposal" cartoon, *South Pasadena Record*, August 10, 1911.

162 **"those favoring annexation":** "Belvedere Antis Bluff Bairdstown Boomers," LAT, September 13, 1911.

162 **"Unexpected Happens":** "Annexation Is Defeated," LAT, September 23, 1911.

162 **"are expected to be a part of Los Angeles":** Ibid.

163 **"There is one subject":** "Campaign Will Be Bitter Fight," LAT, February 15, 1911.

163 **"If you want to start something":** Ibid.

163 **reserved for Caucasians:** Friedricks, *Henry E. Huntington*, 88.

164 **"the lowest tax rates":** "With a Silver Spoon, Full-Grown in a Day," LAT, April 13, 1913.

164 **"Millionaire City" was a West Coast answer to Tuxedo, New York:** Ibid.

164 **Mary Williamson Averell Harriman:** Various, including "Ex-Gov. Averell Harriman, Adviser to 4 Presidents, Dies," *The New York Times*, July 27, 1986.

164 **one-third of its 2,500 acres:** Charles F. Davis, "City in Brief," *Monrovia Daily News*, April 18, 1913.

164 **"it has been suggested":** "Silver Spoon," LAT.

164 **"When my home [in San Marino] is done":** Friedricks, *Henry E. Huntington*, 98.

164 **"All the great joy":** Ibid.

165 **"I can never tell you":** Letter from Henry Huntington to Caroline Densmore (Huntington), The Huntington Library, July 20, 1913.

165 **"The strain and responsibility":** C. Mulholland, *William Mulholland*, 211.

Chapter 16: Mulholland Delivers

166 **Aqueduct Memorial Fountain:** "To Start Big Memorial Fund," *Los Angeles Express*, November 6, 1913.

166 **the goal of laying the first cornerstone:** "Water Memorial Designed to Rise 300 Feet, Cost $500,000," *Los Angeles Express*, May 10, 1913.

166 **"The entire country travels":** "Memorial Fund," *Los Angeles Express*.

166 **Unable to raise $500,000 in building costs:** "Enduring Monument to a Titan's Feat," LAT, May 11, 1913.

166 **aqueduct's official coming out party:** Unless otherwise noted, details of the Los Angeles Aqueduct's opening sourced from C. Mulholland, *William Mulholland*, 243-246; Schedule of events taken from "Official Program," CSUN University Library, November 5-6, 1913.

167 **Panama Canal wouldn't open until 1914:** "Canal History," Suez Canal Authority, www.suezcanal.gov.eg/English/About/SuezCanal/Pages/CanalHistory.aspx.

167 **deliver 258 million gallons:** "Molding Destiny—The Aqueduct," LAT, November 5, 1913.

167 **To handle the crush of attendees:** "Great Crowd Handled without Single Hitch," LAT, November 6, 1913.

167 **drinking cups to sample Sierra's finest from faucets:** Hoffman, *Vision or Villainy*, 171-172.

168 **"Lift your voices":** Ellen Beach Yaw, "California—Hail the Waters!," LAT, November 6, 1913.

168 **"blew the ostrich plumes":** C. Mulholland, *William Mulholland*, 244.

169 **"smiting the rock":** Gen. Adna R. Chaffee quote from author interview with Abraham Hoffman, April 2023. Full quote attributed to Chaffee portrays William Mulholland as "smiting the rock and drawing from its face, pure water which made the desert of Zin a land of fruits and flowers in place of an arid waste." Allusions to scripture to describe Mulholland's prowess peaked during the aqueduct's debut. *See also*: Samuel Parker, "The Aqueduct Dedicatory Poem," *Los Angeles Express*, November 6, 1913.

169 **"like the men of the Bible":** "Tribute to Master Mind of Aqueduct," LAT, November 6, 1913.

169 **"I am sorry that the man":** C. Mulholland, *William Mulholland*, 211.

169 **"I have done nothing more":** "Mulholland the Man of the Hour," LAT, November 6, 1913.

169 **"I'd rather give birth":** Davis, *Rivers*, 100. There are conflicting dates and sources as to when William Mulholland first uttered this phrase.

169 **after an interminable two or three minutes:** Roderick, *San Fernando Valley*, 55.
169 **"that had a sob in it":** C. Mulholland, *William Mulholland*, 245.
170 **"Well, it's finished":** Ibid.
170 **"There it is" and "Thank you":** Ibid., 246.
170 **"stupendous and daring":** "Man of the Hour," LAT.
170 **"We can only share":** "Master Mind," LAT.
170 **"The lands that are immediately contiguous":** Ibid.
170 **thanked city attorney W. B. Mathews:** Standiford, *Water*, 208.
170 **"GLORIOUS MOUNTAIN RIVER NOW FLOWS TO LOS ANGELES' GATES":** LAT, November 6, 1913.
171 **congratulatory telegram from President Woodrow Wilson:** "President Wilson Wires Aqueduct Felicitations," LAT, November 6, 1913.
171 **"California, Hail the Waters!":** Yaw, "Hail the Waters!," LAT.
171 **"busy, credible day":** "Great Crowd," LAT.
171 **"From the standpoint of boosting Los Angeles":** "Pictorial History of the Aqueduct," LAT, November 6, 1913.
171 **"WATER CURES SICK WOMAN":** LAT, November 6, 1913.
171 **"the golden rule":** Standiford, *Water*, 210.
171 **"most" of the Ten Commandments:** McCarthy, "Water," *Pacific Saturday Night*, February 12, 1938, 31.
171 **"Conscience, progress, a chance for every man":** Ibid.

Chapter 17: The Latest Greatest Achievement
172 **"deed" and "control and management":** "What the Course of 'The Times' Shall Be," LAT, August 5, 1917.
172 **Chandler had been managing the paper for years:** McDougal, *Privileged Son*, 84.
172 **large replica cannon on the hood:** Ibid., 45.
172 **"The old general":** Ibid., 84.
172 **Otis would promptly fire the telegraph editor:** Ibid.
173 **"the proper medium for thinkers":** "Course of 'The Times,'" LAT.
173 **"He sits there in senile dementia":** McDougal, *Privileged Son*, 48.
173 **"letter of declaration":** "Course of 'The Times,'" LAT.
173 **"a classic in the annals":** Ibid.
174 **"wonderful brain":** Letter from Moses Sherman to Harry Chandler, Sherman Library, September 24, 1914.
174 **a reference to two palm trees swaying next to its Southern Pacific train depot:** Ingersoll, *Century History*, 353.
175 **"The Padres of old":** Citronia Acres advertisement, LAT, January 3, 1915.
175 **"ANNEXATION is the next step":** Suburban Property advertisement, *Los Angeles Express*, December 2, 1914.
175 **"This land will be worth":** Ibid.
175 **$100 million in estimated earnings:** Davis, *Rivers*, 103.
175 **"My dear General":** Letter from Harry Chandler to Moses Sherman, The Huntington Library, July 27, 1915.
175 **Chandler also forwarded a draft:** Ibid.
176 **"except those having real estate":** C. Mulholland, *William Mulholland*, 250.

176 **"I believe that if we paid"**: Ibid., 253.
176 **the *Record* came out on the side of annexation**: "Vote for Annexation!," *Los Angeles Record*, May 3, 1915.
177 **"The proper thing to do"**: William Mulholland, "Mulholland for Annexation," LAT, May 3, 1915. (Letter dated April 30, 1915.)
177 **"GREATEST ACHIEVEMENT IN HISTORY OF THE CITY"**: LAT, May 30, 1915.
178 **only 223 feet wide**: Calculation by author. Figure is approximate.
178 **"special irrigation district"**: Author interview with Abraham Hoffman, April 2023, and "Flood Control Bonds Close," *The Van Nuys News*, February 23, 1917.
178 **As recently as 2019**: "Annual Water Quality Report: Reporting Year 2019," City of San Fernando, www.ci.san-fernando.ca.us/wp-content/uploads/2020/06/CA000113_WR.pdf.
179 **a troop of "rural police"**: "Van Nuys is Now Part of Greater Los Angeles," *The Van Nuys News*, May 7, 1915.
179 **first customer to receive Owens Valley water**: "Irrigation to Start Saturday," *The Van Nuys News*, May 28, 1915.
179 **"Eighteen Miles of Roses"**: "Handley Ridicules Rose-Lined Roads," *South Pasadena Record*, May 26, 1915.
179 **40,000 blossoms**: "Sixteen Miles of Rose Glory," LAT, May 1, 1914.
179 **"There are twenty to one hundred blooms"**: "Rose-Lined Roads," *South Pasadena Record*.
179 **"a marvelous wonderland"**: "Barbecue, Cabaret and Program Held in Heart of Canyon," *Los Angeles Express*, May 29, 1915.
180 **"'Los Angeles Times' Scenic Automobile Tour"**: "'Los Angeles Times' Scenic Automobile Tour a Beauty," LAT, May 16, 1915.
180 **"Today, you see it completed"**: "Topanga Road Has Auspicious Opening," LAT, May 30, 1915.
180 **"BRINGS SAN FERNANDO VALLEY NEAR TO THE OCEAN BEACHES"**: Ibid.
180 **"Good roads add ten times"**: Ibid.
180 **"Every person in the Van Nuys-Owensmouth tract"**: "All Arrangements Made for Big Event To-Morrow," *The Van Nuys News*, May 28, 1915.
181 **turning left onto Topanga Canyon Boulevard**: Unless otherwise noted, opening of Topanga Canyon mostly taken from "Topanga Road Open May 29th," *The Van Nuys News*, May 21, 1915, and "Topanga Canyon Boulevard Opens a Scenic Route to Autos," LAT, May 16, 1915.
181 **The menu included wild turkeys**: "Topanga Opening Will Have an Outdoor Feed," LAT, May 27, 1915.
181 **wild turkeys were introduced to the Southland**: Caitlin Dempsey, "Where Are Wild Turkeys in California From?," Geography Realm, July 3, 2022, www.geographyrealm.com/where-are-wild-turkeys-in-california-from.
181 **also roamed parts of the Channel Islands**: Tom Batter, "Coexisting with California's Wild Turkeys," CDFW Wildlife Investigations Lab Blog, April 23, 2013, www.calwil.wordpress.com/2013/04/23/coexisting-with-californias-wild-turkeys.

181 **In 1903, there were 300 "horseless vehicles":** "Here Autos Flourish," *Los Angeles Express*, April 25. 1903.

181 **In 1915, there were 27,953:** "60,356 Autos Are Licensed in Southern California," *The Van Nuys News*, May 28, 1915.

182 **"Venice Warns Voters to Absorb Territory Before Los Angeles Swallows It":** LAT, July 16, 1915.

Chapter 18: A Hive of Annexation

184 **"the annexation bee buzzed merrily":** "Merger Topic at Westgate Rally," *Los Angeles Express*, August 25, 1915.

184 **"annexation bee in its bonnet":** "More Suburbs Will Vote on Annexation," *Los Angeles Record*, March 31, 1923.

184 **"Game of the Spider and Fly":** "Annexation Bee Will Sting Sawtelle," *Venice Vanguard*, August 20, 1915.

186 **"the exact counterpart":** Westgate Acres advertisement, *Los Angeles Express*, July 8, 1905.

186 **"Hollywood was a barley field":** Westgate Acres advertisement, *Los Angeles Express*, June 13, 1905.

186 **"regal highway":** Ibid.

186 **"one of the finest automobile courses":** Ibid.

186 **50,000 spectators crammed the throughway:** Loomis, *Brentwood*, 111.

187 **"Take the Los Angeles Pacific cars":** Westgate Acres advertisement, LAT, June 29, 1905.

187 **Sherman proudly stood in the middle of a dozen well-appointed women and children:** Loomis, *Brentwood*, 46.

188 **"It would create":** "Council Appeals for Westgate Annexation," *Los Angeles Express*, May 31, 1916.

188 **"irrigation rate" and "residential rate":** "Knocking at City's Door," LAT, June 30, 1915.

188 **John, who built the ranch and donated the land that became VA property:** Loomis, *Westside Chronicles*, 22.

188 **winning sharpshooting competitions:** "Women Will Test Skill at Shooting," *Los Angeles Express*, September 23, 1915.

188 **sending passengers into "semi-convulsions":** "Wealthy Woman Smashed into Police Car; Loses Diamond," *Venice Vanguard*, October 18, 1915.

188 **reprimanded her for her "shameless" smirking and sentenced her to a day in jail:** "$180 Fine, Day in Jail for Woman Autoist," *Los Angeles Express*, October 21, 1915.

189 **"[Westgate] territory is largely a barren one":** "Suit Ties Up Annexation," *Los Angeles Record*, June 15, 1916.

189 **a Prohibition Era liquor bust at his ranch:** "Gardener Is Locked in Room; Farm Plundered," *Los Angeles Express*, July 6, 1921.

189 **a drunk-driving charge:** "Wolfskill Scion Held in Drunk Case," LAT, May 13, 1937.

189 **the suspicious death of his wealthy sister:** "Body's Finding Thickens Maze," LAT, September 21, 1929.

189 **cause of death labeled "unknown":** Tony Wade, "Back in the Day: Death of Edith Irene Wolfskill Remains a Mystery," *Daily Republic*, February 20, 2015.

190　**Occidental Terrace, Occidental Heights, and Occidental Annex:** Prosser, *SurveyLA*, 122-123.

191　**Candidates who were not "in full sympathy":** "Reorganization of City Departments to Follow Naming of the New Mayor," LAT, September 3, 1916.

191　**"All [Territories] Eventually Will Become":** "City 'Isles' Distinctive; All Eventually Will Become Part of Great Whole," LAT, September 3, 1916.

191　**"We should have city and county consolidation":** "Warning to Long Beach," *Long Beach Daily Telegram*, September 23, 1916.

191　**Their model was L.A.'s eternal rival, San Francisco:** "Movement for a Great Union," LAT, September 28, 1916.

191　**"to invite citizens":** "Last Minute News," *Monrovia Daily News*, September 25, 1916.

191　**Mulholland was recruited to spread the gospel:** Ibid.

191　**"enlarging the field" and "aims":** "Board to Take Up Annexation Plan," *Los Angeles Express*, September 22, 1916.

191　**"the straightening out":** Ibid.

192　**"elimination of local misunderstandings" and "bring within the city":** Ibid.

192　**"WARNING TO LONG BEACH":** *Long Beach Daily Telegram*, September 23, 1916.

192　**"Right now there is a piece":** "L.A. Would 'Take In' Beach," *Venice Vanguard*, September 22, 1916.

192　**"The sooner we clean up":** Ibid.

Chapter 19: Consolidation Battles

195　**"for the advancement":** "Los Angeles County Owns Art Institute Gift of Gen. Otis," *Burbank Review*, April 16, 1920.

195　**It became the Otis Art Institute:** "Otis Institute Stimulates Art," LAT, July 13, 1919.

195　**"I can't stand giggling girls!":** *Among Ourselves: By and For All Employees of the Los Angeles Times*, The Huntington Library, December 1931.

196　**"straightening out":** "Striding Toward Greater City," LAT, September 26, 1916.

196　**"Words of Commendation":** Ibid.

196　**"Representatives of Pasadena":** "Great Union," LAT.

196　**"PASADENA IS READY FOR FIGHT . . . DENIES SENTIMENT IN FAVOR OF CONSOLIDATION":** *The Whittier News*, September 29, 1916.

196　**claiming the *Times* had taken his quotes out of context:** Ibid.

196　**"unalterably opposed to annexation":** "Oppose Annexation," LAT, September 29, 1916.

196　**"until asked to do so":** "Annexation Talk in South Pasadena," LAT, February 15, 1917.

197　**During World War I:** "Prohibition Begins," Research Guides, Library of Congress, www.guides.loc.gov/this-month-in-business-history/january/prohibition.

197　**"There was a time":** "Morals Demand Consolidation," LAT, December 15, 1916.

197 **"evil influence"** and **"easily accessible":** Ibid.
197 **"cannot be reached":** "Consolidation to Better Moral Condition," *Venice Vanguard*, December 15, 1916.
197 **"Morals Demand Consolidation":** LAT, December 15, 1916.
197 **"Group Owensmouth Annexation":** "Three-Angled Voting Today," LAT, February 20, 1917.
197 **"the hole in the doughnut":** Ibid.
198 **"Anti-Strong Drink Law":** Ibid.
198 **more scarce compared to other American cities:** "Not as Bad as Painted," *Los Angeles Herald*, April 2, 1905.
199 **"It is considered necessary":** "Annexation of Near-By Coast District Urged," LAT, June 8, 1917.
199 **long been an object of derision:** Unless otherwise noted, primary sources for Hyperion's history are Sam Gnerre, "Hyperion Treatment Plant," *Daily Breeze*, March 9, 2010; "Sewer Problem Up to Voters," LAT, May 8, 1917; "Death Shadow Checking Law," LAT, March 3, 1910; "Police Launch Runs Afoul in Fish Net," *Los Angeles Herald*, March 3, 1910.
199 **"sewer fish":** "Hunting Japs Before Dawn," LAT, March 3, 1910.
199 **washing out Sherman's Los Angeles-Pacific tracks:** "Sewer Rips Up Railway," LAT, October 8, 1907.
199 **"a large odoriferous splash":** "Pier Is Failing," *Los Angeles Record*, January 4, 1908.
200 **"nuisance":** "Hyperion Sewer One Great Big Nuisance," *Venice Vanguard*, August 7, 1916.
200 **"solid five" city councilmembers:** Various, including "Police Rushed When Billboard Hirelings Break Election Law," *Los Angeles Express*, June 5, 1917.
200 **"the Czar":** The *Los Angeles Record* referred to Councilman Betkouski as "the Czar" throughout 1917.
201 **"The continued growth":** "Intensive Business to Be City's New Policy," LAT, July 3, 1917.
201 **eight successive police chiefs who were hostile to unions:** McDougal, *Privileged Son*, 105.
201 **When the selection process of chiefs switched to a five-person commission:** Ibid.
201 **"Take the tray, Lucy":** C. Mulholland, *Owensmouth Baby*, 107.
202 **"The man who brought":** "Los Angeles Shall Be Ruled Neither by Jackal nor Baboon," *Los Angeles Record*, January 1, 1916.

Chapter 20: Growing Pains and Gains
203 **"Fred, I'm asking you":** Weingarten, *Thirsty*, 218.
203 **"The entire water system":** "Fernando Valley Parched Acqua Duck Breaks Down," *Los Angeles Record*, May 11, 1917.
203 **"There are lots of individuals":** Ibid.
204 **"This would be in addition":** Ibid.
204 **"We relied on them":** Ibid.
204 **"If we had known":** Ibid.

204 **the "Aqua Duck":** The phrase appeared in several *Los Angeles Record* editions.

204 **Scathing cartoons:** "Bill's Acqua Duck Is All Mussed Up Again" cartoon, *Los Angeles Record*, June 1, 1917.

204 **"unfit for human consumption":** "Court Decides for the City in Sweeping, Emphatic Terms," LAT, March 20, 1915.

204 **"excellent quality"** and **"Where are you":** C. Mulholland, *William Mulholland*, 254.

205 **"Oh, I could point you":** Mulholland's exchange with plaintiff's lawyer from Standiford, *Water*, 214.

205 **Harvey Van Norman, the superintendent of the aqueduct's operations, admitted:** "Acqua Duck Man Spills Beans," *Los Angeles Record*, June 1, 1917.

205 **"to develop power":** "The Huntington, Hotel Magnificent, Opens Doors," *Los Angeles Record*, January 30, 1914.

206 **"I am very proud":** "Greater Edison System—Consolidated with the Pacific Light and Power," *The Pomona Progress*, April 1, 1916.

206 **"Mr. Huntington has been the direct means":** Friedricks, *Henry E. Huntington*, 153.

206 **"We have too many laws":** Transcript of Henry Huntington address to the New York Chamber of Commerce, The Huntington Library, November 27, 1922.

206 **"I am now out of business":** Friedricks, *Henry E. Huntington*, 118.

206 **thanks to the affordability of Model T Fords:** Easlon, *Los Angeles Railway*, 23.

207 **"Conditions have changed":** Friedricks, *Henry E. Huntington*, 121.

207 **development slowed to about 200 subdivisions a year:** Ibid., 125.

207 **Henry and Bell kept separate bank accounts:** Author interview with Clay Stalls, June 2023.

207 **"enjoyment and fun":** Thorpe, *Henry Edwards Huntington*, 248.

207 **"THE MAN WHO PAID $50,000 FOR THE GUTENBERG BIBLE":** *The New York Times*, April 30, 1911.

207 **"All the enormous energy":** Ibid.

208 **"I intend to go through":** Friedricks, *Henry E. Huntington*, 19.

208 **Huntington had found his calling:** Ibid., 98.

Chapter 21: Fudge for San Francisco

210 **the first newspaper in the country to launch a regular motion picture column:** Taylor, "It Costs $1000," *Saturday Evening Post*, 62.

211 **"LOS ANGELES THE GLOBE'S MOVING PICTURE CENTER, MILLIONS IN IT":** LAT, January 1, 1915.

211 **"thousands of people":** Ibid.

211 **"Southern California is naturally suited":** This and other quotes in paragraph: "Movie Stars Who Scintillate in Los Angeles," LAT, January 1, 1916.

212 **3,000 people sat "spellbound":** Harry Carr, "Magnificent Film Spectacle Holds Thousands Entranced," LAT, October 18, 1916.

212 **"With 'Intolerance,' David Wark Griffith":** Ibid.

212 **"Culture and the spiritual development"**: Taylor, "It Costs $1000," *Saturday Evening Post*, 62.
213 **Lillian Gish was known to hang out there**: Roderick, *San Fernando Valley*, 87.
215 **"Los Angeles has a right"**: "Sawtelle for the Dual Life," LAT, February 5, 1918.
215 **"I did not want"**: George Garrigues, "Police Seizure of City Hall Starts Sawtelle on Exit Path," LAT, January 10, 1963.
216 **"[took] another whack"**: "The Census and the Quake," LAT, July 6, 1920.
216 **"Had Los Angeles been seeking"**: "Did Los Angeles 'Annex' Its Big Population?," LAT, July 28, 1920.
217 **"phenomenal" Census figures**: Ibid.

Chapter 22: Los Angeles, Inc.
218 **"It's just as well"**: "Who's Who," *Saturday Evening Post*, 234.
218 **"It is a great thing"**: Letter from Moses Sherman to Eli Clark, Sherman Library, January 20, 1923.
219 **"Please let me help"**: Letter from Moses Sherman to Harry Chandler, Sherman Library, ca. 1910.
219 **"the best and 'smoothest' reporter"**: Ibid.
219 **"Your perennial goodness"**: Letter from Harry Chandler to Moses Sherman, Sherman Library, February 10, 1917.
219 **"SHERMAN HEADS NEW COMMISSION"**: LAT, March 1, 1910.
219 **"Gen. M. H. Sherman"**: Ibid.
220 **"from the mountains to the ocean"**: Charles F. Hayden, "Los Angeles to Be City of Three Millions in Twenty-Five Years," LAT, May 30, 1920.
220 **"really Los Angeles"**: G. Gordon Whitnall, "World Metropolis Here Logical, Inevitable," LAT, May 30, 1920.
220 **"unfair to force property owners"**: "Propose Major Street System for California," *Los Angeles Record*, October 14, 1920.
221 **"Thus far we have just 'happened'"**: Whitnall, "World Metropolis," LAT.
221 **"Nobody ever PLANNED Los Angeles"**: Benmar Hills Burbank advertisement, *Los Angeles Express*, October 27, 1923.
221 **"order out of chaos"**: Hayden, "City of Three Millions," LAT.
221 **"making this great development"**: Ibid.
222 **"great truck boulevard"**: Ibid.
222 **"comprehensive system of highways"**: Ibid.
222 **"so that ships"**: Ibid.
222 **"The life of these [smaller] cities"**: Whitnall, "World Metropolis," LAT.
222 **"natural process" and "natural Los Angeles"**: Ibid.
223 **"have stuck the name"**: "Olympiad Here If Bonds Carry," LAT, August 29, 1920.
223 **"As the largest city"**: Ibid.
223 **"Feel confident that if Los Angeles"**: Ibid.
224 **"a calamity"**: "Mayor to Urge New Bond Vote," LAT, September 3, 1920.
224 **Sitting on over fifty boards of directors**: Gottlieb and Wolt, *Thinking Big*, 125.
224 **"I am not sure"**: Berges, *Life and Times*, 43.

225 **"[Chandler] was really the chap"**: Ibid., 44.

225 **"If the plans are developed"**: "To Center All Aviation Here," LAT, September 5, 1919.

226 **eliciting an open letter from Goodyear's chairman:** Letter from Goodyear Tire & Rubber Co. to Harry Chandler, reprinted in LAT, December 4, 1931.

226 **Chandler also convinced the heads of Ford, General Motors, and Chrysler to set up assembly plants:** "Timeline: History of the Los Angeles Times," KCET.org., October 9, 2018, www. kcet.org/shows/inventing-la-the-chandlers-and-their-times/timeline-history-of-the-los-angeles-times.

226 **"impressed with Los Angeles' water supply"**: "Plan for Huge Factory Here," LAT, September 26, 1919.

226 **second in the nation in the issuance of building permits:** "Down the Decades," LAT.

226 **"Most Useful Citizen"**: Taylor, "It Costs $1000," *Saturday Evening Post*, 8.

226 **"Midas of California"**: Kit Rachlis, "The Fall of the House of Chandler," LAT, June 17, 2001.

226 **"Governor of Southern California"**: Bray, "Harry Chandler," *American Newspaper Journalists*.

226 **eleventh richest man in the world:** Gottlieb and Wolt, *Thinking Big*, 125.

227 **"If he has been a despot"**: Bray, "Harry Chandler," *American Newspaper Journalists*.

227 **"Chandler Denies He Is a Bolshevik Fiscal Agent"**: McDougal, *Privileged Son*, 87.

227 **"a proportionate share"**: "Annexation of Sawtelle in High Court," *Los Angeles Express*, April 14, 1921.

Chapter 23: HARRYMOSESLAND

229 **"HUGE ELECTRIC SIGN"** and **"This gigantic sign"**: "Another Unit in Hollywoodland Is Opened, Huge Electric Sign Blazons Name of District Across Sky," *Los Angeles Evening Express*, December 8, 1923.

230 **"The most wonderful salesman"**: Letter from Moses Sherman to Eli Clark, Sherman Library, July 27, 1923.

231 **"It was confidence"**: "Hollywoodland Tract Open," *Hollywood Daily Citizen*, March 31, 1923.

231 **choice of four old-school architectural styles:** *Saga of the Sign*, 4.

231 **"Will your family"**: Ibid.

231 **"wonderful ideas"**: Letter from Moses Sherman to Harry Chandler, Sherman Library, July 16, 1923.

232 **"to give a nice party"**: Ibid., July 2, 1923.

232 **"I am getting"**: Letter from Moses Sherman to Eli Clark, Sherman Library, July 27, 1923.

232 **"You know"**: Ibid.

232 **"Woodruff is spending money"**: Letter from Moses Sherman to Harry Chandler, Sherman Library, July 24, 1923.

232 **"This is all wrong"**: Ibid.

233 **"old, worn out and sick"** and **"Please let's not buy"**: Ibid., ca. 1923.

233 **"The reason I have not"**: Ibid.

233 **Chandler commissioned a twenty-six-year-old designer named John Roche to create a brochure for Hollywoodland:** Various, including Lynn Simross, "Man Behind the Hollywood Sign," LAT, January 18, 1977.
234 **"Do it":** Ibid.
234 **"We just put it up":** Ibid.
234 **"We just did things then":** Ibid.
234 **"The week-end of September 15th":** "Sales Records High at Tract in Foothills," LAT, September 23, 1923.
234 **"swamped with live prospects":** Ibid.
234 **"It will be the most valuable property":** Letter from Moses Sherman to Harry Chandler, Sherman Library, July 24, 1923.
235 **"It has become a veritable 'show place'":** "Another Unit in Hollywoodland," *Los Angeles Express*. Ironically, the sign was only meant to last for eighteen months.
236 **"They're getting thirsty":** Ben Macomber, "The Truth About Los Angeles," LAT, November 13, 1923.

Chapter 24: Moving Mountains
237 **"so situated as to be":** Hadley Meares, "In Over Their Heads," Curbed Los Angeles, February 5, 2019, www.la.curbed.com/2019/2/5/17434640/william-mulholland-dam-collapse-water-los-angeles-history.
237 **"dangerous to life":** Ibid.
237 **"The Weid Canyon Dam":** Ibid.
238 **"common-sense genius":** Allen Kelly, "Common-Sense Genius To Build City's Owens River Aqueduct," LAT, July 7, 1907.
238 **"Lake Hollywood is rapidly becoming":** Sydney Woodruff, "Lake Is Set in Heart of Hills," LAT, March 23, 1924.
238 **"The attempt to minimize":** Letter from Fred Eaton to Howard Robertson, CSUN University Library, September 7, 1919.
239 **"half-regretted the demise":** "William Mulholland," New Perspectives on The West, *PBS - The West - William Mulholland*, January 16, 2009, www.shoppbs.pbs.org/weta/thewest/people/i_r/mulholland.htm. This source quotes Mulholland as saying "troublemakers" instead of "sons of bitches," but scholars point out that media in Mulholland's day regularly substituted euphemisms for Mulholland's coarse language. A similar quote attributed to Mulholland appears in: Frederick Faulkner, "Owens Valley: Where the Trail of the Wrecker Runs," reprinted from the *Sacramento Union*, March 28 to April 2, 1927. In hand-written notes, scholars filled in the paper's three dashes of a Mulholland expletive with "sons of bitches."
239 **"HEARST PAPER FANS FLAMES":** LAT, May 23, 1924.
239 **"as hapless victims":** Ibid.
240 **Mr. Volney Craig of the San Fernando Valley stood up and challenged the Chief:** "Claims Ranchers Withhold Water Owned by City," LAT, August 7, 1924.
240 **"It is now planned":** "Seize L.A. Aqueduct," *Los Angeles Record*, November 17, 1924.
240 **"anarchy":** "Aqueduct Is Periled As Anarchy Rules in Inyo," LAT, November 19, 1924.

240 **"If we can call":** Marian L. Ryan, "Los Angeles Newspapers Fight the Water War, 1924-1927," *Southern California Quarterly*, Vol. 50, No. 2, 1968.

240 **"valley of desolation"** and **"Los Angeles had to have more water":** Davis, *Rivers*, 139.

241 **"If I am not on the JOB":** Starr, *Material Dreams*, 159.

241 **"The entire situation":** "How to Settle Water Problem," *Los Angeles Record*, November 19, 1924.

241 **"He speaks insultingly":** Ibid.

241 **"the formation of a gigantic water district":** "Seize L.A. Aqueduct," *Los Angeles Record*.

241 **now $84 million in debts:** Clare, *Beverly Hills*, 170.

242 **"Most of the Angeleno delegation":** "Our Most Vital need," *The San Bernardino Sun*, June 7, 1925.

242 **"Los Angeles city":** Ibid.

242 **"Those cities were annexed":** Ibid.

242 **"We aren't ready to be annexed":** "Must Have Ownership," *Santa Ana Register*, May 21, 1925.

243 **seven Rhode Islands:** Calculation by author. Mulholland's proposed sphere of folding in portions of San Bernardino, Orange, and Riverside Counties accounts for the approximate 9,000-square-miles figure. Rhode Island is 1,214 square miles per its website, www.RI.gov.

243 **"worthless hills":** "Highway Taps Scenery," LAT, December 28, 1924.

243 **"It is a living monument":** L. J. Burrud, "Drive is Connecting Link," *Los Angeles Evening Express*, December 27, 1924.

244 **"Mulholland Hills lie directly":** Mulholland Hills brochure, CSUN University Library, 1922.

244 **The roadway's actual engineer:** "Mulholland Drive Formally Opened," *The Van Nuys News*, December 30, 1924.

244 **"thousands of men":** "New Drive Is Opened," LAT, December 28, 1924.

244 **The fanfare came fast and furious:** List of events taken from "Mulholland Highway Festival Official Program," *The Girard News*, CSUN University Library, December 27, 1924.

244 **donated 1,000 gallons of gasoline:** "Guns of World War for Fiesta," LAT, December 21, 1924.

244 **shower an audience of Hal Roach's *Our Gang* production with roses:** "High Way Fete to be Free," LAT, December 26, 1924.

244 **choreographed by Cecil B. DeMille:** "Road Fete Leaders Named," LAT, December 17, 1924.

244 **Natalie Kingston performed her seductive Peacock Dance and Betty Blythe, star of *The Queen of Sheba*, reenacted her "Baghdad Number":** "High Way Fete," LAT.

244 **fluttering divas flanked Old Bill:** Sitton and Deverell, *Metropolis*, 48.

245 **An estimated 100,000 people partook:** "Guns of World War," LAT.

245 **32,000 motorists test-drove:** "Mulholland Drive," *The Van Nuys News*, December 30, 1924.

245 **"The rumors come directly":** "Deny Rumor of Owens Attack," *Los Angeles Record*, December 24, 1924.

245 **"notified the world":** "Official Map of Mulholland High Way," *Venice Vanguard*, December 26, 1924.
245 **longest scenic mountain boulevard in the world lying entirely within city limits:** "Highway Taps Scenery," LAT.
245 **"fruit basket and vegetable garden"** and **"People now come":** "Mulholland Drive," *The Van Nuys News*.
245 **"material increase":** "Prosperity's New Highway," *The Girard News*, CSUN University Library, December 27, 1924.
245 **"Photographs of and from the highway":** Ibid.
246 **"One scarcely knows":** "Highway Taps Scenery," LAT.
246 **"He Saw the Mountain and Cut It Away":** "The Modern Mahomet!," *The Girard News*, CSUN University Library, December 27, 1924.
247 **In a publicity photo from March 1924:** Photo published in C. Mulholland, *William Mulholland*.
248 **Los Angeles City Council dropped the whole idea:** "Harry Chandler Land 'Escapes' Assessments," *Los Angeles Record*, July 8, 1927.
248 **"CITY HONORS MULHOLLAND; Dedicates New Dam in Name of Engineer":** LAT, March 18, 1925.
248 **The Ancient Order of Hibernians:** "Fetes to Mark City's Tribute to St. Patrick," *Illustrated Daily News*, March 17, 1925.
248 **"wisdom"** and **"genius":** "City Honors Mulholland," LAT, March 18, 1925.
248 **"showed the delicacy":** Ibid.
248 **planted the first oranges in Southern California:** Ibid.
248 **Hurlburt parted an American flag to reveal the dam's bronze tablet:** Ibid.
249 **"My associates are in the habit":** Ibid.
249 **"Somewhere between Cahuenga pass":** "To Construct Statue to Bill Mulholland," *Los Angeles Record*, December 31, 1924.

Chapter 25: Beauty and the Baron
250 **"Nowhere on earth":** "Railroads Bankrupted," LAT, April 24, 1919.
250 **"People do not have a proper appreciation":** Transcript of "Miss Emma Quigley Oral History," The Huntington Library, April 21, 1967. Quigley was Henry Huntington's secretary and assistant.
250 **"This benefaction is in its extent":** "Huntington's Gift Praised," LAT, May 12, 1923.
250 **In a photograph from this era:** Photo accompanying "Huntington's Gift Praised," LAT, May 12, 1923.
251 **"The shock has been great":** Letter from Henry Huntington to Jacques Seligmann, The Huntington Library, April 1, 1922.
251 **"Mrs. Huntington has been seriously ill":** Letter from Henry Huntington to William E. Dunn, The Huntington Library, July 24, 1924.
252 **"went down stairs yesterday":** Letter from Henry Huntington to Joseph Duveen, The Huntington Library, April 22, 1926.
252 **"Miss Maybe is as much a tyrant":** Ibid., May 17, 1926.
252 **"My dear Elise":** Letter from Henry Huntington to Elise Ferguson, The Huntington Library, May 5, 1925.
253 **"There is very little danger":** Friedricks, *Henry E. Huntington*, 151.

254 **"Very few private collectors"**: "Obituary: Mr. Henry E. Huntington," *The Daily Telegraph*, May 24, 1927.

254 **"Probably no man"**: "Henry E. Huntington Answers Final Call," *Pasadena Evening Post*, May 23, 1927.

254 **"No single individual"**: Minutes from the Directors of the Huntington Land and Improvement Company meeting, The Huntington Library, August 5, 1927.

254 **"lasting monument"**: Thorpe, *Henry Edwards Huntington*, 464.

254 **"aggressive railway building"** and **"done more than anything else"**: Ibid., 223.

254 **"Others have made millions"**: "Henry E. Huntington," LAT, May 24, 1927.

255 **"Those [cultural] treasures"**: Ibid.

255 **The museum now houses:** Ryan Carter, "$40 Million Gift to Huntington," *Daily News*, October 7, 2023.

255 **"I have been approached"**: Friedricks, *Henry E. Huntington*, 16.

Chapter 26: White Spots

256 **"unfit for human consumption"**: "Annexation Views," *Hollywood Daily Citizen*, January 28, 1924.

257 **East Beverly and Beverly Park received consideration:** Nathan Masters, "How the Town of Sherman Became the City of West Hollywood," KCET. org., December 1, 2011, www.kcet.org/shows/lost-la/how-the-town-of-sherman-became-the-city-of-west-hollywood.

257 **"It's not right"**: Helen Starr, "Rich Neighbors Make Sherman Folk Ambitious," LAT, August 23, 1925.

257 **the Rodeo Land and Water Co., which managed Beverly Hills's water:** Clare, *Beverly Hills*, 132.

257 **"laxative qualities"**: "Beverly Hills' Thirst for Autonomy Saves the Day," LAT, January 30, 1994.

257 **The entertainers cavorted door to door throughout Beverly Hills:** Ibid.

258 **the Beverly Hills Eight were honored with a bronze and marble obelisk called "Celluloid":** Clare, *Beverly Hills*, 10.

258 **"I think they are going to make"**: Letter from Moses Sherman to Arnold Haskell, Sherman Library, December 16, 1927.

258 **"Venice of America"**: "Playa Del Rey is Formally Born," LAT, July 17, 1902.

258 **"millionaires colony of villas"**: Grafton Tanguary, "Moses Hazeltine Sherman and Eli P. Clark," *The Jonathan Club Magazine*, December 3, 2016, www.hollywoodlandgiftedpark.com/the-history-of-moses-hazeltine-sherman-and-eli-p-clark-by-grafton-tanguary-contributor-the-jonathan-club-magazine.

259 **sidewalks and utilities were going in at the Venice of America tract:** "In Venice Park Tract," LAT, July 31, 1904.

259 **Kinney designated his community "Venice"**: "Building Notes," LAT, July 31, 1904.

259 **inspired by the Canal of Venice exhibition at the 1893 World's Fair:** Marty Schatz, "The Lost Canals of Venice," Venice Heritage Museum, www. veniceheritagemuseum.org/the-lost-canals-of-venice.html. Kinney was also inspired by a visit to Venice, Italy: Crump, *Red Cars*, 78.

259 **Kinney rushed to complete his plans before Henry Huntington could finish Naples:** Stanton, *Venice Beach*, 14.

260 **"You will not lose":** "Prominent Citizens of Santa Monica Tell Why They Oppose Annexation," *Venice Vanguard*, December 6, 1924.

260 **"Consolidation of Venice and Santa Monica":** "Prosperity Seen in Bay Cities Union," *Venice Vanguard*, September 24, 1925.

260 **"Annexation Means Slavery":** Stanton, *Venice Beach*, 143.

260 **"VENICE VOTES TO ANNEX TO LOS ANGELES":** *Los Angeles Record*, October 3, 1925.

261 **"a gigantic parade":** Ibid.

261 **Two couples from Venice lampooned the law:** "Here's Where It Pays to Watch Your Step," LAT, April 19, 1926.

261 **"so-called moral conduct":** "Majority for Dancing Zone is Large; Venice Voters Favor Measure 3 to 1," *Venice Vanguard*, May 1, 1926.

261 **"Many waitresses who are off ":** "Waitresses' Union Backs Sunday Dance," *Venice Vanguard*, April 24, 1926.

261 **"late afternoon rush":** "Heavy Vote Cast; Police-Fire Raise Venice Dance Win," *San Pedro Pilot*, May 1, 1926.

261 **many restaurants had "No Negroes" signs or mandates:** Cecil Brown, "Life on the Avenue," LAT, June 18, 2006.

262 **"as a result of complaints":** Ibid.

262 **"torture plot":** "Ku Klux Torture Plot Charged in Raid Probe," *Los Angeles Express*, May 12, 1922.

262 **"Negroes informed of the plot":** Ibid.

262 **"The Ku Klux Klan":** Chandler Owen, "The New Year," *California Eagle*, December 30, 1922.

262 **"in full regalia":** "Klansmen Visit Eight Churches," *The Girard News*, CSUN University Library, December 27, 1924.

262 **"Enthusiastic applause greeted":** Ibid.

263 **"COMMUNISTS IN DRIVE TO AROUSE NEGRO HATRED":** Fred R. Marvin, LAT, June 30, 1923.

263 **"within colored churches":** Ibid.

263 **had been warning of communist infiltration among Black people:** Gage, *G-Man*, 68.

263 **"The negro masses":** Marvin, "Communists in Drive," LAT.

263 **"It is one thing":** This and subsequent quotes in paragraph: "The Soul of the City," LAT, June 24, 1923.

265 **"shall not sell or lease property":** "Realtors Adopt An Important Resolution," *The Whittier News*, October 27, 1923.

265 **"other than the white or Caucasian race":** Ibid.

265 **"Restrictions just sufficiently high":** Monte Vista advertisement, LAT, November 2, 1923.

265 **"Men and women":** Western Avenue Crest advertisement, *Los Angeles Express*, March 8, 1924.

265 **"perpetually restricted":** Goodyear Park advertisement, *Los Angeles Express*, September 30, 1922.

265 **"The white race":** Ibid.

266 **"keep the white spot white":** "Greater City Day Observed," LAT, April 9, 1924.

266 **the highly visible dot:** *Saga of the Sign*, 6.
266 **"Biggest electric sign":** George R. Hannan, "Famed Hollywood Is 'White Spot' of the Hills," *Los Angeles Express*, May 24, 1924.
266 **"Los Angeles and Southern California":** Ibid.
267 **"the utmost contempt":** "Hiram Johnson Warmly Commends Vanderbilt's Expose of Chandler," *Illustrated Daily News*, February 8, 1924.
267 **"With his enormous wealth":** Ibid.

Chapter 27: A Circus Atmosphere
268 **"As one, who for [forty] years":** "Four Years, No Umbrella; Mulholland Has One Now," *Illustrated Daily News*, February 3, 1926.
269 **it was the butt of Vaudeville jokes:** "Welcome, Watts," *Los Angeles Express*, April 6, 1926.
270 **found itself drowning in debt:** "Council Finds Debt Annexed with District," LAT, July 14, 1926.
271 **"Village Residents Not Sure":** "City Is Victim of Elections," LAT, July 2, 1926.
271 **"the last of the veteran showmen":** "Barnes Circus Goes Over Successfully; Tickles Everybody," *Chippewa Daily Herald*, August 18, 1926.
271 **"The late Abbot Kinney":** "Barnes Circus to Move to El Monte," *Monrovia Daily News*, February 18, 1927.
271 **"When we were putting up":** "Barnes Circus to Move," LAT, February 16, 1927.
271 **"I also instructed":** Ibid.
272 **"never a community":** Prosser, *SurveyLA*, 202.
273 **"a continuous stretch":** "Barnes City Fate Before Its Voters," *Venice Vanguard*, September 13, 1926.
274 **Venice's wells were nearly bone dry:** "Water Warning Sounded," LAT, August 3, 1927.
274 **"There is a limit":** J. B. Daniell, "Comment," *Venice Vanguard*, August 3, 1927.
274 **"The people would have the right":** "Water Warning," LAT.
275 **"solemn warning":** Ibid.
275 **"The water department":** "No Danger in Annexations, Council Told," *Los Angeles Record*, September 9, 1927.
275 **"six feet underground":** Kunze, "Hidden Hand," *Los Angeles Record*.
275 **"A dam 150 feet high":** Ibid.
275 **seven concrete dams in the U.S. exceeded 300 feet at that time:** "List of Tallest Dams in the United States," Wikipedia, cross-checked with individual sources of the dams.

Chapter 28: Mulholland Falls
276 **"WATER POURING INTO RESERVOIR, NEW SAN FRANCISQUITO BASIN TO STORE VAST SUPPLY":** LAT, March 20, 1926.
276 **"shoot to kill":** "Fear New Blasts As Second Is Fired," *Los Angeles Record*, May 28, 1927.
277 **"If the leaks":** McCarthy, "Water," *Pacific Saturday Night*, March 12, 1938, 36.

277 **"See you again"**: C. Mulholland, *William Mulholland*, 321.
277 **"Like all dams"**: Wilkman, *Floodpath*, 181.
277 **"clear as glass"**: Ibid.
277 **"Please, God, don't let people"**: C. Mulholland, *William Mulholland*, 319.
278 **"KILL MULHOLLAND"**: Davis, *Rivers*, 182.
278 **"tombstone for flood victims"**: "Remains of Giant Dam in Gorge of Death; Stands as Tombstone for Flood Victims," *Los Angeles Express*, March 14, 1928.
279 **"The tragedy of the people"**: Court Kunze quoted in Standiford, *Water*, 248.
279 **"On an occasion like this"**: Ibid.
279 **"The break has all"**: "Sensation at Dam Disaster Inquest," *Los Angeles Express*, March 21, 1928.
279 **"It's in a place"**: "Water Board to Demand Grand Jury Quiz on Dam," LAT, March 22, 1928.
279 **"I have a suspicion"**: Ibid.
279 **"We vigorously resent"**: "Owens Valley Resents Los Angeles Dynamiting Theory," *The Ventura County Star*, March 24, 1928.
279 **"murderous"** and **"attitude that has prevailed"**: Ibid.
280 **"DAM WAS NOT DYNAMITED"**: *Los Angeles Record*, March 24, 1928.
280 **"We must have overlooked something"**: C. Mulholland, *William Mulholland*, 323.
280 **"Fasten it on me"**: Ibid., 325.
280 **"The destruction of this dam"**: "Dam Jury Raps Mulholland," *Los Angeles Record*, April 13, 1928.
280 **Mulholland did not keep up with newer techniques**: Wilkman, *Floodpath*, 189.
280 **"The construction and operation"**: "Dam Jury," *Los Angeles Record*.
281 **the Southern California Metropolitan Water District, at long last, opened for business**: McCarthy, "Water," *Pacific Saturday Night*, March 26, 1938, 31.

Chapter 29: Past vs. Present
282 **"It was that damned dam"**: Standiford, *Water*, 252.
282 **"Please [do] not tell people"**: Letter from Moses Sherman to Harry Chandler, Sherman Library, April 5, 1928.
282 **"My children are doing"**: Letter from Moses Sherman to Harry Chandler, Sherman Library, May 19, 1928.
283 **"I am not able"**: Letter from Moses Sherman to Arnold Haskell, Sherman Library, March 15, 1927.
283 **transplanting of goat glands by grafting them into men's scrotums**: Brock, *Charlatan*, 4.
283 **claimed that goat hormones cured**: Tom Ladwig, *St. Louis Post-Dispatch*, November 4, 1984.
283 **removal of glands from young billy goats' severed testicles**: Brock, *Charlatan*, 3.
283 **"The glands become absorbed"**: McDougal, *Privileged Son*, 471.
283 **paying four *Times* employees $750**: Ibid., 112.

283 **Harry Andrews died four years after his procedure:** "Manager Ed Andrews of Los Angeles Times Dies," LAT, September 21, 1926, and Brock, *Charlatan*, 59, and "When It Was Residential," Historic Los Angeles: Wilshire Boulevard, www.wilshireboulevardhouses.blogspot. com/2013/07/3173-wilshire-boulevard-please-see-our.html.

283 **"He was trying":** Transcript of interview with Dorothy Chandler by James Bassett, The Huntington Library, December 19, 1972.

284 **Chandler finally saw the light:** Berges, *Life and Times*, 47. Dr. Philip M. Lovell covered health for the *Times*.

284 **"It was really Chandler":** Tom Ladwig, "Brilliant, Innovative and a Certified Quack," *St. Louis Post-Dispatch*, November 4, 1984.

284 **"Gran Benefactor de la Ciudad":** Various, including Ainsworth, *Memories*, 36.

284 **"Mexican Repatriation":** Various, including "Welfare Chief Speeds Mexican Repatriation," *Venice Vanguard*, March 31, 1934.

285 **"People seemed happy":** Author interview with Gustavo Arellano, May 2023.

285 **"overrunning" the city:** "Immigrant Quotas," LAT, November 1, 1927.

285 **75,000 Mexican people:** "Great Migration Back to Mexico Under Way," LAT, April 12, 1931.

285 **"Railroad authorities assert":** Ibid.

285 **"Nativism and anti-immigrant sentiment":** Author interview with Jessica M. Kim, April 2023.

285 **just another "gadget":** Lee Averill, "Gadgetry and Such," *Los Angeles Record*, March 19, 1935.

286 **"a forward-looking people":** Paul R. Spitzzeri, "'To Win a Happy Community Destiny': The Dedication of Los Angeles City Hall, 26-28 April 1928," The Homestead Blog, April 29, 2020, www.homesteadmuseum. blog/2020/04/29/to-win-a-happy-community-destiny-the-dedication-of-los-angeles-city-hall-26-28-april-1928.

286 **Los Angeles City Hall was beamed into millions of living rooms:** Marshall, "Los Angeles in Buildings," KCET.org.

286 **L.A.'s 150-foot limit:** Ibid.

287 **"sacrificing sentiment on the altar":** Fred S. Walburn, "Comment," *Venice Vanguard*, March 17, 1930.

288 **"If this keeps on":** Harry Carr, "The Lancer," LAT, November 13, 1929.

288 **"fresh-kill Jungle Barbecue":** Tarzana advertisement, *Long Beach Daily Telegram*, September 29, 1923.

288 **"white spot":** Tarzana advertisement, *Los Angeles Express*, October 27, 1923.

289 **"devoid of literary value":** Marty Altschul, "History Plays Trick on Tarzana," LAT, March 16, 1969.

289 **the dam was deemed "safe," though several engineers found deficiencies:** "Board Studies Report on Dam," LAT, August 12, 1931.

289 **"menace to the city":** "Engineering Report Still Held Secret," LAT, July 16, 1931, and "Dam Abandonment Decision Pending," LAT, July 29, 1931.

289 **"psychological dam":** "Hollywood Dam Backed by Barrier," LAT, December 28, 1933.

289 **"I am going"**: Letter from Moses Sherman to daughter, Sherman Library, January 23, 1929.

Chapter 30: The Peak and Passing of the Patriarchy
291 **"One long drunken orgy"**: McWilliams, *Southern California*, 136.
291 **One out of three Angelenos owned the dwelling they lived in:** Starr, *Material Dreams*, 70-71.
292 **"Make a Friend for California"**: "Make a Friend for California" notices blanketed the *Los Angeles Times* throughout 1925. Amateur photographers and "junior" *Times* readers were also encouraged to enter photographs and essays in the contest.
292 **"There's only one way"**: Bray, "Harry Chandler," *American Newspaper Journalists*.
292 **"The reason is because it has the *Los Angeles Times*"**: Boyarsky, *Inventing L.A.*, 75.
292 **"If those damn unionists"**: McDougal, *Privileged Son*, 121.
292 **Chandler lent them money to save the studio:** Gottlieb and Wolt, *Thinking Big*, 147-148.
292 **net worth ranged between several hundred million to half a billion dollars:** Siegel, *Dreamers and Schemers*, 195.
292 **"many times a millionaire" and "he hasn't a lazy bone"**: "How Chandler Uses Power to Throttle People's Power Bureau," *Los Angeles Record*, March 7, 1924.
292 **"It is Chandler's unflagging activity"**: Ibid.
293 **assigned twenty-four-hour protection while suspicious characters near his house and office were rounded up and interrogated:** "Bare Plot of Gangsters to Kidnap Harry Chandler," *Los Angeles Express*, November 12, 1930.
293 **"I know nothing"**: "Kidnaping Gang Here: Prominent Men Plot Targets," LAT, November 13, 1930.
294 **flags of Spain, Mexico, and the California Republic:** "City Eagerly Awaits First Gala Day of Great Fiesta," *Los Angeles Express*, September 3, 1931.
294 **"all beaches from Long Beach to Santa Monica"**: "El Camino Dedication Features Fiesta Today," LAT, September 10, 1931.
294 **"billion dollar turnout"**: "Film Stars Ready for 'Billion Dollar Turnout,'" *Los Angeles Record*, September 10, 1931.
294 **dressing as a ranchero:** Siegel, *Dreamers and Schemers*, 115.
294 **The city generated 18,000 temporary jobs and grossed $500,000 in receipts from 500,000 paying customers:** "Fiesta Success Brings Praises," LAT, September 15, 1931.
294 **"While money making"**: "Sesquicentennial Plans," LAT, March 24, 1931.
295 **"We were told"**: "Fiesta Success," LAT.
295 **"much of the depression"**: "'Well, What Good Is It?'," LAT, September 6, 1931.
295 **"DEPRESSION CHARGED TO PESSIMISM"**: LAT, July 26, 1930.
295 **"'CHEER-UP' CAMPAIGN HAS BEEN LAUNCHED TO DISPEL PSYCHOLOGY OF DEPRESSION"**: LAT, June 12, 1931.
295 **"dispel the gloom"**: Ibid.

295 **unemployed marchers called for "Groceries, not Games":** Siegel,
    Dreamers and Schemers, 118.
295 **a full-page personal letter:** Passages excerpted from Harry Chandler,
    "A Message for the New Year," LAT, January 1, 1932.
296 **"Had it not been for the arrival":** Siegel, *Dreamers and Schemers*, 87.
297 **St. Louis in 1904:** Multiple sources regard the poorly run St. Louis
    games as the worst Olympiad ever, including Patricia Claus, "The Worst
    Olympic Games Fiasco in History," Greek Reporter, July 14, 2021, www.
    greekreporter.com/2021/07/14/worst-olympic-games-fiasco-1904-st-louis.
297 **"raises a truly tremendous problem":** Guy M. Butler, "Olympic Athletics,"
    The Observer, April 24, 1932.
297 **a self-contained village:** Details of Olympic Village from Siegel, *Dreamers
    and Schemers*, 127.
298 **"There never has been anything":** "Los Angeles Model for Berlin
    Olympiad," LAT, August 20, 1932.
298 **L.A.'s postcard-perfect climate:** "The Tenth Olympiad—And After," LAT,
    August 14, 1932.
299 **"The greatest Olympic Games":** Basil Foster, "We've Lost—Again!," *Daily
    Herald*, August 17, 1932.
299 **"We came here":** "Germans Give Rolph Medal," LAT, August 15, 1932.
299 **"We do not care":** Terrel DeLapp, "The Olympic Torch," LAT, August 15,
    1932.
299 **stopped at L.A. establishments with "No Mexicans" signs:** Siegel,
    Dreamers and Schemers, 185-186.
299 **"race prejudice has been completely tramped":** "Color," LAT, August 14,
    1932.
300 **500 financiers:** "Games Guests Extend Marts," LAT, August 15, 1932.
300 **"In an era of world-wide depression":** John Kieran, "The Olympic
    Games," *The New York Times*, August 14, 1932.
300 **"the laurels go":** Ibid.
300 **"She can rest":** "Tenth Olympiad," LAT.
300 **For the Thirty-fourth Olympiad:** David Wharton, "Coliseum Turns 100:
    Timeless Los Angeles Cultural Centerpiece Endures As an Icon," LAT,
    June 22, 2023.
301 **"an outstanding leader":** "Gen. Sherman's Career Closes," LAT, September
    10, 1932.
301 **"having his clerks":** Ibid.
301 **"that on the day":** Ibid.
301 **"We are not quitters":** Letter from Moses Sherman to Harry Chandler,
    Sherman Library, July 24, 1923.
302 **"his face aged twenty years":** Standiford, *Water*, 248.
302 **"You are my best friend":** Letter from Moses Sherman to Harry Chandler,
    Sherman Library, 1923 (ca. May 21).

Epilogue
304 **"Hello, Fred":** Standiford, *Water*, 267.
304 **Mulholland's angry pledge in 1928 to outlive his estranged friend:**
    "Bill Mulholland, Man of Action, Few Words, Might Have Been Mayor,"
    Los Angeles Record, July 22, 1935.

304 **"yet I knew we were both dead":** Davis, *Rivers*, 258.

304 **"NEAR DEATH" headlines:** "W. P. Mulholland Hovers Near Death," *Los Angeles Record*, December 21, 1934.

304 **he awoke for a moment:** Standiford, *Water*, 257, and Davis, *Rivers*, 259.

304 **Thousands pilgrimaged to his open casket:** Roderick, *San Fernando Valley*, 68.

304 **"the development of Los Angeles":** "Leaders Join in Tribute to Aqueduct's Builder," LAT, July 23, 1935.

305 **"In these days of alibi artists":** "Mulholland Laid to Rest," LAT, July 26, 1935.

305 **"A man's worth":** Davis, *Rivers*, 104.

305 **Mulholland's one request on his headstone:** C. Mulholland, *William Mulholland*, 331.

305 **"Well done":** "Mulholland Laid to Rest," LAT.

305 **"Chinatown is doomed":** Zuniga, "Old Chinatown," California Historical Society.

306 **"The number of happy morons":** Fred Hogue, "Social Eugenics," LAT, February 16, 1936.

306 **"Hitler, with the support":** Alexandra Minna Stern, "Op-Ed: How the Los Angeles Times Shilled for the Racist Eugenics Movement," LAT, February 28, 2021.

306 **"morally reprehensible" tropes:** "Caltech to Remove the Names of Robert A. Millikan and Five Other Eugenics Proponents from Buildings, Honors, and Assets," Caltech, January 15, 2021, www.caltech.edu/about/news/caltech-to-remove-the-names-of-robert-a-millikan-and-five-other-eugenics-proponents.

306 **"negroes and aliens":** Henry Smith Williams, "Our Vanishing American Race," LAT, June 27, 1915.

306 **third worst in the country "in terms of fairness and reliability":** Bray, "Harry Chandler," *American Newspaper Journalists*.

306 **elite roster of advertisers:** Ibid.

307 **which stalled at around 300,000:** Circulation figure from "The Press: Death of Chandler," *Time*, October 2, 1944.

307 **"A tall and rugged oak":** "Harry Chandler Laid to Rest," LAT, September 27, 1944.

307 **"The Apostle to Millionaires":** Kevin M. Kruse, "How Corporate America Invented Christian America," *Politico Magazine*, April 16, 2015, www.politico.com/magazine/story/2015/04/corporate-america-invented-religious-right-conservative-roosevelt-princeton-117030.

307 **"Harry Chandler was a man":** "Chandler Laid to Rest," LAT, September 27, 1944.

307 *Time* **magazine credited Chandler:** Bray, "Harry Chandler," *American Newspaper Journalists*.

308 **"did not so much foster":** Ibid.

308 **"I think of Harry Chandler":** Boyarsky, *Inventing L.A.*, 74.

308 **Marian burned all his papers upon his death:** Bray, "Harry Chandler," *American Newspaper Journalists*.

308 **"young and noisy giant of the West":** "Who's Who," *Saturday Evening Post*, 52.

308 **"move fast and break things"**: J. O'Dell, "Facebook Kills Off Its 'Move Fast, Break Things' Mantra," VentureBeat, April 30, 2014, www.venturebeat. com/dev/facebook-has-killed-off-the-move-fast-break-things-mantra.

308 **"A city plan"**: Cheney, *City Planning Commissions,* Conference on City Planning.

308 **went so far as to criticize:** Ibid.

308 **"a detailed sketch"**: Banham, *Los Angeles*, 16.

309 **"I always thought"**: Nita Lelyveld, "Hollywood Not Ready to Split," LAT, July 2, 2002.

309 **"seventy-two suburbs"**: Bob Pool, "L.A. Neighborhoods, You're on the Map," LAT, February 19, 2009.

309 **200 recognized neighborhoods:** "Communities of the City of Los Angeles," Los Angeles Almanac, www.laalmanac.com/cities/ci93.php.

309 **including some 100 neighborhood councils:** Susan Shelley, "It's Time for Los Angeles' Failed Governments to Be Broken Up," *Daily News*, July 16, 2023.

309 **"four square leagues"**: Guinn, "Los Angeles City," *Historical Society,* 173.

310 **"None of the people"**: Fogelson, *Fragmented Metropolis*, 196.

310 **"I don't know"**: Ibid., 195.

310 **"What we are trying"**: Neal Peterson quoted in Friedricks, *Henry E. Huntington*, 9-10.

311 **"15-Minute City"**: Various, including Andy Hirschfeld, "The 15-Minute City: How Walkability is Gaining a Foothold in the U.S.," *YES!* Magazine, and Author interview with Josh Stephens, May 2023.

311 **"real community pride"**: Fogelson, *Fragmented Metropolis*, 135.

311 **"units"** and **"not one great whole"**: Ibid.

311 **people of color make up eighty-seven percent of the most distressed neighborhoods in present-day Los Angeles:** Author interview with Capri Maddox, May 2023.

312 **"We just need more resources"**: Author interview with David Price, May 2023.

312 **stricter annexation laws for local governments:** Cortese-Knox-Hertzberg Local Government Reorganization Act of 2000, www.calafco.org/resources/ cortese-knox-hertzberg-act/ckh-reorganization-act-guide.

312 **Safe Clean Water Program:** Safe Clean Water Program, www.safecleanwaterla.org.

INDEX

PHOTO CREDITS

xvii (left): Public Domain

xvii (right): Mulholland Hills brochure, circa 1922-1926, San Fernando Valley History Digital Library, Special Collections & Archives at CSUN

xix (right), xxi (bottom): Creative Commons. UCLA Special Library Collections, Charles E. Young Research Library

xxii (top): Henry E. Huntington with ducks and swans in the reservoir, circa 1915, photCL 107 vol8 (105), Henry E. Huntington Estate photograph collection, approximately 1900s-approximately 1960s, The Huntington Library, San Marino, California

xxiii (left): Herald Examiner Collection/Los Angeles Public Library

xxiii (right): Harry Chandler posing on Los Angeles dock with others, LAT 01269, Los Angeles Times Company Records, The Huntington Library, San Marino, California

314–315: Public Domain. Lloyd Aldrich, Los Angeles City Engineer